YIELD MANAGEMENT
Second Edition

Edited by

ANTHONY INGOLD,
UNA McMAHON-BEATTIE
AND IAN YEOMAN

CONTINUUM
London and New York

Continuum

The Tower Building
11 York Road
London SE1 7NX

370 Lexington Avenue
New York
NY 10017–6503

www.continuumbooks.com

First published 2000

British Library Cataloguing-in-Publication Data
A catalogue record for this book is available from the British Library.

ISBN 0-8264-4825-9

Typeset by YHT Ltd, London
Printed and bound in Great Britain by Biddles Ltd, Guildford and King's Lynn

Yield Management
Second Edition

Also available:

Principles of Hotel Front Office Operations (Second edition): Baker, Bradley and Huyton
Principles of Hospitality Law (Second edition): Boella and Pannett
The Tourism Development Handbook: Godfrey and Clarke
Sales and Service for the Wine Professional: Julyan
Heritage Visitor Attractions: Leask and Yeoman (eds)
HRM in Tourism and Hospitality: Lee-Ross (ed.)
Fundamentals of Hospitality Marketing: Mawson
Using Computers in Hospitality (Second edition): O'Connor
Supervision and Leadership in Tourism and Hospitality: Van der Wagen and Davies
Environmental Management for Hospitality: Webster
The Management of Service Operations: Wright

Contents

Editors and Contributors

Anthony (Tony) Ingold graduated from the University of London, where he also gained a doctorate in physiological ecology. Trained as a medical microbiologist, he worked for several years on the development of chemotherapeutic treatments for chronic respiratory infections at Brompton Hospital, London. More recently he has worked as a lecturer at a number of institutions, including the University of Birmingham. He is now a freelance lecturer, research consultant and author. Tony has long had an interest in aviation and is a private pilot.

Una McMahon-Beattie is a Lecturer, industrial placement tutor, course director and research coordinator at the University of Ulster. After graduating with an MSc degree in international hotel management from the University of Surrey, Una worked in hotels in London for a number of years. Her last management position was that of financial controller. She is currently lecturing in hotel operations and management and has research interests in a number of areas, including productivity, yield management and work-based learning.

Ian Yeoman is a graduate of Sheffield City Polytechnic, with a degree in catering systems. Upon graduation he held several operational management roles with Forte Hotels. More recently he lectured in operations management at Birmingham College of Food, leaving this post in 1994 to take up a teaching post at Napier University. His most recent research and publications have been concerned with productivity, yield management and problem-solving in the hospitality management field. In 1994 he received the Mike Simpson Citation from the Operations Research Society.

Neil Andrews has been a Lecturer in Information Technology with Dublin Institute of Technology (DIT), since 1995. His field of interest is the Internet, e-commerce, database management systems and information technology for the hospitality and tourism industries. Before joining DIT, he worked as a systems manager for several US organizations developing and integrating hotel and cruise line reservation systems.

Sir Michael Bishop has been Chairman of British Midland plc since 1978.

Gerald L. Barlow is currently a Senior Lecturer in Operations Management in the Department of Business at the University of Central England. His research interests include operational issues associated with service industries, including capacity, inventory and service quality. Gerald has contributed to many operations and hospitality textbooks as well as academic and practitioner periodicals, and conferences.

Mike Boella is a Principal Lecturer at the University of Brighton Business School, where he teaches law, human resources management and international management. He is also a *professeur invité* at the University of Perpignan in France. Mike also teaches at the Ecole Hotelière de Lausanne. He trained for the hotel and catering industry at Portsmouth, later specializing in personnel management, working for Forte, Bass and as a consultant with Price Waterhouse. He has a masters degree from Sussex University. Mike is the author of a number of books, including *Human Resources Management in the Hospitality Industry*, now in its seventh edition. He is also advisory editor to the Croner CCH catering series of publications.

Kevin Donaghy holds a first class honours degree in hotel and tourism management and a DPhil in hospitality management. Kevin has spent fifteen years working in the hospitality sector at management level and has extensive links with the local, national and international hotel sector. His research interests are in the areas of yield management and revenue optimization and he has worked with the national and international hotel sector in Athens, Jordan, Beirut, South Africa, the UK and Ireland. Kevin now owns KPD solutions, a specialist management consultancy and training company in Northern Ireland which works with clients both nationally and internationally in the hotel and tourism sector.

David A. Edgar is the Head of Division of Business Information Management at Caledonian Business School, Glasgow Caledonian University, Scotland. He is an active researcher in strategic management and knowledge management, with particular interests in the nature of value creation in organizations and the role of knowledge and knowledge management. Most current research has revolved around the strategic use of knowledge management to gain and sustain competitive advantage and the revision of business approaches in a knowledge-driven economy.

Sir Rocco Forte is chairman of RF Hotels, his luxury hotel company established in 1996 following the hostile takeover of Forte plc. Oxford educated, Sir Rocco is a fellow of the Institute of Chartered Accountants and was knighted in 1994 for services to the UK tourism industry, including his work with the British Hospitality Association and the World Travel and Tourism Council. Sir Rocco enjoys shooting, fishing and running and has completed several marathon runs for charity.

Alan Fyall is a Lecturer in Marketing at Napier University in Edinburgh. Alan has researched and published widely in the areas of sustainable tourism, services marketing, heritage tourism and more recently tourism marketing consortia. Publications to date include works in *Tourism Management*, *Journal of Hospitality and Leisure Marketing* and *Annals of Tourism Research*. In addition, Alan has presented papers at conferences in Europe and the United States. He holds a master of philosophy from the University of Wolverhampton and has extensive teaching experience.

Philip Goulding is a Lecturer in Tourism Management at Napier University in Edinburgh, specializing in the areas of tourism operations and tourism development. Philip graduated first from Birmingham University, then from Strathclyde University

(MSc in tourism), after having spent several years working in the travel trade and incoming tourism sectors. His research interests revolve around demand management and seasonality, especially with respect to the Scottish tourism industry.

Jerry Hartley is Director of Hospitality and Consumer Management Studies at Birmingham College of Food. Jerry graduated in hotel and catering management at the University of Surrey and subsequently completed an MBA programme at the University of Bradford Management Centre. He has a number of years of experience in the hotel industry in the field of conference and function sales and management, as well as over ten years' teaching experience. His research interests focus on the area of conference and function management and he has published both within the UK and internationally in this field.

Ian S. A. Hood has worked in the rail industry as an operational research consultant for eleven years. This has involved a wide variety of business issues. Particular emphasis has been on passenger modelling, train performance modelling, revenue allocation, operational modelling and passenger demand forecasting.

Julian Hoseason is an Honorary Lecturer to Anglia Polytechnic University based at City College Norwich, and leads the HND/degree programmes in travel and tourism management. His main area of teaching covers tour and operations management. Other teaching and research interests are in heritage tourism and the economic location of attractions in Europe.

Jeremy R. Huyton has worked in the global hotel industry for seventeen years, in Britain, Africa, Australia and the Caribbean. Since taking up an academic career, Jeremy has taught accommodation management and management studies in both the United Kingdom and Hong Kong, having had a four-year secondment to Hong Kong Polytechnic University. It was during his time in the Far East that he became very interested in the dynamic hotel industry in China. Having recently completed his PhD, studying hospitality education in China, he has been internationally acknowledged as a leading expert in this field.

Nick Johns is Reader and Director of Research in the Hotel School, City College, Norwich, a regional college of Anglia Polytechnic University. He is well known for his work on the quality and productivity of hospitality operations and has also published extensively on hygiene and environmental issues. Nick is currently engaged in developing a new approach to service quality assessment in small hospitality enterprises. He is an associate editor of the *International Journal of Contemporary Hospitality Management* and is at present working on a book on research methods specifically for managers of service industries.

Peter Jones holds the Forte Chair of Hotel Management at the University of Surrey and is responsible for the Centre for Hospitality Industry Productivity Research. He is the author or editor of nine textbooks and over 30 journal articles, and has presented at conferences in eleven countries on five continents. He is currently researching a number of topics related to chain operations, including hotel yield management performance.

Sheryl E. Kimes is an Associate Professor of Operations Management at the Cornell University School of Hotel Administration. She has a PhD in production and operations management from the University of Texas at Austin. At Cornell, she teaches courses in quantitative methods, yield management and restaurant revenue management.

Eric Laws is the author of numerous texts in tourism management and he now resides in Australia. His work includes *Tourism Marketing: Service and Quality Management Perspectives* (1991), *Tourist Destination Management: Issues, Analysis and Policies* (1995) and *The Inclusive Holiday Industry* (1996).

Anna Leask is a Lecturer in Tourism Management at Napier University Business School. Anna studied at Aberdeen University, graduating with an honours degree in geography, after which she graduated from Strathclyde University with an MSc in hotel administration with tourism. Anna then worked for various properties in a management capacity, including Swallow Hotels and Glasgow Royal Concert Hall, before taking up a lecturing post. She is currently involved in a number of research and consultancy projects within the tourism field, particularly in the area of heritage management. Her co-edited text, entitled *Heritage Visitor Attractions: an Operations Management Perspective*, was published in February 1999.

Darren Lee-Ross has lectured on management and human resources management subjects on a range of degree and postgraduate programmes in a number of universities in the UK and Australia. He has a BSc (Hons) and a PhD and is currently Senior Lecturer in Management Studies at James Cook University, Australia. His research interests include health service quality assessment, attitudes and work motivation, and the study of organizational subcultures.

Hilary Main is a Senior Lecturer at Swansea Business School and specializes in marketing information systems and web-based marketing. Her key research areas are in the use of IT in the hospitality and tourism sectors and she has published in international journals and delivered key papers at international conferences. She is a business consultant for the travel sector for the FI group.

Breffni Noone is a Lecturer in Hospitality Management at the Dublin Institute of Technology (DIT). Breffni is a graduate of Trinity College Dublin with a first degree in Management and a higher diploma in Hotel and Catering Management from DIT. Prior to graduating from Dublin City University with an MBS, Breffni worked in operations management in hotels in Ireland and France. In addition to her teaching at the DIT, Breffni currently works as a consultant with the DIT Tourism Research Centre. Her research interests include revenue management, information technology and activity-based management information systems.

Robert Raeside is a Senior Lecturer in Mathematics at Napier University. He took up lecturing after the completion of his PhD, which involved a study of forecasting human populations. Robert's main research interests are in demography, forecasting and operational research, and he is currently supervising a number of research students in these areas. Recently, Robert has been involved with a number of consultancies in the area of quality improvement.

Peter Rand is Chairman and Chief Executive of the Peter Rand Group, Coventry. Peter graduated in hotel and catering management at the University of Surrey. Following management positions in the hotel industry, including general management with De Vere Hotels, Peter set up the first venue-sourcing company in the UK in 1973. His company now handles events throughout the world. Peter's particular interest is in raising the profile and standard of the conference industry. He was Founder President of the Meetings Industry Association and runs training courses on conference and banqueting related subjects for many of the largest UK hotel groups, universities and other meetings venues.

Sarah Thomas gained her first degree in hospitality management at Bournemouth University and later a postgraduate diploma in marketing. At the present time she is completing a PhD on managerial cognition and productivity within the UK hotel industry. She worked as a hotel manager for several years and is currently employed as a lecturer at Birmingham College of Food. Her main teaching areas are operations management, research methods and human resource management. Her publications to date have been in the areas of soft systems facilitation, productivity, yield management and human resource management.

Fiona Whelan-Ryan is a Lecturer in Hospitality Management and Course Tutor for the BA programme in hospitality management at the Waterford Institute of Technology. Fiona received an honours degree in management from the University of Dublin and a higher diploma in hotel and catering management from Dublin Institute of Technology. She was awarded an MBS from Dublin City University for full-time postgraduate research in the area of yield management and its application in hotels. Fiona lectured in DIT and took up her current post in 1996. She lectures in rooms division management, marketing and sales and II as applied in the hospitality industry. Her primary research interests are in yield management and marketing and sales.

David Windle is a Lecturer in the School of Mathematical and Physical Sciences at Napier University. His research interests are in all aspects of management science, especially multicriteria decision-making.

Foreword

As someone who fell in love with the airline industry as a starstruck teenager more years ago than I care to remember, I have always taken tremendous pleasure in seeing it advance and improve.

It therefore comes as a great pleasure to me to write the Foreword to the revised second edition of this text, only four years after the appearance of the groundbreaking first edition. It is most welcome to see that universities and colleges are examining a business issue as crucial as yield management. For the absolute and fundamental conundrum faced by any business, in any market, is how to maximize revenue while at the same time offering a service or product which is competitively priced – satisfying the overriding consumer desire to get value for money. The past decade has shown that this problem is nowhere more acute than in my industry. The airline business is hugely competitive. Maximizing revenue in such a price-sensitive area is a major issue.

At British Midland, we have long recognized the importance of yield management. In fact I believe a skilful and sensitive approach to this issue has helped to ensure that we have continued to register modest profits over the past few years while many in the industry have posted significant losses.

Effective yield management for us is making the best possible use of our data to ensure as accurate a forecast of demand as possible. It is a science and not an art. Accurate forecasting means higher load factors and less waste. For the consumer, it means that we can offer more discounted tickets as we can better predict the likely business demand on any particular service. But yield management is an issue that demands constant improvement. We have recently invested in a brand new state of the art computerized system. It is bigger and better than our earlier capability. It will further enhance our excellence in this crucial area.

I am sure that this book will continue to improve understanding of yield management throughout the tourism and hospitality industries. I am also pleased that it has become the definitive academic and industrial work in this area, demonstrated by the need for this second edition.

Sir Michael Bishop
British Midland Airways

Introduction

Needless to say, Ian and Anthony were delighted when David Barker from Continuum Publishers told us that our book was selling steadily and that it would be useful to produce a second edition. We met to discuss this project at the Third Annual International Conference on Yield Management, held at the University of Ulster, and we decided that we would like to bring in someone with fresh ideas; moreover, Ian was finishing his doctoral dissertation, so could not commit so much time. With this in mind we decided to ask Una McMahon-Beattie to join us, she being Northern Ireland's foremost academic in the subject.

We are pleased that some continuity has been maintained from the first edition by Sir Michael Bishop agreeing once again to provide the Foreword to the work and we are delighted to welcome Sir Rocco Forte as the new contributor of our Endnote. Both are well known and well respected entrepreneurial leaders in industries where yield management is not only used, but probably essential to profitable operation. We thank them both for their insights. We also wish to thank all the contributors who have worked so hard to update their work, sometimes substantially, and to those new contributors who have agreed to work with us to provide completely new chapters. Once again, we have contributions from around the world, bringing a global perspective to the book.

Readers who are familiar with the first edition will see some similarities but will also note many differences. These changes have been introduced to bring the new edition up to date in the fast changing world of yield management. Some changes have also been made to address the limitations of the first edition, which have been pointed out in various reviews of the book over the past couple of years. These changes are noted below.

The principles are once again set out by Sheryl Kimes in her authoritative chapter, which has been considerably revised and updated. The economic and legal aspects are covered by David Edgar and Mike Boella, respectively. These are followed by Robert Raeside and David Windle's essential chapter on quantitative methods used for yield calculation and forecasting.

Part II, on models of yield management, is again headed by Eric Laws, who reviews pricing decisions in the inclusive holiday sector of the tourism industry. This is followed by a new chapter from Peter Jones, who reviews definitions of yield management, proposes a new model that might be used and demonstrates how this can be used to measure the impact of yield management on performance in hotels. Also new is a chapter by Ian Hood, who has devised a model for yield management implementation and monitoring for the railway industry.

The implications of how managers make decisions are reviewed by Ian Yeoman and Anthony Ingold. A completely new chapter has been added reviewing the interaction between yield management and productivity, by Una McMahon-Beattie, Anthony Ingold and Darren Lee-Ross. This is followed by Nick Johns's work on computerized yield management systems, drawing on the experiences of the airline industry. There follows a new chapter by Breffni Noone and Neil Andrews, which provides a timely look at the effects that new technologies are having on yield management. Finally in this section, there is another new chapter reviewing the interaction between marketing operations and yield management, concentrating particularly on the small hotel sector. This chapter addresses one of the omissions of the first edition of this book, and is by Hilary Main.

The Service Sector Studies section has been expanded to include a number of new areas. The chapter on yield management and the airline industry has been rewritten and includes much new material relating to yielding in airline alliances and yielding cargo. The chapter is by Anthony Ingold and Jeremy Huyton. Gerald Barlow has contributed a new chapter on yield management in the budget airline industry, concentrating on the operation of easyJet. This is followed by a completely updated look at revenue management in Scottish visitor attractions by Philip Goulding and Anna Leask. Una McMahon-Beattie and Kevin Donaghy have updated their chapter on yield management practices in UK hotels. Jeremy Huyton and Sarah Thomas have also reviewed their contribution, which examines yield management implementation and application in the UK hotel industry with a case study of the Warwick Hilton Hotel.

Three new chapters follow, with Fiona Whelan-Ryan introducing the concept of applying yield management to the restaurant industry. This is followed by an authoritative review of capacity management in the cruise industry by Julian Hoseason, an expanding and important sector of the tourism industry. Gerald Barlow takes us into the world of the football industry, showing how football clubs operate and how they could apply the principles of yield management to their operations.

The last chapter is once again by Jerry Hartley and Peter Rand, who provide an authoritative insight into the complexities of managing capacity in the conference industry; again, this chapter has been revised and updated.

We hope that this new revised and expanded edition will prove as popular and useful to its readers as the first edition.

Anthony Ingold, Birmingham
Una McMahon-Beattie, Belfast
Ian Yeoman, Edinburgh

DEDICATIONS

(Anthony Ingold) To Lorraine

(Una McMahon-Beattie) To Graham and James

(Ian Yeoman) To my mother

PART I
THE PRINCIPLES OF YIELD MANAGEMENT

1

A Strategic Approach To Yield Management

Sheryl E. Kimes

INTRODUCTION

Yield management originated with the deregulation of the US airline industry in the late 1970s. People's Express, one of the new airlines that emerged, offered customers a low-priced ticket with minimal amenities. Major airlines, such as American and United, decided to compete with People's Express by offering a few seats at even lower fares but maintaining higher fares on the remainder of their seats. In this way, they attracted the price-sensitive People's Express customers while still maintaining their other higher-paying passengers. As a result, many People's Express passengers switched to the major carriers, and People's Express eventually declared bankruptcy. Former People's Express chairman Donald Burr attributes many of People's Express's problems to the lack of a yield management system (Anon., 1992; Cross, 1997).

Yield (or revenue) management, a method for managing capacity profitably, has since gained widespread acceptance in the airline and hotel industries. The term 'yield' originated in the airline industry and refers to yield (or revenue) per available seat mile. The term is easily applied to other industries by altering it to yield (or revenue) per available time-based inventory unit. Yield management is a method which can help a firm to sell the right inventory unit to the right type of customer, at the right time and for the right price. Yield management guides the decision of how to allocate undifferentiated units of capacity to available demand in such a way as to maximize profit or revenue. The problem then becomes one of determining how much to sell at what price and to which market segment.

Research in yield management has previously addressed the theoretical and practical problems facing airlines and hotels, among other industries, but has given little consideration to other industries. Many industries are similar enough to hotel and airline operations that they should be able to apply yield management principles. Indeed, many industries use various yield management-type practices, but the application has so far been mostly tactical. I believe that a broad theory of yield management

3

would permit other industries to gain the benefits of strategic yield management that they currently lack.

The objective of this chapter is to develop the framework for such a theory. I discuss the necessary conditions for yield management, the strategic levers available for yield management, how they have been applied in traditional yield management settings and how they, along with some tactical tools, can be applied to other industries.

DEFINING YIELD MANAGEMENT

Yield management is the application of information systems and pricing strategies to allocate the right capacity to the right customer at the right place at the right time (Kimes, 1989; Weatherford and Bodily, 1992). In practice, yield management has meant setting prices according to predicted demand levels so that price-sensitive customers who are willing to purchase at off-peak times can do so at favourable prices, while price-insensitive customers who want to purchase at peak times will be able to do so. The application of yield management has been most effective when it is applied to operations that have the following characteristics: relatively fixed capacity, predictable demand, perishable inventory, appropriate cost and pricing structure, and demand that is variable and uncertain.

Relatively Fixed Capacity

Yield management is appropriate for capacity-constrained service firms. Firms not constrained by capacity can use inventory as a buffer to deal with fluctuations in demand, but capacity-constrained firms must make do with what they have. Capacity can be measured in both physical and non-physical units. For example, physical capacity may be measured by the number of seats, the number of rooms or the number of square meters. Non-physical capacity is usually time-based and reflects the notion of a physical capacity used for certain periods of time. Examples include room-nights (for hotels), seat-hours (for restaurants) and tee-times (for golf courses).

Capacity is generally fixed over the short term, although some firms are able to change their capacity by adjusting the amount of space or time available. For example, airlines can change the size of their planes and restaurants can reconfigure their dining rooms or use outdoor seating during summer months.

Predictable Demand

Demand for capacity-constrained firms consists of customers who make reservations and walk-in customers. Both forms of demand can be managed, but different strategies are required. In sum, customers who make reservations and those who walk in constitute an inventory from which managers can select the most profitable mix of customers. To forecast this demand and manage the yield it generates, a manager needs to compile information on the percentage of reservations and walk-ins, customers' desired time periods and likely service duration. Tracking customer arrival patterns requires an effective computerized or manual reservation system.

Perishable Inventory

One might think of inventory as physical, but the inventory of capacity-constrained service firms should be thought of as time – or, in this case, the time during which a unit of capacity is available. If an inventory unit is not occupied for a period of time, that part of the firm's inventory perishes. This is the key to the strategic framework, and it is the element that has been missing in most approaches to yield management. Instead of counting the number of customers or calculating the average yield per customer, managers should measure yield per available time-based inventory unit (RevPATI). This measure captures the time factor involved in capacity-constrained service firms.

Many companies evaluate managers and employees based on average sales per customer. This is equivalent to hotels' measuring effectiveness by average daily rate without paying attention to occupancy. While knowing sales per customer or contribution margins of menu items is valuable, those measures do not provide the information on yield generation that RevPATI would give.

Appropriate Cost and Pricing Structure

Industries using yield management should possess a cost structure that features relatively high fixed costs and fairly low variable costs. Like hotels and airlines, other capacity-constrained industries must generate sufficient revenue to cover variable costs and offset at least some fixed costs. The relatively low variable costs associated with many capacity-constrained industries allow for some pricing flexibility and give operators the option of reducing prices during low-demand times.

Time-Variable Demand

Customer demand varies by time of year, by week, by day, and by time of day. For some firms, demand may be higher on weekends, during summer months, or at particular times of day. Managers must be able to forecast time-related demand so that they can make effective pricing and allocation decisions to manage the shoulder periods around high-demand periods. A special factor for firms using yield management is that they have to predict the length of time a customer will use the service. For example, in restaurants while it is usually true that lunch is short and dinner is long, if managers can accurately predict customer duration, they can make better reservation decisions and give better estimates of waiting times for walk-in customers.

STRATEGIC LEVERS OF YIELD MANAGEMENT

This section is adapted from Kimes and Chase (1998). Many industries appear to possess the conditions necessary for yield management, but there is little evidence of most industries using a strategic approach for using the demand-management mechanisms at hand. A successful yield management strategy is predicated on effective control of customer demand. I have alluded to the two strategic levers that managers have at hand to manage demand and, thus, revenue. Those are duration management and demand-based pricing (Kimes and Chase, 1998).

		Price	
		Fixed	Variable
	Predictable	Quadrant 1: Cinemas Stadiums/arenas Convention centres	Quadrant 2: Hotels Airlines Rental cars Cruise lines
Duration	Unpredictable	Quadrant 3: Restaurants Golf courses Internet service providers	Quadrant 4: Continuing care Hospitals

Figure 1.1 Typical pricing and duration positioning of selected service industries

Price is a fairly obvious target for manipulation, and many operators already offer price-related promotions to augment or shift peak-period demand (e.g. early bird specials, special promotions). More sophisticated manipulations of price include time-of-day pricing, day-of-week pricing and price premiums or discounts for different types of customers. Managing duration is a bit more complicated. On the production side, managers must streamline and control their service-delivery process, as well as understand customer-arrival patterns and determine ways of influencing customer duration.

A TYPOLOGY OF YIELD MANAGEMENT

Different industries are subject to different combinations of duration control and variable pricing (see Figure 1.1) (Kimes and Chase, 1998). Industries traditionally associated with yield management (hotels, airlines, car rental firms and cruise lines) are able to apply variable pricing for a product that has a specified or predictable duration (Quadrant 2). Cinemas, performing arts centres, arenas and convention centres charge a fixed price for a product of predictable duration (Quadrant 1), while restaurants, golf courses and most Internet service providers charge a fixed price but face a relatively unpredictable duration of customer use (Quadrant 3). Many health-care businesses charge variable prices (e.g. Medicare versus private pay), but do not know the duration of patient use, even though some may try to control that duration (Quadrant 4). The lines dividing the quadrants are broken because in reality no fixed demarcation point exists between quadrants. Thus, an industry may have attributes from more than one quadrant.

Successful yield management applications are generally found in Quadrant 2 industries, because they can manage both capacity and customer duration. Other industries can shift to Quadrant 2 strategies to achieve some of the revenue gains associated with yield management by manipulating duration and price. Although many companies use some of the tools described in Kimes and Chase (1998), a strategic framework with which to evaluate and position such efforts has not yet been developed.

Duration Management

Managers of capacity-constrained firms typically face an unpredictable duration of customer use, which inhibits their ability to manage revenue. To allow for better yield management opportunities, managers must increase control over the length of time customers use their service. To do this, they can refine the definition of duration, reduce the uncertainty of arrival, reduce the uncertainty of duration or reduce the amount of time between customers.

Refining the Definition Of Duration

Duration is how long customers use a service and is measured either in terms of time (i.e. the number of nights or number of hours) or by event (i.e. a meal or a round of golf). When duration is defined as an event rather than as time, forecasting the length of customer use becomes particularly challenging. Thus, if duration for all industries could be defined in time, rather than events, better control of duration would be likely to result.

Uncertainty of Arrival

In order to increase duration control, companies must ensure that customers honour their reservations. If customers do not arrive, or arrive late, the company may be faced with unused capacity and, therefore, less revenue. Since many capacity-constrained firms have perishable inventory, they must protect themselves from no-shows. Firms can use both internal (not involving customers) and external (involving customers) approaches to decrease uncertainty of arrival. Internal approaches include the forecasting of arrivals and no-shows and overbooking models (for example, Rothstein, 1971, 1985; Schlifer and Vardi, 1975; Lieberman and Yechialli, 1978). External approaches to reducing arrival uncertainty shift the responsibility of arriving to the customer. The deposit and cancellation policies used at many capacity-constrained service firms, such as cruise lines, restaurants and resorts, are excellent examples of external approaches.

Uncertainty of Duration

Reducing duration uncertainty enables management to gauge capacity requirements better and hence to make better decisions as to which reservation requests to accept. Both internal and external approaches can be used for this purpose. Internal approaches include accurate forecasting of the length of usage and the number of early and late arrivals and departures, and improving the consistency of service delivery (Kimes *et al.*, 1998). External approaches for handling uncertainty of duration generally reach the customer in the form of deposits or penalties. Although penalties may work in the short term, they risk incurring customer wrath and hurting the company in the long run. For this reason, internal approaches are generally preferable (Kimes and Chase, 1998).

Reduce Time Between Customers

Reducing the amount of time between customers (changeover time reduction) by definition means that more customers can be served in the same, or a shorter, period of time. Although changeover time reduction is not normally considered a tool of yield management, it is a tactic which can be used to increase revenue per available inventory unit. Such tactics play an important role in the yield management strategy. Changeover time reduction has become a common strategy for airlines. Southwest Airlines and the Shuttle by United both boast of 20-minute ground turnarounds of their aircraft (compared to the average of 45 minutes at most airlines) and have been able to increase the utilization of their planes (Kimes and Young, 1997). Many restaurants have instituted computerized table management systems which track tables in use, the progress of the meal and when the bill is paid. When customers leave, the table management system notifies bussers, and the table is cleared and reset (Liddle, 1996). The result is an increase in table utilization and hence revenue per available seat hour.

Price

To use yield management effectively, companies must develop logical differential pricing policies. Industries actively practising yield management use differential prices and charge customers using the same service at the same time different prices depending upon customer and demand characteristics. Passengers in the economy section of a flight from New York City to London may pay from nothing (for those using frequent flyer vouchers) to over $2000. The fares vary according to the time of reservation, the restrictions imposed or the group or company affiliation. In contrast, Quadrant 1 and 3 industries use relatively fixed pricing and charge customers using the same service at the same time the same price.

Optimal Price Mix

Companies must be sure that they offer a logical mix of prices from which to choose. If customers do not see much distinction between the different prices being quoted, a differential pricing strategy may not work. Determining the best mix of prices is difficult because management often has little information on price elasticities. The lack of price elasticity information usually results in pricing decisions based solely on competitive pressures.

Development of Rate Fences

The possession of a good pricing structure does not ensure the success of a variable pricing strategy. Companies must also have a logical rationale, or, in industry terms, 'rate fences' that can be used to justify price discrimination. Quadrant 2 industries often use rate fences, such as when the reservation is booked or when the service is consumed, to determine the price a customer will pay. Rate fences refer to qualifications which must be met in order to receive a discount (Hanks *et al.*, 1992; Dolan and Simon, 1996). Physical rate fences include tangible features such as room type or view for hotels, seat type or location for airlines, or table location for restaurants. Non-physical rate fences include cancellation or change penalties, and benefits based on when the reservation was booked, desired service duration, group membership or affiliation and time of usage.

It is common practice for companies to adopt differential pricing schemes without rate fences. Hotels use top-down pricing in which reservation agents quote the rack rate (generally the highest rate) and only quote lower rates if customers ask for them. Knowledgeable customers may know to ask for the lower rate, but inexperienced customers may not. Customers view this practice in a highly unfavourable way (Kimes, 1994).

NECESSARY INGREDIENTS FOR A YIELD MANAGEMENT SYSTEM

In order to implement a yield management system, a company must possess the ability to segment the market based on willingness to pay, information on historical demand and booking patterns, good knowledge of pricing, a well developed overbooking policy and a good information system. Each of the necessary ingredients will be discussed below.

Market Segmentation

In order to be able to use yield management effectively, a company must be able to segment its customers into those who are sensitive to price and those who are insensitive to price. Airlines have done an excellent job of segmenting their passengers by willingness to pay. The restrictions associated with low fares (i.e. Saturday night stays, advanced purchase requirements and cancellation penalties) encourage price-conscious travellers to book ahead if they wish to obtain lower rates. Business travellers, who are typically more time-sensitive, are unable to qualify for the lower rates. The hotel industry has also experimented with similar ideas. For example, Marriott has instituted low rates available to customers who book at least three weeks ahead of time and who are willing to accept non-refundable rates (Hanks *et al.*, 1992).

Historical Demand and Booking Patterns

Accurate forecasts are essential to a yield management system. Extensive information on demand and booking patterns by rate level and length of usage is necessary for forecasting. Most firms have information on historical sales patterns, but may not track when customers make their reservations. Without this type of information, it is almost impossible to make accurate forecasts.

Booking curves can be developed which show the increase in reservations over time. Booking curves, which show the number of reservations on hand for various days before customer arrival (often referred to as reading days), are the foundation of any yield management system. The booking horizon for different types of businesses varies. For example, reservations are made far in advance for resort hotels, but may be made at the last minute for an airport hotel. If managers know their booking patterns, they will be better able to decide which reservations to accept and which to deny.

Pricing Knowledge

Many people believe that yield management is a pricing method by which firms change their price thousands of times a day. In reality, companies using yield management rely on opening and closing already-existing rate classes. Some theoretical work on dynamic pricing has been published, but computational intensity has so far prevented widespread use of dynamic pricing models. Many airline and hotel firms are actively studying the possibility of developing dynamic pricing approaches to yield management.

Yield management is essentially a form of price discrimination. As with other businesses such as telephone service and cinemas, when demand is low, discounted prices are available, but when demand is high, discounted rates are unavailable. By offering multiple rates, firms hope to increase their revenue (see Cross, 1997, for a good explanation of the advantages of multiple rates). If firms price their services incorrectly, yield management systems may end up making incorrect decisions about rate and availability restrictions.

Most firms that practice yield management rely on competitive pricing methods. Global distribution systems (such as Sabre and Apollo), electronic commerce sites and shopping services help companies determine the prices that their competitors are offering.

Overbooking Policy

A logical overbooking policy is essential to any good yield management system. Companies overbook to protect themselves against the possibility of no-shows. To develop an overbooking policy, a firm must collect information on no-show and cancellation rates over time. Companies can develop other methods, such as guarantees, customer reminders or deposits, to reduce the likelihood of no-shows. In addition, firms must develop internal methods for dealing with displaced customers. If employees are not trained in how to handle this potentially unpleasant situation, both customer and employee satisfaction may suffer.

Information System

For a yield management system to be successful, it must be integrated with the other information technology (IT) systems of the company. Without system integration, the same data may be entered into multiple systems and each system may be operating without complete information. The lack of computer integration is one of the biggest obstacles facing successful yield management implementation. Although some firms (most notably in the airline industry) have successfully addressed this issue, most yield management systems are not well integrated with other IT systems.

UNRESOLVED ISSUES AND THE FUTURE

Although yield management has met with success in many industries (Hanks *et al.*, 1992; Smith *et al.*, 1992; Geraghty and Johnson, 1997; Metters and Vargas, 1999), many issues remain unresolved. Major unresolved issues include the best and appropriate uses of forecasting, information system integration, pricing, customer satisfaction and incentive systems. In addition, other areas, such as expansion into other areas of business, regional or city-wide yield management and integration with e-commerce, offer great potential.

Forecasting

A detailed and accurate forecast is the key ingredient for any yield management system but little research on the best forecasting method, the best level of aggregation and the best constraining method exists. Recent research in the hotel and airline industries shows that simple exponential smoothing and pick-up methods provide the most accurate forecasts (Weatherford, 1998; Kimes and Weatherford, 1999) and that disaggregated forecasts provide more accurate results than aggregated forecasts (Weatherford *et al.*, 1999). With the exception of the PODS studies (Skwarek, 1996), little published research on the choice of unconstraining method exists. Without good forecasting, yield management systems may result in erroneous recommendations and poor performance.

Information Systems Integration

A yield management system requires an additional computer system which must be integrated into the IT structure of a company. Companies using computerized yield management systems have faced severe integration problems and are frequently unable to rely on two-way interfaces between their yield management system and other IT systems (Inge, 1998). Until such issues are resolved, the implementation of yield management will be difficult.

Pricing

Most yield management systems assume that the set of prices are given and that the role of the yield management system is to determine which prices are open and which are closed. Airlines and hotels are actively researching dynamic pricing and are trying to determine how to apply optimal pricing in real-time. A 1 per cent increase in price can result in a net income gain of 10–15 per cent (Dolan and Simon, 1996). Clearly, efforts to determine the structure and application of the optimal price mix are worthwhile and can result in a high return.

Customer Satisfaction

Long-term studies on the impact of yield management on customer satisfaction and loyalty have not been conducted. If yield management results in a serious decline in customer satisfaction and repeat business, the use of yield management may be unwise. If customers perceive that firms are behaving in an unfair manner, they are less likely to patronize that firm (Kahneman *et al.*, 1986). Customers are more likely to view yield management practices as fair if they are provided with full information on restrictions associated with discounted rates and if customers are given sufficient benefits to offset rate and booking restrictions (Kimes, 1994).

Incentive Systems

Some companies that have tried to implement yield management have been unsuccessful because of a lack of attention to appropriate employee incentive systems. Incentive systems which help to align the goals of employees and managers with the goal of maximizing revenue must be developed if a yield management system is to be truly successful (Hensdill, 1998).

Expansion to Other Parts of the Business

Yield management has typically been applied to the reservations of individuals, but in the hotel industry, for example, this effectively precludes groups, tour operators, corporate accounts and other non-rooms revenue (food and beverage, recreation, retail). Some hotel chains are seeking to develop total hotel yield management in an attempt to maximize their total revenue rather than just their rooms revenue.

City-Wide Yield Management

In a related issue, some companies (notably Disney and Marriott) are trying to do more than maximize the revenue of a single hotel. For example, Disney controls over 20,000 rooms in Orlando, Florida. Rather than maximize the revenue for each of their hotels, Disney tries to maximize the revenue over all hotels. Similarly, Marriott has developed revenue management clusters in which the revenue for all Marriott-affiliated brands is maximized for a particular city or region. Maximizing revenue across hotels requires a sophisticated campus-wide system approach in which business can be easily transferred from one unit to another.

Integration with E-commerce

E-commerce will significantly change the way in which companies sell their capacity. E-commerce businesses such as priceline.com, expedia.com and other bid-based companies give capacity-constrained firms an opportunity to sell their capacity directly to consumers and profitably and efficiently to dispose of unsold perishable inventory. E-commerce also offers the potential of dynamic, customer-based, pricing which may alter the way in which yield management is practised.

CONCLUSION

Yield management offers the potential of increased revenue to any capacity-constrained firm. A good yield management system helps to coordinate complex information which can then be used to make better pricing and duration control decisions. If yield management is to be truly successful, companies must seriously address both the technical and non-technical implementation issues and must be prepared to embrace and anticipate future technological changes.

REFERENCES

Anon. (1992) 'A conversation with Don Burr'. *Scorecard*, fourth quarter: 6–7.

Belobaba, P. P. (1987) 'Air travel demand and airline seat inventory management. PhD Thesis, Massachusetts Institute of Technology.

Cross, R. G. (1997) *Revenue Management: Hard-Core Tactics for Market Domination*. New York: Broadway Books.

Dolan, R. J. and Simon, H. (1996) *Power Pricing*. New York: The Free Press.

Geraghty, M. K. and Johnson, E. (1997) 'Revenue management saves National Car Rental'. *Interfaces*, **27** (1), 107–27.

Hanks, R. D., Cross, R. G. and Noland, R. P. (1992) 'Discounting in the hotel industry: a new approach'. *Cornell Hotel and Restaurant Administration Quarterly*, **33** (2), 40–5.

Hensdill, C. (1998) 'The Culture of Revenue Management'. *Hotels*, March, 83–6.

Inge, J. (1998) 'Revenue management systems: "must-have" or luxury?' *Hotel and Restaurant Technology Update*, fall: 4–10.

Kahneman, D., Knetsch, J. and Thaler, R. (1986) 'Fairness as a constraint on profit seeking: entitlements in the market'. *American Economic Review*, **76** (4), 728–41.

Kimes, S. E. (1989) 'Yield management: a tool for capacity-constrained service firms'. *Journal of Operations Management*, **8** (4), 348–63.

Kimes, S. E. (1994) 'Perceived fairness of yield management'. *Cornell Hotel and Restaurant Administration Quarterly*, **35** (1), 22–9.

Kimes, S. E. and Chase, R. B. (1998) 'Strategic levers of yield management'. *Journal of Service Research*, **1** (2), 156–66.

Kimes, S. E., Chase, R. B., Choi, S., Ngonzi, E. N. and Lee, P. Y. (1998) 'Restaurant revenue management'. *Cornell Hotel and Restaurant Administration Quarterly*, **39** (3), 32–9.

Kimes, S. E. and Weatherford, L. R. (1999) 'Forecasting methods for hotel revenue management: an evaluation'. Working paper.

Kimes, S. E. and Young, F. (1997) 'The Shuttle by United'. *Interfaces*, **27** (3), 1–13.

Lee, A. O. (1990) 'Airline reservations forecasting: probabilistic and statistical models of the booking process'. PhD Thesis, Massachusetts Institute of Technology.

Liddle, A. (1996) 'New computerized table management reduces guests' waits, empty seats'. *Nation's Restaurant News*, 5 August, 22.

Lieberman, V. and Yechialli, U. (1978) 'On the hotel overbooking problem: an inventory problem with stochastic cancellations'. *Management Science*, **24**, 1117–26.

Metters, R. and Vargas, V. (1999) 'Yield management for the nonprofit sector'. *Journal of Service Research*, **1** (3), 215–26.

Rothstein, M. (1971) 'An airline overbooking model'. *Transportation Science*, **5**, 182–92.

Rothstein, M. (1985) 'OR and the airline overbooking problem'. *Operations Research*, **33** (2), 237–48.

Schlifer E. and Vardi, Y. (1975) 'An airline overbooking policy'. *Transportation Science*, **9**, 101–14.

Skwarek, D. K. (1996) 'Competitive impacts of yield management system components: forecasting and sell-up methods.' MIT Flight Transportation Lab Report R96–6.

Smith, B. C., Leimkuhler, J. F. and Darrow, R. M. (1992) 'Yield management at American Airlines'. *Interfaces*, **22** (1), 8–31.

Weatherford, L. R. (1998) 'Forecasting issues in revenue management'. Presentation at spring INFORMS Conference, Montreal.

Weatherford, L. R. and Bodily, S. E. (1992) 'A taxonomy and research overview of perishable-asset revenue management: yield management, overbooking pricing'. *Operations Research*, **10** (5), 831–44.

Weatherford, L. T., Kimes, S. E. and Scott, D. A. (1999) 'Aggregation and disaggregation in forecasting for hotel revenue management'. Working paper.

2

Economic Theory of Pricing for the Hospitality and Tourism Industry

David A. Edgar

INTRODUCTION

This chapter aims to introduce the student to the economic theory underlying the concept of yield management. Using a pricing decision framework the elements of demand, supply and price are explained relative to the hospitality and tourism industry.

While economic theory tends to be universal in nature it is essential to understand the context within which the theory is adopted. Before we examine the elements of the pricing framework it is therefore useful to place the theory within the context of the hospitality and tourism industry. Hospitality and tourism falls within the category of service industries.

Service industries differ in characteristics from primary or manufacturing industries in terms of a number of key areas:

- services themselves are unstorable, but their experience or consequences may be longer lasting;
- consumption and production are generally simultaneous and inseparable;
- services have a high degree of intangibility but are not necessarily exclusively intangible;
- there is a high degree of customer and culture specificity and intimacy.

Obviously different service operations and markets display these characteristics in differing degrees and as such each characteristic should perhaps be viewed as an element of a continuum (Van Dierdonck, 1992, Bitran and Lojo, 1993) ranging from low perishability to high perishability, low simultaneity to high simultaneity, low intangibility to high intangibility, and low customer intimacy to high customer intimacy. Hence, individual hospitality and tourism operations and markets can be composed of a vast array of elements of the service continuum in differing degrees. As such, the pricing decisions of managers will vary depending upon the continuum mix of each product[1] or market.

This chapter provides the tools for understanding the nature of demand, supply and pricing within organizations based upon economic principle. The underlying theory should be considered in the context of a range of operations and not accepted as being consistent for all operations or markets within the hospitality and tourism industry.

THE PRICING DECISION FRAMEWORK

> To be successful, the hotelier must keep the bar full, the house full, the storeroom full, the wine cellar full, the customers full, and not get full himself. (Garvey, 1986)

Based upon this rather simple premise, considering the major implications imposed by a changing hospitality environment, and accepting that the key measure of an organization's success is financial performance, pricing in the hospitality and tourism industry has major implications for how organizations react to change and what resulting performance they achieve (Lewis and Chambers, 1989; Crawford-Welch, 1991).

In economic theory, price is the main factor used to explain the links between supply and demand for a product (Wolfe, 1993). Therefore, a price decision framework provides an excellent vehicle for explaining the dynamics of the economics of yield management.

Pricing Decision Framework

The price at which hospitality and tourism products are offered for sale affects the demand for those products (Relihan, 1989) and therefore revenue and profit. From pricing theory (Kuncher and Hilleke, 1993) the profit maximizing price of a product depends on market reactions and marginal costs, i.e. both the market and the company's internal cost structure are determinants of a product's price. This leads to the framework adopted for this section. The framework, shown in Figure 2.1, was constructed by Kuncher and Hilleke (1993), and while not dedicated specifically to the hospitality and tourism industry, does represent the key elements of pricing and therefore forms an excellent means of examining the economics of yield management. From Figure 2.1 there are two key elements to price, the market side or demand, and the company side or supply.

The market side represents the consumer's ability and willingness to buy the product based upon the perceived value of the purchase at the purchase price and the resulting opportunity cost (i.e. the next best or alternative usage of the resource). Such willingness and ability to buy leads to the volume of achieved sales. The company side represents the logistics of providing the product including the costs of production and gross profit requirements.

In order to understand fully the nature of pricing decisions it is necessary to focus on the market side (demand) and company side (supply) in more detail before determining pricing and yield techniques.

DEMAND: THE MARKET SIDE

The market side revolves around the relative perceived value of a product and the consumer's willingness and indeed ability to buy that product. The perceived value will lead to the level of consumer price threshold, i.e. how much the consumer values the

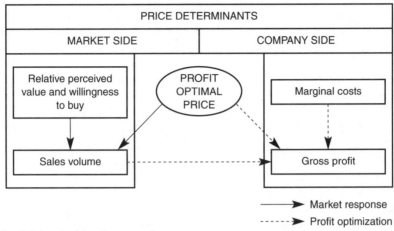

Figure 2.1 Pricing decision framework
Source: Kuncher and Hilleke (1993)

product and therefore how much he or she is willing to pay, subject to the law of diminishing marginal utility, or the value placed on each additional unit consumed.

Such value is obviously related to the nature of the product and alternative sources available. Rather than focusing on a debate as to which theories of demand and definitions of product are most pertinent, this section determines the grounding theory of demand allowing later sections to explore the elasticity of demand, representing different types of product.

Sales volume represents the amount consumed at various price levels and when combined with the value (price) indicates the turnover generated. This relationship reflects the principles of the demand curve D1 indicated in Figure 2.2a. From Figure 2.2a total turnover is calculated by multiplying Q1 and P1, or Q2 and P2. The revenue can be increased in two ways, either lower price and raise volume, or raise price and accept lower volumes. These are called MOVEMENTS ALONG the demand curve. As demand is an independent variable, these movements can only result from an increase or reduction in price. Such characteristics are the basics of yield management and are examined in more detail later. What should be noted here is that the price–volume relationship can vary considerably between and even within markets, making the pricing decision difficult, yet critical (Relihan, 1989). Often the hospitality and tourism product is produced and consumed on site, and is the result of an experience. The experience will determine whether the consumer recommends the product to others or consumes the product at a specific cost, i.e. price.

In addition to such movements *along* the demand curve, the curve can also *shift* to the right or to the left. When the curve shifts to the right it represents an increase in demand, while a shift to the left represents a decrease in demand. The cases of such shifts stem from changes in the business environment that move the environment away from *ceteris paribus*, the most common being those shown in Table 2.1. Hence, a shift in the demand curve to the right can result in a greater revenue generation without a reduction in price (Figure 2.2a D2) or a potential to raise price and maintain volume, perhaps raising profitability.

While these principles assume a single demand curve it would be unwise to think hospitality and tourism organizations have only one product or market. There are a

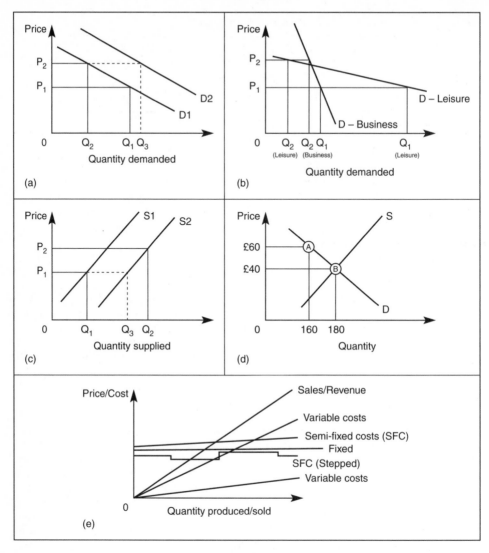

Figure 2.2 The demand curve: (a) The demand curve; (b) Price elasticity of hotel demand; (c) The supply curve; (d) Price equilibrium; (e) Cost dynamics: stepped and gradual fixed costs

wide range of markets serviced by operators in the industry, each with a different 'perceived value' for the product on offer and as such each with a different willingness or ability to pay. This willingness and ability to pay is termed 'elasticity of demand'.

DEMAND: THE ELASTICITY MIX

Most hospitality and tourism businesses serve a wide variety of clientele groups. It is feasible that every operation could have a different mix of consumers, even those operating under the same company or brand name. Of the same accord, it is important to acknowledge that the same consumer can fall into different target market categories.

Table 2.1 Shifts caused by common environmental changes

Environmental change	Increased demand (shift to the right)	Decreased demand (shift to the left)
Advertising/promotion	Successful advertising	Negative promotion
Change in fashion, trends, tastes	Fashionable	Unfashionable
Change in income	Increase	Decrease
Price change of complement products	Decrease	Increase
Price change of substitute products	Increase	Decrease

The corporate business traveller during the week becomes a leisure traveller when on holiday or at weekends. Different occasions find the same consumer having different expectations and needs (Buttle, 1986). Such a concept is termed elasticity of demand. Elasticity of demand has three commonly adopted measures – *price* elasticity, *income* elasticity and *cross* elasticity – representing the relationship between the elasticity measure and quantity demanded.

Price elasticity represents the relationship between a change in price and a change in quantity demanded. Income elasticity represents the relationship between a change in consumer income and quantity demanded. Cross elasticity represents the relationship between the change in the price of product x and the quantity of product y demanded. The calculations for each form of elasticity are:

$$\text{Price elasticity} = \frac{\text{Percentage change in quantity demanded}}{\text{Percentage change in price}}$$

$$\text{Income elasticity} = \frac{\text{Percentage change in quantity demanded}}{\text{Percentage change in income}}$$

$$\text{Cross elasticity} = \frac{\text{Percentage change in quantity demanded of } x}{\text{Percentage change in price of product } y}$$

The most relevant elasticity measure for the purposes of yield management is price elasticity of demand. The formula provides a result of <1, >1 or 1. A result of <1 indicates a market that is highly elastic, i.e. a change in price will have little effect on quantity demanded, the lower the result, the less price sensitive the market. A result of >1 indicates an elastic market, meaning a more price-sensitive market, while a result of 1 indicates unitary elasticity, i.e. a direct relationship between the change in price and the quantity demanded.

The elastic and inelastic markets are shown in Figure 2.2b, where the business market is depicted as price inelastic, i.e. a percentage rise in price is greater than the percentage fall in quantity demanded. In the leisure market, where demand is more elastic in nature, the percentage change in price is less than the percentage change in quantity demanded, meaning that if price is raised or lowered, demand levels alter considerably (Hanks *et al.*, 1992).

Now consider that an operation has a mixture of business and leisure markets all with varying degrees of elasticity as shown in Figure 2.2b. The pricing decision becomes critical to ensure that price-insensitive consumers, i.e. those who are highly inelastic, pay full tariff and do not trade down, and that a price is reached where less of the price-sensitive markets are attracted. Combine this with the nature of environments and the problems of seasonal markets and it becomes highly evident that an understanding of the nature of hospitality and tourism units is essential in implementing yield management strategies.

While the demand–price relationship is useful in determining the revenue generating potential of an organization, it is of little use in determining the actual profitability of the organization unless it is combined with elements of supply.

SUPPLY: THE COMPANY SIDE

From the company side, the emphasis shifts to being more operational in nature and focuses on the nature of marginal costing and supply. Marginal costs are the incremental cost per unit added to production or sales. Hence, the marginal cost is the cost of selling one extra bed night or one extra meal and is essentially the difference in variable cost between each incremental sale. The marginal cost relationship will lead to gross profit, in that the greater the margin between marginal cost and revenue, once fixed costs are covered, the greater the gross profit. The nature of hospitality unit costs warrants more detailed analysis and is therefore examined in the next section of this chapter. However, before we determine in more detail the nature of costs, the supply curve is introduced and the basics of price equilibrium are determined, representing the foundation of market forces.

As the demand curve indicated the quantity demanded of a product at a specific price, the supply curve indicates the quantity of a product supplied at each price (Figure 2.2c). Supply represents an inverse relationship to demand, in that as price increases suppliers are willing to supply more. This represents a *movement along* the supply curve.

The supply curve also *shifts* to the left and right as a result of elements affecting operational issues. If the curve shifts to the left supply is decreasing; if it shifts to the right supply is increasing. The most common issues causing shifts in supply are shown in Table 2.2. When supply is reduced, the product becomes scarce and commands a higher price, while when supply increases the product becomes more available making it difficult to command higher prices. Supply curve S2 in Figure 2.2c represents an increase in supply. The nature of most hospitality supply relative to yield management implies fixed supply in the short term. The key issue therefore relates to the combination of supply and demand, i.e. capacity management.

Figure 2.2d shows demand and supply for the same product on the same diagram. Point B is the price equilibrium of demand, i.e. all that is produced is consumed at the price charged. If the organization prices the product at £60 there will be excess capacity A to B (20 units), requiring a price reduction (i.e. a movement along the demand curve), or an increase in perceived value to attract the market (i.e. a shift of the demand curve to the right). Alternatively, a reduction in supply, i.e. a shift to the left, may make the product more scarce, thus shifting the equilibrium to point A and allowing an equilibrium price of £60.

Maximizing room rates and supplementary spend is clearly one of the biggest day-to-day challenges facing the hospitality unit. The over-supply in many markets (Fine,

Table 2.2 Common issues causing shifts in supply

Operational issue	Increased supply (shift to the right)	Decreased supply (shift to the left)
Change in government funding	Provide subsidies/lower tax	Raise tax/cut subsidies
Change in costs of production	Lower costs	Higher costs
Seasonality	In season	Out of season
Change in working practices	Good techniques	Poor techniques
Change in technology	New technology	Obsolete technology

1993), combined with generally poor economic conditions, forces many managers to price their products as low as possible in an attempt to raise volume and therefore profit.

It is clearly evident that the pricing technique used will have major implications on how well the hotel can adapt to changing environmental and economic conditions. Crawford-Welch (1991) classifies pricing into one of four categories: (a) cost pricing, based on methods such as cost plus mark-up, contribution or break even; (b) competitive pricing, based on meeting local competition; (c) market demand pricing; and (d) customer pricing techniques, based upon customer expectations and cognitive issues.

The most commonly used method of pricing, perhaps reflecting the product-driven approach to pricing by hotels, is where a room rate is determined by a combination of location, view, square footage and appointment (Orkin, 1990), revolving around the cost pricing techniques. The three most evident methods appear to be: (a) 'rule of thumb', where the rack rate is calculated by charging £1 per night per £1000 construction costs; (b) the Hubbart formula, where the average room rate is calculated by totalling the undistributed expenses with the required return and the rooms' operating expenses, less the net income from other departments, then dividing the whole lot by the number of room nights; and (c) the marginal costing method, where the average room rate is calculated by adding the required return to total costs and dividing by the expected number of room nights.

While in simple, less dynamic and less segmented markets such pricing methods prove effective, a more demand-driven strategy is required for modern hospitality operations (Orkin, 1990). This leads to the notion of examining the nature of hospitality and tourism cost dynamics in more detail before focusing on yield management and the alternative demand-driven approaches to enhancing performance through pricing.

SUPPLY: HOSPITALITY AND TOURISM COST DYNAMICS

The nature of costs is of key importance to the means of pricing and therefore to operational performance. In order to determine the nature of such costs it is necessary to establish the types of costs that exist, i.e. the cost dynamics, and the elements of hospitality costs. As the hospitality industry is multisegmented and multifaceted in nature, it is useful to focus on a sector of the industry to explain the dynamics of costs through examples. In keeping with the yield management theme and recognizing the

Yield Management

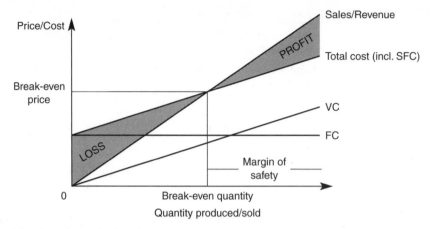

Figure 2.3 Cost dynamics: break-even

importance and value of the accommodation markets, this section uses hotels as the subject for explaining cost dynamics.

Cost Dynamics

It is common practice to divide hotel costs into categories of fixed, semi-fixed and variable costs, although some authors dispute the terminology of such categories (Davies, 1990). Each cost category displays distinct characteristics over the short and longer term.

Fixed costs can be seen as those costs that over the short term remain constant and are characterized by elements of the operation not affected by changes in the volume of guests or sales. Fixed costs include such items as rent, rates and loan interest repayments, and are a large cost to hotel operations (Orkin, 1990), representing on average 13.4 per cent of UK hotel revenues in 1992 (Miller, 1992). In terms of the methods of hotel ownership established by Harrison and Johnson (1992), it would appear that the closer to full owner or operator status, the higher the likely fixed costs incurred. This may explain the increased activity by some groups to seek alternative ownership patterns, such as franchising and management contracting.

Semi-fixed costs are costs that remain constant for a period of time and then change either in incremental steps or gradually over time. Examples here are permanent staffing levels or the purchase of new machinery.

Variable costs are the costs that fluctuate with the degree of production or sales and are most evident in the area of raw materials and seasonal staffing. However, variable costs will not necessarily increase and decrease directly in proportion to output (Wijeyesinghe, 1993). This provides a number of profit-making opportunities in relation to margin and contribution, discussed below under 'the elements of hotel costs'.

Figure 2.2e shows the cost dynamics in diagram form. Commonly, the costs are split simply into fixed costs and variable costs.

Adding fixed, semi-fixed and variable costs provides an indication of the hotel's total cost, which when combined with sales allows a break-even chart to be produced, as in Figure 2.3. The break-even chart illustrates that profit is made above the intersection of

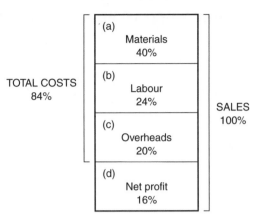

Figure 2.4 Hotel cost relationships
Source: Kotas and Davis (1976)

sales and total costs, representing the margin of safety. A reduction in sales revenue or increase in operating costs would move this point to the right, reducing the profitability of the organization and the margin of safety. Hence, for an organization to be profitable it should seek to exploit and expand the margin of safety. However, one should consider that such calculations often represent one point in time and, while providing useful information on a holistic level, they should not be treated in isolation, i.e. basic profit or loss does not provide sufficient detail of individual units of sale. Hence it is necessary to examine the elements of hotel cost.

Elements of Hotel Costs

Kotas and Davis (1976) provide a simplistic breakdown of the relationship of hotel costs relative to sales and profitability, which while dated provides a useful framework for understanding the need to examine elements of costs. Figure 2.4 shows this breakdown. From Figure 2.4 the relationship between costs, sales and profitability is clearly evident, although different operators will obviously have variations in the size of each cost. Sales can be seen to represent all costs plus profit or, similarly, profit can be seen as sales less costs. While this relationship is acceptable when adopting a holistic approach to a hotel's cost–profit relationship, it neglects to account for the complex package that makes up the sales structure of a hotel, i.e. room revenues, catering, telephone, services, etc. The result is that, when related to costs, the margins will vary throughout the hotel and thus the contribution that each department achieves will vary.

Based upon the former, probably the two most important cost elements in understanding the nature of the pricing decision of hotels and hospitality and tourism operations are the concepts of marginal costing and contribution. These in effect expose the nature of costs and revenue structures, by accounting for the high fixed cost base and the importance of covering variable costs relative to seasonality and demand elasticity. Based upon these key areas it is possible to determine the optimal price.

GAINING THE OPTIMAL PRICE: MARGINS AND CONTRIBUTIONS

The contention so far is that profit is the primary goal of any organization. The level of profit obtained can be expressed in a number of forms, the most simple of which, and indeed the foundation of all forms, is based upon the equation:

Profit = Total revenue − Total costs

Here total revenue is composed of the price of a product multiplied by the quantity of the product sold, and the total cost is represented by all costs associated with the operation. It therefore becomes evident that, to increase profit, revenue could be increased, by increasing price, quantity sold or both. However, the impact of price changes on profitability depends on, among other things, price elasticity (Orkin, 1990), income elasticity and the possibility of substituting for the product. It will also depend on supply variables such as the relative competitive position of the company (Ardel and Woods, 1991; Norrbin, 1993).

Alternatively, to raise profits, costs can be reduced in terms of: (a) fixed costs such as alternative forms of ownership; (b) semi-fixed costs, i.e. reducing full-time staffing levels; or (c) variable costs, i.e. cheaper food or smaller portions. The danger when reducing costs is a reduction in quality, as the market side established the price and therefore the revenue generated is based upon the consumer's perceived value and willingness to pay. Based on this premise, the most attractive way to raise profit would be to increase revenue while operating at maximum efficiency. This is the foundation of yield management.

Pricing within this context takes two key forms: pricing based on marginal cost and pricing based on contribution.

Marginal Costing

Much has been written from a technical perspective about the advantages and benefits of marginal costing and marginal income (Bonnisseau and Cornet, 1990; Naish, 1990; Kelly and Gopalan, 1992; Vohra, 1992). This section seeks to simplify the concept in relation to hospitality and tourism operations.

Marginal costing can be defined as 'the increase or reduction in total cost, at a given volume of output, resulting from an increase or reduction of one unit of output' (Boardman, 1978), while marginal revenue can be seen as the additional revenue obtained from producing one extra unit of output, the marginal income being the profit or difference between the marginal revenue and marginal cost.

The theory is that, for a short period, additional sales can be added to the normal sales volume profitably even at prices too low to cover a proportionate share of fixed overhead (Boardman, 1978). This is because the operations overheads have been met by previous sales, so as long as the remaining units sold cover the variable cost of offering those units then additional profit is being made. This is perhaps more clearly shown through the use of an example.

If a hotel sells on average 40,000 bed nights in a year, and the total costs amount to £800,000 (£300,000 fixed costs and £500,000 variable costs), then the total cost per bed night is £20. If the average achieved room rate per bed night is £45 then a net profit of £25 per bed night is made, or £1 million per annum. This may be regarded as the normal business of the hotel, and every sale is expected to bear its cost burden. Once the normal business of the hotel has been met then any additional room sales contribute to profit, as long as the price charged is greater than £12.50 (£500,000 ÷ 40,000), allowing room rate to be cut by as much as 70 per cent and hoping to attract additional spend in the supplementary areas, such as restaurant, bar, services. Marginal costing and marginal income can thus be very useful tools for the unit manager and form the basis of many hotel strategies, ranging from packaging to short break markets.

Contribution

The difference between the selling price per unit of additional sales and the marginal cost of those sales is the contribution per unit to fixed expenses and profit, generally referred to simply as the 'contribution'. If the selling price is greater than the marginal cost, identified earlier, then there will be a contribution to profit from additional sales. However, if the marginal cost is greater than the selling price the extra business will result in a loss (Boardman, 1978; Hughes, 1989). In a period when losses are being made owing to high fixed expenses a positive contribution may reduce the loss without actually resulting in a profit. This can be essential for survival and is well worth striving for during slack periods of demand.

While marginal income techniques and contribution may appear similar, they represent two inverted approaches. Marginal income ensures the hotel's fixed and variable costs have been covered by the existing volume of output before allowing additional units of output, essentially representing additional variable cost only, to be sold more cheaply as long as the variable cost is covered, thus making a profit. The contribution concept attempts at least to cover variable costs and go some way to contribute to fixed costs and, it is hoped, profit. Obviously, the most desirable method for hotel units is the marginal income approach, and this is where yield management can be of benefit.

ECONOMIC THEORY AND YIELD MANAGEMENT

The management of capacity or yield management has been identified as one strategy that can be adopted by hoteliers in order to balance demand and supply (Jones and Lockwood, 1989; Jones, 1993). It is a technique which focuses management decision-making on the maximization of returns from the sale of the central hotel product, accommodation (Brotherton and Mooney, 1992), and shifts the managerial focus from product orientation to demand orientation (Moje, 1990). Indeed, a survey by NOP (1993) established that filling rooms was the number one priority of 88 per cent of UK hotels.

Focusing management attention on the basic principles of pricing and controlling inventories yield management has proven a useful tool for maximizing revenues (Reliham, 1989; Jones and Hamilton, 1992), particularly in the airline industry, where its roots lie (James, 1987; Williams, 1987; Carter, 1988, Larsen, 1988; Kimes, 1989; Berge, and Hopperstad, 1993).

To a great extent, development and application in the hotel sector is still at an evolutionary stage of development (IHA, 1992; Donaghy *et al.*, 1994) with debate concerning the applicability of the concept to the hotel industry (Verchere, 1993) and in particular the segmented nature of hotel markets (Dunn and Brooks, 1990).

While airlines and hotels are similar in that they both operate with fixed capacity and perishable inventories, Kimes (1988) and Orkin (1988) have drawn attention to the specific problems in hotels of lack of a distinct rate structure, multiple night stays, multiplier effect and decentralization of information – problems rare in airlines. Hanks *et al.* (1992), however, establish that hotels provide ideal conditions for implementing yield management, as they display low variable costs, high fixed costs, perishable inventories, variable patterns of demand, an ability to forecast future patterns of demand and an ability to segment customers on their varying needs, behaviour and willingness to pay (Kimes, 1994). Whatever the argument, the underlying principles of yield management are simple – to maximize revenue.

In hotels, the most commonly adopted measure of the effectiveness of practices and policies applied to maximize revenue, i.e. yield management, is the realized revenue divided by the revenue potential. This can be applied to room, restaurant or bar sales. Perhaps the most prominent measure is that of room sales. In this area it should be recognized that many combinations of occupancy and average room rate could generate equal revenue and yield percentages. However, not all these combinations are necessarily equally beneficial for overall profitability. A combination of lower occupancy and higher rates, or higher occupancy and lower rates, may be equally desirable owing to lower room servicing costs of the former or higher potential food and beverage revenues related to the latter (Jones and Lockwood, 1989). Hence, while yield management's primary focus is often regarded as the maximization of sales revenue (Orkin, 1988), it is a 'concept of further extension in terms of the development of an optimum business mix to maintain profitable product–market alignment'.

The application of yield management within a hotel environment is therefore essentially an attempt to enhance a hotel's ability to operate a flexible, adaptive and predictive market response strategy which seeks to match variable market conditions with the selection of products offered, i.e. segmented markets. Yield management should therefore be viewed simply as the practice of maximizing profits from the sale of perishable assets: it is 'not a computer system (although computer systems can be used to support it) nor a set of mathematical techniques. It is an approach to increasing revenues and improving service by responding to current demand' (Lieberman, 1993). Bearing this in mind, the next section determines the methods based on economic pricing theory by which hotels attempt to 'increase revenues and improve service by responding to demand' and in the process maximize profitability.

Yield management is the revenue generation side of the profitability equation. There are a number of yield strategies that appear to have emerged over the past decade to raise revenue. These include discounting, segmentation, packaging, differentiation through value added, repositioning, knowledge management and offering short breaks, often adopted in some form of strategy mix.

Discounting

Discounting is the term given to hotel rooms that are offered for sale at rates below rack rate, rack rate being the published room rate. One may expect that the hotel industry would apply structured and logical rules for discounting, this is generally not the case (Hanks *et al.*, 1992; Rice, 1993). Although the practice of discounting is widespread, it may not be the most profitable way to fill rooms (Egan and Haynes, 1992). Hotels in different locations have different levels of discounts, with discounts varying widely throughout the year (Carroll, 1986) and the degree of discounting varying according to both property size and hotel location. The larger the property the higher the room rates and discounting percentage. Rates in most cities, which have the most expensive hotels, also show above average discounting (MacGill, 1992). However, as Walker (1993) established, discounting may be a feasible option for large hotel groups to gain market share, as 'in tough economic times the high price player can cut rate to hold occupancy, a move the low price operator cannot counter by suddenly adding more upscale facilities'. Indeed, MacGill (1992) identifies that by using discounting strategies to get people into the hotel, occupancies have fallen to a lesser degree than profits, essentially due to the additional supplementary spend, i.e. contribution.

While discounting seems to be a feasible option for larger hotel groups, it is certainly not a viable one. Discounting is damaging to the bottom line. The relationship between pricing strategies and bottom line results has been shown to be quite intricate, and discounting has not produced favourable profit results (Hanks *et al.*, 1992). It could, however, be argued that the very nature of demand and the demand curve forces hotels to discount to satisfy as many guests as possible and maximize revenues from existing demand.

It should also be remembered that if discounting does take place, considerable occupancy must be gained to compensate for revenue lost through reduced rates, market segments must be kept apart and differing rates justified. Wolfe (1993) estimated that if the hotel cuts its rack rate by 3 per cent and accepts a reduction in gross profit percentage of 5 per cent then sales must be increased by 150 per cent to make the same cash profit. It can therefore be seen that improving occupancy is one thing, but the problem facing most hotels is how to rebuild achieved room rates (Gordon, 1993). Essentially, what is needed, as identified by Orkin (1990) is 'a way to offer full rates and discounted rates concurrently'. To a great extent this can be achieved by segmenting the market.

Segmentation

The economics of supply and demand require that hotels are segmented to maximize revenue and attempt to cover the property's large fixed cost base (Hanks *et al.*, 1992). Different customers are charged different prices, capturing more revenue and satisfying more customers. The key to the concept is to have a meaningful segmentation strategy in place that differentiates customers who are willing and able to pay higher prices from those who are willing to change their behaviour in exchange for lower price points (Reliham, 1989; Hanks *et al.*, 1992). As such, market segmentation allows improved product pricing through the development of separate pricing structures (Berry *et al.*, 1991) and through products especially designed for different market segments. Single businesses can serve multiple market segments, but such businesses must ensure hotel operations are flexible enough to meet the expectations of different users throughout the week (Teare *et al.*, 1989; Russo, 1991; Quain, 1992).

The incompatibility of different market segments was identified by the airlines long before the hotel industry recognized the issue as either a problem or an opportunity. These incompatibilities become most apparent between the key segments of business and leisure travellers who might occupy the same seat (or hotel room) but have paid very different prices in return for forfeiting certain degrees of flexibility or choice. This segmentation phenomenon has been stimulated by recognition of the increased marketing potential of product branding aimed at specific markets, resulting in a hotel market that is highly sophisticated (EIU, 1991), and with the key companies using a combination of segmentation strategies and techniques to keep segments apart.

Packaging

What appear to be bargain rate packages can be used as a strategy to generate substantial new business from markets unwilling to pay rack rate. The success of such packages appears to hinge on the means by which items are 'bundled' together (Guiltinan, 1987) in an attempt to 'tangiblise the intangible' (Buttle, 1986). Often these items would be of little value to the full rate payer or would add more perceived value to the product as a package as opposed to individually either through ease of purchase or value in cash retail terms (Orkin, 1990). Examples here are what appears to be a free bottle of wine, chocolates or flowers in the hotel room for a honeymoon couple, or the use of a leisure centre or typing facilities for a business traveller.

Differentiation Through Value Added

'Goods manufacturers seek competitive advantage through features that may be visually or measurably identified, cosmetically implied or rhetorically claims by reference to real or suggested hidden attributed that promise distinction from competitive goods' (Levitt, 1980). The same, he says, is true with services. Therefore, in the highly competitive hotel market, the level and quality of service delivered is the key differential attribute (Lovelock, 1991). This is commonly achieved through differentiation of physical facilities, market level and more recently possession of BS 5750.

Repositioning

The intention here is simply to recognize that as the industry has had to focus on maximizing returns from existing products rather than developing new facilities, making an underperforming hotel respond to market dynamics may involve a total repositioning (Bohan and Cahill, 1992) or possibly even the decision to close during certain times of the year (Cahill, 1987).

Before we establish the final yield method, short breaks, it is useful to establish that technology plays an increasing role in yield management in terms of manipulating room rates and providing detailed and up-to-date information. However, technology itself is not a method for improving yield, it is a tool that can be used in conjunction with the methods identified in this section and should be treated as such. Similarly, while no detailed or direct mention has been made of the need to market hotels, the view of Dev (1990) is shared here: 'a hotelier who does not consider marketing as a major part of the hotels operation is doomed to failure'.

Knowledge Management

From the previous discussion it is clearly evident that a core element of the ability to maximize returns from operations lies in the ability to gather and manage information. Such information can be used to raise revenues, inform on cost control and ultimately enhance the manager's ability to manage yield through the balance of economic understanding and social awareness. While knowledge management is not the premise of this chapter, it is an area that will prove critical to the future of yield management and to the ability of organizations to gain maximum yield from all resources, including knowledge.

Offering Short Breaks

Short breaks are to a great extent a creature of the nature of hotel operations cost structure, environmental change and the off-peak/seasonality drive for demand (Edgar *et al.*, 1994). They are widely recognized as a key growth market for hotels and have distinct market characteristics essentially evolving from the off-peak weekend break to a market in their own right. Major city centre hotels had targeted the business market, which meant high occupancy percentages between Monday and Thursday. Additional revenue was therefore sought, and by using an attractive pricing policy the short break market evolved (Davies, 1990). Short breaks are economically worthwhile as long as variable costs are met. In reality, many short breaks provide the opportunity to secure considerable additional revenue and to contribute significantly to profits. Senior and Morphew (1990) identified that the survival of traditional operators will require them to extend their horizons and move from short-term tactics – pricing and product augmentation – to long-term strategies. The provision of short breaks provides such a strategy. Hence, as customers become more sophisticated in manipulating the current pricing system of hotels, hotels will eventually be forced to modify their pricing structure (Hanks *et al.*, 1992) and can react by combining the key elements of yield management through the provision of short breaks.

CONCLUSION

The management of capacity, or yield management, represents an intricate and complex relationship between demand, supply and marginal cost. It is based on the premise of ensuring maximum profitable revenue generation from markets of varying price elasticity evolved from different attitudes and capabilities to pay.

While the economic underpinning of the concept of yield management is universal, it should be taken within the industrial context in order to be fully understood. As such, a range of yield management methods can be employed based upon these economic foundations, including discounting, repositioning, differentiation, segmentation, packaging and offering short breaks. An understanding of the economics of pricing and its relation to yield management provides the manager with an excellent tool to implement capacity management strategies.

NOTE

1. Product in this text is defined as a good, service or combination of goods and services offered to the hospitality and tourism consumer.

REFERENCES

Arbel, A. and Woods, R. H. (1991) 'Inflation and hotels: the cost of following a faulty routine'. *The Cornell HRAQ*, February **31**(4), 66–75.

Berge, M. E. and Hopperstad, C. A. (1993) 'Demand driven dispatch: a method for dynamic aircraft capacity assignments, models and algorithims'. *Operations Research*, **41**(1), 153–68.

Berry, W. L. (1991) 'Factory focus: segmenting markets from an operator's perspective'. *Journal of Operations Management*, **10**(3), 363–87.

Bitran, G. R. and Lojo, M. (1993) 'A framework for analyzing service operations'. *European Management Journal*, **11**(3), 271–82.

Boardman, R. D. (1978) *Hotel and Catering – Costing and Budgets*, 3rd edn. London: Heinemann, p. 153.

Bohan, G. and Cahill, M. (1992) 'Determining the feasibility of hotel market repositioning'. *Real Estate Review*, **22**(1), 63–74.

Bonnisseau, J. and Cornet, B. (1990) 'Existence of marginal cost pricing equilibria: the non-smooth case'. *International Economic Review*, **31**(3), 685–708.

Brotherton, B. and Mooney, S. (1992) 'Yield management'. *International Journal of Hospitality Management*, **11**(1), 23–32.

Buttle, F. (1986) 'Hotel and food service marketing: a managerial approach', London: Cassell.

Cahill, M. (1987) 'Seasonal resorts: the off-season challenge'. *The Cornell HRAQ*, August, 86–95.

Carroll, J. D. (1986) 'Discounting hotel rack rates'. *The Cornell HRAQ*, August, 13.

Carter, R. (1988) 'Screen Dreams'. *The Business Traveller*, April, 33–5.

Crawford-Welch, S. (1991) 'International marketing in the hospitality industry for the 1990s'. In R. Teare and A. Boer (eds), *Strategic Hospitality Management*. Cassell, London: p. 182.

Davies, B. (1990) 'The economics of short breaks'. *International Journal of Hospitality Management*, **9**(2), 103–6.

Davis, J. (1989) 'Globalization of hotel market is going strong: segmentation is meeting the needs of the 1990s'. *National Real Estate Investor*, **31**(13), 59–76.

Dev, C. S. (1990) 'Marketing practices of hotel chains'. *The Cornell HRAQ*, November, 54–63.

Dunn, K. D. and Brooks, D. E. (1990) 'Profit analysis: beyond yield management'. *The Cornell HRAQ*, **31**(3), 80–90.

EIU (1991) 'Special Report', No. 1180. Economist Intelligence Unit.

Edgar, D. A., Litteljohn, D. L., Allardyce, M. and Wanhill, S. (1994) 'Commercial short holiday breaks: the relationship between market structure, competitive advantage and performance'. In *Tourism State of the Art*, Oxford: John Wiley & Sons, pp. 323–42.

Egan, P. and Haynes, J. (1992) 'The anatomy of a failure: a hotel'. *Real Estate Review*, **22**(1), 75–9.

Fine, M. (1993) 'The tough work of rate management'. *Lodging Hospitality*, **49**(1), 34.

Garvey, J. (1986) 'Outlook and opportunities in market segmentation'. In R. C. Lewis, T. Beggs and M. Shaw (eds), *The Practice of Hospitality Management*. AVI Publishing Company Inc., pp. 451–5.

Gordon, R. (1993) 'Long-term outlook bright for the UK hotel industry'. *Caterer & Hotelkeeper*, 1 July, 21.

Guiltinan, J. (1987) 'The price bundling of services'. *Journal of Marketing*, **51** (April), 74–85.

Hanks, R. D., Cross, R. G. and Noland, R. P. (1992) 'Discounting in the hotel industry: a new approach'. *The Cornell HRAQ*, February, 15–23.

Harrison, L. and Johnson, K. (1992) *UK Hotel Groups Directory*. Hotel & Catering Research Centre, Huddersfield University. London: Cassell.

Hughes, H. L. (1989) *Economics for Hotel and Catering Students*. London: Stanley Thomas.

I. H. A. (1992) 'Yield revenue management'. International Hotel Association Congress, Bangkok, pp. 1–52.

James, G. W. (1987) 'Fares must yield to the market'. *Airline Business*, January, 16–19.

Jones, P. (1993) 'Managing capacity'. In P. Jones and A. Pizam (eds), *The International Hospitality Industry: Organisational and Operational Issues*. London: Pitman, p. 148.

Jones, P. and Hamilton, D. (1992) 'Yield management: putting people in the big picture'. *The Cornell HRAQ*, **33**(1), 89–95.

Jones, P. and Lockwood, A. (1989) 'Approaches to the measurement of accommodation performance'. *International Journal Contemporary Hospitality Management: Launch Conference Proceedings* **2** (April), pp. 45–56.

Kelly, T. and Gopalan, R. (1992) 'Managing for profit'. *LIMRA's Market Facts*, **11**(6), 47–50.

Kimes, S. E. (1994) 'Perceived fairness of yield management', *The Cornell HRAQ*, **35**(1), 22–4.

Kimes, S. E. (1989) 'The basics of yield management', *The Cornell HRAQ*, **30**(3), 14–19.

Kotas, R. and Davis, B. (1976) *Food Cost Control*. London: International Textbook Company Ltd.

Larsen, T. D. (1988) 'Yield management and your passengers'. *ASTA Agency Magazine*, June, 46–8.

Levitt, T. (1980) 'Marketing success through differentiation of anything'. *Harvard Business Review*, January/February, 73.

Lewis, R. C. and Chambers, R. E. (1989) *Marketing Leadership in Hospitality: Foundations and Practices*. New York: Von Nostrand Reinhold, pp. 353–87.

Lovelock, A. (1991) *Services Marketing*, 2nd edn. London: Prentice Hall.

MacGill, J. (1992) 'Desolation row'. *Scottish Business Insider*, September, 45–8.

Millar, B. (1992) 'In times of gloom there's still good news for the hotel lobby'. *The Scotsman*, Tuesday 15 September, p. 25.

Moje, H. I. (1990) 'Yield management in the lodging industry'. MBA Thesis, Central Michigan University.

N. O. P. (1993) 'Market Report 1993'. *Hotel and Restaurant Magazine*, November, 15–30.

Naish, H. (1990) 'The near optimality of mark-up pricing'. *Economic Inquiry*, **28**(3), 555–85.

Norrbin, S. C. (1993) 'The relationship between price and marginal cost in US industry: a contradiction'. *Journal of Political Economy*, **101**(6), 1149–64.

Orkin, E. B. (1988) 'Boosting your bottom line with yield management'. *The Cornell HRAQ*, **28**(4), 52–6.

Orkin, E. B. (1990) 'Strategies for managing transient rates'. *The Cornell HRAQ*, February, 34–9.

Quain, W. J. (1992) 'Analyzing sales mix profitability'. *The Cornell HRAQ*, April, 57–62.

Relihan, W. J. (1989) 'The yield management approach to hotel room pricing', *The Cornell HRAQ*, **30**(1), 40–5.

Rice, F. (1993) 'Why hotel rates won't take off – yet'. *Fortune*, **128**(8), 124–8.

Russo, J. A. (1991) 'Variance analysis: evaluating hotel room sales'. *The Cornell HRAQ*, **31**(4), 60–5.

Senior, M. and Morphew, R. (1990) 'Competitive strategies in the budget hotel sector'. *International Journal of Contemporary Hospitality Management*, **2**(3), 2–9.

Teare, R., Davies, M. and McGeary, B. (1989) 'The operational challenge of hotel short breaks'. *Journal of Contemporary Hospitality Management*, **1**(1), 19–23.

Van Dierdonck, R. (1992) 'Success strategies in a service economy'. *European Management Journal*, **10**(3), 365–73.

Verchere, I. (1993) 'Airlines try the flexible approach on seats'. *The European*, 17–23 December, p. 24.

Vohra, R. (1992) 'Marginal cost pricing under bounded marginal returns'. *Econometrica*, **60**(4), 859–76.

Walker, B. H. (1993) 'What's ahead: a strategic look at lodging trends'. *The Cornell HRAQ*, **34**(5), 28–34.

Williams, I. (1987) 'Dark science brings boost to airline profits'. *Sunday Times*, 27 November, p. 94.

Wolfe, A. (1993) 'How to profit from premium priced brands'. *Marketing Business*, June, 28–32.

3

Legal Aspects

Mike Boella

INTRODUCTION

Yield management is a management technique operated by many different industries which is concerned with maximizing an enterprise's effective use of its resources. Its aim is to maximize business bottom-line profit through managing a complex of factors which includes pricing, sales volumes, operating margins and gross profit contribution. Kimes (1989) defines yield management as 'the process of allocating the right kind of capacity to the right kind of customer at the right price'. Many of these issues are discussed elsewhere in this book. This chapter sets out to look at the legal context in which managers, attempting to maximize yield, operate.

Within the hospitality and tourist industries typical examples of yield management practice are:

- decisions about rack rate and discounted pricing;
- timing of offers;
- timing of acceptance of bookings;
- overbooking statistics and practices;
- which customers to book out (in the USA, to 'walk', and in airline jargon, to 'bump').

In some cases these decisions are driven by low occupancy, so discounted offers are made to attract customers at off-peak times. In other cases decisions are driven by excess demand and patterns of customer behaviour, particularly the frequency of 'no-shows', i.e. customers who have reserved but who do not arrive to take up their reservation.

'No-shows' may result from a variety of different reasons, including multiple bookings by individuals and travel agents, guests leaving earlier or staying longer than forecast, change of plans (sometimes notified, sometimes not) and travel problems caused by strikes or weather conditions. As a consequence of these 'no-shows' many operators adopt overbooking practices. This chapter looks at the key legal issues concerned with overbooking, including the law of contract, statutes which regulate what operators can and cannot do, the responsibility of agents and customers' liabilities.

A major challenge in setting out to look at the legal implications of any management practice from an international legal perspective is that there is no such thing as 'international' law in such a context. There is only a multiplicity of different legal systems and regimes. Within the United Kingdom alone we have two major legal systems, consisting of English law and Scottish law. Within the European Union each member state has its own systems and traditions, admittedly increasingly circumscribed, as Lord Denning stated twenty years ago, by the 'incoming tide' of Community law. The United States, like many other federal states, has a multiplicity of laws at individual state level and at federal level.

As a consequence of there being no such thing as 'international' law in this area of business, one system has of necessity been chosen as a basis for discussing the many issues which arise in the context of 'yield management'. As the book is written in the English language it is likely that the majority of readers live and operate within a country whose legal system has strong traditional connections with the United Kingdom. To readers from other legal traditions the author apologizes but trusts that the examples used illustrate the type of issues likely to be encountered in any legal system.

When a business sets out to maximize yield, a number of issues arise which can have legal consequences for the enterprise and the customer and perhaps intermediaries as well, such as travel agencies and tour operators.

CONTRACT LAW

The relationship between an enterprise and its customer, in most jurisdictions, starts with contract law. In English law, and in many other jurisdictions which are based on English law, contract law is based on certain 'common law' principles. These have been determined over hundreds of years through the decisions of judges. For a contract to be enforceable in English law there are several 'essentials of a valid contract'. These are:

- offer and acceptance;
- consideration, i.e. something of value such as money;
- intention to create a legally enforceable contract;
- capacity of the person to enter into a contract;
- legality of the objective;
- possibility of performance.

If any of these essentials is absent no enforceable contract exists.

In all contracts for services such as hotel accommodation, restaurant bookings and travel products all the above essentials are normally present and a contract is enforceable upon both parties to any contract. Most contracts in English law do not have to be in writing, and this applies to contracts for most hospitality and tourism services.

This contrasts with French law, where a contract for hotel services, among others, has to be confirmed in writing. At the time of writing it has still to be tested in the French courts as to whether a credit card transaction (by telephone) will be accepted as evidence of the contract. As with English law, conditions such as room release time have to be specified. Otherwise the operator leaves himself or herself open to an action for breach of contract.

Offer and Acceptance

In most cases, under English law, it is the customer who makes the *offer*, in response to an advertisement, a feature in a guidebook or a brochure. It is the provider of the service, such as the hotel, restaurant, carrier or tour operator, who *accepts*.

Where a company is operating within a 'yield management' context or philosophy the crucial element to consider is the *offer and acceptance*. This is because of the need, from the enterprise's point of view, to leave as much flexibility as possible. For example, if a guest books a single room, and the hotel has accepted that booking, this leaves the hotel with virtually total freedom to allocate whichever room it wishes. If, on the other hand, a customer has booked a room with a 'sea view' the hotel's ability to manoeuvre is reduced – within the contract the hotel can only allocate the customer one of its rooms with a sea view. If the customer has been even more specific, i.e. he has booked a double bedded room, with bathroom containing a shower and a sea view, the hotel's room for manoeuvre is further restricted. To allocate a room not fulfilling the customer's requests amounts to a breach of contract.

The same principle applies in the United States of America. As quoted by Wilson *et al.* (1994), 'A promise by a hotel to deliver a room in the future in return for payment or a promise to pay constitutes a binding contract. The hotel is obligated to deliver the room and the traveler is obligated to pay for it.' As in English law no deposit is required – the mutual promise of offer and acceptance is sufficient, unless as part of the offer process it is clearly stated that a deposit is required to confirm the reservation.

In the case of travel companies, clauses are normally inserted into contracts which leave them with a degree of flexibility to maximize profitability. This might include consolidating a number of undersubscribed holiday destinations into one destination, in order to reduce transport and other running costs. A typical clause in a contract might be:

> Although it is unlikely, the company reserves the right to make changes to the travel arrangements you have booked. Most changes are likely to be minor and you will be informed as soon as any information becomes available. If a major change is required, e.g. change of departure airport or time of more than 12 hours, you will be given the option to accept the change or to cancel your arrangements without penalty. In addition compensation will be paid, as follows

Such a clause gives the operator maximum flexibility, while generally remaining within the law (see also the Package Travel, Package Holidays and Package Tours Regulations 1992, below). Companies will also normally include a paragraph concerned with *forces majeures*, i.e. unpredictable circumstances such as natural disasters, political upheaval or disease etc.

Deposits

In English (and US) law, as was stated above, deposits, or advance payments, are not necessary to confirm the existence of a contract. A contract will be binding if the essentials of a valid contract (listed above) are present. However, an operator can make it a condition of the contract that an advance payment, deposit or card number is provided, as a condition of the contract. If the customer fails to meet this condition then the customer cannot sue for breach of contract.

Where an operator fails to perform his or her part of the contract, and the customer has paid a deposit, the deposit has to be returned, except in those cases where 'frustration' of the contract may have arisen (see below). The customer, however, would be advised to accept it with the condition that the acceptance does not prejudice any subsequent action on his part.

In France there is an interesting situation in that the law provides for a number of forms of prepayment. One, known as *arrhes*, is a deposit which acts as a guarantee provided by the customer and is not refundable in the case of cancellation. However, should the hotelier cancel the contract double the deposit has to be paid to the customer. The second is *dépôt*, which is a form of prepayment and is refundable upon cancellation. If the hotelier fails to provide the goods or services he or she only has to refund the money paid. French hoteliers and restaurateurs are therefore very careful as to which form they use.

As in English and US law the French can, by contract, impose cancellation penalties with time periods applying, e.g. 25 per cent cancellation fee if a cancellation is received within one week of the contracted arrival date.

Frustration

A contract is frustrated where circumstances outside the control of one of the parties to the contract prevent it being performed. Generally frustration arises where the contract is impossible to perform through no fault of either party (*Taylor* v. *Caldwell [1863] 3 B & S 826*). In many overbooking situations explanations are offered to customers which appear to be seeking the concept of frustration, such as 'last night's storm flooded the top floor'. It is unlikely that many defences based on the principle of frustration would succeed, as most are not true in the first place! Where a contract is frustrated the customer does not have an automatic right to a refund of any money paid in advance. The business which has incurred expenses prior to the time at which the contract was frustrated may be able to recover those expenses up to a limit of the sums paid or payable to him under the contract. If, however, no money was paid or became payable prior to the frustrating event, the business will not be able to recover any expenses at all (the Law Reform [Frustrated Contracts] Act 1943).

Unfair Contract Terms

It is quite in order to attempt, through the contract, to give onself maximum flexibility and to minimize one's liabilities by writing in clauses which have that effect. However, not all limitation and exclusion clauses will have legal effect. Under the Unfair Contract Terms Act 1977 and the EU Unfair Terms Directive (93/13), certain unfair or unreasonable clauses in contracts and conditions of sale are void in law. The Directive applies to terms which have not been individually negotiated. Terms which have been determined in advance by the supplier, and where the consumer has not had the opportunity to influence the particular term, are covered. Unfair terms will not be binding on the customer. Operators therefore have to ensure that such terms are brought specifically to the attention of customers, by highlighting them in contracts and/or by ensuring that staff bring them to the customer's attention.

Modifying Contracts

Once entered into contracts can only be modified, should one of the two parties wish to modify the contract, by mutual agreement, i.e. both parties must agree to any new terms. Otherwise the contract must be performed within the terms of the contract or a breach of contract may ensue.

Breach of Contract

A breach of contract may occur in several different ways. First, a business such as a hotel may realize some time ahead that it can no longer fulfil its commitments. As a consequence it may write to the customer, or customers, attempting to cancel the booking. This can constitute an 'anticipatory breach'. An example is where a banqueting centre, having accepted a booking for a small party, receives a request for a much bigger and more profitable event. It may wish to cancel the earlier and smaller booking. It can only do so by mutual agreement. If the contract is breached upon performance, e.g. accommodation of a much lower standard than that agreed is provided, or no accommodation is provided, this constitutes an 'actual breach'.

Where the breach is fundamental, i.e. one of a *condition* which is at the heart of the contract, then the injured party (the customer) may refuse to perform his or her part of the contract, e.g. to pay or to accept a room. Where the term breached is a *warranty* (less than fundamental), the injured party may have rights to a reduction of the price to be paid.

Invitation to Treat

In many businesses the goods and services available for sale are advertised, promoted or put on display in order to communicate their availability to potential customers. In most such cases this activity constitutes an 'invitation to treat', which is different from an 'offer'. Hotel brochures, airline timetables, car hire company tariffs, restaurant menus and self-service cafeteria displays are all examples of 'an invitation to treat'. A hotel brochure or a travel timetable falls short of an 'offer', usually because it does not contain sufficient information to constitute an offer. For example, a hotel brochure, a car hire company tariff or an airline timetable does not usually state or imply that accommodation, a car or seats are available on a particular date. All the accommodation, cars or seats may have already been reserved (see *Partridge* v. *Crittenden (1968) 1 WLR 1204 (QBD)*).

In some cases, however, an advertisement can possibly constitue an 'offer'. For example, advertisements containing vouchers offering free goods or services or price reductions can be an 'offer' (see *Carlill* v. *Carbolic Smoke Ball Co. [1893] 1 QB 256*

(CA)). So if a restaurateur or hotelier wishes to attract trade at certain off-peak times he or she may advertise free bottles of house wine or a free bedroom for every couple dining at the restaurant. As a result of the *Carbolic Smoke Ball* case the advertisement may well constitute an offer. To be safe in such circumstances the restaurateur may be advised to put a limit on the offers, e.g. the first 50 to apply.

False Statements and Misrepresentation

Wording of advertisements, brochures and other promotional and contractual material has to be considered very carefully, as false statements, carelessness and recklessness can result in torts (civil wrong) and even criminal offences being committed.

In some cases travel agents or other providers may make *false statements* which form a term of the contract (*Jarvis* v. *Swan's Tours [1973] 1 All ER 71 (CA)*). In such cases the client may sue for breach of contract. *Misrepresentation* instead occurs where a provider makes a statement of fact upon which the client relies, and as a result enters into a contract. Misrepresentation may arise under the common law of tort or under statute law, the Misrepresentation Act 1967.

In the United States many overbooking cases have alleged fraud or misrepresentation, because the damages to be recovered are greater than those for a simple breach of contract (Wilson *et al.*, 1994). A case based on misrepresentation is only likely to succeed if, on the basis of the facts available at the time of the booking, it was known that the booked accommodation was not going to be available (*Wells* v. *Holiday Inns, Inc. USA 1981*). In another case in the United States, however, where a hotel, as a standard procedure, overbooked by 15 per cent, the court found the hotel guilty of fraud, because it had accepted a booking and repeatedly confirmed to the travel agency concerned that the rooms were available.

Where heavy overbooking occurs it is, of course, arguable that the operator knows that the booking may not be honoured. In English law this could be perceived as inducing someone to enter into a contract by deception or misrepresentation. In the United States a court stated:

> The fact that it conceals such practices in its advertising and otherwise, and by virtue of its failure and refusal to take reasonable steps to avoid harm to the Plaintiffs herein is tantamount to willful and wanton misconduct which gives rise to and provides a proper basis for each of the plaintiff's claims for damages (*Nader* v. *Allegheny Airlines, Inc. (1973)*). (Reproduced from Wilson *et al.*, 1994)

Withholding Information

To withhold information from a potential customer, which may be necessary for him or her to make an informed offer or acceptance, may constitute a tort in English law and may well run foul of several statutes as well. In the United States many states have laws which make it a violation of consumer protection law to 'fail to disclose to a buyer or prospective buyer any fact, the disclosure of which may have influenced the buyer or prospective buyer not to enter the transaction. As Enghagen and Healy (1996) write about the situation in the United States, 'Pursuant to federal regulations, airlines are not only required to disclose their overbooking practices, they are mandated to offer bumped passengers compensation for their trouble.'

Negligent Misrepresentation

In English law negligent misrepresentation arises out of statute law, i.e. the Misrepresentation Act 1967. This statute gives protection to those who have entered into contracts, whereas the torts of deceit and negligent misstatement may arise before a contract has been entered into. In the case of misstatements it is better to bring an action under section 2(1) of the 1967 Act, as it is for the defendant to justify his or her actions rather than the plaintiff to prove fault.

Unfair and Deceptive Acts and Practices

In the United States both federal and state law prohibits unfair and deceptive acts and practices – similar in some respects to the English Trade Descriptions Acts and the Unfair Contract Terms Act 1977, which respectively prohibit misleading and false descriptions and make void certain contract conditions.

Innocent Misrepresentation

In English law, even if a provider is neither negligent nor fraudulent, i.e. misleading information is given innocently, a customer may still have remedies under section 2(2) of the Misrepresentation Act 1967.

Remedies for Misrepresentation

First, fraudulent, negligent and innocent misrepresentation all enable the customer to *rescind* the contract, i.e. treat it as at an end. Second, damages may be sought.

Pro-Forma Bookings

In many cases bookings for travel, accommodation, banqueting, conference or restaurant services are made by companies using 'pro-forma' orders. The booking may, in turn, be confirmed by a provider using a standard pre-printed confirmation. In many cases the two documents differ in certain respects and the question often arises as to which of the two documents has legal effect. An example could be that of a customer making a booking from his or her office, using a standard order form. In this the order may specify a particular type of room. The hotel may acknowledge the booking using its standard form, which reserves the right to allocate any room in the hotel. In English law *the last document* to be issued is the legally binding one, so in the above case it is the hotel which has the right to allocate any room.

Criminal Legislation

Criminal legislation specifies what acts are criminal – for example, to knowingly make a misleading statement or claim regarding a product or service may not just make a contract unenforceable, or subject to damages, on the part of the person making the misleading claim (in civil law) but it also renders the person committing such an action liable for criminal penalties such as fines or even imprisonment. The main criminal legislation follows.

Trade Descriptions Act 1968

The Trade Descriptions Act 1968 creates criminal offences, i.e. it provides for punishment of those guilty of committing offences under the Act. This distinguishes it from civil law, which provides for damages rather than for punishment.

The main provisions of the Act, as far as hotels, restaurants and travel organizations are concerned, are contained in section 14(1):

It shall be an offence for any person in the course of any trade or business –

(a) to make a statement which he knows to be false; or
(b) recklessly to make a statement which is false;

as to any of the following matters, that is to say –

(i) the provision in the course of any trade or business of any services, accommodation or services;
(ii) the nature of any services, accommodation or facilities provided in the course of any trade or business;
(iii) the time at which, manner in which or persons by whom any services, accommodation or facilities are so provided;
(iv) the examination, approval or evaluation by any person of any services, accommodation or facilities so provided;
(v) the location or amenities of any accommodation so provided.

For an action to succeed under section 14 of the Trade Descriptions Act it is necessary to prove that the defendant knew the statement to be false, or that he or she was reckless as to whether it was true or false (*Sunair Holidays Ltd* v. *Dodds (1970) 1 WLR 1037 (CA)*).

The case most commonly sited in this respect is *British Airways Board v Taylor (1976) 1 WLR 15 (HL)*. In this case British Overseas Airways Corporation (BOAC), the predecessor to British Airways, confirmed a customer's reservation on a specified flight, on a particular time and day. BOAC operated an overbooking policy, i.e. more passengers were booked on flights than there were seats available. The passenger arrived to take up his seat but BOAC could not carry him because there were more passengers than seats, as a result of the overbooking policy. BOAC was prosecuted for breach of section 14(1) of the Trade Descriptions Act 1968 in that it recklessly made a statement about the provision of services which was false as to the time and manner in which the service was to be provided. Upon appeal, the House of Lords held that BOAC's letter to the passenger and the ticket were a statement of fact that the passenger's booking on the flight in question was certain. This statement in view of section 14(1) was false, since the passenger was exposed to the risk that he might not get a seat upon that particular flight.

The Package Travel, Package Holidays and Package Tours Regulations 1992

For many operators in the tourist industry creating packages is their *'raison d'être'*. For others, a major way to maximize yield from their existing core products is to develop and promote products in conjunction with other products, i.e. to create a package. For some operators, such as hoteliers, the package may merely consist of adding an attraction such as a 'murder weekend' to the main products of accommodation, food and drink. In other cases, however, packages are extremely complex, consisting of different modes of travel and transfers, services of couriers and guides, accommodation, entertainment, sport, cultural and educational events and excursions, food and drink.

As the package travel industry developed some saw that there was a need to harmonize the rules governing package travel so that operators from different countries (within the European Union, in particular) operated within a similar legal regime. It also became necessary to introduce measures to give the consumer protection from abuses and from business failures. The European Union Directive on Package Travel, Package Holidays and Package Tours was adopted in 1990. The Directive was implemented in the United Kingdom by the introduction of the Package Travel, Package Holidays and Package Tours Regulations 1992. The Directive covers 'packages' which consist of:

> the pre-arranged combination of at least two of the following components when sold or offered for sale at an inclusive price and when the service covers a period of more than twenty-four hours or includes overnight accommodation:
>
> (a) transport;
> (b) accommodation;
> (c) other tourist service not ancillary to transport or accommodation and accounting for a significant proportion of the package;
> and
> (d) the submission of separate accounts for different components shall not cause the arrangements to be other than a package;
> (e) the fact that a combination is arranged at the request of the consumer and in accordance with his specific instructions (whether modified or not) shall not of itself cause it to be treated other than pre-arranged.

From this definition it is apparent that 'package' may include a wide range of 'products' offered by operators in the tourist industry and not just the traditional 'package holiday'. A conference which involves travel and excursions would fall within the definition, as would a weekend at a hotel with an inclusive activity such as tennis coaching. Business and educational services are excluded. The following is a brief description of the main features of the regulations, which cover a number of different issues.

● The brochure must not contain any misleading information, and where a brochure is provided, there should be information about transport, accommodation, meals, itinerary, passport and visa requirements for British citizens and any health formalities, deposit to be paid and method of settling the balance, minimum number of persons for the package to take place, and arrangements for security of money paid over and for repatriation in case of insolvency of the operator (n.b. a brochure does not have to be provided).

- The consumer has an implied right to transfer his or her booking where there is some substantial reason preventing the consumer from proceeding with the package.
- Contracts providing for price revisions are automatically void unless they provide for decreases as well as increases. The term in the contract must state how the revised price is calculated and this must relate only to transport costs, including fuel costs, taxes and fees such as airport taxes and exchange rate fluctuations.
- Where an operator is obliged to make changes to any of the 'essential terms' (due to factors outside the operator's control) the consumer must be notified as quickly as possible. The operator should indicate in the contract what might be considered 'essential terms' and what might be 'significant alterations'. Where a significant change has been made the consumer may cancel without penalty or accept a rider to the contract which states the alterations and any impact on price.
- Where an operator is obliged to cancel or to make significant alterations the regulations entitle the consumer to take a substitute package, and where the substitute is cheaper to have the difference paid to him or her, or to have all money already paid refunded. The consumer may be compensated for non-performance of the contract except where the package was cancelled because the number required was not reached or where the package was cancelled for reasons beyond the control of the organizer.
- Where (after departure) a significant proportion of the services contracted for are not provided or the operator knows that they will not be provided the operator must make suitable alternative arrangements, at no cost to the consumer, and provide for compensation for the difference between the two levels of service. Where alternative arrangements cannot be made or where the consumer has reasonable grounds for rejecting them the consumer must be transported back to the place of departure or another place agreed by the consumer.
- The organizer is liable for the performance of the contract whether or not he or she is providing the services directly or through other parties, and the organizer is responsible for trying to remedy any defects in the performance of the contract.
- The organizer must provide evidence of security for the refund of money paid by consumers and for the repatriation of the consumer in case of insolvency. Such money should be secured by bonding, insurance or money held in trust (or some variants of these), unless the money is secured in another member state or where the package is covered by the Civil Aviation (Air Travel Organisers Licensing) Regulations 1972.

Overbooking in Practice

In order that hotels, carriers and other similar types of business can maximize occupancy, load factors and profits, and perhaps also offer lower prices to customers, many argue that overbooking is an essential part of normal business practice. It has been a part of many sectors of the tourist and hospitality industries for so long that few people within these industries question its ethical basis. It is argued that when conducted properly, i.e. based on sound knowledge of business patterns, it should not often result in dissatisfied customers. However, there are occasions when the statistical forecasting necessary to underpin an effective yield management system will not run 'true to form' and more customers will show than predicted.

In such cases the business has to consider its courses of action, first to maintain the customer's goodwill and second to avoid the risk of legal action. It is argued that where a customer is 'booked out' or 'bumped', as long as what the customer gets (e.g accommodation) is equal to or better than that originally booked, the customer will not have grounds for legal action because the contract has been performed. On the other hand, dependent upon the precise nature of the contract, the business may be in breach of contract, at the least. At worst, it may also have breached criminal statutes. What the business therefore needs to do is to set out to persuade the customers concerned to modify the contract. In law, effectively, this means that a new contract has to be negotiated. Airlines do this by 'buying off' or compensating the 'bumped' passengers with offers of cash, hotel accommodation or additional tickets for future occasions. Hotels likewise have various practices, including finding alternative accommodation and providing transport, paying for phone calls and offering upgraded or complimentary rooms on subsequent visits.

From a practical point of view the first question to answer is who it is best to 'book-out'. The question of how to choose a particular customer or customers to be booked out should depend upon future long-term goodwill issues as well as legal issues. From a legal point of view the hotel staff should look first for sound legal reasons for their choice. If a customer was asked to confirm by letter or fax and has not done so that may provide a sound reason. If a customer arrives after room release time that provides another reason. On the other hand, where customers have been very specific about their requirements, e.g. type and position of room, it is unwise to book them out as there may be difficulty in matching precisely their specific requests. Where a number of customers have booked in together it may be unwise to split them as a major part of their purpose may be to meet regularly and easily in the particular hotel.

Where a hotelier fails to provide accommodation contracted for the customer may treat the contract as at an end. The customer may book into another hotel of similar standard and sue the first hotel for the costs of the second hotel. If there is available only a hotel of higher standard the customer could sue for the higher cost.

What Damages Are Recoverable?

A customer may claim, in addition to the contract price, damages for disappointment incurred by the failure of the provider to meet the standards provided for *(Jarvis* v. *Swan's Tours (1973) 1 All ER 71 (CA))*. In this case the plaintiff was awarded damages for disappoinment and distress caused to him by his loss of enjoyment of the holiday. Following from this case, a customer may be awarded damages greater than the contract price. In addition, as a result of another case *(Jackson* v. *Horizon Holidays Ltd (1973) 3 All ER 92 (CA))*, people who book for the benefit of others are able to recover damages not only for their own disappoinment but also for the benefit of those for whom the contract was made.

It should go without saying that staff concerned with handling overbooking situations should be carefully trained in how to select the 'unlucky' customers, what arrangements to make and, in particular, how to inform them without giving grounds for legal action.

The Business's Remedies when Customers Fail to Show

Overbooking practices have arisen as a direct response to customer behaviour, i.e. making bookings and then not arriving to take up the service contracted for. In the worst cases customers, particularly airline passengers, make a number of bookings even though they need only one. In many such cases the customer is in breach of contract and the business concerned could sue for any damages suffered. The business, however, is still expected to mitigate the loss suffered (see *British Westinghouse Electric and Manufacturing Company* v. *Underground Electric Railway Co. of London (1912) AC 673 (HL)*). Whether to sue customers or not in such situations will depend upon the circumstances, including the likely damages to be awarded by the court. For example, in the case of a restaurant the actual damages awarded are unlikely be the total costs likely to have been incurred by the customer, but rather the actual loss suffered, perhaps around 60 per cent of the anticipated bill.

Some operators are looking at ways of reducing the incidence of 'no-shows'. Hyatt is reported to be experimenting with an administration fee for guests who change their length of stay (akin to insurance companies charging for changes to policies) and National Car Rental is reported to offer discounts to customers who make advance reservations and agree to pay a cancellation fee should they cancel (Wilson *et al.*, 1994).

Agencies

A special relationship exists between a customer and the provider of a service such as a hotelier or travel agent. A special relationship exists where a customer is trusting the provider of the service to exercise such a degree of care as the circumstances require, and it is reasonable for the client to rely on the provider's advice. So, if a provider gives advice which he or she knows, or should have known, that the customer will rely upon, the provider may be liable should the advice be false. This liability arises out of *Hedley Byrne & Co. Ltd* v. *Heller & Partners Ltd (1964) AC 465 (HL)*, in which Lord Morris defined a 'special relationship': 'If someone possessed of a special skill undertakes (irrespective of contract) to apply that skill for the assistance of another person who relies on such skill he voluntarily undertakes the responsibility of so acting.'

The principle applies to the hotel, restaurant and tourist industries, in that if a provider states that certain services are on offer at particular prices, and the statement proves to be false, the customer may bring an action for negligent misstatement. Most businesses acting as agencies, such as travel agencies, set out to limit their liabilities, making it clear that they are acting only as agents for the supplier. In most cases this means that the contractual relationship is between the customer and the supplier of the service. An example of such a clause follows:

> Where the company acts as a retailer we act only as agent for the suppliers providing transportation, sightseeing, accommodation or other services comprising your booking. All coupons, receipts, tickets and other documents are issued subject to the terms and conditions specified by the supplier. By accepting the coupons, receipts

and tickets and/or utilizing the services, you agree that neither we nor any of our affiliated companies shall have any obligation to you whatsoever for the operation of the travel arrangements.

CONCLUSION

This chapter has set out to introduce the main legal issues which may arise each time a business enters into a contract with a customer, but particularly when managers and owners set out to maximize the yield of their businesses. In essence owners and managers have responsibilities to a number of different stakeholders in their business, who include the owners, the suppliers, the trading partners, the staff and finally and most importantly their customers. Reconciling these responsibilities is no easy matter and maximizing yield has posed many ethical and legal problems, some of which, some argue, are still unresolved today. In some countries the risk of extensive damages being awarded against operators is always present. In the USA, for example, it is argued that many hotels run the risk of 'class actions', i.e. actions which open the way for many others to bring actions which may involve multiple damages, lawyers' fees and injunctions. Damages could be significant because every customer who had been booked out in recent years could conceivably bring an action for damages (see Wilson *et al.*, 1994).

The law, in setting out to provide the customer with ever more protection, has made 'maximizing yield' ever more challenging for many businesses; the Package Travel, Package Holidays and Package Tours Regulations 1992 is just one example. Whichever way an owner or manager turns now, in order to maximize yield, he or she will find that the law has set traps for the unwary. I hope that this chapter has identified some of the legal pitfalls.

REFERENCES

Boella, M. J. and Pannett, A. J. (1999) *Principles of Hospitality Law*, 2nd edn. London: Continuum.

Enghagen, L. K. and Healy, E. P. (1996) 'The case against overbooking'. *Journal of Hospitality and Leisure Marketing*, **4** (1), 55–6.

Kimes S. E. (1989) 'The basics of yield management'. *Cornell Hotel and Restaurant Administration Quarterly*, **30**, (3) 14–19.

Wilson, R. H., Enghagen, L. K. and Sharma, P. (1994) 'Overbooking: the practice and the law'. *Hospitality Research Journal*, **17** (2), 93–105.

4

Quantitative Aspects of Yield Management

Robert Raeside and David Windle

INTRODUCTION

The reservation manager has to decide how many rooms to sell to groups or individuals at promotional (discount) prices and for how long these discounts will be offered. Typically, discounted rooms are available to groups who book in advance, or individual early bookings, and are usually associated with some loss of customer flexibility. The decision is one of how many rooms should be offered at a discount price to ensure as high an occupancy as possible, while attempting to secure as many full price paying customers as possible. This is made difficult because the demand cannot be determined with certainty. Some groups or individuals who reserve rooms may not appear, and of those who do the duration of their stay will vary, some cutting short their stay, while others may wish to stay longer. It is undesirable to over-book as this would mean a loss of goodwill and often 'transfer' costs are incurred in booking the customer into a rival hotel or offering some other compensation for 'bumping'.

Thus the crux of the problem in yield management or perishable-asset review management (PARM), as Bodily and Weatherford (1995) call it, is: 'the optimal revenue management of perishable assets through price segmentation'. Cross (1989) defines the problem as: 'using price incentives and inventory controls to maximise the value of existing processes'. Approaches to solving the yield management problem stem from scientific foundations in operational research, statistics and economics.

The problem is one of matching a probabilistic and sometimes unknown demand to a set of finite resources in a manner which will optimize profits or utilization (these need not be equivalent). In the sphere of hospitality and tourism management this is a difficult optimization problem. In some ways yield management is the reverse of the inventory control problem, in that the decision is not how much to stock, but rather, given a fixed capacity, how demand should be managed to ensure optimal usage and revenue maximization. This decision is made more difficult because of the uncertain level of demand, especially as new products and services are continually being developed. Demand is affected by competition from rival organizations, seasonal factors such as holiday and weekend effects and the extent to which customers are influenced by fashionable trends. Adding to these factors external influences, such as exchange rate fluctuations, political upheavals and the vagaries of the weather, produces a major managerial problem.

Kimes (1989) gives six attributes of the yield management problem:

1.   A relatively fixed capacity – capacity cannot be increased or decreased readily in hospitality and tourism.
2.   Demand can be segmented into classes, such as mid-week breaks, weekend demand, business users, those requiring luxurious accommodation.
3.   Inventory is perishable – if the room is not used the revenue for that period is lost.
4.   The product can be sold well in advance.
5.   There can be substantial fluctuations in demand.
6.   Variable costs are much less than fixed costs – for a hotel room even a discount in excess of 50 per cent may cover fixed costs for that room and contribute to profit.

There are two ways of approaching this problem: either to make the best estimate of demand and use management strategies to cope with the inevitable uncertainty in it; or to improve the estimate through better forecasting. In this chapter these areas are explored and examples of the use of different quantitative techniques are given.

QUANTITATIVE APPROACHES TO ENSURE OPTIMAL CAPACITY UTILIZATION

In the forefront of the development and application of quantitative methods for yield management has been the airline industry, where a variety of different methods have been used. These methods range from simple rule-based heuristics to sophisticated mathematical programmes with hundreds of decision variables. Airline companies which have used quantitative methods to aid the management of seat allocations have had a great deal of success and examples are documented in Rothstein (1971), Glover *et al.* (1982) and Belobaba (1989). Kimes (1989), reviewing several of the methods which have been used, states that: 'One of the key elements of the yield management problem is that it must be solved repeatedly. Because of this, any solution method must be fast, fairly accurate and not too expensive.' With this notion of the need for robust and workable methods in mind some of the solution approaches will now be discussed.

Mathematical Programming

This approach works best when dealing with static problems, i.e. those problems which when solved are not updated when additional information becomes available. Linear programming can be used to allocate resources between different groups, which might, for example, be discount classes (see Alstrup *et al.* (1986) and Glover *et al.* (1982) for some applications). Using linear programming in its most basic form, the classes must be assumed to be distinct and demand must be known.

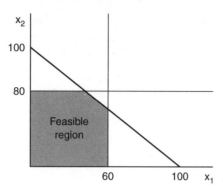

Figure 4.1 Linear programme

The objective is to maximize revenue (R) subject to the constraints on capacity. This is formulated as:

Maximize $R = \sum_{i=1}^{n} r_i x_i$

Subject to:

$$\sum_{i=1}^{n} x_i \leq C$$
$$x_i \leq d_i$$
$$x_i, d_i \geq 0$$

Where: i is the rate class; r_i is the revenue per unit of i; x_i is the number of units of i; C is the capacity of the service; d_i is the demand for units of i.

To give a trivial example, suppose that a 100-room hotel has two rate classes, a full price of £80 and a discounted tariff for early booking or group booking of £50. The maximum demand for full and discounted price rooms is thought to be 60 and 80 respectively. The decision variables are the number of full price rooms (x_1) and the number of discount price rooms (x_2). The linear program is:

Maximize $R = 80x_1 + 50x_2$

Subject to:

$$x_1 + x_2 \leq 100$$
$$x_1 \leq 60$$
$$x_2 \leq 80$$
$$x_1, x_2 \geq 0$$

Graphically this problem is represented as in Figure 4.1.

The optimal solution to a linear programming problem is at one of the vertices (corners) of the area of feasible solutions. The optimal combination is to allocate 40 rooms to discount class and 60 to full price to yield a revenue of £6,800. The maximum revenue of £6,800 is formally called the value of the objective function. In the above example the optimal solution was obvious from the statement of the problem, but if the allocation was required for a period of a week for three rate classes the problem becomes more complex. There would be three rate classes on each of seven days giving a total of 21 decision variables which must assume integer values. A computer-based solution would then be required. Given that the decision variables must assume integer values, a special form of linear programming, called integer programming, is required (see Winston, 1987). Furthermore, the demand for accommodation is assumed to be deterministic, which is very rarely the case, and probabilistic linear programming should be used.

Kimes (1989) shows that the problem is formulated as:

$$\text{Max } R = \sum_{j=1}^{m} \sum_{i=1}^{n} p_{ij} \, r_{ij} \, x_{ij}$$

Subject to:

$$\sum_{j=1}^{m} \sum_{i=1}^{n} x_{ij} \leq \sum_{j=1}^{m} C_j$$

Where: i is the rate class; j is the unit being purchased (i.e. the room); $x_{ij} = 0$ if item j is not sold at rate i, $= 1$ if item j is not sold at rate i; p_{ij} is the probability of selling item j at rate i; r_{ij} is the revenue obtained from selling item j at rate i; C_j is the number of items of j available.

This is computationally very intensive. For example, if there were three rate classes in a 100- room hotel then to optimize allocation for one day would require 300 decision variables and 300 probability estimates. Additionally, a rather restrictive assumption is made that the demands for full price and discounted rooms are independent.

In studies on optimizing airline booking, dynamic programming and network models have been used (see Rothstein, 1974; Glover *et al.*, 1982; Alstrup *et al.*, 1986). William-son and Belobaba (1988) make use of a greedy algorithm to allow 'virtual nesting' of bookings in which the value of each fare class depends on the overall ticket revenue. Some approaches allow the parameters to be updated and changed over time (Alstrup *et al.*, 1986). Within the limitations of this chapter these approaches are not pursued, other than to point out that in general mathematical programming is not suited to the requirements of many hoteliers because, unlike the airline companies, they do not tend to have abundant computer resources and tend to be more customer-centred.

Other approaches based on economic methods and marginal revenue may have more appeal and these are discussed next.

Marginal Revenue Approaches

To decide how many units to sell at discounted cost and how many to reserve for full price paying customers, Bodily and Weatherford (1995) advocate the use of a simple decision rule.

The total contribution, which must be maximized, can be written as:

$$q_d \, R_d + X R_f \qquad \text{if } q_d + X < q_c$$
$$q_d \, R_d + (q_c - q_d) \, R_f \text{ if } q_d + X \geq q_c$$

Where: R_f is the revenue a full tariff generated; R_d is the revenue a discount tariff generates; q_c is the capacity of the service; q_d is the maximum number of discounts.

The basic idea is to increase the availability of discounted spaces (q_d) until the risk of exceeding capacity when the number of full price customers are added becomes unacceptably high. If the probability of 'spoilage', i.e. of having empty spaces ($q_d + X < q_c$), is p then the decision rule is given by:
Continue to offer discounted spaces until:

$$pR_d + (1-p)(R_d - R_f) > 0.$$

This can be simplified to:

Reserve an additional discounted customer if:

$$p > \frac{R_f - R_d}{R_f}$$

For example, suppose that a reservations manager was managing a hotel with 100 rooms of the same type and there was a policy of letting some rooms at a 40 per cent discount. Rooms would be offered at the discount price provided that the probability of not reaching capacity was greater than 60 per cent.

The spoilage probability can be estimated from the forecast demand. If the forecast demand for full price paying customers has a continuous probability distribution then the '>' sign can be replaced with an equals sign to give an exact relationship.

Suppose that in the above example the demand for rooms was normally distributed with an expected level of 60 rooms and a standard deviation of 15 rooms and that the full price of each room contributes £150 to fixed costs. The number of rooms to be discounted would be obtained from the probability of spoilage.

The probability of spoilage is to be equal to:

$$\frac{150 - 90}{150} = 0.4$$

If X rooms are retained for full price sale, X is found from the inverse of the normal probability distribution.

$$\left[\frac{60 - X}{15} \right] \leq \phi(0.4) = 0.255.$$

Thus $X = 60 - 0.255 \times 15 = 60 - 3.825 = 56.175$. Thus 56 rooms should be retained at full price and 44 offered at discount. The situation is illustrated in Figure 4.2.
The expected revenue is obtained from:

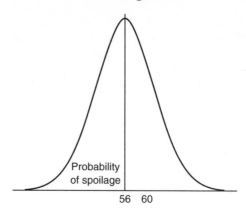

Probability
of spoilage

56 60

Figure 4.2 The probability of spoilage

$$EC = Yr_f + q_d r_d - c_v (Y + q_d)$$

Where Y is found from:

$$Y = \overline{D} - s_D \phi \left(\frac{C - q_d - \overline{D}}{S_D} \right) + (C - q_d - \overline{D}) \left[1 - \Phi \left\{ \frac{C - q_d - \overline{D}}{S_D} \right\} \right]$$

Where: $\overline{D}$ is the expected demand; s_D is the standard deviation of demand; c_v is the variable cost; r_f is the full price; r_d is the discounted price; q_d is the quantity discounted; C is the capacity; and Y is the number of rooms sold at full price.

In Table 4.1 the expected revenue for different combinations of discounted and full price rooms is given, confirming the optimum to be 56.

Over-booking is a problem and many hotels go to great lengths to prevent this happening. If demand exceeds capacity then the more valued full price paying customers may be lost to discounted customers. In order to reflect the cost if capacity is exceeded if more full price customers arrive the revenue associated with full price paying customers is often increased to incorporate costs associated with loss of goodwill, finding someone to 'walk' and the loss of their revenue. If this revenue is R_g the decision rule becomes:

Table 4.1 Expected revenue

Number of full price rooms	Number of discounted rooms	Expected revenue £
100	0	8,697.43
70	30	10,921.31
56	44	11,251.63
30	70	10,281.53
0	100	8,499.98

$$\text{Reverse an additional discount customer if } p > \frac{R_g - R_d}{R_g}$$

Not all those who book will actually turn up and Bodily and Weatherford (1995), using decision trees, show that the form of the solution remains unchanged.

A simpler approach for deciding how many discounts to offer is given in Weatherford and Bodily (1992). Another discounted unit is offered provided that the probability of overbooking, Pr(*ob*) (i.e. the probability that discounted demand plus full price demand will exceed capacity), is greater than the ratio of reduced price contribution R_d to the full price contribution R_f, i.e.

$$\text{Allow discount if Pr}(ob) > \frac{R_d}{R_f}$$

Thus the closer the discounted price is to the full price the more q_d, (the quantity discounted) approaches the capacity of the facility C.

In the approaches outlined above it was assumed that there was no correlation between the demand for full and discounted price accommodation. This is most unlikely in practice. Brumelle *et al.* (1990) attempt to overcome this problem by advancing a rule for situations where there is a positive correlation between the number of discounted customers (q_d) and the number of full price paying customers (q_f) and where discounts are issued first and there is no overlap in the time period during which discounts and full price are offered. Their rule is:

$$q_d = \max\{0 \leq q \leq C : \Pr[q_f > C - q | q_d \geq q] < P_d/P_f\} \text{ where } C \text{ is the capacity}$$

To illustrate how this rule operates consider a hotel with 100 rooms with a forecast demand (or room occupancy in this case) for a particular period which is normally distributed with mean 60 and standard deviation 10. The full price rooms cost £100 and a discount of 25 per cent is available for early booking. We can then write:

$$\Phi\left[\frac{q_f - (100 - q)}{10}\right] = 75/100$$

Hence,

$$\frac{q_f - (100 - q)}{10} = \phi(0.75) = 0.575$$

Thus $2q = 100 - 5.75 = 94.25$. The hotel will not therefore discount more than 47 rooms. Brumelle *et al.* (1990) also proposed a decision rule which incorporates the loss of goodwill and compensation if overbooking occurs. This is a modification of the above in which a term P_g is added to the full price to give the rule that the optimum number of discounted customers (q^*) is:

$$q^* = \max \{0 \le C{:}\Pr[q_f > C - q | q_d \ge q] < \frac{P_d}{P_f + P_g}\}$$

In the above decision rules it has been assumed that there are two classes of customers: those who pay full price and those who will only pay the discounted price. In reality it is more likely that all customers want the discounted price and as the discounts become unavailable a proportion will accept the full price. This is known as diversion, and Pfeifer (1989) allows for this in proposing the following rule to determine the number of discounts:

$$\text{Book another discounted customer provided } p_1 p_2 < \frac{P_f - P_d}{P_f};$$

where p_1 is the probability that the $q + 1$ customers will only accept the discounted price; p_2 is the probability that $Q - q - 1$ full price units will satisfy all subsequent demand from those who want full price and those who would prefer the discount but would accept the full price if none were available. In practice estimating the probabilities $p1$ and $p2$ is extremely difficult.

Brumelle *et al.* (1990) advance the rule for determining the number of discounts as:

$$q^* = \max \left\{0 \le q \le C{:}\Pr[Y{+}U(q) > C - q | q_d \ge q] < \frac{(P_d - \gamma P_f)}{P_f}\right\}$$

They assume that as discounts become unavailable vertical upgrade can occur with a probability of γ. $U(q)$ is the number who take the upgrade option if discounts are cut off at q. As before there are difficulties in estimating the required probabilities.

In the above there has been some discussion of overbooking. This, however, is often not a very big issue owing to current quality improvement and customer care initiatives. Many companies have managerial policies to prevent overbooking. However, this means that 'no shows' carry a large cost especially if possible full price paying customers have been turned away and a customer who has reserved a discounted place fails to turn up. Bodily and Pfeifer (1991) discuss survivorship further in relation to the issue of overbooking. They give a simple rule when to incorporate no-shows, as book another person if:

$$p > \frac{C_o}{R + C_o}$$

Where p is the probability of a 'no-show', R is the revenue from each surviving customer and C_o is the cost of overbooking. Often p is estimated by expert judgement based on past experience of no-shows. If the likelihood of spoilage (no-show) is not dependent on when the booking was made then the binomial distribution may be used. The rule then becomes, book another customer provided that:

$$\sum_{i=0}^{N-1} \frac{B!}{i!(B-i)!} \, p^i \, (1-p)^{B-i} > \frac{C_o}{R + C_o}$$

Where B is the number of bookings made and N is the number of units available (the capacity). If N is large, say greater than 30, the binomial distribution may be approximated by the Normal distribution. To overcome the restrictive assumption that the probability of surviving is independent of when the booking was made, Bodily and ·Pfeifer (1991) extend the above model to allow for time varying probabilities and estimate the mean number of survivors (m) from:

$$m = \sum_{i=j}^{J} b_i \, p_i$$

Where: j is the number of periods prior to the use of the facility and J is the maximum number of periods in advance that a booking can be made; b_i is the number of current bookings that were booked j periods previously; p_i is the probability that each current booking made j periods previously will survive.

The variance (s^2) of the distribution of survivors is given by:

$$s^2 = \sum_{i=j}^{J} b_i \, p_i \, (1 - p_i)$$

In this approach it is assumed that the probabilities of surviving are broadly similar from one period to the next. Booking rules can now be constructed but these are more complicated as the reservations and cancellations require updating every period and so this is not pursued here. Bodily and Pfeifer further generalize their approach and allow for survivor probabilities being conditional on factors such as economic or weather conditions. This becomes very complex and many practitioners estimate the average level of no-shows and then use judgement to correct for weather and economic effects. Since these external influences are erratic and hard to predict, judgemental approaches are likely to be as accurate as the more complex analytical methods.

One way to reduce the number of survivors or at least receive some revenue from the no-shows is to have non refundable reservations, and if this is the case Bodily and Pfeifer (1991) state that the decision rule takes the form.

Book another customer if:

$$P > 1 - \frac{R}{p_s(C_o + R)}$$

Where P is the probability of spoilage and p_s is the probability that the $B + 1$ booking will survive given that the number of survivors is greater than equal to the capacity. (This can be amended to allow for cases where other penalties on no-shows are used, such as non-refundable deposits.)

In practice a customer's willingness to pay full price increases as the availability date draws closer, and for the hotelier a threshold curve can be used to reduce the number of discounts available as the availability date approaches. If there is unused capacity discounts can always be offered, but this runs the risk of annoying the full price payers

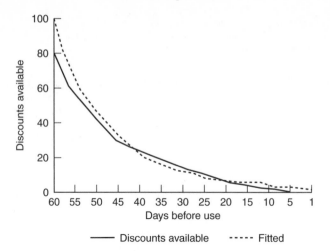

Figure 4.3   Threshold curve

and in practice late discounts are often only available on the day of use. Threshold curves are discussed briefly in the next section.

THRESHOLD CURVES

The construction of threshold curves tends to be based on past experience and observation of demand by the company and tends to be proprietary. The idea is to construct a curve showing how the number of discounts available should be reduced as the date of use draws nearer. Such a curve is illustrated for a 100-room hotel in Figure 4.3.

The dividing line need not be absolute and limits at ±2 standard errors can be placed on the line to reflect the statistical uncertainty in this procedure. For observed demand the yield manager can estimate the threshold line by fitting the model:

$$\text{Discount level} = \beta_0 e^{-\beta_1(t-t_0)}$$

Where e is the exponential constant and t is the time from the period when bookings first opened (t_0). By taking natural logarithms (ln) this model may be fitted using ordinary least squares:

$$\ln(\text{discount level}) = \ln(\beta_0) - \beta_1 t$$

For the data in Figure 4.3 this gives the equation of the threshold curve as:

$$\text{Discount level} = 97.5 e^{-0.074(t-60)}$$

This 'fitted' curve is displayed in Figure 4.3.

More complex curves can be used but their estimation is more difficult, often requiring specialist statistical and computing skills. Several threshold curves may be constructed if there are different discount bands. An alternative, but interesting, approach is to construct a threshold curve after considering the probability distributions of customers who extend their stay, new reservations and 'walk-ins' (i.e. those without a reservation). This is illustrated in an article by Williams (1977).

These methods may not find the optimal booking level, but nevertheless Kimes (1989) states that the approach is 'simple to use and gives good results' a view supported by Reliham (1989). However, a major problem is the timely update of the curves when patterns of demand change. This stresses the need for fairly accurate forecasting and this is the subject of the next section.

FORECASTING DEMAND FOR FACILITIES

If demand could be forecast in a reliable and accurate manner then a plan could be drawn up to develop or reduce facilities to cater optimally for this demand. In forecasting there are two approaches to this problem, 'top-down' and 'bottom-up'. In the 'top-down' approach the total number who will use the facility is predicted and this number is decomposed into the demand for different parts of the facility. Consider, for example, the case of an international hotel in a major city. The number of customers in a particular month could be predicted and classified into business users and tourists, and their length of stay and type of room could be estimated. There is, of course, a risk of losing accuracy using this method, but the degree of accuracy does tend to be better than the alternative approach of taking the lowest level unit, the room, for example, and predicting the demand for it. The whole area of forecasting tourism is given good treatment by Frechtling (1996).

The forecasts can be made using judgemental or quantitative methods or a mixture of the two. Judgemental approaches make use of expert opinion, whether individually or in panel form, and often consider various 'what if' scenarios. Such approaches are particularly useful when considering the development of new facilities or service, the effects of some untested promotion or the effects of competition. Since this chapter is primarily a review of the various quantitative methods that are employed in yield management the judgemental approaches, although useful, are not pursued here. Interested readers should refer to Peterson (1990), Goodwin and Wright (1993) and Frechtling (1996).

Quantitative approaches can be based on extrapolation, in which it is assumed that historical trends will continue into the future, or causal models based upon some relationship between independent variables and demand. Consider first of all the simplest case of extrapolative forecasting based on a constant level; for example, the demand for bed and breakfast rooms on weekdays. The daily demand is given in Table 4.2.

Table 4.2 Constant demand series

Day	1	2	3	4	5	6	7	8	9	10	11	12	13	14	15	16
Demand	110	80	70	120	150	100	80	130	170	120	11	9	90	140	75	115

The data should first be graphed. A graph of daily demand is illustrated in Figure 4.4. Note that on days 11 and 12 demand was virtually zero. An attempt should be made to explain this – was the hotel partially closed or did the dates coincide with some national

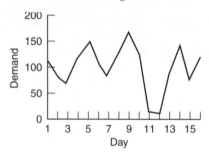

Figure 4.4 Demand for rooms

celebration? In any event it is advisable to treat these as 'outliers' and remove them from the data set. Alternatively the values could be replaced by average demand for the four days around them. This initial examination of data is an essential step in producing forecasts and observed data should be checked for: 'odd values', trend and seasonal fluctuations before selecting a forecasting method. Also of concern in choosing a forecasting method is the time horizon and accuracy requirements. Chatfield (1985) discusses these issues further.

To forecast the demand for the next day a naive forecast can be generated by assuming that the demand for the next day will be the same as that for the previous day, i.e.

$$F_{t+1} = D_t$$

Where: F_{t+1} is the forecast at time $t + 1$; D_t is the observed demand at time t.

Another way might be to use the average of past demand, or more sensibly an average of the most recent demands. This is the method of moving averages. A four-period (day) moving average forecast is given by:

$$F_t = \frac{D_t + D_{t-1} + D_{t-2} + D_{t-3}}{4}$$

Simple exponential smoothing, which is similar to moving averages, but with forecasts revised in the light of the most recent experience, may also be used. The one step ahead exponentially smoothed forecast is given by:

$$F_{t+1} = \alpha D_t + (1 - \alpha) F_t\text{-x}$$

Where α is called the smoothing constant and assigned a value between 0 and 1 which is chosen to minimize one step ahead forecast errors in the historical data set. The larger the value of α, the more weight is given to the recent history, and so the model is more responsive to change.

Consider the above example of weekday demand for bed and breakfast with the very low values of demand in periods 11 and 12 removed. Once the data have been examined it is easy using a spreadsheet to construct the model. This has been done using *Excel* for a naive method, a four-period moving average and simple exponential smoothing with $\alpha = 0.1, 0.3$ and 0.5. The results are displayed in Table 4.3.

Table 4.3　One step ahead forecasts

Day	Demand	Naive	Error	MA(4)	Error	ES(α = 0.1)	Error	ES(α = 0.3)	Error	ES(α = 0.5)	Error
1	110										
2	80	110	−30			110	−30.00	110	−30.00	110	−30
3	70	80	−10			107	−37.00	101	−31.00	95	−25
4	120	70	50			103	16.70	92	28.30	83	37.5
5	150	120	30	95	55	105	45.03	100	49.81	101	48.75
6	100	150	−50	105	−5	109	−9.47	115	−15.13	126	−25.63
7	80	100	−20	110	−30	109	−28.53	111	−30.59	113	−32.81
8	130	80	50	113	17.5	106	24.33	101	28.58	96	33.59
9	170	130	40	115	55	108	61.89	110	60.01	113	56.80
10	120	170	−50	120	0	114	5.70	128	−7.99	142	−21.60
11	90	120	−30	125	−35	115	−24.87	126	−35.60	131	−40.80
12	140	90	50	128	12.5	112	27.62	115	25.08	110	29.60
13	75	140	−65	130	−55	115	−40.14	122	−47.44	125	−50.2
14	115	75	40	106	8.75	111	3.87	108	6.79	100	14.9
Forecasts		115		105		112		110		108	
MAPE		37.39		24.17		25.05		27.96		31.53	

Five forecasts have been produced. To determine which is the most likely forecast the performance of past forecasts is often used in the assessment. The mean absolute percentage error (MAPE) is the most commonly used performance measure, although not necessarily the best, to assess forecast error. The MAPE is given by:

$$MAPE = \frac{1}{n} \sum_{i=1}^{n} \left| \left(\frac{O_i - F_i}{F_i} \right) \right|$$

Where O is observed value; F is forecast value; n is number of forecasts.

In Table 4.3 the MAPEs are written below the forecasts. The moving average has the best (smallest) MAPE followed by exponential smoothing with α = 0.1. In practice when using exponential smoothing the value of α is often chosen so that the MAPE obtained from one step ahead forecasts of observed data is minimized. In assessing the performance of the method it is useful to compare the MAPEs of the selected forecast method and the naive MAPE. The method would only be used if it was better than the naive estimates.

Other commonly used measures are the mean absolute deviation (MAD), mean square error (MSE) and root mean square error (RMSE):

$$MAD = \frac{1}{n} \sum_{i=1}^{n} |O_i - F_i|$$

$$MSE = \frac{1}{n} \sum_{i=1}^{n} (O_i - F_i)^2$$

$$RMSE = \sqrt{\frac{1}{n} \sum_{i=1}^{n} (O_i - F_i)^2}$$

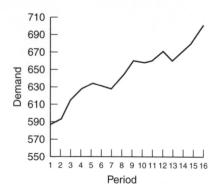

Figure 4.5   Demand

For a more complete discussion of error measures see Armstrong and Callopy (1992), Fildes (1992), Witt and Witt (1992) and Watson (1994).

If there is a trend, either upwards or downwards, it has to be accounted for. One way of doing this is by using Holt's method, which decomposes the series into a level and a trend in making the forecast. Producing a forecast involves the following steps:

Step 1: Obtain a smoothed estimate of the level.

$$A_t = \alpha D_t + (1 - \alpha)(A_{t-1} + T_{-1})$$

Where A_t is the smoothed value at time t; D_t is the observed value at time t; α is the smoothing constant for the level, often chosen to be between 0 and 0.3.

Step 2: Obtain a smoothed trend estimate by:

$$T_t = \beta(A_t - A_{t-1}) + (1 - \beta)T_{t-1}$$

Where T_t is the smoothed trend estimate; β is the trend smoothing constant, often chosen to be between 0 and 0.1.

Step 3: Generate the forecast from:

$$F_{t+m} = A_t + mT_t$$

Where F_{t+m} is the forecast m periods into the future.

Suppose that, for example, a forecast for the next four periods of the demand for rooms in a hotel is required. The historical demand is given in Figure 4.5 and Holt's method in Table 4.4.

Values of $\alpha = 0.3$ and $\beta = 0.1$ were used in Table 4.4. In practice values of the smoothing constants would be chosen to minimize the MAPE. As in the case of simple exponential smoothing the forecasting procedure has to be initialized. The level of demand for period one was used as the prediction for period two and the first estimate of the trend was obtained from the difference between the level of demand in periods two and one. The forecasts are displayed graphically in Figure 4.6. In such situations

Table 4.4 Demand series with trend

Period	Demand	Level	Trend	Forecast	Absolute % error
1	588				
2	594	588.0	0.0		
3	617	596.7	0.9	588.0	4.9
4	628	606.7	1.8	597.6	5.1
5	633	615.8	2.5	608.5	4.0
6	631	622.1	2.9	618.4	2.0
7	627	625.6	3.0	625.0	0.3
8	642	632.6	3.4	628.6	2.1
9	660	643.2	4.1	636.0	3.8
10	655	649.6	4.3	647.3	1.2
11	659	655.4	4.5	653.9	0.8
12	668	662.3	4.7	659.9	1.2
13	658	664.3	4.4	667.0	1.4
14	670	669.1	4.5	668.8	0.2
15	682	676.1	4.7	673.6	1.2
16	702	687.2	5.4	680.9	3.1
17				692.6	
18				697.9	
19				703.3	
20				708.6	

with trend, linear regression is often used to fit a straight line to the data and extrapolated to give forecasts.

The regression model $D_t = \beta_0 + \beta_1$ *Period* was fitted to the above data using *Excel* to estimate the values of β_0 and β_1. This gave the forecasting model:

$$F_{t+m} = 592 + 6.2 \times (t+m)$$

The regression line provided a good fit to the data, accounting for 92 per cent of the observed variance in the data, (given by the R^2 value), and the estimates of the βs were statistically significant.

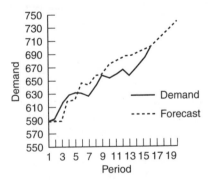

Figure 4.6 Forecasts

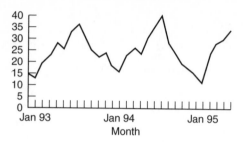

Figure 4.7 Demand for rooms

So far the discussion has been of level and trend; clearly, in hospitality and tourism seasonal fluctuations are important. Winter's method extends exponential smoothing to incorporate seasonality. When using this method a smoothed estimate of the level (A_t) is first obtained from:

$$A_t = \alpha \frac{D_t}{S_{t-p}} + (1 - \alpha)(A_{t-1} + T_{t-1})$$

Where α is the smoothing constant for the level having a value between 0 and 1; D_t is the observed level; T_{t-1} is the previous trend estimate; S_{t-p} is the seasonal estimate for the season p periods previously.

The trend estimate is then computed from

$$T_t = \beta(A_t - A_{t-1}) + (1 - \beta)T_{t-1}$$

Where β is the smoothing constant for the trend and takes a value between 0 and 1.

The seasonal estimate is then given by:

$$S_t = \gamma \frac{D_t}{A_t} + (1 - \gamma)S_{t-p}$$

Where γ is the smoothing constant for the seasonality estimate and assumes a value between 0 and 1.

The forecast m periods into the future (F_{t+m}) is given by:

$$F_{t+m} = (A_t + pT_t)S_{t-p+m}$$

For example, if the historical demand for rooms in a hotel is as given in Figure 4.7, a seasonal forecast is required. The application of Winter's method to these data is displayed in Table 4.5 with smoothing constants for α, β and γ equal to 0.4, 0.1 and 0.3 respectively.

Initialization of the forecast procedure is similar to Holt's method, with the first seasonal estimate given a value of one. The forecasts are displayed graphically in Figure 4.8.

Table 4.5 Seasonal demand series

Date	Period	A_t	T_t	S_t	Forecast	Absolute % error
Jan 93	15					
Feb 93	13	15	−2	1	15	13.33
Mar 93	20	15.80	−1.72	1.08	13	53.85
Apr 93	23	16.97	−1.43	1.11	15	51.29
May 93	28	19.44	−1.04	1.13	17	62.85
Jun 93	25	19.88	−0.89	1.08	18	35.85
Jul 93	33	23.64	−0.43	1.12	20	61.01
Aug 93	36	26.80	−0.07	1.10	26	40.13
Sep 93	31	27.28	−0.01	1.04	30	2.44
Oct 93	25	25.97	−0.14	0.99	29	14.90
Nov 93	22	24.39	−0.29	0.97	29	23.85
Dec 93	24	24.36	−0.26	1.00	27	9.74
Jan 94	18	21.66	−0.51	0.95	25	28.23
Feb 94	15	18.25	−0.80	0.95	21	28.28
Mar 94	23	18.78	−0.66	1.12	17	35.79
Apr 94	26	20.06	−0.47	1.16	18	44.11
May 94	23	20.29	−0.40	1.13	19	23.66
Jun 94	30	22.66	−0.12	1.15	19	59.29
Jul 94	34	25.86	0.21	1.18	25	34.29
Aug 94	40	31.01	0.70	1.16	30	31.90
Sep 94	28	30.36	0.57	1.01	36	22.04
Oct 94	24	28.45	0.32	0.95	36	32.59
Nov 94	19	24.89	−0.07	0.91	34	43.91
Dec 94	16	21.64	−0.39	0.92	29	44.40
Jan 95	14	18.67	−0.64	0.89	21	34.47
Feb 95	10	14.37	−1.01	0.87	17	41.30
May 95	23	15.93	−0.75	1.22	12	89.44
Apr 95	28	18.99	−0.37	1.26	14	100.84
Mar 95	30	21.60	−0.07	1.21	17	81.08
Jun 95	33	24.12	0.19	1.22	19	75.96
Jul 95					29	
Aug 95					28	
Sep 95					25	
Oct 95					24	
Nov 95					23	
Dec 95					23	

Alternatively, multiple regression may be used with dummy variables to represent the seasonal effects. If the demand was seasonal with four quarters then the seasonal fluctuations can be modelled with three dummy variables coded as follows:

$Q2$ = 1 if referring to quarter 2, 0 otherwise.
$Q3$ = 1 if referring to quarter 3, 0 otherwise.
$Q4$ = 1 if referring to quarter 4, 0 otherwise.

Yield Management

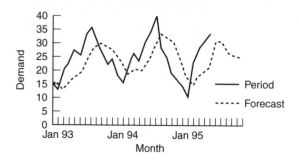

Figure 4.8 Demand for rooms

Table 4.6 Quarterly demand

Year	Quarter	Demand	*Advert*	*DInc*	*Q2*	*Q3*	*Q4*	*Trend*
1991	1	120	35	280	0	0	0	1
	2	80	11	180	1	0	0	2
	3	400	11	370	0	1	0	3
	4	200	16	290	0	0	1	4
1992	1	75	32	190	0	0	0	5
	2	120	10	220	1	0	0	6
	3	270	12	280	0	1	0	7
	4	155	21	260	0	0	1	8
1993	1	120	72	240	0	0	0	9
	2	150	31	270	1	0	0	10
	3	660	19	353	0	1	0	11
	4	270	14	290	0	0	1	12
1994	1	200	75	285	0	0	0	13
	2	280	41	300	1	0	0	14
	3	800	17	420	0	1	0	15
	4	320	10	350	0	0	1	16

Quarter 1 would be represented as the base level and incorporated into the constant term with associated values of zero for variables *Q2*, *Q3* and *Q4*. (If calendar months were to be represented in this way then 11 dummy variables would be required.)

One advantage of using regression analysis is that additional variables may be incorporated into the model to explain and forecast demand. Consider the following example in which a hotel wishes to model the demand for rooms. The pattern of demand is seasonal with quarterly periods and the forecasters believe that the level of observed demand is influenced by the number of advertisements (*Advert*) placed and the average level of customers' disposable income (*DInc*). The data are given in Table 4.6.

Fitting a multiple regression model of the form:

$$D_t = \beta_0 + \beta_1 Advert + \beta_2 DInc. + \beta_3 Q2 + \beta_4 Q3 + \beta_4 Q4 + \beta_5 Trend$$

to the data yielded:

$$D_t = -229.73 - 1.96Advert + 1.48DInc. - 34.83Q2 + 142.15Q3 - 80.33Q4 + 13.53Trend$$

This would suggest that demand is depressed relative to quarter one for quarters two and four and is inflated in quarter three.

However, although this model was a good fit to the observed data with an adjusted R^2 value of 82 per cent, the magnitudes of the standard errors were such that only the coefficients of disposable income and trend were significant. Thus there is no evidence that advertising promotions are influencing sales, or that the seasonal effects are statistically important.

Explanatory variables such as the number of advertising promotions or the average level of disposable income may help to explain demand but they are not very helpful in forecasting as these values must in turn be forecast. Explanatory variables are, however, useful in some situations, allowing 'what if' type questions. For example, the impact on demand for rooms given a fall in the level of disposable income could be determined. Dummy variables can also be used to incorporate special events such as festivals or conventions into time-based forecasting models.

More complex (but not necessarily more accurate) univariate forecasting methods have been investigated for tourism and associated industries. Notable among these has been the application of the auto regressive integrated moving average (ARIMA) models, as originated by Box and Jenkins in 1976. There is a much cited example of the application of this methodology to predicting airline passengers (see Montgomery and Johnson, 1976). This more complex procedure, which requires a time series of substantial length (greater than fifty observations for non-seasonal applications and far more if the intention is to model and forecast a seasonal structure), and the use of specialized software, is outside the scope of this chapter, but the interested reader is referred to O'Donovan (1983).

Other approaches to demand forecasting take an econometric perspective and some of these are described by Witt and Witt (1992). These methods involve the use of regression analysis to estimate the demand function:

$$D = f(X_1, X_2, \ldots X_k)$$

Where D is demand to be estimated; $X_1, X_2, \ldots X_k$ are the explanatory variables; and f is some function, often linear, which relates the explanatory variable(s) to demand.

Typical variables which can be used are population size, gross national product, income, family size, price of product or service, trend and dummy variables to indicate such features as time of year, dates of promotion periods, changes in competition, destination and so forth.

Witt and Witt (1992) give a model for intentional tourism demand as:

$$\ln \frac{V_{ijt}}{P_{it}} = \alpha_1 + \alpha_2 \ln \frac{Y_{it}}{P_{it}} + \alpha_3 \ln C_{jt} + \alpha_4 \ln CS_{it}$$
$$+ \alpha_5 \ln EX_{ijt} + \alpha_6 \ln TA_{ijt} + \alpha_7 \ln TAS_{it}$$
$$+ \alpha_8 \ln TS_{ijt} + \alpha_9 \ln TSS_{it} + \alpha_{10}DV1_t$$
$$+ \alpha_{11}DV2_t + \alpha_{12} DV3_{it} + U_{ijt}$$

Where V_{ijt} is the number of tourist visits from origin i to destination j in year t; P_{it} is the origin i population in year t; Y_{it} is the personal disposable income in origin i in year t; C_{jt} is the cost of living for tourists in destination j in year t; CS_{it} is the weighted average of the cost of living for tourists in substitute destinations for residents of origin i in year t; EX_{ijt} is the rate of exchange between the currencies of origin i and destination j in year t; TA_{ijt} is the cost of air travel from origin i to destination j in year t; TAS_{it} is the weighted average of the cost of travel by air to substitute destinations from origin i in year t; TS_{ijt} is the cost of surface travel from origin i to destination j in year t; TSS_{it} is the weighted average of the cost of surface travel to substitute destinations from origin i in year t; DV_n ($n = 1,2,3$) are dummy variables and U_{ijt} is a nuisance term. A full discussion of the variables and the model is given in Witt and Witt's book.

Estimating the parameters of this model requires the collection of historical data for the explanatory variables and associated levels of demand. Ordinary least squares regression or, more reliably, the maximum likelihood method is then used. Readers should consult Madalla (1992) for an in-depth discussion.

However, Witt and Witt (1992) found when reviewing published econometrics-based forecasts of international tourism that their performance was somewhat disappointing. They stated: 'the random walk model is ranked more highly in terms of forecasting accuracy than econometric models in the context of international tourism'. In 1982 a forecasting competition found surprisingly that in terms of forecast accuracy simple models outperformed more complex methods (see Makridakis *et al.*, 1982, for further details).

Several researchers have found that combining forecasts made by different methods can greatly increase forecast accuracy (see Clemen, 1986; Bunn, 1988; Watson, 1994). The average of a forecast made by using judgement, simple time series and an econometric model may well produce more accurate and reliable forecasts. In general, a sensible course of action for producing forecasts might be to use simple quantitatively produced forecasts as inputs into decision-making where they will be amended in the light of expert knowledge.

Methods of obtaining point forecasts have been outlined, but a measure of the uncertainty of these forecasts is also required. A crude approximation of a 95 per cent prediction interval can be obtained by taking the forecast plus or minus twice the standard deviation of the errors in fitting the model. Montgomery and Johnston (1976) and Wheelwright and Makridakis (1989) detail some other approximations.

Employing quantitative methods to improve forecasts and allow more informed discussion will help to improve demand estimates. These demand estimates can then be refined using the simple rules outlined in the earlier part of this chapter. This should then allow the capacity-constrained organization to ensure a high yield from its resources and ultimately an improved contribution. However, it should be borne in mind that the use of quantitative methods is an aid to decision-making and not a replacement for it, and that the experience and knowledge of those who manage the resources should not be devalued.

REFERENCES

Alstrup, J., Boas, S., Madsen, O. and Vida, L. R. (1986) 'Booking policy for flights with two types of passengers'. *European Journal of Operational Research*, **27**, 274–88.

Armstrong, J. S. and Collopy, F. (1992) 'Error measures for generalizing about forecasting: empirical comparisons'. *International Journal of Forecasting*, **8**, 69–80.

Belobaba, P. P. (1989) 'Application of a problematic decision model to airline seat inventory control'. *Operations Research*, **37**(2), 183–97.

Bodily, S. E. and Pfeifer, P. E. (1991) 'Overbooking decision rules'. *Omega*, **20**, 129–33.

Bodily, S. E. and Weatherford, L. R. (1995) 'Perishable-asset revenue management: generic and multiple-price yield management with diversion'. *Omega*, **23**, 173–85.

Box, G. E. P. and Jenkins, G. M. (1976) *Time Series Analysis: Forecasting and Control*. San Francisco: Holden-Day.

Brumelle, S. L., McGill, J. I., Oum, T. H., Sawaki, K. and Tretheway, M. W. (1990) 'Allocation of airline seats between stochastically dependent demands'. *Transportation Science*, **24**, 183–92.

Bunn, D. W. (1988) 'Combining forecasts'. *European Journal of Operational Research*, **33**, 223–9.

Chatfield, C. (1985) 'The initial examination of data'. *Journal of the Royal Statistical Society*, Series A, **148**, 214–53.

Clemen, R. (1986) 'Linear constraints and the efficiency of combined forecasts'. *Journal of Forecasting*, **5**, 31–8.

Cross, R. G. (1989) 'Yield management: new horizons for a dark science'. Paper presented at the Yield Management Multi-industry Conference, Charlotte, NC.

Fildes, R. (1992) 'The evaluation of extrapolative forecasting methods'. *International Journal of Forecasting*, **8**, 81–98.

Frechtling, D. C. (1996) *Practical Tourism Forecasting*. Oxford: Butterworth-Heinemann.

Glover, F., Glover, R., Lorenzo, J. and McMillan C. (1982) 'The passenger-mix problem in the scheduled airlines'. *Interfaces*, **58**(3), 73–9.

Goodwin, P. and Wright, G. (1993) 'Improving judgmental time series forecasting: a review of the guidance provided by research'. *International Journal of Forecasting*, **9**, 147–61.

Hanke, J. E. and Reitsch, A. G. (1992) *Business Forecasting*. Needham Heights, MA: Allyn & Bacon.

Kimes, S. E. (1989) 'Yield management: a tool for capacity-constrained service firms'. *Journal of Operations Management*, **8**(4), 348–63.

Madalla, G. S. (1992) *Introduction to Econometrics*. New York: Macmillan.

Makridakis, S., Anderson, A., Carbone, R., Fildes, R., Hibon, M., Lewandrowski, R., Newton, J., Parzen, E. and Winkler, R. (1982) 'The accuracy of extrapolation (time series) methods. Results of a forecasting competition'. *Journal of Forecasting*, **9**, 5–22.

Montgomery, D. C. and Johnson, L. A. (1976) *Forecasting and Time Series Analysis*. New York: McGraw-Hill.

O'Donovan, T. M. (1983) *Short Term Forecasting: an Introduction to the Box–Jenkins Approach*. Chichester: John Wiley & Sons.

Peterson, R. T. (1990) 'The role of experts' judgment in sales forecasting'. *Journal of Business Forecasting*, **9**(2), 16–21.

Pfeifer, P. E. (1989) 'The airline discount fare allocation problem'. *Decision Sciences*, **20**, 149–57.

Reliham, W. J. (1989) 'Yield management approach to hotel room pricing'. *Cornell Hotel and Restaurant Administration Quarterly*, May, 40–5.

Rothstein, M. (1971) 'An airline overbooking model'. *Transportation Science*, **5**, 180–92.

Rothstein, M. (1974) 'Hotel overbooking as a Markovian sequential decision process'. *Decision Sciences*, **5**, 389–94.

Watson, M. C. (1994) 'The practice of forecasting in commercial enterprises with focus on the Scottish electronics industry'. PhD Thesis, Napier University.

Weatherford, L. R. and Bodily, S. E. (1992) 'A taxonomy and research overview of perishable-asset revenue management: yield management, overbooking, and pricing'. *Operations Research*, **40**(5), 831–44.

Wheelwright, S. C. and Makridakis, S. (1989) *Forecasting Methods for Management*. New York: John Wiley and Sons.

Williams, F. E. (1977) 'Decision theory and the innkeeper: an approach for setting hotel reservation policy'. *Interfaces*, **7**(4), 18–30.

Williamson, E. L. and Belobaba, P. P. (1988) 'Optimization techniques for a seat inventory control'. *AGIFORS, 28th Annual Symposium Proceedings*, 153–70.

Winston, W. L. (1987) *Operations Research: Applications and Algorithms*. Boston: PWS-Kent Publishing Company.

Witt, S. F. and Witt, C. A. (1992) *Modelling and Forecasting Demand in Tourism*. London: Academic Press.

PART II
MODELS OF YIELD MANAGEMENT

5

Perspectives on Pricing Decision in the Inclusive Holiday Industry

Eric Laws

INTRODUCTION

The inclusive holiday industry has achieved spectacular growth in the decades since the end of the Second World War. Foreign holidays are now readily available and affordable to many people in Western and other industrialized societies. Most countries throughout the world are eager to develop further their inbound tourism for the employment and foreign currency benefits it brings. The package holiday industry's success can be explained in part by its managers' policy of emphasizing low prices, thus expanding the market, but this has resulted in several problems which are increasingly being recognized within the industry and by other interest groups. Concern has been expressed about the consequences of yield and volume control policies in causing unsustainably low profit margins, and about the effects on destination communities of the rapid and insensitive expansion of their tourism sectors in the face of demand pressures. The policies which have led to the growth of the inclusive holiday industry now require re-evaluation and perhaps revision if it is to continue the pace and scale of its development.

This chapter introduces a critical evaluation of the yield and capacity management policies commonly adopted by tour operators and retail travel agencies to manage their revenue flows and their market share. It examines the nature and evolution of market place responses to low price holiday offers, and focuses attention on the consequences for all organizations in the holiday industry. It argues that the analytical and policy focus should be the entire industry. The objective of this chapter is to focus attention on low prices as a significant factor constraining the holiday industry's ability to function systemically as a network of long-term business relationships creating the types of holiday products and experiences which are enjoyable for clients, rewarding for entrepreneurs and staff, and welcomed by destination area residents, local businesses and politicians.

Yield Management

THE DEVELOPMENT OF THE INCLUSIVE HOLIDAY INDUSTRY

During the second half of the twentieth century tourism became one of the major industries in the world. The number of people travelling abroad for all reasons in 1992 was 476 million (World Tourist Organization, 1994). The proportion of the United Kingdom population who had ever taken an overseas holiday rose from 34 per cent in 1970 to 70 per cent in 1990 (British Tourist Authority, 1992). A number of factors have been identified to account for this success, summarized as:

- technological developments in transport;
- improvements in business communication and reservation systems (CRS) and telecommunications;
- increases in standards of living in the countries of tourist origin;
- investment in tourism infrastructure development in destination areas;
- the creativity of travel agents in tour operators (based on Burkhart and Medlik, 1981; Pearce, 1989; Poon, 1993; Holloway, 1994; Page, 1994).

The first two developments noted above (transport, CRS and telecoms) have enabled tour operators to increase the range of destinations offered, as well as to hold or reduce the cost of holidays. In combination with the third factor, improved standards of living (especially higher discretionary income, longer paid holidays and changing demographics and patterns of work), this has resulted in much wider social access to holidays. The holiday industry's development has also coincided with greater general awareness of overseas travel resulting from television and media coverage of heritage, ecology and other place-related topics.

Destination areas have responded to the economic opportunities offered by the increasing demand for tourism services by investment in support infrastructure such as airports, and by providing specialized training for employment in the tourism industry. Entrepreneurs in the destination areas have developed hotels (and many other types of businesses) which both rely on tourist demand and contribute to the ability of an area to function effectively as a destination. Retail travel agents and tour operators offer easy access to distant destinations from countries of tourist origin, in particular by providing packaged holidays enabling clients to buy all the elements needed for a holiday in one transaction. The demand for these inclusive holidays has been stimulated by the industry's marketing, including its advertising and pricing practices. These have tended to favour certain members of the holiday industry system, particularly the tour operators and retail travel agents at the expense of those in destination areas, and have led to the commoditization of holiday products where clients tend to discriminate by price (Urry, 1990; McCannel, 1992; Boniface and Fowler, 1993).

The general public in Britain is the target of a plethora of holiday advertising which has three main thrusts: images and descriptions of place-evoking appeals such as culture, climate, scenery, or activity; appeals based on service style and quality; and offers emphasizing low prices. Two general rationales lie behind this approach to yield management: the increasingly urgent need as departure date approaches for holiday companies to sell the remaining capacity they have contracted on flights and in hotels; and their wish to defend (or to increase) market share. It is shown below that bargain offers not only stimulate demand, but also have three effects with long-term significance, altering its demographic profile and temporal characteristics, and providing opportunities for power plays between the various organizations in the holiday industry system.

HOLIDAY INDUSTRY PRICING POLICIES

Companies can adopt a variety of approaches to pricing, but they should be evaluated in the context of its overall aims, as McCarthy and Perreault (1988) have pointed out: 'Managers develop a set of pricing objectives and policies in the context of the company's objectives. The policy explains how flexible prices are to be, the level at which they will be set over the life cycle of the service, and to whom and when discounts will be allowed.'

The complexity of yield management decisions for a tour operator has been high-lighted by Holloway and Robinson (1995). Robinson is the Group Marketing Manager of First Choice, one of Britain's leading tour operators, and the authors note that the company 'produced some 2,300 brochure pages for the summer 1995 season. Most featured a price panel with perhaps 100 separate prices, making a total of almost a quarter of a million prices.' First Choice's pricing is based on a straightforward cost-plus approach, but also reflects specific objectives such as to regain market share in specific resorts, or to achieve an overall price advantage.

They conclude that 'the brochure price is determined, but so too is the proposed policy on early booking discounts, child discounts, late sales reductions, travel agent commission incentives and the like. This is because the overall profitability target of the programme must be set against the actual sales price likely to be achieved' (Holloway and Robinson, 1995).

Price setting for yield management is therefore based on setting various price thresholds, reflecting assumptions about price-related differences in buying behaviour, particularly with respect to seasonal and departure airport preferences, and responses to late or early booking reductions. This can be assessed from analysis of the company's (or industry's) historic data (Relihan, 1989).

Seasonal Pricing

One of the most common ways of setting holiday price differentials is the seasonal banding typical of tour operators' brochures and familiar to all who purchase inclusive holidays, in the form of price and departure date price matrices. This is represented schematically in Figure 5.1. The peak season, when little discounting is offered and many holiday-makers are willing to pay premium prices, is shown as a broad vertical column, flanked by two shoulders of unequal width representing the early and late seasons. The more restricted nature of demand during the shoulder seasons limits opportunities to charge premium prices, but offers scope to stimulate market demand through a variety of discounting practices.

Departure Supplements

One of the crucial factors for the success of an area as a destination is the ease of access to it from origin points, particular by direct flights. Charter airlines incur a range of costs when positioning their aircraft away from the main base for these flights, and it

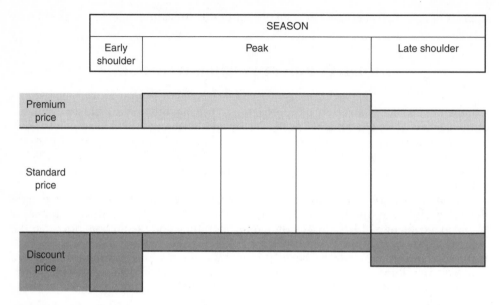

Figure 5.1   Seasonal price banding

Table 5.1   Supplements to fly to Majorca by season and airport of departure

Departure airport	Low season supplement £	High season supplement £
London Gatwick	0	41
Luton	0	41
Edinburgh	9	114
Glasgow	0	118
Aberdeen	3	89

Source: Trend (1994)

might be expected that this will be reflected in the supplements charged by tour operators for regional departures. Other technical considerations, such as the use of smaller aircraft, are also factors (Laws, 1996). However, as Table 5.1 indicates, price differentials for regional departures represent another opportunity for price engineering, rather than directly reflecting any extra costs incurred. Table 5.1 also shows that the regional pricing structure further distorts the basic holiday price by the differential application of seasonal price banding to each departure airport.

Price reductions for late booking are a widespread holiday industry response to its unsold capacity, and are typically offered shortly before departure. This has proved an effective way to tackle one of the problems characteristic of the services sector, the inability to store inventory (Cowell, 1986). Tour operators consider it better to obtain some revenue for a particular holiday (which can be defined by departure date and airport, duration and resort of stay) which they have not been able to sell at the price offered in the brochure. One common approach is to invite clients to pay a stated price, for example £100 per week, for a known departure and duration, but leaving the hotel and even the resort to the tour operator's discretion. From the customer's perspective, this introduces a higher than normal element of uncertainty (or risk) into the holiday purchase transaction, a point which is developed in a later section of this chapter.

Each of the three price boundary approaches discussed above has contributed to the expansion of the market base of clients for holidays, by the combination of low prices and the high visibility of travel agency windows featuring price discounted holidays. However, the benefits for tour operators of increased numbers of clients through the late booking discount mechanism have to be set against difficulties which have resulted. These include customers who did not obtain the quality of holiday which they had hoped for, an apparent shift away from the traditional early booking of holidays in favour of waiting for these late offers to be made and approaches to managing both the supply and distribution channels which have tended to favour the major tour operators and the vertically integrated holiday companies strongly.

CUSTOMER PERSPECTIVES ON PRICE POLICIES

Responses to Late Offers

During the 1960s and 1970s, there was a highly publicized annual rush to buy holidays as soon as the next season's brochure was launched. Queues formed outside travel agencies early each new year, to buy holidays for the summer ahead: early purchase gave the clients the highest probability of getting their preference for destination, hotel, duration and departure date. In contrast, a trend had emerged in the 1990s to delay the purchase of package holidays. This can be understood as representing customers learning the new rules of selling, and adapting these to their own benefit when purchasing holidays. In the case of inclusive tours, the pattern of early booking which formed the basis of buyer behaviour (and consequent price adjustment tactics to shift unsold volume as departures dates approached) has altered under the influence of reduced price offers (Vellos and Becherel, 1995).

Now there is a noted resistance to buying holidays early in the belief that a high proportion of capacity will remain unsold, thereby increasing the likelihood of reduced price offers, and of being able to buy a holiday which closely matches that desired. A travel industry manager commented critically, 'getting a package deal at a knock down price is now a national sport'. Other criticisms focus on the way that discounting is shifting holiday destination preferences. For example, flat rate discounting (a prominent feature of retailer tactics) favours long haul destinations, because the technique produces a greater cash saving when compared to the typically lower priced European holiday. When combined with seasonal price banding for areas such as the Caribbean, the effect has been to redistribute the peak travel season. A senior manager commented, 'All the hard work done by the tour operator and the hotelier working together in terms of spreading demand across the season is wiped out by the stroke of a felt tip pen in a travel agent's window' (Heape, 1994).

The duration of the interval between clients making a booking and taking their holiday has been important to tour operators, since it provides an opportunity for them to function as 'bankers' of their clients' deposit. The industry practice is for tour operators to settle their suppliers' invoices at about the time that the client receives services from the charter airline and hotel. The number of clients, and the consequent aggregate value of their deposits, has enabled tour operators to place money on the overnight market, with the result that interest received accounts for a significant element in their revenue. This source of income is at risk from the shift towards later bookings. In response to this threat, tour operators have recently begun to offer incentives for early booking, including free child places and three weeks for the price of two.

Influencing Holiday Purchases

A growing body of tourism research has examined the factors which influence tourists' holiday choices, their behaviour and satisfaction experienced; a collection of papers on these themes has been edited by Crotts and Van Raaij (1995). Understanding the factors leading to choice of holiday supplier (tour operator and travel retailer) and of holiday destination is critical to the continuing success of each. From the point of view of individual companies, their objectives in the market place are to attract clients against the competition of other holiday suppliers, in order to ensure that holiday-makers buy from them, rather than competitors. Tour operators and travel agents also seek to encourage clients to buy early (in order to obtain the 'banker' benefits outlined above). The customers' priorities, however, are to obtain the type of holiday they want (for example, skiing, cultural city centre or beach-based), in a destination which appeals to them, at a suitable time and price.

For certain travellers, the decision about which destination to visit is so proscribed by the purpose for which travel is undertaken that it scarcely qualifies as a choice; examples include travel for family reasons or to attend business meetings. Both of these travel purposes can be fulfilled by the purchase of a packaged holiday to that destination, offering the advantages over making independent arrangements of simplicity, convenience in booking, and relative cheapness. More generally, the decision to go on holiday opens up a choice from the entire spectrum of vacation resorts and hotels. At an intermediate level, a requirement for specific destination attributes limits the choice; for example, the holiday-maker who wishes to go powder skiing is restricted to a limited range of mountain resorts (Laws, 1995).

Increasingly, destinations also market themselves actively; of the 290 travel brands advertising on British television channels in the year to June 1995, 57 were UK tourist offices or resorts (Laser, 1995). However, although destinations actively promote their place benefits, it is tour operators which dominate the determination of the prices which customers consider when purchasing their holidays. Complaining about the declining attractiveness of Newquay, a bed and breakfast operator identified the comparative price advantages and more powerful publicity of overseas resorts as key factors. While a week's bed and breakfast in Newquay cost £112, and 'the train from London can cost up to £110.00 return for a standard class fare ... a seven night holiday in Majorca ... including bed, breakfast and flights, is advertised at under £200.00' (Leith, 1995).

High and Low Involvement Buying Behaviour

The purchase of a holiday represents a deliberate decision, in which individuals (or a group such as a family) invest part of their limited resources. The price paid for a holiday is constrained by the customer's budget considerations, but is often treated as a priority expenditure in planning personal or family expenditure. This implies both that the tourist has chosen not to spend money (and time) on alternative products, and that he or she cannot visit alternative destinations during that vacation. (The exception is that some holidays, such as cruising, multi-stop itineraries and coach tours, are designed to include a selection of destinations in one holiday.)

The variations in the importance of any category of purchase between different customers can be understood by investigating their degrees of interest and 'involvement'. Cohen (1986) defined involvement as 'a state of arousal that a person experiences in regard to consumption related activity'. Involvement is considered likely to be high when the purchase has functional and symbolic significance, and entails some risk (Asseal, 1987). Four features of holidays which make it likely that many tourists will experience a high degree of involvement in choosing their holiday are:

- holidays are expensive;
- they are complex both to purchase and to experience;
- there is a risk that they will not prove satisfying;
- the choice of destination (or type of holiday) reflects the holiday-maker's personality.

The significance of regarding holidays as a high involvement purchase is the implication that considerable care will be invested in the choice of destination or type of holiday. Potential tourists often undertake detailed and extended study of brochures, reading and watching holiday advertising and visiting travel agencies for advice to identify suitable places to visit, given their individual interests and the time and budget available.

This rationalist model of holiday destination choice has much less validity in the conditions which have characterized much of the market for packaged holidays, when tour operators or travel retailers emphasize prices rather than destination attributes in their promotions. This shifts the customers' attention to a comparison of prices rather than of what each destination offers, potentially resulting in a reduced 'commitment' to the resort visited. Under these conditions, there is more likely to be a mismatch between the tourists' holiday expectations and their destination experiences, resulting in dissatisfaction and complaint. This difficulty is exacerbated by two factors, one internal to the holiday industry, the other characteristic of contemporary society. Discounted, and particularly late offer, holidays often involve relatively low quality holiday components. These may include inconvenient departure and arrival times, and unspecified hotel (or other) accommodation. While clients sometimes benefit under these trading conditions from accommodation better than they had anticipated, the reverse is often the case, mainly because those who booked early have opted for the superior accommodation and the better locations.

The industry has regularly experienced a high incidence of complaints about low standards of accommodation, poor resort location and associated difficulties, particularly with respect to late booked holidays. At the same time, there is growing management emphasis, in tourism no less than other sectors of the economy, on product and service quality (Gronroos, 1990; Normann, 1991). This situation has to be considered in the context of growing consumer rights awareness (Prus, 1989), and the 'meta-context' of scepticism about the underlying values and institutions of Western societies (Hughes, 1993).

The overall effect of price discounting by tour operators and travel retailers is to shift buyers' attention to the affordability of holidays, thereby widening the customer base but reducing the discrimination shown between alternative destinations. A further consequence is that consumers sometimes purchase holidays to inappropriate destinations. For example, young family groups or the elderly visit resorts where the range of entertainment is geared to youths, with resultant disappointment for each type of visitor. This has negative connotations during the vacation for the hotel, the resort and the tour operator, who have to respond to complaints. The travel retailer also becomes a target of complaint when the client returns, a situation which recent European legislation is likely to accentuate (Rogers, 1993).

ANALYSING CUSTOMER RESPONSES TO PRICE POLICIES

Price Relativities as a Signal of Product Quality

It is an axiom of life in a consumer society that a range of products are available at any one time, which, although they perform similar functions, are offered at different prices. For any type of product there is a range of prices and a range of quality: their features or specifications vary, as does their durability and the attention paid to both functional and aesthetic aspects of their design, yet all products of that type perform similar core functions. All four door passenger cars offer families the ability to drive to local and distant destinations with reasonable reliability and in fair comfort. But new four door saloons range in price from a few thousand pounds to over a hundred thousand. Most motorists recognize (or believe they do) the superiority of, say, a Bentley turbo over a standard family car, just as most travellers can accept the idea that the superior aspects of a journey to New York by Concorde compared to the experiences of flight in the economy cabin of airlines are reflected in the price differential between the two.

Kimes (1994) has suggested that consumers seem to accept yield management in the airline sector, where they receive specific benefits if they accept certain restraints. However, she raised the question of how customers react to it in other industries, suggesting that 'a customer who pays more for a similar service and cannot perceive a difference in the service may view the situation as unfair'. Kimes developed her argument on the basis of a reference price, derived from market prices and the customer's previous experience. Figure 5.2 conceptualizes the range of psychic outcomes for inclusive holiday customers of different combinations of price paid and quality experienced. At a normal (or reference) price, a high standard of service and amenities will please the client, but those same standards will only satisfy clients paying premium rates. Customers enjoying normal or superior standards on a holiday for which they paid low prices will be pleased, or delighted. In contrast, customers receiving normal levels of service in return for high prices will feel at best exploited, and if standards fall further, they are likely to experience (and express) anger. Low levels of service or amenities are likely to provide negative responses, whatever the price paid for them.

Satisfaction and Dissatisfaction

A more formal analysis highlights the significance of evaluating customers' consumption experiences and examining them against the expectations which led to their purchase of a particular service (Ryan, 1995). Various factors have been identified

PRICE PAID FOR TOURISM SERVICE
HOLIDAY AMENITIES AND SERVICE QUALITY

		High	Normal	Low
PRICE PAID FOR HOLIDAY	High	Satisfied	Exploited	Angry
	Standard	Pleased	Satisfied	Exploited/ angry
	Low	Delighted	Satisfied	Exploited/ angry

Figure 5.2 Customer consequences of differing price and quality combinations

which, in combination with individual personality and their previous experience, determine customer expectations. These include formal marketing communications such as advertising messages or brochures, the opinions of friends or other people who have experienced the service and, significantly, the price of one service relative to the alternatives.

Consumer satisfaction is the outcome when expectations are matched by service experience; conversely, dissatisfaction occurs when there is a mismatch, and expectations are not fulfilled by the service delivered (Engel *et al.*, 1986). Aggregate dissatisfaction among many consumers is a serious matter to the firm providing a service, as the implication is that customers will take their future business elsewhere. They are also likely to discuss their negative experiences with friends, thereby further undermining the company's market place credibility (Laws, 1991).

Dissatisfaction can be understood as cognitive dissonance (Festinger, 1957), a psychological condition making it unlikely that the customer will purchase from that supplier in the future. In extreme cases, the customer will complain formally, thereby imposing a burden on the company which will have to respond in a considered way (in case the dispute reaches the courts or an arbitration process for ultimate resolution). The company may decide (or be ordered) to pay the disappointed client financial compensation. Arbitration involves the travel retailer as the first point of recourse, and this has introduced a new dynamic into the network of organizations contributing to the package holiday industry. Letters to the travel trade press indicate that increasingly travel retailers are reluctant to act as agents for tour operators that are the subject of frequent complaints by customers. Court cases, or those pursued through the consumer pressure groups and on radio, TV or press consumer programmes, also attract widespread attention, thereby further threatening the company, and ultimately undermining the credibility and desirability of the industry's products (Rogers, 1993).

Changing Price Levels and Changes in Market Demand

It is suggested above that price-led marketing has expanded the overall demand for holidays, and it is often asserted that this has brought 'less desirable' clients into the market. The meaning of this is generally left unspecified, but two features are apparent.

Less desirable clients include low spenders, such as youths, the elderly or people with low incomes. Although their presence imposes demands on the resort's infrastructure, tour operators and the resort-based businesses cannot sell low-spending clients the lucrative extras such as souvenirs, excursions and entertainment in the quantities which better-off clients regard as essential elements of their augmented holiday. The second suspicion is that many people buying the cheapest holiday packages are more likely to indulge in undesirable behaviour on arrival, including heavy drinking and noisy late night carousing. The concern often has another dimension, as it reflects an unproven general assumption that there is a direct link between detrimental client behaviour in a resort and low-priced access to it through the medium of cheap inclusive holidays.

Some destination managers have indicated that they do not wish to host such groups, and are actively trying to attract clients who will spend more, and are assumed to be more sensitive to the destination's culture, while less likely to offend local people (or other visitors) by their behaviour. A newspaper report entitled 'Tourists? We only want the cream on Jersey, thank you' illustrates these concerns. Following an attempt to open the Channel Islands to package tourists, hoteliers refused to reduce their room rates to the level which the tour operator had offered, between £13 and £23 a day, and the island airport declined to offer a 25 per cent reduction on landing charges. Explaining the resistance, an Executive of the Jersey Hotel and Guest House Association said, 'Airtours wanted to offer holidays so cheap that you have to wonder whether the people they brought over here would have any money to spend when they arrived ... we don't want to down grade the island as a cut price destination' (Leith, 1995).

Supplier resistance such as this is becoming more common, and overall it implies a limit to the ability of tour operators to price their holidays very cheaply. Some relatively new destinations, such as Dubai, take the view that setting high prices will minimize any social disruption through undesirable behaviour of visitors (Laws, 1995), while some traditional destinations have adopted a policy of moving upmarket, as the case study of Majorca below indicates.

Economic Modelling of Clients' Responses to Price Adjustments

In common with most companies, those supplying inclusive holidays generally set their prices in accordance with the assumption that they face a downward sloping demand schedule for their products (Lancaster, 1974; Bull, 1991). In this model of economic behaviour, a limited number of clients are assumed to be willing or able to pay high prices. Their price behaviour has a rational base, and can be explained by their need to travel at a particular time (for example, during school holidays, or during the most favourable snow conditions). As the price is reduced, the holiday becomes affordable to a larger number of clients, thereby increasing sales volume. The gamble is that the trade-off (or ratio) between price reduction and volume gained (represented by the slope of the demand schedule) will result in increased revenue.

Rather than continuous, small changes to price, companies generally set a few distinct price bands, defined by assuming behavioural rules of the type discussed above. This approach is based on the assumption of discontinuities in the demand schedule, with discrete segments in the market place. This enables one type of product to be sold at differing prices, where each lower price segment in the market has different characteristic behaviour, such that boundary rules can be set which exclude higher priced segments, thereby protecting their higher revenue value. An earlier section of this chapter discusses typical 'rules' relating to the holiday season, departure airport and time interval between booking and departure. However, each lower price segment may be overlapped slightly by the preceding higher band, indicating that such banding rules are somewhat fuzzy, and are consequently difficult both to define and to apply rigidly.

Broadening the Market for Cruise Holidays

The significance of the foregoing discussion is that a significant reduction in price provides access to the product by a market segment which is not only larger, but has different characteristics. Ideally, the shift from one price band to a lower one occurs after the higher payers have bought; then the lower price has the effect of bringing the product to a new group of potential purchasers, with different behavioural character-istics. One example of this is the way that cruising holidays are being marketed to a broader market. In 1995, Airtours claimed to have achieved its aim of gaining around 60 per cent of cruise bookings from clients who had not cruised before.

The marketing director is reported to have said, 'The ship has been fully refurbished and we have made the product affordable and less formal. We have applied the Airtours sales and marketing formula, so anyone who has enjoyed our other holidays will enjoy our cruises. We have a well thought out formula. The ship is the right size to give us the economies of scale we need to offer affordable fares, which is always the starting point for customers.' Commenting on this, the Director of PSARA remarked that Airtours has a tightrope to walk: 'On one hand, they are telling customers there is no mystique about cruising, its just a package holiday in which the hotel floats. On the other hand, it must try not to take away the elegance of cruising because they would be selling themselves and the industry short' (Cooney, 1995).

PRICE COMPETITION AND COOPERATION IN THE HOLIDAY INDUSTRY

Origin Market Effects

Price-based marketing practices have two consequences for the companies producing and selling holidays in origin markets, achieving shifts in the balance of market power within a sector (one tour operator gaining market share from another through the power of lower prices), or in terms of altering the existing balance of channel dominance between tour operators and retail travel agents. The leading British trade body for the industry, the Association of British Travel Agents (ABTA), has 2,396 travel agent members, 484 tour operators and 221 members in both categories (ABTA, 1994).

Description and analysis of the inclusive holiday industry generally views it from the perspectives of channel management theory which had been developed to examine the distribution systems for food, fast moving consumer goods or consumer durables (Bucklin, 1967). The issues for channel members are about dominance and control: retail travel agents have traditionally been regarded as weak because of their small size relative to the tour operators, and their reliance on the tour operator for products to sell, although they are developing ways of gaining influence; for example, by refusing to rack the brochures of tour operators paying low commission, or those about which many complaints are received. An aspect of competition leading to changes in channel dominance is the effect of discounting in favouring the larger companies, particularly the multiple-branch retail agents. 'Discounting advantages are quickly negated by competitive response, but then there is no doubt that multiples take bookings from independent agents. Through acquisition of extra retail outlets and through heavy discounting, the major multiples are steadily increasing their share of business' (Heape, 1994). Discussing the advantages of larger companies, Heape also pointed to the fact that the tour operators who own retailers do not pay extra commission on the sales made by their retail partners. 'Therefore their products can be priced very competitively compared to other operators.'

Traditionally, economists have considered that incumbent firms in a market gain advantages from insurmountably high fixed costs barring entry to a market. Baumol and Willig (1981) defined entry barriers as 'anything that requires an expenditure by a new entrant into an industry, but requires no equivalent cost upon an incumbent'. Another feature of contestable markets is that exit costs are minimal, as other businesses, incumbents or new entrants, will be willing to buy the business assets. Price discounting provides the package holiday with a tool for structural changes by undermining the profitability of some companies to the point where it is no longer viable for them to stay in the industry. A director of Airtours reported that 'I have about 20 proposals a week land on my desk from companies who want us to purchase them because they know we have lots of money and are ambitious' (Skidmore, 1995). Sheldon (1986), discussing the relationship between industry structure and pricing policy, noted a polarization in the industry, with a few large firms, and many small ones, and pointed to the relative short lives of many small companies. However, several large tour operators have failed, and many mergers or acquisitions have been recorded in the industry.

Destination Effects

More attention must be focused on the fact that pricing decisions by tour operators and travel retailers have consequences not only for the companies which take them, but also for their partners, the hotels and destinations that are the principal suppliers of the holiday experience. The raid growth of the industry during the 1960s and 1970s resulted in a proliferation of hotel developments, particularly in the Mediterranean resorts. Many of these hotels were built to low design criteria, and they were often aesthetically unappealing in the context of idyllic settings. As the hotel stock grew, and as more destinations became accessible, tour operators were able to drive contract room rates down. The cumulative effect of repeated seasons of low contract rates paid by tour operators to hotels has eroded their ability to improve standards of service or invest in upgraded facilities, but this period has coincided with a period of increasing consumer awareness (Morgan, 1994; Vellos and Becherel, 1995). More effective deployment of consumer rights has alerted media attention to the dissatisfaction and complaints arising from low standards in holiday accommodation. Hoteliers have responded by showing a preference to deal with tour operators who do not exert such severe cost controls, notably those from other European countries. This has given rise to the phenomenon of one set of guests in a hotel being afforded preferential treatment in terms of better rooms or a more varied dinner menu, further exacerbating the dissatisfaction.

Hoteliers have also responded by adopting overbooking policies (Lamnert *et al.*, 1989), because the slender margins on room revenue lead to a need to sell all available capacity and to take the maximum advantage of the additional sources of revenue from clients, such as bar sales. Overbooked hotels result in the need for tour operators to switch their clients, often after arrival in the resort, to alternative hotels, and often result in complaints or claims for compensation by disgruntled clients.

Cooperation in the Holiday System

Additional insights into the complexity and the dynamics of relationships between inclusive holiday industry participants can be gained by adopting the theoretical perspectives of network (Gummesson, 1987) or relationship (McKenna, 1994) marketing, and by viewing the holiday industry systematically. Systems theory emphasizes the interdependency of the elements which together make up the industry, notably the tour operators, travel retailers, airlines, hotels and destination organizations and communities (Mill and Morrison, 1985; Leiper, 1990; Laws, 1996). Systems analysis also focuses attention on the consequences for all stakeholders of the way the system functions, and of any policy or operational changes. These approaches highlight as critical issues for examination the mutual dependency of all organizations in a holiday system, and the environment within which the industry operates, rather than the legitimate but lower order issue of competition between individual member companies. The case study of Majorca demonstrates how cooperation in emphasizing the quality of customers' experiences offers the promise of long-term benefits to all participants in the holiday system.

Majorca

Majorca provides an example of a destination which experienced many of the problems outlined in this chapter, but it has adopted a systematic policy response which illustrates that these difficulties may be countered by setting clear objectives and by working in alliance with the companies that bring holiday-makers to it. Majorca was one of the first destinations for mass tourism in the Mediterranean, but visitor numbers began to fall at the end of the 1980s, suggesting that it was losing its appeal due to over-familiarity, falling standards relative to alternative Eastern Mediterranean or long-haul destinations and adverse publicity in its main origin markets featuring the unruly behaviour of some visitors.

Majorca's problems were exacerbated, since 90 per cent of its visitors were clients of charter-based inclusive tour operators, bringing high volume, low yield business. Furthermore, pressure during the 1970s and 1980s from the large overseas tour operators had forced hotel rates down, and although this strategy succeeded in attracting large numbers of visitors, the low room rates meant that hotels could not afford to modernize or refurbish their facilities in line with competing destinations. The situation was further worsened since another response to the increased arrivals through the 1980s had been the building of low-grade hotel stock, and as a result Majorca gained a reputation for building activity, blocked views and the spreading of hotels to previously unspoiled areas. These difficulties of environmental deterioration were compounded by frequent, and highly publicized, flight delays from Northern Europe across French airspace, and the tour operators' tendency to alter clients' accommodation arrangements on arrival.

Coordinated approaches were adopted to improve visitors' experiences and to obtain increased financial benefit from each visitor.

- From 1985 onwards, development controls limited building permits to four star or better properties, with a maximum height of three storeys, and required 30 square metres of land per guest.
- In Magaluff, measures to improve the quality of the environment included tree planting, pedestrianization and a public sea front esplanade to replace privately owned hotel and cafe frontages.
- A wider customer mix was sought by attracting tour operators from the Netherlands and Switzerland, and by inviting quality press visits to other aspects of Majorca, drawing attention away from the established resort areas near Palma in favour of the modern, architecturally more sensitive resorts on the east coast.
- Overseas youth tour operators cooperated by repositioning their services as well organized and behaved. Large same-sex groups were prohibited, and representatives' roles were redefined: they no longer lead drinking competitions!
- Thomson embarked on a programme to invest £10 million in ten three star properties. Detailed specifications were prepared covering food, facilities, entertainment, room decor and service standards expected from staff.

The improvements to Majorca's tourism standards should be seen in the context of the Spanish government's four-year improvement plan (1991–5) for tourism, focusing on the appropriate development of the industry in the light of Spain's heritage and other resources. The intention is to improve the product rather than expand capacity (Laws, 1995, based on Morgan, 1991; Jenner and Smith, 1993; articles in *Travel News*, March 1990 and the *Travel Trade Gazette*, May 1990; and interviews with tourism managers).

CONCLUSION

This chapter has reviewed the pricing practices of tour operators and travel retailers against the background of growth and competition which has characterized origin markets in recent decades. It has pointed to changes in package holiday buying behaviour in response to low price and late sales offers, and has examined the causes and consequences of consumer disappointment which may result from purchasing inappropriate holidays.

The combined effects of relatively low levels of service, overbooking and rowdy destination behaviour have reduced the attractiveness of budget holidays, and these might ultimately undermine the viability of this type of product. It should be a matter of concern to the industry that heavily discounted holidays distort the market by creating unsustainable long-term price expectations, since the low rates do not provide a sound basis for investment in the upgrading of hotel or resort facilities (in fact the opposite results, since standards are forced down, at least in relative terms, as the resort's cash flow is reduced).

A more forward looking policy has been implemented in some resorts, as the case study of Majorca indicated. This illustrated the benefits of adopting a systematic approach, recognizing the mutual dependency of all organizations contributing elements to the package holiday industry and focusing attention away from low prices.

REFERENCES

ABTA (1994) *Members Handbook*. London: Columbus Press.

Asseal, H. (1987) *Consumer Behaviour and Marketing Action*. Boston: Kent Publishers.

Baumol W. and Willig, R. (1981) 'Fixed costs, sunk costs, entry barriers and sustainability of monopoly'. *Quarterly Journal of Economics*, August.

Boniface P. and Fowler, P. (1993) *Heritage and Tourism in the Global Village*. London: Routledge.

BTA (1992) *Annual Report*. London: British Tourist Authority.

Bucklin, L. (1967) 'The economic structure of channels of distribution'. In B. E. Mallen (ed.), *The Marketing Channel*. New York: Wiley.

Bull, A. (1991) *The Economics of Travel and Tourism*. London: Longman Cheshire.

Burkhart, A. J. and Medlik, S. (1981) *Tourism: Past, Present and Future*. London: Heinemann.

Cohen, J. B. (1986) *Involvement, Separating the State from Its Causes and Effects*. Quoted in W. L. Wilkie, *Consumer Behaviour*. Chichester: Wiley.

Cooney, M. (1995) 'Airtours plots a course for a growing market'. *Travel Weekly*, March, 6.

Cowell, D. (1986) *The Marketing of Services*. London: Heinemann.

Crotts J. and Van Raaij, W. (eds) (1995) *Economic Psychology of Travel and Tourism*. New York: Haworth Press.

Engel, J. F., Blackwell, R. D. and Miniard, P. W. (1986) *Consumer Behavior*. Chicago: Dryden Press.

Festinger, L. (1957) *A Theory of Cognitive Dissonance*. Stanford, CA: Stanford University Press.

Gronroos, C. (1990) *Service Management and Marketing*. Lexington, MA: Lexington Books.

Gummesson, E. (1987) *Marketing, a Long Term Interactive Relationship*. Gothenburg: Anderson Sandberg Dhein.

Heape, R. (1994) 'Outward bound'. *Tourism Society Journal*, **83**, 4–5.

Holloway J. C. (1994) *The Business of Tourism*, 4th edn. London: Pitman.

Holloway, J. C. and Robinson, P. (1995) *Marketing for Tourism*, 3rd edn. Harlow: Longman.

Hughes, R. (1993) *Culture of Complaint*. New York: Warner Books.

Jenner, P. and Smith, C. (1993) *Tourism in the Mediterranean*. London: EIU Research Report.

Kimes, S. E. (1994) 'Perceived fairness of yield management'. *Cornell Hotel and Restaurant Administration*, **35**(1), 22–9.

Kotler P. H. (1982) *Principles of Marketing*. Englewood Cliffs, NJ: Prentice Hall.

Lamnert, C. U., Lambert, J. M. and Cullen, T. P. (1989) 'The overbooking question: a simulation'. *Cornell Hotel and Restaurant Administration Quarterly*, **30**(3), 15–20.

Lancaster, K. (1974) *Introduction To Modern Micro Economics*. Chicago: Rand-McNally.

Laws E. (1991) *Tourism Marketing: Service and Quality Management Perspectives*. Cheltenham: Stanley Thornes.

Laws, E. (1995) *Tourist Destination Management: Issues, Analysis and Policies*. London: Routledge.

Laws, E. (1996) *The Inclusive Holiday Industry*. London: Thomson International Business Press.

Laser (1995) Company presentation to Chartered Institute of Marketing Travel Industry Group.

Leiper, N. (1990) *Tourism Systems*. Palmerston North: Massey University Press.

Leith, E. (1995) 'The holiday's over'. *Mail on Sunday Review*, October, 6–8.

MacCannell, D. (1992) *Empty Meeting Grounds: the Tourist Papers*. London: Routledge.

McCarthy, J. E. and Perreault, W. D. (1988) *Essentials of Marketing*. New York: Irwin.

McKenna, R. (1994) *Relationship Marketing: Successful Strategies for the Age of the Customer*. Reading, MA: Addison Wesley.

Middleton, V. T. C. (1988) *Marketing in Travel and Tourism*. Oxford: Heinemann.

Mill, R. C. and Morrison, A. M. (1985) *The Tourism System*. Englewood Cliffs, NJ: Prentice Hall.

Morgan, M. (1991) 'Dressing up to survive: marketing Majorca anew'. *Tourism Management*, March, 15–20.

Morgan, M. (1994) 'Homogeneous products, the future of established resorts'. In W. Theobald (ed.), *Global Tourism: the Next Decade*. Oxford: Butterworth-Heinemann.

Normann, R. (1991) Service Management, Strategy and Leadership in Service Business. Chichester: Wiley.

Page, S. J. (1994) *Transport for Tourism*. London: Routledge.

Pearce, D. (1989) *Tourist Development*. Harlow: Longman Scientific.

Poon, A (1993) Tourism, Technology and Competitive Strategies. Wallingford: CAB International Press.

Prus, R. C. (1989) *Pursuing Customers: an Ethnography of Marketing Activities*. London: Sage.

Relihan, W. (1989) 'The yield management approach to hotel pricing'. *Cornell Hotel and Restaurant Administration Quarterly*, **30**(1), 40–5.

Rogers, P. (1993) A Practical Guide to the Package Travel Regulations. London: Landor Travel Publications.

Ryan, C. (1995) *Researching Tourist Satisfaction*. London: Routledge.

Sheldon, P. (1986) 'The tour operating industry, an analysis'. *Annals of Tourism Research*, **13**, 349–56.

Skidmore, J. (1995) 'Airtours plays down need for acquisitions'. *Travel News*, April.

Trend, N. (1994) 'Local airport blues'. *BBC Holidays*, July, 50–1.

Urry, J. (1990) *The Tourist Gaze*. London: Sage.

Vellos, F. and Becherel, L. (1995) *International Tourism*. Basingstoke: Macmillan.

WTO (1994) *Year Book of Tourism Statistics*. Madrid: World Tourist Organisation.

6

Defining Yield Management and Measuring Its Impact on Hotel Performance

Peter Jones

INTRODUCTION

Yield management (more commonly now referred to as rooms revenue management) is the single most researched topic in the hospitality operations literature (Jones and Lockwood, 1998). It has been widely adopted throughout the industry, although implementation may not always be precise; nor are common procedures adopted (Griffen, 1996; Jarvis et al., 1997). It is therefore surprising that there are few detailed studies of the effectiveness of this approach to managing hotels' fixed capacity, or more precisely the nature and extent of financial performance improvement (if any). This chapter addresses this issue.[1]

This chapter sets out to identify the extent to which the adoption and implementation of yield management improves a hotel's performance. To do this a classical social-scientific research methodology has been adopted: define the problem, identify the key variables, hypothesize their relationship, measure the dependent and independent variables, remove extraneous variables and draw conclusions. Despite previous studies and many existing definitions, it was found necessary to adopt soft systems analysis in order to define the problem, identify variables and hypothesize relationships. In order to test these, detailed case study research of three hotels was conducted. This study demonstrates how difficult it is to prove conclusively that yield management (YM) improves a hotel's operating performance. However, emerging evidence suggests that YM leads to 1–8 per cent performance improvement.

DEFINING YIELD MANAGEMENT

There are many definitions of yield management. Sheryl Kimes has defined it as 'a method that can help a firm sell the right inventory unit to the right customer at the right time' (Kimes, 1997). Jauncey et al. (1995) conducted a literature review of nine

YM studies dating back to 1988 and concluded that 'YM is concerned with the maximisation of room revenue through the manipulation of room rates in a structured fashion, so as to take into account forecasted patterns of demand.' Donaghy *et al.* (1997) suggest that 'YM is a revenue maximization technique which aims to increase net yield through the predicted allocation of available bedroom capacity to pre-determined market segments at optimal price.' These definitions describe the *purpose* of yield management, but fail to differentiate it from reservation practices that existed prior to YM implementation. For instance, is it to be assumed that, prior to YM, hotels were deliberately selling the 'wrong' room, to the 'wrong' customer, at the 'wrong' price? It is also the case that, prior to YM, hotels manipulated room rates by discounting, forecast patterns of demand and clearly identified market segments. Hence YM is not *meaningfully* defined by its purpose, since hotels have always tried to make as much money as they could out of their fixed capacity.

YM needs to be defined by its 'systems structure', i.e. how it enables revenue maximization. Very few existing definitions begin to identify this. However, the main industry association (the American Hotel and Motel Association) states that YM 'is a set of demand-forecasting techniques used to determine whether prices should be raised or lowered and a reservation request should be accepted or rejected in order to maximise revenue'. This provides a clearer picture of yield management, but does not identify how YM is different from pre-YM reservation practices.

Also in the literature there is frequent reference to the fact that hotels adopted and adapted YM from the airline business. But rarely is a key difference between airlines and hotels highlighted. Unlike in the airline business, in the hotel business a single reservation can have a 'displacement' effect. This is because instead of an airline customer reserving a seat on a specific flight, the hotel customer reserves a room for one *or more* nights. Hence a hotel reservation may span time periods for which demand is high and a high rate can be quoted (such as midweek in a business hotel), along with slack periods when the room rate would be lower (such as weekends in a business hotel).

Given the range of alternative definitions of yield management and their failure to differentiate between airlines and hotels or YM and non-YM hotel practices, a research methodology designed to distinguish structure and function seems appropriate (for a more detailed review of the YM literature and exposition of soft systems analysis applied to YM see Jones, 1999). Soft systems analysis (SSA), developed by Checkland (1981), is such a methodology. Naughton (1984) describes SSA as 'beginning with a mess' – in this case the profusion of overlapping, alternative views of YM. The second stage of SSA involves the development of a 'rich picture' of the situation, from which emerge patterns. In this study, rich pictures were developed of a number of hotels' YM systems, through observation of meetings and operational activity, discussion with a wide range of employees and review of relevant documentation. An example of such a rich picture is given in Figure 6.1.

Such hotels were generally large, four or five star properties situated in large cities. Stage 3 of SSA involves identifying the emergent properties of the system through iteration until 'relevant systems' are identified. In this study the relevant system was defined as 'a system for identifying and securing the most profitable customers for hotels'. Following classical SSA methodology, this needs to be further clarified as a 'root definition' and tested against the 'CATWOE' checklist: customers (C), actors (A), transformation processes (T), *Weltanshauung*, or viewpoint (W), owners (O) and environmental constraint (E). The definition that is proposed from this analysis is as follows:

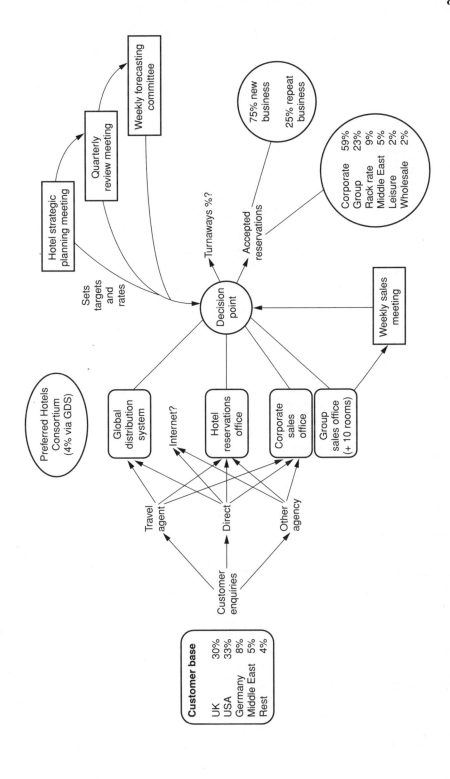

Figure 6.1 Rich picture of sample hotel

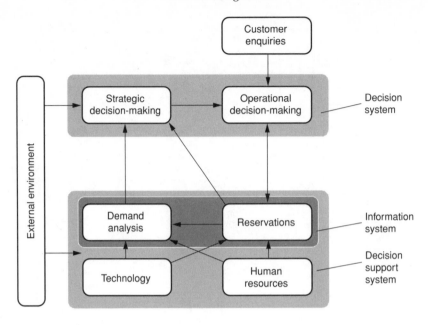

Figure 6.2   Hotel yield management system

> Yield management is a system for hotel owners to maximise profitability through
> their senior management in hotels identifying the profitability of market segments,
> establishing value, setting prices, creating discount and displacement rules for
> application to the advanced reservations process, and monitoring the effectiveness
> of these rules and their implementation.

This definition emphasizes the strategic role of yield management in managing
profitability. Increasingly the hotel industry, and the relevant academic literature, is
placing greater emphasis on the profitability of each market segment, not just the sales
value of their custom.

   Finally, the system is conceptualized as a model. Models almost always simplify the
complexity and sophistication found in the real world. This is true in this case. The
important point is that a hotel needs to have each element of the model in place for it
to have the potential to put YM successfully into practice.

   The model is shown in Figure 6.2. It comprises two relevant systems: the decision-
making system, which is largely concerned with yield management; and the
decision-support system, which is concerned with the advanced reservation process and
pre-existing yield management. Hence this system's configuration clearly identifies how
YM is different to prior ways of managing capacity. The 'system-in-focus' has two
subsystems: The strategic decision-making subsystem is concerned with making long-
term decisions about market segmentation and demand from which 'rules' are drawn
up, while the operational decision-making system focuses on applying these rules in
response to customer enquiries. The two major day-to-day decisions that are made
relate to what price to quote and the displacement effects of reservations.

- annual business plan:
  - develop marketing plan
  - agree dept/budgets
  - agree pricing policy
- quartley review meeting
  - review business plan
  - identify special events
  - update competitor analysis

- weekly forecasting meeting
  - discuss performance
  - preview next 3 months
  - adopt short term measures
- agree daily overbooking status

- demand forecasting
  (based on actuals
  and estimates)
- group demand
  analysis
- daily competitor check

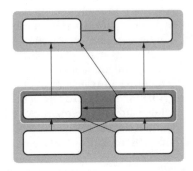

- offer made on rate
  category
- some rate negotiation
- turnaways sometimes
  noted

- global distribution system
- Fidelio reservation system in-house
- Fidelio property management system

- reservations manager
  + 4 reservationists
- F.O. team of 8
  + receptionists
- corporate sales office of 6
- group sales team of 10
- sales teams rewarded by
  incentive scheme
- ad hoc recognition by GM

Figure 6.3   Yield management system in sample hotel

In order to illustrate further how this works in practice, the hotel illustrated as a rich picture in Figure 6.1 is now illustrated by the YM model in Figure 6.3. This demonstrates how powerful the model is in capturing the specific and unique features of a single hotel and its approach to YM.

ANALYSIS OF PERFORMANCE IMPROVEMENT

From the analysis above, it emerges that performance improvement derives from three main factors. First is a better understanding of customers and their perception of value, in relation to competing brands or properties, so that aggregate demand may be increased. Second is a YM system's ability to handle data more efficiently and manipulate these data more accurately so that better forecasts of demand can be made and price adjustments can be made in the short term. Third, using the same forecasts, YM foresees the displacement effects of reservations.

This task of data capture and manipulation is performed by specialized computer systems designed for YM (the technology in the YM systems model). Such technology has given confidence to hotel managers and reservation managers to take more 'risks', i.e. to defer taking a reservation now for one night in the belief that a reservation for more nights will be made later, or a reservation at one price can be refused as later one at a higher price will be made. It is therefore to be expected that potential revenue performance improvement will affect both occupancy and achieved room rate (ARR). A higher occupancy will be achieved either through perceived higher value or lower levels of displacement; and higher ARR will be achieved as hotels manipulate rates to match demand. In reality it is likely that all three may apply, and identifying their separate influence is highly problematic.

The extent to which YM improves revenue performance has been little researched. Suppliers claim it will give an increase in average achieved room rates of between 3.5 and 5 per cent within the first twelve months (Goymour and Donaghy, 1995). One marketer claims that a YM system can earn properties $5–10 more per room night, depending on how well the property was managed before YM was introduced (Rowe, 1989). In the late 1980s, Hilton hotels introduced a YM system and it was reported that one hotel experienced a $7.50 increase in transient average rate with no reduction in occupancy in the first month (Orkin, 1988). Bob Regan, President of Revenue Dynamics, reported that three hotels using his companies system experienced a 5–8 per cent improvement in room revenue (Boyce, 1991). In 1999, one supplier's website cited increased revenues of 3–7 per cent and profit increases of 50–100 per cent (tims Revenue Optimization Systems, 1999).

Despite these claims, objective long-term measurement of such performance improvement has rarely been carried out and is not published in the research literature. In order to conduct such an investigation, a case study methodology was adopted. Such an approach has been criticized as being a weak social science methodology, based on concern for bias derived from the involvement of the researcher in constructing the evidence, lack of generalization owing to the relatively small number of cases and the difficulty of interpreting large amounts of data (Yin, 1995). None the less, case study research is used extensively and has some advantages. Notably, the wide range of sources that are used – interviews, documentation, archival records and observations – provide highly valid data. Such studies are also holistic, multidimensional and in-depth. Finally, case studies are valuable when the researcher has little control over events.

In order to test the proposal that hotel revenues will improve after the implementation of a YM system, a number of methodological problems have to be overcome. First, the properties selected as case studies have to have adopted and *fully implemented* a yield management system. As the Jarvis *et al.* (1997) study demonstrated, some hotels believe they have adopted YM, when in fact they have not fully done so. In order to resolve this issue, three four star, branded hotels were selected from the same chain. The brand is American, but operated in the UK on a corporate franchise. This chain was selected because it was identified from the soft systems analysis that it had the most sophisticated YM system of all five chains in the preliminary study and certainly met all those criteria established by Jarvis *et al.* (1997), as well as additional factors suggested by the Griffen (1996) study.

Second, there need to be accurate measurement of the dependent variable (room revenue) and the independent variables (occupancy and achieved room rate) both before the implementation and after it. Given that these variables are all key performance measures of hotel operation, such data would be readily available. Greater control over the research would be achieved if it were designed as a longitudinal study, i.e. a hotel that was yet to implement YM was studied for some time prior to implementation and for some time afterwards. But this is very time-consuming and costly, so historic data sets were used. The lowest level of aggregation in data would be the most desirable, which could be weekly or monthly sales performance. But the time frame over which data need to be compared pre- and post-implementation is long. It is suggested by those implementing YM that it takes at least six months for the system to 'bed down'. Furthermore, there may be seasonal fluctuations. This suggests that a minimum of three years' data need to be considered: a full twelve months pre-implementation, twelve months during which the system is installed, tested and established, and twelve months post-implementation. Finding hotels that had accurate data for this time frame was not easy within the chain, and all data were aggregated on a calendar month basis.

The third methodological problem is the effect of extraneous variables. During the three years of sales activity to be included in the study a number of factors may have influenced the revenue performance of the hotels, other than YM implementation. These could be either external or internal influences. External influences could be national trends, economic circumstances, national advertising campaigns by the firm or competitors and local developments relating to business demand and competitor behaviour. Internal factors affecting performance could be a change in the management personnel within the property, in-house sales initiatives or refurbishment. In order to investigate these and ensure that their influence was minimized, in-depth interviews were conducted with the management and personnel in the hotels to identify such effects and tentatively measure them. And to overcome national influences, the individual hotels' performance was benchmarked against the industry-wide performance of similar hotels as measured by a UK-based consulting firm (BDO Hospitality Consulting, 1998). However, these data were annualized, so that for comparative purposes, the hotel's annual performance had to be adopted (see below). Furthermore, the make-up of the BDO sample is unknown and more especially the proportion of hotels with a YM system. The chain in this study was not the only one that had implemented YM, so it may not outperform the national average if all other hotels in the BDO sample were as successful at YM implementation as we believe this one to be.

YIELD IMPROVEMENT IN PRACTICE

Three hotels were researched and each was written up as a case study (Choi, 1998). Their performance was benchmarked against BDO Hospitality Consulting's annual study of industry performance, *UK Hotel Industry*. All three hotels were located outside London and hence they were compared with the annualized hotel trends of 'provincial' hotels. This category of hotels' annualized performance is illustrated in Table 6.1, and the rate of growth is illustrated in Table 6.2.

Hotel A is a 170 bedroom hotel located in a busy city on the coast. The hotel adopted YM practices in November 1994, but during the first year of operation experienced problems since records of historical demand patterns were inadequate. Data for seven

Table 6.1 Operating performance of UK provincial hotels

	1992	1993	1994	1995	1996	1997
Occupancy (%)	55.8	59.4	62.7	67.3	70.0	71.7
Average daily rate (£)	40.71	40.37	41.49	42.66	46.37	52.53

Source: BDO Hospitality Consulting (various)

Table 6.2   UK provincial hotels' performance: rate of change

	1993	1994	1995	1996	1997
Occupancy (%)	6.5	5.6	7.3	4.0	2.4
Average daily rate (%)	−0.8	2.8	2.8	8.7	13.3

Source: BDO Hospitality Consulting (various)

years of operation (financial year March to March) were identified. Sales and occupancy data are provided in Table 6.3 and the rate of change in performance is shown in Table 6.4.

The most significant period of growth in occupancy (27 per cent) was in 1993/4, but this period began six months prior to YM's implementation. In the first full trading year after implementation occupancy grew by only 0.28 per cent. Likewise in 1992/3 and 1993/4, the hotel experienced a significant drop in average rate (9.56 per cent and 5.78 per cent fall respectively), although it was able to improve rate significantly in the first full year of YM implementation, 1994/5, with a 10.82 per cent increase. In order to understand more fully the reasons for these fluctuations in performance, the hotel data are compared with industry data. These show that in 1992 the hotel had slightly below average occupancy at an average daily rate (ARR) 20 per cent higher than the industry average. The significant drop in rates in 1992 and 1993 brought this rate more in line with the industry norm, so that by 1994 Hotel A's ARR was £41.70, against an industry benchmark of £41.49. The effect of this rate drop was the significant rise in occupancy experienced in 1993/4, up to 68.1 per cent, compared with the industry average of 62.7 per cent. From 1994 onwards, Hotel A consistently has a higher occupancy than the industry norm and achieves a higher ARR. But whether this is due to the adoption of YM is not at all clear. It is apparent that in 1993/4 the hotel changed its approach to rooms revenue management by creating a 'fair' room rate, closer to the industry norm and stimulating occupancy. This is consistent with the chain's approach to YM.

The impact of this can be examined by examining the relative contribution made by occupancy and ARR to the performance improvement. Between 1993/4 and 1997/8

Table 6.3   Hotel A annualized operating performance

	1991/2	1992/3	1993/4	1994/5	1995/6	1996/7	1997/8
Rooms sold	32,427	33,271	42,256	42,260	43,721	45,142	46,819
Occupancy (%)	52.26	52.62	68.10	68.29	69.30	73.40	75.70
Average rate (£)	48.90	44.26	41.70	46.21	47.31	51.31	35.25
Sales revenue (£ million)	1.59	1.47	1.76	1.95	2.07	2.34	2.49

Source: Choi (1998)

Table 6.4   Hotel A operating performance – rate of change

	1992/3	1993/4	1994/5	1995/6	1996/7	1997/8
Occupancy (%)	2.60	27.00	0.28	1.48	5.92	3.13
Average rate (%)	−9.56	−5.78	10.82	2.38	8.45	3.78
Sales revenue (%)	−7.21	19.66	10.83	5.93	13.34	6.33

Source: Choi (1998)

occupancy improved from 68.10 per cent to 75.70 per cent (an 11.16 per cent increase) and ARR from £41.70 to £53.25 (a 27.70 per cent increase). If occupancy had risen at this rate at the 1993/4 ARR, the revenue improvement would be £190,277, whereas maintaining the occupancy rate at 1993/4 levels but improving ARR creates a revenue improvement of £488,057. Hence 71.95 per cent of the performance improvement derives from the better management of ARR. This is to be expected in a well managed YM system.

But the sustained performance above the industry norm post-1994 may be attributed to factors other than simply YM. With 170 rooms, Hotel A is larger than the industry norm (approximately 120 rooms). It attracts a significant proportion of the business market, partly due to its size and related conference facilities, and partly because it is located in a strong local economy. It is also the case that the brand has been consistently developed, advertised and promoted within the UK during the period 1994 onwards, so that this marketing spend may contribute to above average performance.

Hotel B is a large city centre hotel in the west of England. It has 289 rooms. This hotel adopted YM in 1995, but the general manager of the hotel expressed the view that it was not until early 1997 that the system was fully operational, following the appointment of a new reservations manager. Data for five years of operation (financial year March to March) were identified. Sales and occupancy data are provided in Table 6.5 and the rate of change in performance is shown in Table 6.6.

Over these five years it is clear that the year on year performance of the property has been steady ranging between 12 and 18 per cent. But whereas this improvement derived largely from improving occupancy up to 1996, from there on occupancy flattens out and improved ARR becomes more significant. However, when compared with the industry average, until 1996 Hotel B was at or below average occupancies, whereas thereafter it was 5 per cent better than the average, while its ARR matched quite closely the industry ARR. The slightly better ARR of this property is likely to be due to its size and conference facilities.

In this hotel, therefore, the impact of YM appears to be that full implementation has enabled occupancy to be better managed, while rates are maintained. This can be checked by identifying the relative contribution of these two factors to the overall

Table 6.5 Hotel B annualized operating performance

	1993/4	1994/5	1995/6	1996/7	1997/8
Occupancy (%)	55.84	62.24	69.32	74.70	75.20
Average rate (£)	43.85	43.87	45.33	50.76	56.54
Sales revenue (£ million)	2.58	2.87	3.36	3.96	4.47

Source: Choi (1998)

Table 6.6 Hotel B operating performance – rate of change

	1994/5	1995/6	1996/7	1997/8
Occupancy (%)	11.50	11.40	7.80	0.70
Average rate (%)	0.00	3.30	12.00	11.40
Sales revenue (%)	11.50	17.00	18.00	12.70

Source: Choi (1998)

performance. The impact of this can be examined by examining the relative contribution made by occupancy and ARR to the performance improvement.

Between 1993/4 and 1997/8 occupancy improved from 55.84 to 75.20 per cent (a 34.67
per cent increase) and ARR from £43.85 to £56.54 (a 28.94 per cent increase). If
occupancy had risen at this rate at the 1993/4 ARR, the revenue improvement would be
£895,504; whereas maintaining the occupancy rate at 1993/4 levels but improving ARR
creates a revenue improvement of £747,480. Hence 45.5 per cent of the performance
improvement derives from the better management of ARR. This is a much lower
proportion than for Hotel A, which may be accounted for by the fact that YM
implementation was slow. Certainly, all the improvement in 1997, when the new
reservations manager was appointed, derives from better rate performance and little or
no occupancy improvement.

Given the difficulty of identifying any clear YM effect from the two previous case
studies, a third hotel was studied that had different characteristics and had implemented YM more recently. *Hotel C* is not a city centre property, but a country resort
hotel with 94 rooms and a golf course. It was rebranded and refurbished in July 1996
and YM was introduced in August 1997. Hence *monthly* data over three years are
compared: 1995/6 pre-refurbishment and rebranding (providing the benchmark for
performance improvement), 1996/7 pre-YM implementation and 1997/8 post-YM
implementation. Occupancy and ARR for these years are illustrated in Tables 6.7 and
6.8.

Between 1995/6 and 1996/7 the number of rooms sold improved by 37.3 per cent, but
by only 3 per cent between 1996/7 and 1997/8. It is clear that rebranding and
refurbishment led to a significant improvement, whereas YM has had little impact on
occupancy. ARR increased by 17.75 per cent after the rebranding (from £51.57 to
£60.72), and by 6.13 per cent after YM implementation (from £60.72 to £64.44). If the
pre- and post-YM implementation years are compared, two-thirds (67 per cent) of the
performance improvement derives from a higher ARR, and one-third from improved
occupancy.

Table 6.7 Hotel C occupancy (percentages)

	Aug	Sep	Oct	Nov	Dec	Jan	Feb	Mar	Apr	May	Jun	Jul
1995/6	61	70	49	42	47	26	41	43	33	36	70	55
1996/7	62	80	62	55	53	46	63	77	73	58	91	70
1997/8	60	95	69	66	62	42	64	77	60	63	93	64

Source: Choi (1998)

Table 6.8 Hotel C average rate (£)

	Aug	Sep	Oct	Nov	Dec	Jan	Feb	Mar	Apr	May	Jun	Jul
1995/6	51.38	49.88	48.81	44.65	48.02	36.99	37.76	32.48	43.05	64.73	63.73	76.88
1996/7	67.32	62.44	56.26	57.35	61.90	51.72	53.21	50.97	57.95	65.59	65.36	74.28
1997/8	74.08	62.23	59.48	56.08	63.40	55.64	52.82	59.25	61.57	68.26	73.35	82.13

Source: Choi (1998)

YIELD IMPROVEMENT: MYTH OR REALITY?

It is clear from the data analysis of the three hotel case studies that it remains extremely difficult to be sure that any change in performance derives from the implementation of a YM system. Despite attempts to remove extraneous variables from the study, in practice this is almost impossible. In the case of Hotel C, it is clear that rebranding and refurbishment had a significantly greater impact on performance than YM. In addition, records of financial performance do not exactly match YM implementation time periods. Indeed, there is a great deal of uncertainty about how long it takes for the system to be fully operational.

However, in discussion with senior managers in each of the properties, it is clear that their *perception* is that YM is extremely effective. In Hotel A the sales manager, front office manager and rooms revenue manager all agreed that YM greatly helps to improve the hotel's performance. They base this assertion on their personal knowledge of the local market and the level of competition. For instance, the revenue manager was certain that the hotel's 'market share' had improved significantly since YM. He also calculated that the hotel was operating at 20 per cent yield premium. Management staff in Hotel B were also convinced of YM's benefits. In their case they cited rate efficiency as evidence for this – their hotel was operating at only 20 per cent below corporate rate. Hotel C managers were equally enthusiastic. The general manager stated that the hotel was running at 12 per cent yield premium over its competitors due to YM. This hotel also estimated its relative market share in its locale.

What is clear is that, post-YM implementation, all hotels appear to be achieving better ARR, although even this depends on which years are compared. Managers also agreed that performance improved largely owing to YM's impact on rate-setting and rate control. Some managers identified that the reduction in discounting that accompanied the 'fair rate' pricing may have deterred some business, but this was more than offset by the improved ARR.

This research is ongoing. Subsequent to this study, another chain has released data that it collects to compare those hotels in which it has so far implemented YM against the performance of those without the system. The chain tracks on a monthly basis average rate, yield and percentage yield variance of its 'experimental group' with YM of approximately 40 properties, against its control group of slightly smaller size. Consistently YM hotels outperformed non-YM hotels on a monthly basis but this varied widely from under 1 to 5 per cent better yield.

CONCLUSION

Despite attempting to measure the impact of YM on hotel performance, this study produces inconclusive results. The case study approach provides a great deal of detailed and qualitative information that enables exploration of the issues, but has not provided a large enough sample in which any clear link can be established.

The research may also have been improved by benchmarking each hotel's performance in a different way. For instance, it may have been desirable to compare the individual hotels with the performance of the chain as a whole. However, the company was reluctant to release chain-wide data. In addition, these data would comprise a mixed sample of early implementers of YM and of late implementers (see below), so that comparisons would again not be clear. Likewise, hotel performance may vary widely from area to area, so benchmarking each hotel against other similar hotels in the immediate market place might provide better insight. Certainly the hotel managers' perception of improvement was based on their local knowledge and how well they thought they were doing compared with their competitors. Obtaining such data is of course problematic, unless several chains are prepared to collaborate in such a study.

Despite this, a number of conclusions may be drawn:

- There is growing evidence from a number of sources that yield management may improve yield performance by around 4 per cent in the UK.
- Such improvement largely derives from better management of the average rate achieved (rather than better management of occupancy).
- Yield improvement varies over time, probably in relation to the strength of demand. Most improvement is seen with respect to those periods when demand is strong.
- It takes some time for a YM system to be fully operational so that performance improvement may lag six to eighteen months behind implementation.
- Hotels have invested heavily, in terms of both financial investment and human resources, without having any clear system in place to monitor the impact that the YM system will have on operational performance.

There is still a lot we do not know. For instance, we do not know if such performance improvement applies to all categories of hotel. Probably it does not, largely because one and two star hotels tend to have less discretion over their room rate. We do not know if performance improvement varies from location to location, such as by city or country. Almost certainly it does, as levels of demand and seasonality will vary by location. We do not know if such improvement is sustainable over time. Certainly, the competitive advantage that YM hotels gain over non-YM hotels will only last as long as some hotels do not have the technology. No study has attempted to identify whether the whole sector's performance has improved as a result of YM. And it would be even more difficult to do than the hotel study described in this chapter.

In conclusion, yield management leads to improved performance in the short term. It is therefore clearly the 'right thing to do'. But the sophistication of a hotel YM system means that improvement is also dependent on 'doing things right'. Not all hotels are necessarily optimizing all the benefits that might result from YM. In the end, long-term success will continue to depend on a hotel or a chain outperforming its competitors on a range of factors – location, service, management expertise – and not just one single technology: YM.

NOTE

1. This chapter is adapted from a paper presented jointly by the author and Kyung-Ho Choi at the CHRIE International conference in Alburquerque, New Mexico, in 1999.

REFERENCES

BDO Hospitality Consulting (1994, 1995, 1996, 1997, 1998) *UK Hotel Industry*. London: BDO Hospitality Consulting.
Boyce, D. (1991) 'Maximise yields'. *Caterer and Hotelkeeper*, 24 January, 27.

Checkland, P. B. (1981) *Systems Thinking, Systems Practice*. Chichester: John Wiley.

Choi, K.-H. (1998) 'Contribution of yield management to performance improvement in the hotel sector'. MSc Dissertation, University of Surrey.

Donaghy, K., McMahon-Beattie, U. and McDowell, D. (1997) 'Yield management practices'. In I. Yeoman and A. Ingold (eds), *Yield Management: Strategies for Service Industries*. London: Cassell.

Goymour, D. and Donaghy, K. (1995) 'Reserving judgement'. *Caterer and Hotelkeeper*, 26 January, 64–5.

Griffen, R. K. (1996) 'Factors of successful lodging yield management systems'. *Hospitality Research Journal*, **19**(4), 17–27.

Jarvis, N., Lindh, A. and Jones, P. (1997) 'An investigation of the key criteria affecting the adoption of yield management in UK hotels'. *Progress in Tourism and Hospitality Research*, **4**(3), 207–16.

Jauncey, S., Mitchell, I. and Slamet, P. (1995) 'The meaning and management of yield in hotels'. *International Journal of Contemporary Hospitality Management*, **7**(4), 23–6.

Jones, P. (1999) 'Yield management in UK hotels: a systems analysis'. *Journal of the Operations Research Society*, **50**, 1111–19.

Jones, P. and Lockwood, A. (1998) 'Operations management research in the hospitality industry'. *International Journal of Hospitality Management* **17**(2), 183–202.

Kimes, S. E. (1989) 'The basics of yield management'. *Cornell Hotel and Restaurant Administration Quarterly*, **30**(2), 14–19.

Kimes, S. E. (1997) 'Yield Management: an overview'. In I. Yeoman and A. Ingold (eds), *Yield Management: Strategies for Service Industries*. London: Cassell.

Naughton, J. (1989) *Soft Systems Analysis: An Introductory Guide*. Milton Keynes: Open University.

Orkin, E. B. (1988) 'Boosting your bottom line with yield management'. *Cornell Hotel and Restaurant Administration Quarterly*, **28**(4), 52–6.

Rowe, M. (1989) 'Yield management'. *Lodging Hospitality*, February, 65–6.

tims Revenue Optimization Systems (1999) http://www.tims.fr/increase.html

Yin, R. K. (1995) *Case Study Research: Design and Methods*. London: Sage.

7

MERLIN: Model to Evaluate Revenue and Loadings for Intercity

Ian S. A. Hood

INTRODUCTION

Background

In the years running up to privatization, the various train operators of British Rail looked into how they could design ticket structures by using yield management. They wanted to encourage price sensitive people to travel on the lighter loaded trains without crowding out established and high-fare passengers at peak times. For example, one product that was introduced was the Apex ticket. This is much cheaper than other tickets, but has to be booked at least one week in advance and is quota controlled so that only a few, or none, are available on busier trains.

The break-up of the British Rail network into 25 individual train operating companies (TOCs) has both intensified and fragmented this outlook. TOCs now have more freedom (albeit subject to regulation) to design their own timetables and fares structures that maximize their benefits. At the same time, they are coming under more scrutiny as to the standard of the products they offer; for example, the crowding conditions on peak trains.

There is now also the possibility of competition between TOCs. On flows where two or more TOCs provide services, one is nominated as the 'lead operator'. They set the fares for the 'inter-available' tickets which can be used on any operator's service and which are subject to fares regulation. However, the other TOCs on this flow (the 'minor operators') are additionally allowed to introduce their own tickets which are valid on their services only. Their fares are not subject to regulation. This type of competition is mostly limited to flows where two or more operators were running services prior to privatization. But the plan is to open it up more in the future, giving TOCs more freedom as to where they can run services.

Table 7.1 Choice of tickets available from Bristol to London (summer 1997)

	Train operating company				
	Great Western	Great Western	South Wales and West	Great Western	Great Western
Depart Bristol	07:45, 08:15	08:45	08:47	09:15	10:15
Arrive:					
Paddington	09:20, 09:50	10:15		10:50	12:00
Waterloo			11:17		
Cheapest tickets valid on train	Open = £61.00	Saver = £37.00	Cheap day = £19.50	Super Advance = £27.00	Supersaver = £27.00
			Supersaver = £23.70		Apex = £18.50
			Apex = £16.50		

In this changing environment, the Great Western Trains Company approached AEA Technology to build a model that could help it to design its timetable and fares structure. Since then we have spent over two years developing a model called MER-LIN. In this chapter we describe our methodology and how we approached calibrating the model so that it matches observed behaviour.

Purpose of the Model

Great Western wanted to use the model to help to answer a variety of questions, including:

- What are the effects on loadings and revenue if a ticket's fare and/or restrictions are changed?
- Similarly, what are the effects of changing the timetable?
- Is it worth running another train in the peak to relieve crowding?
- Where might there be risks and opportunities from competition?

Example

As an example of the scenario that has to be modelled, suppose someone wants to travel from Bristol to London. Ideally she would like to depart Bristol Temple Meads station at 08:00. She is faced with the choices shown in Table 7.1 (on a Wednesday in the summer 1997 timetable). The nearest trains to the ideal departure time are the 07:45 and 08:15, but our passenger must buy an Open ticket to travel on them. This is the most expensive standard class ticket and can be used on any train in the return direction, so there is no need to worry about which train to catch home from London. The choice between the early and late trains depends on the passenger's valuations: for example, business passengers might catch the earlier train to ensure arriving on time for an appointment.

The next train is half an hour later (though five minutes quicker) but now she can buy a Saver ticket. This is £24 cheaper, and again there are no return restrictions. However, by waiting an extra two minutes she can catch a train run by South Wales and West. This has very different characteristics: the train itself is smaller, with different seating arrangements, it is an hour slower and it runs into Waterloo rather than Paddington. But also South Wales and West has its own much cheaper tickets and there is a choice of three on this train, depending on the type of journey being made.

- First, if she is travelling back the same day she can buy a Cheap Day Return (£41.50 cheaper than the Open). For the return journey she can only catch a South Wales and West train.
- If, though, she is returning on a later day she can buy the Saver, more expensive but still cheaper than the inter-available Saver. Again she is limited to a South Wales and West train in the return direction.
- Finally, if she knows at least one week in advance when she wants to travel she can buy an Apex ticket. These are the cheapest available, but our passenger must book a seat on both the outward and return South Wales and West trains. These tickets are quota controlled, with a limited number available on each train.

The next train to depart is the 09:15 on which another inter-available ticket is valid: the Super Advance ticket. This is quota controlled but can be booked up to one day in advance. Generally there are quotas on all Great Western trains but there are a few with zero quotas in the peak periods.

The final two choices are available on the 10:15 train, some two and a quarter hours after our passenger would like to depart. The inter-available Supersaver ticket is £10 cheaper than the Saver, but for an extra one and a half hours wait; and Supersavers are not valid on some peak trains on the return journey from London. The Apex ticket is the cheapest ticket valid on Great Western trains; it is quota controlled (generally none available on the peak trains) and must be booked on both the outward and return trains at least one week in advance of the outward journey.

How Do People Choose between Different Travel Packages?

As we can see in the above example, there are potentially many ticket/train combinations to choose from. And, of course, there may be reasonable options by other modes of transport such as car, coach and air. How do passengers make their choice? There are many factors which affect their decision, including:

- when they want to depart or arrive, in both the outward and return directions;
- how long the journey takes;
- the cost of the journey and who is paying;
- the flexibility to change when they want to go;
- comfort of the journey (crowding, seating layout, availability of food and drink, interchanges along the route, etc.);
- the reliability of the service on offer.

No doubt, there are many more. Different types of people value each of these differently. So typically someone travelling on business is less worried about cost and more concerned with journey time. For leisure passengers it tends to be the other way round.

Focus of the Model

At the outset, we set out the limits of our model. First, we decided to concentrate on rail passengers and explicitly to model the rail options only. This is because we have a lot of data on rail passengers – what sorts of people travel at what times – and we have access to research on how they tend to react to some of the factors listed above. All the other modes can be aggregated together (plus the decision not to travel at all) and treated as 'non-rail'.

Because different passengers have different values, we divide them into a number of markets: in standard class we have business, leisure, personal business (for example, job interviews, going to funerals), commuters and other (mainly those who travel on travelcard type tickets and rail staff). We also consider first class passengers independently, treating them in isolation from standard class.

Another dimension to consider is the day of travel. The Friday timetable is slightly different from the other weekdays, and Saturdays and Sundays have their own timetables. Tickets can have different restrictions on different days: notably, Supersavers are not valid on Fridays. And the profile of passengers on these days varies: for example, no commuters at the weekend. So far we have set up two models, Monday–Thursday and Friday, and it is the Monday–Thursday model that we describe in this chapter.

On geographical coverage, Great Western was keen for us to include all four of its routes: Avon (London to Bristol), South Wales (London to Cardiff and Swansea), West of England (London to Plymouth and Penzance) and the Cotswolds (London to Hereford and Cheltenham Spa). So each of the stations on these routes where Great Western trains call is modelled explicitly. But the other stations on the rail network are zoned together – the further from the routes, the larger the zones (so the whole of Scotland is one zone). This produces a total of 76 stations and zones.

METHODOLOGY

Identifying Options on Offer

The first stage in the model is to identify all the ticket and train options on offer to passengers travelling on a particular flow.

We start with the tickets. On any given flow there will be a set of inter-available tickets which are valid on all operators. But there may also be operator specific tickets. MERLIN allows the user to specify one set of operator specific tickets in addition to the inter-available set. In our example it would be South Wales and West tickets comprising Cheap Day Returns, Savers and Apex.

Next we take each ticket in turn and identify the train options available to the passenger. Clearly the choice of sensible options changes during the day. So we divide the day into 15-minute timebands, and look at the options in each of these.

Within each timeband we assume the demand is concentrated on the midpoint; for example, at 05:38 in the 05:30–05:45 timeband. Then we take each ticket in turn and for each one generate the 'opportunities to travel' (OTTs). Each of these is either a direct train or, in the case of interchanging, a series of trains that can be caught with this ticket. So in our example the 08:15 train to Paddington is a valid OTT for the Open ticket and the 08:45 train is a valid OTT for both the Open and Saver tickets.

We had to decide how wide a choice of OTTs we should allow the model to consider. Initially we limited it to two, the nearest early and the nearest late OTTs, in order to speed up the processing time and limit the memory and hard disk space requirements. But we found this did not always present a sensible choice, particularly when there was a faster OTT just a few minutes earlier or later. So we extended the choice to four OTTs.

One further complication is that tickets can have different restrictions depending on whether the passenger is travelling on their outward journey leg or return journey leg. For example, Savers cannot be used in the outward direction on some peak trains at London but can be used on any train in the return direction.

So within each timeband we end up with:

- for each journey leg;
- for each ticket on offer;
- the two early OTT and two late OTT choices.

Attaching a Generalized Cost to Each Option

The next step is to measure the attractiveness of each ticket/OTT combination. The measure we use is generalized cost (GC) which combines several characteristics of the rail journey by converting them into monetary value. The basic formula is

$$GC = \text{distance}^{\pm} \times \{ (\text{value of time} \times (GJT + (P \times (\text{shift in departure time} + \text{opposite direction penalty})))) + \text{fare} + \text{advance purchase penalty} \}$$

The components are described below.

Distance is the distance of the OTT. It is included here as a way of controlling how people react to the differences between the options on offer. Without it, the model predicts that people react to a £1 difference between two options on a £5 journey in the same way as they do to a £1 difference on a £50 journey. Intuitively, this is not correct. At the other extreme we could say people react in the same way to proportional differences, so that a £1 difference in a £5 journey is the same as a £10 difference on a £50 journey. Again, this does not seem correct. The x value is therefore introduced to produce an effect between these two extremes.

Value of time varies by market such that business passengers have higher values than leisure passengers. GJT is the generalized journey time, which is made up of on-train journey time plus a penalty for changing trains if appropriate. P shows how passengers weight a shift from their ideal departure time compared with on-train journey time. This varies according to market: business passengers are far less willing to wait for a train with cheaper tickets than leisure passengers.

As well as building in the effect of restrictions on having to shift departure time in the outward direction, we also want to include the effect of restrictions in the return direction (the opposite direction penalty). Initially we tried ignoring this but found that the model was over-predicting the choice of the cheaper tickets.

This is potentially a complicated area. We are assuming that people make their choice of ticket on the basis of its restrictions in both directions together. But do people always know in advance when they want to return? And are they more willing to shift from this time than they are on the outward journey leg?

What we would like to know is the distribution of return departure times given the outward departure time. Then we could calculate how many people would be affected by the return restrictions. Unfortunately, we do not have this information. Instead we tried calculating the effect of return restrictions by estimating the average shift in departure time, weighted according to when all passengers want to return. We then reduce this by 40 per cent to account for its lower weighting in the decision.

But averaging in this way means we add the same penalty throughout the day. This masks the impact of return restrictions, since those affected will have a much higher penalty, whereas those unaffected will have a zero penalty. To get round this we calculate three penalties: for those returning in the morning peak, those in the off peak and those in the evening peak. This then means we end up with three separate generalized costs to be fed into the model for these three groups of people.

Having calculated the return restrictions penalty for those in the outward direction, we had to decide how to cope with modelling passengers travelling back in the return direction. Our initial idea was to impose the ticket choice predicted by the model in the outward direction. But we do not know how this varies throughout the day. So we decided to reverse the process, this time calculating three outward penalties. This seems to work reasonably well: we checked a few sample flows and found that the ticket choice predicted by the model was fairly consistent between the two directions.

The fare we use for a ticket is the return fare.

For those tickets that have to be bought in advance we add a further penalty (the advance purchase penalty). This is a monetary value which measures the inconvenience of:

- having to book in advance;
- being tied to specific outward and return trains;
- not always being able to book on the first choice train owing to quotas being exceeded.

We have separate penalties for business and leisure, and also for Apex (up to seven days in advance) and Super Advance (up to one day in advance). But further, we found early on that our predictions in and around the peaks were too high and so we had to introduce separate peak, shoulder peak and off peak penalties. We reasoned that this was because the quotas were being hit more often in the peaks, and some people must view these tickets as simply off peak products.

Predicting the Choices: the Logit Model

Having calculated the generalized costs, we now feed them into a logit model to predict ticket and OTT choice. We do this for each 15-minute timeband separately.

In the model, the choices faced by passengers are put into a decision tree structure. At the lowest level, the choice within each ticket is between the four OTTs and is modelled as

$$\text{proportion choosing the } i\text{th OTT} = \frac{\exp(-\lambda GC_{i\text{th OTT}})}{\sum_{n=1}^{4} \exp(-\lambda GC_{n\text{th OTT}})}$$

Here γ is the spread parameter which controls how sensitive people are to one choice (OTT) being better than another.

The next decision up the tree is which ticket to choose. For this we first need to calculate the generalized cost of each ticket, which is a combination of the corresponding costs of the four OTTs. So for ticket I

$$GC_{tkt\,I} = \frac{-1}{\lambda}\left(\ln\left(\Sigma^4_{n=1}\exp\left(-\lambda GC_{nth\,\text{OTT for tkt I}}\right)\right)\right)$$

Then we apply the following equation.

$$\text{proportion choosing ticket I} = \frac{\exp(-\lambda\theta GC_{tkt\,I})}{\Sigma\,\exp(-\lambda\theta GC_{tkt})}$$

where θ is another spread parameter contolling the sensitivity of ticket choice.

In doing this calculation, we separate the walk-up tickets from the advance tickets. So all the proportions of the walk-up tickets add up to 1, and all the advance tickets add up to 1. So finally the choice between walk-up and advance purchase is then modelled at the top level of the tree structure. This is calculated by combining the generalized costs of the relevant tickets, to give a cost for walk-up and a cost for advance purchase. Then we apply:

$$\text{proportion choosing walk-up} = \frac{\exp(-\lambda\theta\mu GC_{\text{walk-up}})}{\exp(-\lambda\theta\mu GC_{\text{walk-up}}) + \exp(-\lambda\theta\mu GC_{\text{advance}})}$$

where μ is a third spread parameter.

Applying Quotas

Having calculated the proportions making each choice, we apply the demand to calculate how many people choose each train and with which ticket. But we have a potential problem in that some quotas may be exceeded.

In our generalized cost formulation we included the advance purchase penalty partly to measure the inconvenience of having to choose another train owing to quotas being filled. But this does not prevent the model from exceeding quotas on certain popular trains. As a result we have to take the excess demand and recycle it through the model, but with a few differences

- we remove the excess ticket/OTT option from the choices available;
- we remove tickets from the choices available if they require more advance notice in booking (so Apex can choose Super Advance but Super Advance cannot choose Apex);
- we remove the advance purchase penalty from the generalized cost formulation, since these people have already made the effort of trying to book in advance;
- we remove some of the demand, assuming they are put off travelling by rail, by calculating how much worse their next option is compared to their previous in terms of fare and *GJT*, and applying elasticities accordingly.

We repeat this process several times, since passengers' second choice may cause new quotas to be exceeded.

Estimating the Change in the Rail Market

As mentioned in the Introduction, we do not explicitly measure other modes of transport. But a new fares or timetable option may affect the size of the rail market. So, instead, for each flow (e.g. Bristol to London) we calculate the average fare paid and average *GJT* and compare these with the base case. We then apply an elasticity to each – which is the ratio of the percentage change in rail demand to the percentage change in the factor (fares and *GJT* in this case). And because each market responds differently (e.g. leisure are price sensitive whereas business are journey time sensitive) we apply separate elasticities for each one.

HOW GOOD IS THE MODEL? CALIBRATION

Benchmark Data

As can be seen, there are many variables which contribute to the choice model. These need to be calibrated so that the model predictions match observed behaviour. The benchmark data we use for this include

- *Train counts:* the senior conductor on GW trains counts the number of standard class passengers and first class passengers at various points along the train's journey. We use the counts at Paddington since these are the highest – and so most crucial – loadings for GW. But they can be dominated by commuters in the peaks who currently have no choice to make between tickets (all season tickets are inter-available). So for each train we also choose a monitoring point further down the route where seasons make up a smaller proportion.
- *Quota take-up:* for Apex, Super Advance and Advance tickets we know the average number of bookings on each train.
- *Ticket sales:* for each flow we know how many of each ticket were sold. And for all journeys made on GW trains we know the total number made by each ticket.

Process

To calibrate the model we wanted to divide GW's trains into groups where the choices faced by passengers are similar. First we split them into their four constituent routes: Avon, Cotswolds, South Wales and West of England. Although there is some inter-action, especially between London and Reading, they generally serve their own flows. They face different types of competition from other TOCs: Avon and South Wales from South Wales and West running a few trains to and from Waterloo, Cotswolds from Thames Trains and West of England from South West Trains running trains between Exeter and Waterloo.

Then we split by direction: up to or down from London. In the up direction the restrictions are in the morning peak when most passengers are on their outward

Table 7.2 Minimum targets for matching against train counts for Monday to Thursday

Counts	Targets
Standard class	90% of trains within 37 (i.e. 10% of capacity)
(both at Paddington and along route)	98% if trains within 56 (i.e. 15% of capacity)
First class	90% of trains within 17 (i.e. 15% of capacity)
(at Paddington)	98% if trains within 22 (i.e. 20% of capacity)

journey leg and can buy an expensive ticket or wait for a cheaper one. In the down direction there are a few restrictions early in the morning but most of them are in the evening peak. At this time there are passengers returning home as well as travelling out. And there are two shoulders to this peak: late afternoon and late evening.

As a starting point, we set our parameters to what we thought were sensible values. Where they existed, we used values suggested by various research studies and recommended in the Passenger Demand Forecasting Handbook (an industry-wide document sponsored by the TOCs). We then concentrated on the train counts – which is a test of both train and ticket choice – to fine tune these parameters. This mainly involved the P factors and demand profiles.

Performance

Our minimum targets for matching against the train counts for Monday–Thursday are shown in Table 7.2. At the time of writing, we have almost reached these targets. Taking Avon as an example, we show the profile of train counts versus MERLIN's predictions at the end of this chapter. During the calibration process we have learnt several lessons, including the following:

- The logit model is not good at recognizing when one option is clearly worse than others and is chosen by next to no passengers. This happens when none of the elements of generalized cost is better and at least one is worse; for example, there are no return restrictions with Savers so no one would choose to buy a more expensive Open ticket if he or she was making the outward journey leg in the off peak. We therefore remove such options from the choice set.
- The discrete nature of the 15-minute timebands can artificially favour certain trains. We assume that all demand within a timeband is centred on the mid-point; for example, 14:53 for the 14:45–15:00 timeband. In this case, for London–Reading passengers their nearest trains are the 14:48 Thames train or 15:00 Great Western train. Combining the shifts of five and seven minutes respectively with the P factors produced significant proportions of passengers choosing the slower Thames train. We therefore allowed passengers to shift up to eight minutes at no cost, so covering the whole of the 15 minutes in the timeband.
- The choice of four OTTs closest to departure time can be too limiting when there are a few that are clearly better. For example, from Penzance to London there are a few through trains, but there are other OTTs that involve changing at Plymouth. In this case a more sophisticated choice is needed. We therefore allowed the two furthest OTTs to be replaced by faster OTTs, as long as they depart within four hours of the ideal departure time.
- People seem to be unwilling to shift their departure time earlier to catch the last Supersaver train prior to the evening peak restrictions. This is probably

reasonable: leisure passengers travelling on their outward journey leg may be unable to leave early from work, as are business passengers returning home. We therefore had to increase the *P* factor for shifting departure times back in the evening peak. Conversely, we had to make it more difficult to shift later in the morning peak (business passengers prefer arriving early than late).

- The train counts tend to underestimate the loadings on very busy trains. When it is impractical to count people, senior conductors record a default 'full and standing' which is assumed to be 115 per cent load factor. On a small number of trains we believe the loadings between London and Reading are higher than this.

- As we expected, we have had to introduce 'rolling stock factors' to prevent the model from over-predicting the attraction of Great Western's current competition on longer distance journeys. This measures (at least) two disadvantages of the competition: the perceived quality of the rolling stock and the lack of awareness of the availability of their tickets. We found we needed a smaller penalty on the Exeter–London route where South West Trains provides a reasonably frequent – and hence well known – service.

CONCLUSION: WHAT THE MODEL CAN AND CANNOT ASSESS

Building a train and ticket choice model of this size has proved to be very difficult. There are many parameters that we have had to set, some with little hard knowledge as to what they should be. Probably the most troublesome have been the demand profiles – when people ideally want to travel. Currently there are 150 of them (five distance bands, to/from/non-London, ten markets).

So how good is the model? The test is not just how closely the predictions match observed behaviour, but also how sensible the values of the parameters are. At the time of writing we are coming to the end of the calibration for the Monday–Thursday model. The predictions are close to observed behaviour and, encouragingly, the parameters seem sensible. Possibly the weakest area, though, is the *P* factors, which we have had to force higher than previous research has suggested.

We plan to carry out further tests. First is to move on to the Friday model – when the timetable is slightly different, Supersaver tickets are not valid and the profile of passengers is very different. Second is to compare the model's predictions for past timetable changes with what was observed to happen.

After all this development, can the resultant model be used for its original purposes? We believe it is well suited for assessing the effects of changes to the timetable, the fares structure and the capacity of trains (on crowding implications). In addition, it is useful for assessing the impact of new competition, e.g. what might happen if a competitor introduces a new ticket. However, this is likely to depend heavily on perceptions and marketing, which are included in our 'rolling stock factor' and which we have found to vary from route to route. The downside of the model is its run-time. It produces very large data sets (in excess of 100 MB) and with a Pentium 200 takes over two hours to run. This is something we intend to improve on in the future.

PART III
DECISION SUPPORT

8

Decision-Making

Ian Yeoman and Anthony Ingold

INTRODUCTION

Kimes (1989) describes yield management as the process of allocating the right type of capacity to the right kind of customer at the right price so as to maximize revenue or yield. The assumption of a management role places an individual in the mainstream of an organization's decision-making activity with authority to make decisions and to organize and develop the organization's decision-making capability (Jennings and Wattam, 1994). The purpose of this chapter is to explain the management process of decision-making through Kimes's definition of yield management. The chapter outlines the decision process using examples from airlines, corporate hotels and independent hotels.

This chapter sets out models of decision-making following the principles of Gore's (1995) study of hotel managers' decision-making models. Gore examined the rational/ normative model, bounded rational paradigm and expert model of decision-making. The authors have expanded on these models to include a chaos paradigm. These models are expanded to highlight behavioural attributes of decision-making in yield management.

DECISION-MAKING

Yield management, as a process of managing capacity, must be viewed within the context of an organization's need to improve its decision-making (Jennings and Wattam, 1994). This need arises because:

- In general, organizations face a scarcity of resources and need to make the most effective use of the resources available to them.

- Increasingly both private and public sector organizations face competition through successive governments exposing more organizations and their decisions to market disciplines, beginning in the 1980s.
- Issues such as consumer safety and ethics frequently raise public concern over the degree of social responsibility demonstrated by organizations in their decision-making. Both public and private sector organizations often find themselves judged by the wider society, not only for the results of decisions they have made, but also for how those decisions were arrived at.
- The need for survival, maintaining market share and profits are great influences on an organization to improve decision-making.

Previous studies of decision-making in the hospitality industry have been inconclusive in formation of satisfactory models in this area. Gore's (1995) study was unsatisfactory in the terms of determining a hospitality decision-making model. Gore states: 'there is some evidence to support Klein's RDP model but support for the rational and bounded rational model is much stronger'. Gore suggests that further research is required in hospitality management decision-making; hence the purpose of the present study.

Yield management and capacity management strategies are discussed within appropriate models of decision-making within the hospitality industry through case studies.

YIELD MANAGEMENT: A RATIONAL/NORMATIVE DECISION MODEL

The sequence of activities shown in Figure 8.1 specifies a rational/normative model of decision-making. The process provides a logical means of making a decision. The model is typical of the rational/normative models that have been proposed in the decision-making literature of corporate planning and management science (Jennings and Wattam, 1994). A rational/normative model describes how decisions should be made, rather than how they are made. The model is a proposal of how ideally to make a decision. The ability of this decision-making process to deliver 'best' decisions rests upon the activities that make up the process and the order in which they are attended to.

An understanding of the normative model of decision-making is examined through a case study of a 500-bedroom, four star central London hotel application of a yield management system (for the purpose of confidentiality, the hotel has been renamed the 'Westland'). For the purpose of this case study, personnel were interviewed before and after the process of yield management to determine whether the rational/normative model of yield management had been a success. Members of the yield management team, hotel manager and regional director were interview participants. Each interview lasted approximately one to one and a half hours.

The Westland hotel is part of a major international hotel chain, with two properties in Greater London. The hotel chain operates its own central reservation system, but travel agents also have access via a global distribution (Sabre). The Westland hotel in 1995 was faced with a problem situation of a forecast occupancy of 36 per cent for the summer quarter. The regional director of the company gave the general manager the objective of increasing occupancy to at least 66 per cent. The hotel, therefore, went about increasing occupancy by decreasing the average room rate. The room rate dropped from £58.00 to £26.00, with the consequence of a sharp decrease in operating profit. The hotel management team decided to address the problem situation of rooms

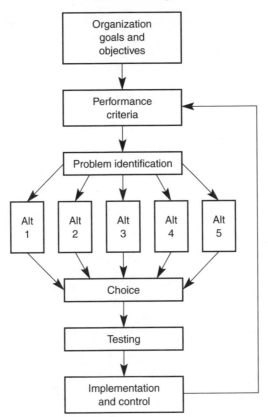

Figure 8.1 The decision-making process: a normative model
Source: Jennings and Wattam (1994)

revenue through the implementation of a yield management system. Using the model in Figure 8.1, the organizational goal was stated as: 'on high demand days for accommodation, maximum revenue yield to be achieved, whereas on identified low demand days market potential revenue yield to be targeted'. The prime reason for implementing a yield management system was to focus management on to rooms management within the hotel and, by using a rational/normative model, the hotel management team had a structured approach to the problem situation.

Once the objective of yield management had been agreed, aims were required as the following:

- On high demand days, the aim was to maximize average room rate to increase revenue.
- Plan for group reservations. Use a band of four group tariffs depending on demand.
- On low demand days, maximize occupancy and optimize average room rate.
- Yield is measured by the formula: (total actual room revenue × 100) ÷ optimum room revenue = yield (per cent).

- The success of the yield management depends on the 'yield management' team, consisting of the executive assistant manager (rooms division), reservations manager and sales manager.
- The yield management team must ensure systems for forecasting and feedback.
- An incentive scheme to be used based upon achieved yield forecasts. Incentive schemes to be based on the yield management team and front office/reservations teams.

With these aims in mind, a yield management software system was utilized within the reservations department of the hotel. Once a system had been installed the appropriate staff were trained in the software's operation (with an understanding of the aims of a yield management system).

Criteria that influence the rational/normative model, both tangible and intangible, were identified as:

- *Business ethics*. The hotel was concerned about overbooking and the implications of this on customer perception of the hotel. The hotel management was also concerned about the potential situation of booking out 'hotel company credit card holders'. Was overbooking compatible with the company's 'customer care programme'?
- *Profit*. Pressure applied by the regional director of the hotel company to achieve a budgeted profit.
- *Customer tolerance*. Dealing with angry customers who had to be booked out and the consequent effect on customer perception of service.
- *Legality*. When the hotel enters into a contract to provide accommodation, should the hotel break the law when using a yield management system for overbooking (Boella, 1996).
- *Incentives*. The drive to achieve a bonus through maximizing yield results in a motivator for the yield management team and front office/reservation personnel.

The rational/normative model of decision-making is concerned with an evaluation of different options. Options can be forecast for an optimum solution using mathematical modelling techniques; this approach allows the yield management team to discuss a cost–benefit analysis for each option within the criteria already mentioned.

Once the yield management process had been implemented, how effective had the normative model of decision-making been? What was the effect of the various criteria on the model? The conclusions that can be drawn include the following:

- *The drive to achieve yield*. The most overriding pressure to achieve yield came from the regional director, whose influence was described as manipulation and cohesion. This seemed to defeat the purpose of the team approach to yield management. The yield management team felt as if they were simply trying to justify suggested directions of the regional director. The process of yield management was only a framework and the team felt as if they were 'just going through the motions' and 'trying to satisfy the boss'. The regional director showed a leadership style similar to that of 'system 2, Benevolent Authoritative' (Likert, 1961), where the manager has superficial, condescending confidence and trust in subordinates, imposes decisions, never delegates, motivates by reward and sometimes involves subordinates in problem-solving, though in a paternalistic manner. The general manager of the Westland hotel was seen as weak and under the 'thumb of the regional director'; therefore, the general manager wasn't held in high esteem by the yield management team.

- *Organizational climate*. The aims of the normative model were not consistent with the aims of the actors in the problem situation. The normative model is based upon rational decision-making, whereas the situation that was presented was a political process of decision-making. The organization had a strict hierarchy of decision-making, and the team approach to yield management was not consistent with this. The culture could be described as a 'power and role cultures' (Handy, 1985); here there was only one major source of power and influence, e.g. the regional director within the boundaries of this defined role. The regional director was seen as trying to satisfice his superiors.
- *The customer*. A conflict situation arose in terms of priorities between the yield management team and front office staff. As the yield management team's primary objective was to achieve the required yield, the yield management team pushed for this objective, whatever the cost. This led to several situations, when the front office staff felt that customer care and the hotel's image was affected. Front office felt that on a number of occasions the overbooking levels were intolerable. The yield management team also had conflict with the human resource director, who at that time was promoting a customer care package. Front office personnel felt a conflict of interest between the programmes of customer care and yield management. The staff felt that the programmes were incompatible, and led to confusion among the priorities of the front office team. Front office personnel stated that their greatest fear was dealing with guests who had to be booked out.
- *Group decisions*. Because of the role of the regional director, the issue of legitimacy of decisions was raised by the yield management team. It was felt that the regional director took decisions that were autocratic, without regard for the feelings of the yield management team. Therefore the decisions that were taken by the team were to satisfice the regional director, not the issue of yield management. Hence the team members did not feel bound by the decisions. If the group did not feel bound by the decisions they had made, a question must be asked of the quality of decisions taken by the yield management team. The group also only looked for limited information in order to make satisficing decisions. Finally, participation in the group decisions was very much a 'groupthink scenario' (Janis, 1982). This was evident through statements of a degree of self-censorship by the group, group members did not express the misgivings they had about particular yield management decisions. Stemming from this self censorship, the team members shared the illusion of group unanimously. Many team meetings had a strong degree of silence and only luke-warm approval of the decisions that were taken was expressed.

Work reported by Arnold *et al.* (1991) goes some way towards an understanding of satisficing decisions relating to individuals. This work introduces the notion of subjective expected utility (SEU). What this concept suggests is that individuals act in similar ways, which can be viewed as rational in that they make decisions on the basis of expected outcomes and the value they place on those outcomes. Thus choices will be made between alternatives according to the effects they are judged to have in terms of outcomes and according to the value the individual ascribes to the outcomes.

The yield management team members had a high element of agreement with the decisions they made. Therefore, low morale was evident in the group's perception by others. Limitations of rational/normative model of decision-making involve the understanding of conflict. Some of the decision strategies used by people can be thought of as conflict-confronting and conflict-avoiding. That is, some decision processes confront and resolve conflict by considering the extent to which one is willing to trade off more of one valued attribute for less of another valued attribute. Choice heuristics may not be stored in their entirety in memory, but may exist only as fragments – subparts which are put together constructively at the time of making the decision. Hence, yield managers take decisions by referring to their subconscious, which is not taken into account by the rational/normative model.

The satisficing attribute is one of the oldest heuristics identified in decision-making literature (Simon, 1955). Ackoff (1981) states that the heuristic is concerned with:

> a course of action that yield an outcome that is good enough ... We call this approach clinical because it relies heavily on past experience and current trial and error for its inputs. It is qualitatively, not quantitatively, orientated, it is rooted deeply in common sense, and makes extensive use of common sense, and it makes extensive use of subjective judgements.

Ackoff (1981) states that most managers follow this heuristic. If so, the rational/normative model is not appropriate (in the context of this study) in decision-making as managers will not place a value on all choices that are available to them, they will find a decision that satisfices. The satisficing heuristic also overlaps the favourite choice heuristic, as the regional director is trying to get the yield management to select his favoured solution to the problem.

Decisions can never be taken in isolation: many social and political factors influence decision-making (Tetlock, 1985). The three major causal of factors are the problem situation, people and the context of decisions. At a more detailed psychological level of analysis, these three major types of factor influencing strategy choice affect the availability, accessibility, processability and perceived benefits of various decision strategies. Therefore the Westland case study has highlighted that decisions are not made in isolation, and hence the rational/normative model of decision-making is flawed in decisions for the real world. The rational/normative model (Simon, 1981) does not consider time pressures, which are an important attribute in management decision-making, thus underlining another fault with the model.

This case study also highlights the weight given to qualitative against quantitative reasoning. Because the most important influence was the attitude of the regional director, group members listened to his arguments against the quantitative information presented through the yield management system. Tversky *et al.* (1988) make similar observations relating to qualitative and quantitative thinking.

The complexity of the decision task in yield management makes the rational/normative model inappropriate in decision-making. For example, the number of alternatives available, the number of attributes or dimensions of information on which alternatives vary and time pressure all add to the complexity.

YIELD MANAGEMENT: AN EXPERT MODEL

A case study of an expert model of decision-making is examined through the yield management process of a large international airline. For the purpose of confidentiality, the airline has been renamed TransEuropean.

Gore (1995) states that:

> Klein (1989) [*Klein et al. (1993)*] proposed the recognition-primed decision making model (RPD) which describes the decision making observed from studies of fire ground commanders, tank commanders and design engineers. Klein's model proposes that individuals frequently take decisions through a process in which they recognise their situation as similar to a previous experience. This recognition therefore 'primes' the individual with a possible course of action or option to the current situation. Klein suggests that the decision maker usually evaluates options serially until an acceptable solution is found.
>
> Klein concludes that decision makers could recognise ways that situations and circumstances were usual and would include usual/typical responses. Klein deduced that very few decisions are made using 'analytical processes', for example generating a variety of options and contrasting their strengths and weaknesses.

Kleins *et al*'s (1993) recognition-primed decision-making model is drawn from the Tversky and Kahneman (1973) propositions on heuristics, which are stated as follows:

> that cognitive biases that stem from the reliance judgmental heuristics are not attributable to motivational effects such as wishful thinking or the distortion of judgements by payoffs and penalties. Therefore, even yield managers within an expert model of decision making are prone to some biases – when they think intuitively. For example, the tendency to predict the outcome that best represents the data, with insufficient regard for prior probability, has been observed in the intuitive judgements of those who have extensive training in statistics. Although the statistically sophisticated avoid elementary mistakes, their intuitive judgements are liable to similar fallacies in more intricate and less transparent problems.

What is surprising according to Tversky and Kahneman (1973) is the failure of people to infer from lifelong experience. Fundamental statistical rules of mathematical modelling are not learned from everyday experience because the relevant instances are not coded appropriately.

> The lack of an appropriate code also explains people usually do not detect the biases in their judgements of probability. A person could conceivably learn whether his judgements are externally calibrated by keeping a tally of the proportion of events that occur among those to which he assigns the same probability.

Other instances of subjective reasoning are better characterized as applications of individuals' personal mental models of given situations (Yates, 1992). Examples, including the representatives, availability and anchoring-and-adjustment heuristics, are well described in a number of research journals (Tversky and Kahneman, 1973; Tversky *et al.*, 1988). These are cases of an individual's conception of how various factors literally bring about the occurrence of a given event. Or, in other cases, individuals' mental models appear to be little more than collections of their beliefs that various factors are statistically associated with the target. It is widely accepted that much of management decision-making is automatic behaviour, and runs without continuous attention control. This automatic behaviour is controlled by a hierarchy of stored schemata (Yates, 1992). Most management decision-making is guided by arranged schemata with built-in decision criteria that have evolved on the basis of experience, and that are not subjected over and over to conscious risk analysis; hence the foundations of Klein *et al*'s (1993) rapid recognition-primed decision-making model.

An expert can be described as: 'a trained by practice, well informed, skilful, person having special skill or knowledge' (Swannell, 1986). Do experts and non-experts interpret risk in different ways? (Yates, 1992). One common factor seems to be the perceived degree of control a person has in affecting an outcome. Important heuristics are situations that are indicators of hazard that trigger largely automatic responses in skilled behaviour. Since behaviour of this sort occurs only after prolonged experience or practice, the hazard indicators are likely to be highly situation specific, and hence Klein *et al*'s RDP model has one fundamental flaw and is only appropriate to the fire-fighter experts from Klein *et al*'s 1992 study. The case study presented next examines this dimension.

The case study examines the role of 'experts' in yield management within TransEuropean. To test Gore's (1995) study of decision-making of hospitality managers, three managers were interviewed from three different levels of management involved with yield management decisions within this airline. The interviewees were asked four days prior to the interviews to think about the decisions they made within the following framework: routine versus non-routine, administrative, tactical and strategic. Throughout the interview, critical incident technique and protocol analysis were used to establish heuristics that the yield managers used.

The organizational structure of the department is described below. The YOs (yield officers, the most junior managers) are responsible for the operational decisions of yield management within the airline. In the airline situation, yield management can be defined as determining the 'net yield per passenger kilometre'.

The YO is involved in forecasting the yield per passenger for a particular flight. A typical aeroplane is divided up into different products and different classes giving different yields. The role of the YO is connecting the class of passenger to the fare he or she has paid. The primary role of the YO is to manage capacity, as the YOs take the capacity as fixed. They have no authority to change pricing.

The decisions a YO takes include the following:

- the type of aircraft for a particular route;
- the level of passengers for different classes;
- the relationship between ticket holders (packages) in each class;
- the relationship between cargo and passengers, e.g. load factors;
- the level of overbooking for each flight, no-shows, cancellations;
- the number, and frequency, of flights on a particular route.

The constraints on a YO include:

- baggage handling capacity;

- political agreements, e.g. the number of slots available for TransEuropean at John F. Kennedy airport;
- seasonal factors, e.g. low and high season;
- political atmosphere, e.g. war;
- time, e.g. aircraft turnaround;
- availability of aeroplanes, plus a variety of other constraints.

Generally, YOs are graduates, with a management science background. The role of YO is seen a learning ground for all graduate 'high flyers', which involves day-to-day operational decision-making. Six YOs report to the yield managers (YMs, middle managers). The YMs report to the yield executives (YEs, executive managers), of whom there are two, long haul and short haul.

YOs' roles are concerned with forecasting. In order to do this a management science approach is used to model options. This approach uses the techniques of operations research, statistics and systems thinking. A management science approach models simulations based upon mathematical models. Computer software is used to deal with the large quantity of mathematical calculations that are required. By taking this approach the YO can simulate the effect of different criteria to achieve different yields. Models are changing constantly, when criteria in the real world change. Therefore the YO is modelling different situations for $D - 1$, $D - 3$, $D - 5$, $D - 30$, etc. (the D represents departure, and the number how many days before departure). The forecast is more accurate the closer to departure date. Historical information and market intelligence are used for the forecasting criteria. The software used for forecasting also has links with the airline's reservation system; therefore information is as accurate and up to date as possible.

The YM acts as a team leader for six YOs, and his or her functions include:

- focusing on the 'bigger picture' by analysing the detail of market behaviour provided by the YOs;
- responsible for a geographic area, e.g. 'North Atlantic routes';
- identifying revenue-generating opportunities and planning how to exploit them;
- developing and interpreting quality monitors;
- team leadership;
- decision-making in the terms of capacity and scheduling;
- liaison with sales executives to identify sales opportunities.

The YEs manage yield in strategic and long-term parameters.

The heuristics and behavioural influences were identified as follows. A large influence on the YO decision-making was that of 'career choice decisions'. Sociologists (Jennings and Wattam, 1994) argue that there will be factors outside the control of the individual, arising out of the structure of society, which has influence on managers' decision-making. This factor limits the range of choices an individual is willing to take. The direct consequence of this attribute is on the quality of decision-making. Decisions are made to satisfice the YE, not necessarily optimal decisions.

TransEuropean has a bureaucratic structure; therefore managers tend to focus on information which is quantitative. This agrees with the research of Hegarty *et al.* (1988), who examined organizational structure and the processing of information. Managers of

Table 8.1 Quotations from yield personnel about decision-making

Yield executive	Yield manager	Yield officer
'I make split-second decisions which I don't share with others.' I mean, I don't justify to others'.	'I make decisions which I think my boss finds politically acceptable.'	'I make recommendations for scenarios.'
'Work is my life, that's what the wife says.'	'Competition is about not being seen to be a loser or soft touch.'	'Sometimes I think the airline thinks I am just an extension of the computer.'
'The organization is constantly changing, you have always got to be the "tiger" within the department.'	'Decision-making is systematic, that is a strength.'	'Who listens?'

bureaucratic organizations spend considerably more time processing and disseminating quantitative as against qualitative information because of the culture of the organization.

Slovic (1972) proposes a principle of 'concreteness':

> namely that decision makers will tend to use only that information that is explicitly displayed in the stimulus object and will use it only in the form in which it is displayed. The argument is that in order to reduce the cognitive strain of integrating information, any information that has to be stored in memory, inferred from the display, or transformed will be discounted or ignored. Note that this explanation of a display effect on decision behaviour involves same information-processing considerations used in explaining the task complexity on choice.

In the case of YOs, this is reflected in the comments that graphic displays accounted for a consistency in decision-making. The graphic displays produced 'concreteness', which enabled the YOs to make decisions on quantitative information rather than qualitative.

The expert model case study has highlighted the fact that likelihood judgement deficiencies (Yates, 1992) are not independent of the significance of focal events on the person making the judgements. Most often, people inflate the chances whose occurrence they would prefer seeing and deflate the unappealing events. The YO is promoting favoured options which may not be the optimal solution. The YO is promoting a solution that is 'acceptable'.

Related to this are personal role biases, which are distinct from value biases and overconfidence (Russo and Schoemaker, 1992) in the YE's own judgement. Individuals tend to judge that if they think their own actions have a role in a situation the chance of a favourable outcome is improved. Hence the YEs took decisions that had bias because of their role and accountability for capacity within the airline.

One of the strengths of a formal yield system highlighted by the decision-makers in the case study is that it allows feedback on forecast scenarios which is reflected in other findings (see the chaos paradigm and incremental model).

Table 8.2 Constraints model of policy decision-making

	Cognitive	Affiliative	Emotive
Yield executive	'What you can't do and what you can do.'	'Yield management is the association of guts and luck.'	'The competition is alarming ... for top spot.'
Yield manager	'Optimization.'	'Balancing is the corner of yield management decisions, you never know when you need to call in favours.'	'Go for it ... is usually the response on the London/Paris route. What I mean is, I can always overbook.'
Yield officer	'It can be a game.'	'You think about the terminal manager's reaction.'	'Frustration is one of the major disadvantages of the job ... you bottle up a lot.'

Janis (1989) presents a constraints model of policy decision-making and identifies some of the situations of heuristics highlighted by the yield managers. The model classifies decisions into three types of simple, error-prone decision rules: cognitive rules, affiliative rules and emotive rules. These rules are highlighted in Table 8.2.

The examples of heuristics associated with Janis's model highlight how decisions are made using the RDP model rather than a traditional model of decision-making. The mental process of heuristics highlights the failure of traditional models of decision-making. Decision-makers in TransEuropean use their experience to make decisions, rather than analytical strategies. The yield managers use situational assessment and mental stimulation to generate a specious course of action rather than to compare all options analytically.

The distinction of decision-making types at different levels has been examined by Rasmussen (1983). He distinguished skill-based behaviour, which runs mostly automatically; rule-based behaviour, which operates through the application of consciously chosen from fully pre-programmed rules; and knowledge-based behaviour, under which all sorts of conscious problem-solving are grouped. This three-level decision making is compatible with risk homeostasis theory and zero-risk theory. The YO concludes he is in a zero-risk post, as all the decisions involved scenario management which were based upon rules behaviour, whereas the decision-making of the YE is a high-risk situation, as he is accountable for the decisions of others. The YEs used knowledge-based rules of behaviour in making decisions about yield. They were the managers who took decisions based upon the data supplied by the YOs. The YMs felt the only decisions they could take involved the hiring and firing of YEs, as they took most operational decisions. The YMs use mental processes to see if the scenarios will work rather than contrasting the strengths and weaknesses of the different options.

The search for an optimal solution requires decisions not to be evaluated until all the analysis is completed. This never happens, as it would be an infinite problem. Therefore, a recognitional strategy enables the yield manager to be continually prepared in decision-making, resulting in satisficing decisions.

YIELD MANAGEMENT: A CHAOS PARADIGM

Decision-making of all kinds rests on some assumptions about our ability to predict the future. Yield management is a process of forecasting; better and more accurate forecasting, it is hoped. Chaos theory suggests that a range of phenomena are inherently unpredictable. As a consequence, to try to foresee the future may be a futile and wasteful activity; we may need to take decisions knowing what we can forecast accurately rather than forecasting for inaccuracy. A chaotic situation (Jennings and Wattam, 1994) is characterized by the absence of regularities which prevent the accurate prediction of what will happen next. An important concept underpinning chaos theory is that of non-linearity. The chaos theory process proposes that events can be discrete and that, despite having full information about past events, the next occurrence may follow a pattern different from previous occurrences. Fundamental to the concept of chaos is the perspective that many events in both the physical and social worlds are complex and hence intrinsically difficult to predict with any certainty.

Chaos theory suggests that attention should be given to short-term forecasting and short-term decisions, as there is a chance of 'getting it right'. Therefore chaos theory points to the failings of traditional approaches and suggests that any faith in them is misplaced. However, in many hospitality organizations these methods are highly regarded and the ideas and solutions generated by such methods are afforded a higher status than those arrived at by less conventional methods. Chaos theory proposes that even decisions taken with full adherence to more traditional methods contain elements of guesswork and inaccuracy.

To illustrate the application of yield management in the hospitality industry, a case study is applied to two hotels: the Arnside Hotel and Alpine Lodge. The managers of these hotels were interviewed for approximately one to one and a half hours. The Arnside Hotel (the name of the hotel has been changed for reasons of confidentiality) is a 53-bedroom, three star hotel with extensive banqueting of up to 2,000 covers and four restaurants, including steak, carvery, novel cuisine and brasserie restaurants. The hotel has been recently refurbished, with all public areas upgraded. The hotel has just completed the development of an 18-hole golf course with clubhouse. Future plans include a leisure club with indoor swimming pool. The hotel is owned by Arnside Estates, with the Arnside being seen as the flagship hotel. Traditionally the hotel has had a focus on food and beverages, but with addition of 34 new bedrooms in the past year, the area of rooms management cannot be neglected. As the hotel is independently owned, it is part of a marketing consortium with a central reservations system.

Traditionally the hotel had followed a pricing policy parallel to that of their larger competitors. The rate was set at 10 per cent below those of the market leader. This strategy had been highly successful, as with only 19 bedrooms there was a greater demand for accommodation than supply. That situation changed with the additional bedrooms and the opening of a new three star hotel with 200 bedrooms nearby (the Alpine Lodge). Arnside Estates had financed the additional bedrooms through a bank loan; therefore, if the hotel was to repay the loan, the average room rate would have to stay at approximately £52.00.

The Alpine Lodge (the name of the hotel has been changed for reasons of confidentiality) decided to enter the market with a rate cutting package. The hotel had a price promise of 'at least 20 per cent cheaper than the competition'. The immediate dramatic effect of the Alpine Lodge following this policy was a decrease in occupancy for the Arnside. The Alpine Lodge kept up this policy for nine months; therefore the

Arnside was gradually losing business. The only way the hotel could counterattack was to match the Alpine Lodge's rates.

The medium-term effect of this strategy was that Arnside Estates now had cash flow problems. This resulted in Arnside Estates defaulting on the bank loan and eventually facing bankruptcy. The company secretary attributed the downfall of the hotel to the lack of a systems approach to rooms inventory. An unattributed reason for the Arnside Estates downfall could be the characteristic of overconfidence (Russo and Schoemaker, 1992). Cognitive reasons why Arnside Estates had overconfidence include:

- *Availability.* The hotel management team were having difficulty in imagining all the ways that events unfolded. This is called availability bias (Fischoff *et al.*, 1978): 'what's out of sight is often out of mind'. This is because we fail to envision important pathways in the complex net of future events, e.g. we would not forecast chaos.
- *Anchoring.* A second reason for overconfidence relates to the anchoring bias, a tendency to anchor on one value or idea and not adjust away from it sufficiently or appropriately.
- *Conformation.* A third cognitive reason for overconfidence concerns the hotel management mental search process. When making forecasts, the hotel management team leaned towards one perspective, and the natural tendency would be to seek support for their initial view rather than to look for refusal evidence. Unfortunately, the more complex and uncertain a decision is, the easier it is to find one-sided support. Realistic confidence requires seeking refusal evidence, as well as confirming evidence.
- *Hindsight.* Hindsight makes us believe that the world is more predictable than it really is. What happened often seems more likely afterwards than it appeared beforehand, since we fail to appreciate the full uncertainty that existed. Hindsight instils an illusion of omniscience.

The Alpine Lodge was able to use a yield management system to force a competitor hotel out of business. It achieved this through only discounting heavily on 15 per cent of rooms, inventory stock. The yield management system assisted the Alpine Lodge to take more effective decisions. The general manager of the Alpine Lodge commented that 'a yield management approach to rooms inventory adds structure to an otherwise chaotic situation'.

This overconfidence of the future is mentioned by Kimes (1996) in a study of People Express airline, which collapsed, partly at least, through a lack of a yield management system. The Alpine Lodge had a systematic approach to yield management which overcame overconfidence through the following attributes:

- *Accelerated feedback.* A yield management system allows instant feedback on scenarios of decisions about pricing and volume.
- *Counter-argumentation.* By using a team approach to yield management decisions, with a supporting organizational culture which allowed 'openness', overconfidence is reduced.
- *Murphy's Law.* 'If anything can go wrong, it will go wrong.' By using Murphy's Law to predict potential problems the Alpine Lodge yield management team had contingency plans.

YIELD MANAGEMENT: A CHAOS PARADIGM × RATIONAL/ NORMATIVE DECISION MODEL = LOGICAL INCREMENTALISM

A study of decision-making by Quinn (1980) identifies a decision-making process that is proactive, where decisions are made on an incremental basis. Compared to the normative model of decision-making, logical incrementalism is a process that lacks a clear structure, which is appropriate for an economic and political environment where a chaos theory approach is more suitable. In the context of this model, evaluation and choice are implicit in the development of the solution. Therefore, yield management is suggested as a logical incremental process of decision-making using the principles of rational decision-making but in a chaos situation. Decision-makers adapt to different situations depending upon a variety of factors. One of the most important attributes identified by Payne *et al.* (1993) is flexibility. The flexibility of organizations can determine their chances of success in a competitive and turbulent environment. Flexibility, at the individual level, flexibility to response (adaptivity), is generally viewed as a mark of intelligence.

A fundamental feature of the logical incremental model is the lexicographic heuristic. The lexicographic procedure determines the most important attribute and then examines the values of all alternatives on that attribute. The alternative with the best value on the most important attribute is selected, depending on the stage of the model in time. For example, the best decision is selected depending on the circumstances and timing of the decision. The yield manager is able to apply lexicographic heuristics within the context of environment of the decisions.

The application of the logical incrementalism model to the hospitality industry is reflected in the application of yield management by Falcon plc (the name of the company has been changed for reasons of confidentiality). The 'actors' mentioned in the case study were interviewed for approximately one to one a half hours. Falcon plc is a large multinational hospitality company with representation in over 30 countries worldwide. The range of hotels are classified into a selection of branded hotels, ranging from budget hotels to luxury hotels.

The European division decided to implement a yield management system. The project coordination was managed by a yield management executive (YME), working across all brands of the hotel chain. The first stage was the introduction of the yield management system for the budget brand of hotels. This was successful for the following reasons:

- Fixed price accommodation.
- All purchases of accommodation by consumers via a central reservation system; therefore 100 per cent central control of rooms inventory.
- Only one yield management executive reporting to the budget brand central reservations manager. Therefore decisions could be taken quickly.
- Hotel managers had no authority on managing rooms inventory, they were only concerned with delivery of brand standards.
- Yield management decisions were not concerned with pricing but with length of stay of the consumer.
- Holder of the largest market share in budgeted brand hotel sector.

As the implementation of a yield management system had been successful in the budget brand, the next stage was the implementation of a yield management system for the roadside motel brand. This brand had over 80 properties throughout Europe, but differed from the budget brand in the following ways:

- Motel managers had total responsibility for profit and loss and therefore made rooms inventory decisions.
- A higher degree of service than the budget brand.
- A wider range of food and beverage products.
- Price discrimination, e.g. discounting.
- Only 24 per cent of accommodation was purchased by consumers via a central reservations system; 76 per cent of reservations were made direct to the motel.

The motels were all identical within the brand, and this was a success factor for the roadside motel chain. Therefore the introduction of a yield management system would have to be different from that for the budget brand because of the difference in the product–service mix. A decision was made to appoint a rooms inventory supervisor (RIS) for every 25 motels. From the start, this caused problems because the RISs were based at the central reservations office. The relationship of the RISs with the general managers of motels was indifferent: some motel managers delegated authority to the RIS but some didn't. This led to conflict, as managers came to view the RIS function as another layer of bureaucracy. The yield management software did not integrate with the central reservation system; hence data had to be keyed manually into the yield management software. Communication between the RIS and the hotel manager was via a fax and telephone, which caused delay and resulted in slow decisions being taken. Because of these problems, the full benefits of yield management were not successfully attained.

This failure to adapt is highlighted by Payne *et al.* (1993), who state that being adaptive requires both various types of knowledge and the ability to execute strategies. Deficits in either of these lead to failure of adaptivity. The deficits in the types of knowledge displayed by the YME include difficulties in assessing the task and the context factors characterizing the decision environment, lack of knowledge of appropriate strategies, not being able to assess the effort and/or accuracy of a strategy in a particular situation and not knowing the desired accuracy–effort trade-offs.

The YME had difficulty in assessing the environment or the effect of implementing the yield management system in the branded roadside motel chain. The YME was unable to forecast the reaction of the hotel managers to the implementation of the yield management system, e.g. he showed a lack of understanding of human decision-making. This mistake is common in the implementation of new decision process, as individuals fail to adopt a strategy that considers the human dimension of decision-making with different environments. Research shows that managers over-generalize in the implementation of strategy for different situations (Ginossar and Trope, 1987) and they find the understanding of people difficult to predict, which results in systems failure. Baron (1988) argues that over-generalizing the applicability of normally reasonable judgements heuristics is a typical cause of failure of adaptivity in decision-making. That is, individuals often apply rules or heuristics that are generally useful across a wide variety of situations to a new situation where those rules may not be appropriate. Klayman and Ha (1987) argue that people rely overly on 'positive test strategy' that often works very well but can lead to systematic errors in some situations. They suggest that the use of more optimal strategies may require that the relationship between task variables and strategy performance be highly transparent.

Experts in a domain (e.g. yield management) often develop specific rules for recurring, highly familiar tasks. Holland *et al.* (1986) point out that such specific rules still compete with more general heuristics for application, rather than substituting for them. Therefore, the same experts who avoid biases by using a specific rule to deal with a highly familiar task fall prey to over-generalizing a more generic heuristic when dealing with a task containing unfamiliar elements (managers who have a degree of independence).

Other behavioural reasons why the implementation of a yield management system didn't succeed include the severe time pressures and heavy levels of distraction the YME was faced with. The reduction in time span of making any decision at whatever level will decrease the consideration given to that decision by the YME (Jennings and Wattam, 1994). This therefore increases the risk of taking inappropriate decisions. Time pressure is a very interesting task variable because managers often take important decisions under time pressure because they don't have enough time to make a considered decision, as happened in the YME case (Simon, 1981).

With the implementation of a new system within the roadside motel chain, hotel managers felt that too much information was been provided for them, which results in an information overload, and hence an increase in complexity and perceived uncertainty. Information overload occurs from the mechanism of selective information acquisition. Do hotel managers respond to complex information environments by focusing on the most important complex information or do they get distracted by irrelevant or less important information? Gaeth and Shanteau (1984) found that managers were adversely influenced by irrelevant factors, which sums up several comments from hotel managers themselves who were updated with information from head office, resulting in the 'couldn't see the forest for the trees' phenomenon.

The YME also had problems with interference from other senior managers within the organization, who wished to take control of the shorter-term decisions. These senior managers believed that a decision is critical, and hence yield management decisions were regarded as tactical. This process is typical of hierarchical organizations, and suggests that Falcon plc suffers from inertia.

Simultaneously, the yield management system was implemented in one luxury hotel in London (renamed the Royal Duke for purpose of confidentiality). The rooms division manager (RDM), with great enthusiasm, was allocated responsibility for the implementation of the yield management system within the hotel.

The Royal Duke is a five star, 200-bedroom hotel in Central London in a strong financial position, historically the hotel has also been very successful. But the forecasting of bed nights in the short to medium term is seen as very unpredictable. The demand for accommodation in London can be related to that of the Lornez (Jennings and Wattam, 1994) butterfly effect, where initial minor variations in input have a very major effect on outputs. This is sometimes referred to as sensitivity to initial conditions, because unless starting conditions are absolutely identical then outcomes will follow an unpredictable course. Hotels face widely fluctuating demand patterns (Kimes, 1989). Demand varies by season of the year, by day of the month and by time of the week. For example, any political changes in the world have a major effect on accommodation in London. These include a slump in demand from American consumers at about the time of the Gulf War in 1991 and the US Air Force bombings on Libya in 1986. The London market is also sensitive to changes in foreign exchange, especially from the American and Japanese markets. This demonstrates that planning in the medium to long term can be very difficult.

The hotel hoped to improve the system by implementing a yield management system. Hence, the Royal Duke hoped to manage fluctuating demand. Yield management in the London accommodation market can be used to help to temper some of the demand fluctuations by helping to increase occupancy during slow times and by increasing revenue during busy times. If the RDM knows when demand peaks and valleys are going to occur, she will be better able to plan for them.

The RDM concluded that in order to succeed in a 'chaos situation' for a yield management system, certain existing systems would need improvement. The RDM identified the following areas:

- *Booking patterns.* The hotel must be able to identify booking patterns by market segment. Good information systems are required to establish booking patterns.
- *Overbooking policy.* The hotel must have clear systems and procedures for dealing with overbooking.
- *Multiple-night stays.* A yield management system must be able to handle consumer accommodation patterns.
- *Employees.* For the success of implementation, employees must understand the advantages of a system, and the potential problems they will have to face, e.g. overbooking. Top management within the hotel must show a commitment to yield management.

The Royal Duke highlights some of the accuracy trade-offs that occur in the yield management process (Payne *et al.*, 1993). The local accuracy–effort assessments are reduced, as the RDM constructs heuristics on the spot, which are based on local momentary accuracy–effort assessments. When an individual notes that all values on an attribute appear to be similar and shifts to another attribute, that in effect reflects a trade-off of the low benefits from continued processing of that attribute versus the costs. The local accuracy–effort assessments are avoided because of the systematic process of yield management decision-making (Huyton *et al.*, 1996).

One of the most important underlying concepts in decision-making psychology (Payne *et al.*, 1993) is the idea that individuals learn about the structure and risk of the task as they gather information, and that they may then change their processing to take advantage of what they have learned. People may, in fact, often begin working on a task using some approach that generally has proved successful for them in the past, knowing that they can adjust their processing as they learn. These notions of noticing and exploiting regularities are very similar to the idea of interrupts and reactions to interrupts. For instance, once the RDM had begun to work on a particular goal, she did not blindly follow the original direction to completion. This reinforces yield management as a logical incremental model of decision-making.

A yield management system provides feedback on decisions, the effect of this at the Royal Duke was that this increased the use of normative decision strategies in a chaos paradigm (Payne *et al.*, 1993). Accurate feedback increases the number of acquisitions and marginally increases the time spent on information gathering in the beginning. Accurate feedback also leads to more alternative-based processing, which according to Payne *et al.* (1993) leads to managers being willing to take more risks.

The success of the yield management operation at the Royal Duke can be associated with the motivation of the RDM, who put effort into restructuring the yield management psychological decision processing so that a more accurate decision strategy could be utilized with only a reasonable amount of effort. The RDM could see the potential benefits of such a decision-making process; therefore, she put in extra effort to ensure the success of the yield management system.

YIELD MANAGEMENT AS A MODEL FOR DECISION-MAKING

The findings of this research have limitations owing to the small size of the sample, the number of people interviewed and the problems of qualitative research. Therefore any conclusions that are drawn must be within the framework of the constraints of the research.

Gore's (1995) study of models of decision-making of hotel managers was inconclusive because: 'there is some evidence to support Klein *et al*'s RDP model but support for the rational and bounded rational model is much stronger'.

What did this research conclude? The rational/normative model of decision-making seems to be inappropriate in the real world of yield management decision-making, as it doesn't consider the following identified aspects: time pressures, qualitative versus quantitative reasoning, political factors, social factors, information (availability, accessibility and processability), groupthink and the satisificing heuristics of decision-making. No evidence was found that supported the rational/normative model of decision-making.

The expert model was examined using Klein *et al*'s (1993) RDP framework because Klein *et al* suggest we make decisions based upon heuristics rather than the evaluation of options. This research supports this notion, as examples of heuristics that were identified include: career choice, concreteness, judgemental deficiencies, personal role biases, overconfidence, constraints (cognitive, affiliative and emotive) and hierarchy role heuristics (skill, rule and knowledge).

The environment for which we make decisions is discussed through a chaos paradigm, which, although not conclusive, supports the argument that yield management allows hospitality managers a mechanism for making yield management decisions in a chaotic environment. An organization using yield management may have a competitive advantage.

The final model considered is that of an equation model: a chaos paradigm $\times$ rational/normative decision model = logical incrementalism. This model states that we take decisions in a chaos vacuum, for which yield management is seen to be a rational/normative decision model. But as managers do not take decisions using that model because of heuristics, it is proposed that the yield management process is that of 'logical incrementalism'.

As with Gore's (1995) study, the results are subjective and a further larger study of decision-making in the hospitality industry is required. Yield management allows hospitality managers to engage in analytical decisions about inventory, but the environment of decision-making plays a greater influence on management heuristics than any system of decision-making.

REFERENCES

Ackoff, R. L. (1981) 'The art and science of mess management'. *Interfaces,* **11**(1), 20.
Arnold, J., Robertson, I. T. and Cooper, C. L. (1991) *Work Psychology.* London: Pitman.
Baron, J. (1988) *Thinking and Deciding.* Cambridge: Cambridge University Press.

Boella, M. (1996) 'Legal implications of yield management'. In I. Yeoman and A. Ingold (eds), *Yield Management, a Strategy for Service*. London: Cassell.

Fischoff, B., Slovic, P. and Lichtenstein, S. (1978) 'Fault trees: sensitivity of estimated failure probabilities to problem representation'. *Journal of Experimental Psychology: Human Perception and Performance*, **4**, 330–44.

Gaeth, G. J. and Shanteau, J. (1984) 'Reducing the influence of irrelevant information on expected decision makers'. *Organisational Behaviour and Human Performance*, **33**, 263–82.

Ginossar, G. and Trope, Y. (1987) 'Problem solving in judgement under uncertainty'. *Organisational Behaviour and Human Decision Processes*, **39**, 23–51.

Gore, J. (1995) 'Hotel managers' decision making: can psychology help?' *International Journal of Contemporary Hospitality Management*, **7**(2/3), 19–23.

Handy, C. B. (1985) *Understanding Organisations*. London: Penguin Books.

Hegarty, M., Just, M. A. and Morrison, I. R. (1988) 'Mental models of mechanical systems: individual differences in qualitative and quantitative reasoning'. *Cognitive Psychology*, **20**, 191–236.

Holland, J. H., Holyoak, K. J., Nisbett, R. E. and Thagard, P. R. (1986) *Induction: Processes of Influence, Learning and Memory*. Cambridge, MA: MIT Press.

Huyton, J., Peters, S. and Yeoman, I. S. (1996) 'The implementation of a yield management system for the hotel industry'. In I. Yeoman and A. Ingold (eds), *Yield Management, a Strategy for Service*. London: Cassell.

Janis, I. L. (1982) *Victims of Groupthink*. London: Houghton Mifflin.

Janis, I. L. (1989) *Crucial Decisions: Leadership in Policy Making and Crisis Management*. New York: Free Press.

Jennings, D. and Wattam, S. (1994) *Decision Making: an Integrated Approach*. London: Pitman.

Kimes, S. (1989) 'The basics of yield management'. *Cornell Hotel and Restaurant Quarterly*, **29**(4), 15–19.

Kimes, S. (1996) 'Yield management: an overview. In I. Yeoman and A. Ingold (eds), *Yield Management, a Strategy for Service*. London: Cassell.

Klayman, J. and Ha, Y. (1987) 'Confirmation, disconformation and information in hypothesis testing'. *Psychological Review*, **94**, 211–88.

Klein, G. A., Orasnu, J., Calderwood, R. and Zsambok, C. E. (1993) *Decision Making in Action: Models and Methods*. Norwood: Albex Press.

Likert, R. (1961) *New Patterns of Management*. New York: McGraw-Hill.

Mintzberg, H. (1973) *The Nature of Managerial Work*. New York: Harper & Row.

Orkin, E. (1990) *Yield Management*. Orlando, FA: Educational Institute of the American Hotel and Motel Association.

Payne, J. W., Bettman, J. R. and Johnson, E. J. (1993) *The Adaptive Decision Maker*. Cambridge: Cambridge University Press.

Quinn, J. B. (1980) *Strategies for Change: Logical Incrementalism*. New York: Irwin.

Rasmussen, J. (1983) 'Skills, rules and knowledge: signals, signs and symbols, and other distinctions in human performance models'. *IEEE Transactions on Systems, Man, and Cybernetics*, **3**, 257–68.

Russo, J. E. and Schoemaker, P. J. H. (1992) 'Managing overconfidence'. *Sloan Management Review*, **33**(2), 7–17.

Simon, H. A. (1955) 'Rational choice and the structure of the environment'. *Psychological Review*, **63**, 129–38.

Simon, H. A. (1981) *The Sciences of Artificial*. Cambridge, MA: MIT Press.

Slovic, P. (1972) 'From Shakespeare to Simon: speculation – and some evidence – about man's ability to process information'. *Oregon Research Institute Bulletin*, **12**, 3.

Stewart, R. (1982) *Choices of the Manager*. New York: McGraw-Hill.

Swannel, J. (1986) *The New Little Oxford Dictionary*. Oxford: Oxford University Press.

Tetlock, P. E. (1985) 'Accountability: the neglected social context of judgement and choice. *Research in Organisational Behaviour*, **7**, 297–332.

Tversky, A. and Kahneman, D. (1973) 'Judgement under uncertainty: heuristics and biases'. *Science*, **185**, 1124–31.

Tversky, A., Sattath, S. and Slovic, P. (1988) 'Rational choice and the framing of decisions'. *Journal of Business*, **59**, 251–78.

Yates, J. F. (1992) *Risk-taking Behaviour*. Chichester: Wiley.

9

Productivity and Yield Management

Una McMahon-Beattie, Anthony Ingold and Darren Lee-Ross

INTRODUCTION

The need to increase productivity in hospitality has once again been drawn to the attention of the industry by the McKinsey Report (1998), which estimated that labour productivity in the UK hotel sector is currently around 53 per cent of the US level and 60 per cent of the French level. Yield management (YM), with its potential to increase profit through an analytical and systematized intelligence of a company's customer base, market characteristics and capacity, has been identified as one method of improving productivity (Ingold and Lee-Ross, 1999). Given the fact that the process of managing yield has been seen as 'basically a human activity' (Yeoman and Watson, 1996), this chapter examines the potential of YM to increase the productivity of hotel front office staff. Focusing on the corporate sector, where interest in and application of YM is greatest (Donaghy and McMahon-Beattie, 1998), it presents the findings of an exploratory, qualitative investigation into the views of front office managers on the use of YM as a formal means of raising productivity levels.

A DECLINE IN SERVICE INDUSTRY PRODUCTIVITY

Since the late 1980s it has been well documented that the productivity of the service industry is a source of concern for Western economies (Elfing, 1989; Medlik, 1989; Johns, 1996). In our present post-industrial economy, manufacturing has been replaced by the service industry, with hospitality and tourism representing one of its most important sectors. During the same period there was an increasing interest in the concept of YM. Developed by American Airlines after deregulation in the late 1970s (Cross, 1997), it had begun to be adopted in the hotel industry around the mid-1980s. At this time the industry was being confronted with excess capacity, severe short-term liquidity problems and increasing business failure rates (Donaghy *et al.*, 1995). Major chains such as Hyatt, Marriott, Quality Inn and Radisson endeavoured to redress these problems by adopting YM. As such it is likely that the interest in both productivity and YM in hospitality derives from the current fiercely competitive market situation.

DEFINITION AND MEASUREMENT OF PRODUCTIVITY

There are a plethora of definitions of productivity, most of which derive from manufacturing. 'Manufacturing products have a tangible existence as well as an economic one and the economic concept of productivity in terms of wealth generation is easy to grasp' (Stewart and Johns, 1996). At its simplest, Prokopenko (1987) states that the 'concept is always the ratio of output to input, a simple equation of resource conversion'. However, he warns that productivity means different things to different people. Heap (1992) goes further, to suggest that 'most people when faced with the term would have some understanding of its use but would be hard pressed to offer a definition'. This is particularly true in relation to productivity in the service industry sector. Researchers (Jones and Lockwood, 1989; Witt and Witt, 1989) have established that the features and characteristics of services (intangibility, perishability, simultaneity and heterogeneity) have limited the evolution of a universally accepted definition of productivity. Johns (1996) illustrates this point clearly by arguing that 'A "good" service is not like a "good" car, house or tractor. A service such as a financial transaction, a successful purchase or a session at the hairdressers has a degree of "utility" but the encounter itself (for which the customer pays) has no utility and indeed exists only in the customer's mind.' However, Riley (1999) contends that the concern with the nature of the output of services is misplaced. He supports the view that hotels are essentially 'production units' producing clean rooms, meals, drinks and interpersonal interactions, all of which can be counted. The issues of intangibility and the nature of services are a 'red herring' and are only of real importance on the input side. 'It is the output that drives the input not as in the manufacturing model' (Riley, 1999). As such, at operational level in the hotel, it could be argued that since individuals put in their time and effort and utilize resources, it would make sense to regard productivity as outputs (such as meals, drinks, reservations taken), divided by inputs (such as labour time, labour cost, raw material, energy). If this is the case, then productivity in a YM system might easily be measured, for example, by the amount of sales front office staff make during a particular period. However, this would not be done on the basis of occupancy or room rate achieved, where the implicit assumption is that all room nights are beneficial to the hotel regardless of rate. To be effective, the productivity measure would have to take into account sales made on high, medium and low demand days.

INDUSTRY FEATURES HINDERING PRODUCTIVITY IMPROVEMENT

According to the McKinsey Report (1998), there are a number of factors which hold the UK hotel industry back from achieving productivity improvements. These include the predominance of old hotel stock, low penetration of chain hotels and high construction costs for maintenance or building of new hotels. The report recommends that planning schedules for new hotels need to be shorter and greater governmental support for new hotels. Ingold and Lee-Ross (1999) state that these are potentially excellent developments but only corporate hotels 'have the expertise and office abilities to take benefit from these'. They argue that the managers of small independent hotels, a sector which represents the largest number of all hotels in UK, only have a limited understanding of what productivity means. Supporting this view, Lowe (1992) and Ingold (1993) have shown that these hoteliers have much more important objectives than productivity. However, limited understanding of productivity is not confined to this sector. Various reports (Witt and Witt, 1989; Witt and Clark, 1990; NEDC, 1992) have highlighted the fact that hoteliers in general lack the expertise and time to devote to productivity improvement. Indeed, their 'being there, hands-on' style makes them reluctant to spend time on paper work and figure work (Guerrier and Lockwood, 1989). To highlight this further, studies of the use of YM in hotels (Bradley and Ingold, 1993; Donaghy *et al.*, 1997a, 1997b) would suggest that hoteliers even in large groups have only a limited grasp of the factors that affect productivity.

Importance of Labour as an Input

Yeoman *et al.* (1996) have stated that hotel productivity can be affected by a number of factors, including labour, grade and type of hotel, product–service mix, the nature of technological systems and remuneration. Operationally, these tend to be highly interdependent and make it difficult to identify the effect of one particular influence. In practice, most organizations constrain their efforts to measuring and attempting to improve labour productivity. This is understandable, since the hospitality industry is labour-intensive. As Watson (1996) states, 'Service demand human input and productivity gains can only be achieved by increasing the productivity of individuals.' Much of the hospitality research has identified human resources and their management as a key factor in respect of productivity improvement. Training in particular has been seen as a key means of increasing productivity in the workplace (Jewell, 1993). Ranfti (1984) examined the relationship between training and productivity and noted the need for managers to devise a strategy to train effectively. As such, this study focuses on the ability of YM to make front office staff more productive and implicit in this is the need for effective training.

Productivity and Technology

There is no doubt that most product-orientated industries rely on automation and technology to achieve a more productive operation. However, the substitution of technology for human labour in an industry which prides itself on its successful customer–server interactions has always been treated with caution. The most conspicuous use of technology to improve productivity has been in the fast food sector and with developments such as 'cook–chill'. Yet computerized YM offers the opportunity for front office staff to maintain their customer–server interaction in the reservations process while improving their productivity by increasing the net yield of room sales. YM software allows for the efficient computer processing of the extensive data required for effective forecasting and the recommendation of appropriate rates for specific market segments on specific days. There is, however, a general assumption that new technology can deskill or take control away from the staff, with jobs becoming less skilled, more monotonous and more pressurized (MacVicar and Rodgers, 1996), thus resulting in a lowering of productivity by reducing morale and motivation. On the other hand, Lieberman (1993) has argued that a computerized YM system allows employees to make more informed decisions, thus empowering them. This view is supported by Donaghy (1996), who states that the eight managers interviewed in his study were of the opinion that their staff were much more involved in the planning and decision-making process and were more accountable for their decisions in a YM system. This resulted in employees who were more motivated and reduced staff turnover among front office employees. A similar effect was reported at British Midland Airways by Ingold and Huyton (1997) following the introduction of YM. Thus, with the potential of YM simultaneously to increase profit and improve the motivation of staff, it may be argued that the implementation of YM can result in increased productivity for the accommodation division.

However, great caution must be applied when measuring any impacts of technology on productivity. Wolf (1999) reports on studies which reviewed factors affecting productivity in the United States macroeconomy. He reports Greenspan (Chairman of the Federal Reserve) as stating on 28 July 1999 that 'American productivity growth has picked up over the past 5 years or so', citing as evidence 'Non-farm business productivity (on a methodologically consistent basis) grew at an average rate of a bit over 1% per year in the 1980's. In recent years, productivity growth has picked up to more that 2%, with the past year averaging about 2.5%.' In explanation Greenspan said that output had grown beyond what would normally be expected from the increased inputs of capital and labour. He suggests that synergies of new technologies had enhanced productive efficiencies. However, Gordon (1999) puts this apparent increase in productivity down to three factors: improved measurement of inflation, exceptionally rapid output growth and an exceptional growth in productivity in production of computers. Gordon (1999) argues that most of the apparent increase in productivity can be explained by cyclical and economic factors, leaving a real increase of only 0.3 per cent. This final 0.3 per cent can, he argues, be explained by the increased productivity in the production of computers. This was 18 per cent year-on-year from 1972 to 1995 and 42 per cent per year since then. Jorgensen and Stiroh (1999) argue that investment in computing has actually had little effect on productivity in the rest of the US economy. They state that computers have only substituted for other inputs; for example, other inputs of capital. This does not necessarily raise productivity.

Standardization, Productivity and YM

Riley (1999) has stated that 'The assumption that productivity is a function between the level of standardisation, the range of services offered, technological intervention and human capital has a common sense to it.' Greater standardization, he continues, would benefit productivity because the hotelier could employ less skilled staff, there would be an opportunity to mechanize and there would be greater opportunity to adjust resources to demand. It could be argued, however, that YM offers non-standardized hotels, with their wide range of products/services, an opportunity to increase their productivity. Since it more accurately predicts changes in the levels of customer demand, it allows the hotel manager to match human capital and related resources effectively with peaks and troughs in that demand. It also provides an opportunity for these hotels to customize their service range profitably. As Donaghy *et al.* (1995) have stated, 'In a hotel context, YM is concerned with the market sensitive pricing of fixed room capacity relative to specific market segments. The "goal" of YM is the formulation and profitable alignment of price, product and buyer.'

Strategies for Productivity Improvement

A number of different strategies for the improvement of productivity has been described in the literature. Johns and Wheeler (1991) have identified both contractive and expansive strategies specifically for the hospitality industry. Essentially, the aim of a contractive strategy is to reduce input while maintaining or increasing output, while the aim of an expansive strategy is to improve output while keeping inputs constant. Contractive strategies, they argue, are most suitable to back-of-house or production elements of hotel operations, with their emphasis on cost reductions. Expansive strategies are most suitable for front-of-house operations, with their aim being to increase sales revenue while holding costs down. In line with this, if hotel managers can utilize a YM system effectively with the same number of staff in order to maximize revenue, then, theoretically, there is an opportunity to improve productivity.

Heap (1992) encourages a 'top-line' approach which involves all the functions of management and the personnel of an organization. He asserts that improving productivity is not about finding faults and imposing solutions on an unwilling workforce but management and staff working together to build an organization that treats staff with respect and uses their enthusiasm and interest in partnership. As such, if a YM system can incorporate employees in the decision-making process and can contribute to the active development of staff in the form of training, it can potentially improve productivity.

An alternative view is that of Pickworth (1994), who identified three broad approaches to improving operational productivity. First, there are the 'problem-orientated' approaches, which centre on the identification of problems and the manner in which obstacles can be overcome in order to increase productivity. Second, there are 'systems-orientated' approaches, which involve ways in which the service delivery system can be optimized; for example, by greater emphasis on team building, group dynamics and employee participation. Third, 'capacity-orientated' approaches are designed to help to align supply and demand. These may include such things as increased training in sales techniques, flexible working practices and use of empowerment. Indeed, Van der Hoeven and Thurik's (1984) study of European hotels concluded that one factor that influenced productivity was advance bookings, since these enabled managers to plan and match supply and demand. The use of YM would fit well into this third general approach, since it allows the hotelier to make more accurate forecasts of future levels of demand and to match that demand with appropriate labour and materials supply.

METHODOLOGY

In order to examine the effect of YM on the productivity of front office staff, this exploratory research took the form of in-depth interviews with front office managers from one national and one international hotel chain in Northern Ireland. As direct line managers, it was felt that these individuals would be in the best position to observe the effects of YM on the staff who operated the system. Hotel A was a five-star, city centre property, and Hotel B was a four-star unit situated in the country. They both offered a wide range of products and services to business and leisure travellers and both hotels were recently constructed and purpose-built. Formal YM systems have been in operation in the respective hotel chains for at least five years and both managers had at least ten years of experience in front office management. The managers were interviewed with regard to the YM system operating in their hotels, their understanding of productivity and its management in their companies, and YM's ability to raise productivity levels. The interviews lasted two hours, were taped, transcribed verbatim and analysed by theme.

FINDINGS AND DISCUSSION

The front office managers interviewed displayed a sound knowledge of the concept of YM and had received formal YM training carried out by personnel from their own head offices. They recognized that management's understanding of YM is as an essential component of a successful system. Both hotels used *Fidelio* software and the manager in Hotel A was able to point out that this was fundamentally a rate management system and not a YM system. However, this level of knowledge and awareness was not evident in relation to their understanding of the concept of productivity. They defined it vaguely as follows:

> Getting the last out of your system and staff and to do that you have got to know your business. (Manager, Hotel A)

> Making the best of what you've got from everything not just your staff. (Manager, Hotel B)

While staff and their training were identified as the most important factors in increasing the performance of front office, neither manager could offer any details of specific company productivity strategies or ratios used as 'productivity measures' in the hotel in general or in the front office in particular. When the front office manager of Hotel B was asked how he identified 'low productivity', he stated: 'By having a chat with staff and by checking their competency sheet.' These findings would appear to confirm the findings of previous research (Witt and Witt, 1989; Witt and Clark, 1990; NEDC, 1992): that hotel managers possess a general lack of understanding and expertise in relation to productivity management.

The managers indicated that YM had contributed significantly to increased revenue in their units. Both were unable to quantify this in real terms but they felt that they were in a good position to judge this since they had both worked in non-YM hotels in the past. They stated that operation of their YM systems did not require any more staff than would be required in a traditional front office. Accepting their professional judgement, it would appear that YM is a successful expansive strategy which can increase output (revenue in accommodation) while keeping inputs (labour) constant. This is an obvious area for further research. While many software houses and management consultants have made claims of guaranteed percentage increases in revenue, the likely contribution of YM has yet to be quantified by independent researchers.

As indicated above, both managers regarded their staff as having a central role in their YM system. Staff, they agreed, appeared to be more motivated, and the manager of Hotel A could identify certain members of her staff who seemed 'to work harder and achieve better results' after YM training. Indeed, training was viewed by both managers as essential for the effective operation of a YM system. Staff at Hotel A received three weeks of intensive initial training on joining the hotel. This includes all aspects of front office operations and the *Fidelio* system. In Hotel B ongoing YM training is given by the front office manager himself and two departmental trainers. As such, it could be argued that training of staff in YM systems is a key means of increasing productivity. Donaghy *et al.* (1997b) have argued for the need for 'tailored' YM training specific to each individual unit and the needs of its employees. Both companies appear to be achieving this through the head office training of key managers and the on-site and ongoing training of front office staff.

With regard to the use of incentives, both companies were using the output from *Fidelio* to award financial bonuses and star bonds/vouchers for use in major high street stores. For example, the head office of Hotel B has initiated a scheme which measured the percentage of no-shows against the percentage of revenue achieved. However, neither manager saw the use of these incentives as part of any formal company productivity strategy. Once again, this highlights their lack of awareness of productivity management techniques.

In line with Pickworth's (1994) 'capacity-orientated approach' to productivity, both managers pointed out that the forecasting function of a YM system had allowed the hotel to determine required staffing levels for periods of high and low demand. Indeed, the manager of Hotel B stated that the forecast produced by front office had considerable impact on the level of staffing subsequently used in other areas of the hotel, such as food and beverages and housekeeping. Additionally, both managers commented that they felt that staff were more 'empowered' in the current system. While they must generally stay within the rate offered by the system, they were encouraged to get clearance to override the system if they felt that rates were too high or too low for the level of business. As a result, staff had more accountability for the rates achieved by front office. This confirms the findings of Lieberman (1993) and Donaghy (1996).

CONCLUSIONS

Although this is only a preliminary study, it seems that the hotel managers interviewed did have a clear understanding of the concept of yield management, and this is encouraging. However, it is also true that the managers were unsure of any clear definition of productivity and hence probably of the importance of productivity to their type of organization. This seems little changed from the findings of a UK national survey by Ingold *et al.* in 1993 and gives some cause for concern. It seems reasonable to argue that YM may well contribute to front office productivity, in certain types of hotel at least. With the reservations over definitions and measurement of productivity in mind, the authors consider that this is an issue worthy of further research. Linked to this is the important issue of the role of staff training and incentives, since employee inputs and staff costs are almost certainly major players in the input/output equations for front of house productivity. The role of technology also needs to be explored, particularly in the light of the work of Gordon (1999) discussed above. It is also not yet clear at what point/size of hotel it is worth implementing a computerized YM system rather than using a paper-based method. The authors are continuing with this research.

REFERENCES

Bradley, A. and Ingold, A. (1993) 'An investigation of yield management in Birmingham hotels'. *International Journal of Contemporary Hospitality Management*, **5**(1), 13–16.

Cross, R. (1997) *Revenue Management: Hard Core Tactics for Market Domination*. London: Orion Business Books.

Donaghy, K. (1996) 'An investigation of the awareness, current impact and potential implication of yield management among hotel managers'. Unpublished DPhil Thesis, University of Ulster.

Donaghy, K., McMahon, U. and McDowell, D. (1995) 'Yield management: an overview'. *International Journal of Hospitality Management*, **14**(2), 139–50.

Donaghy, K. and McMahon-Beattie, U. (1998) 'The impact of yield management on the role of the hotel general manager'. *Progress in Tourism and Hospitality Research*, **4**, 217–28.

Donaghy, K., McMahon-Beattie, U. and McDowell, D. (1997a) 'Yield management practices'. In I. Yeoman and A. Ingold (eds), *Yield Management: Strategies for the Service Industries*, London: Cassell.

Donaghy, K., McMahon-Beattie, U. and McDowell, D. (1997b) 'Implementing yield management: lessons from the hotel industry'. *International Journal of Contemporary Hospitality Management*, **9**(2), 50–4.

Elfing, R. D. (1989) 'The main features and underlying causes of the shift to services'. *Services Industry Journal*, **19**(3), 337–56.

Gordon, R. (1999) 'Has the new economy rendered the productivity slowdown obsolete?' http://faculty-web.at.nwu.edu/economics/gordon/researchhome.htm

Guerrier, Y. and Lockwood, A. (1989) 'Flexible working in the hospitality industry: current strategies and future potential', *Journal of Contemporary Hospitality Management*, **1**(1), 11–16.

Heap, J. (1992) *Productivity Management: a Fresh Approach*. London: Cassell.

Ingold, A. (1993) Report of two seminars to explore productivity in hotels – November. Unpublished data.

Ingold, A. and Huyton, J. R. (1997) 'Yield management and the airline industry'. In I. Yeoman and A. Ingold (eds), *Yield Management: Strategies for the Service Industries*. London: Cassell.

Ingold, A. and Lee-Ross, D. (1999) 'Productivity: panacea or pain?' *The Hospitality Review*, **1**(3), 55–7.

Ingold, A., Yeoman, I. and Peters, S. (1993) Unpublished research on productivity in hotels.

Jewell, B. (1993) *An Integrated Approach to Business Studies*. London: Pitman.

Johns, N. (ed.) (1996) *Productivity Management in Hospitality and Tourism. Developing a Model for the Service Sector*. London: Cassell.

Johns, N. and Wheeler, K. L. (1991) 'Productivity and performance measurement and monitoring'. In R. Teare and A. Boer (eds), *Strategic Hospitality Management*. London: Cassell.

Jones, P. and Lockwood, A. (1989) *The Management of Hotel Operations*, London: Cassell.

Jorgenson, D. and Stiroh, K. (1999) 'Information technology and growth'. *American Economic Review*, **89**(2), 109–15.

Lieberman, W. H. (1993) 'Debunking the myths of yield management'. *Cornell Hotel and Restaurant Administrative Quarterly*, **34**(1), 34–41.

Lowe, J. (1992) 'Locating the line: the front-line supervisor and human resource management'. In P. Blyton and P. Turnbull (eds), *Reassessing Human Resource Management*, London: Sage, pp. 148–68.

McKinsey (1998) *Driving Productivity and Growth for the UK Economy*, London: McKinsey Global Institute, McKinsey and Company.

MacVicar, A. and Rodgers, J. C. (1996) 'Computerised yield management systems: a comparative analysis of human resource management implications'. *International Journal of Hospitality Management*, **15**(4), 325–32.

Medlik, R. (1989) 'The main features and underlying causes of the shift to services'. *Tourism*, **61** (January/February), 13–18.

National Economic Development Council (NEDC) (1992) *Working Party on Competitiveness in Tourism and Leisure, Sub-Group Report: Costs and Manpower Productivity in UK Hotels.* London: HMSO.

Pickworth, J. (1994) 'A framework of the main variables influencing organisational productivity'. In B. Davis and A. Lockwood (eds), *Food and Beverage Management.* Oxford: Butterworth-Heinemann.

Prokopenko, J. (1987) *Productivity Management: a Practical Handbook.* Paris: International Labour Office.

Ranfti, R. M. (1984) 'Training managers for high productivity: the Hughes approach'. *National Review*, Spring, 24–31.

Riley, M. (1999) 'Redefining the debate on hospitality productivity'. Seminar Series No. 1, 11 February, Centre for Hospitality Productivity Research, School of Management Studies for the Service Sector, University of Surrey.

Stewart, S. and Johns, N. (1996) 'Total quality: an approach to managing productivity in the hotel industry'. In N. Johns (ed.), *Productivity Management in Hospitality and Tourism.* London: Cassell.

Van der Hoeven, W. H. M. and Thurik, A. R. (1984) 'Labour productivity in the hotel business'. *Services Industries Journal*, **2**(2), 161–73.

Watson, S. (1996) 'Productivity through people'. In N. Johns (ed.), *Productivity Management in Hospitality and Tourism.* London: Cassell.

Witt, C. A. and Clark, B. R. (1990) 'Tourism: the use of production management techniques'. *Services Industry Journal*, **10**(2), 306–19.

Witt, C. and Witt, S. (1989) 'Why productivity in the hotel sector is low'. *International Journal of Contemporary Hospitality Management*, **1**(2), 28–33.

Wolf, M. (1999) 'Not so new economy'. *Financial Times*, 4 August, 12.

Yeoman, I., Ingold, A. and Peters, S. (1996) Productivity in the hotel industry: a cognitive case study. In N. Johns (ed.), *Productivity Management in Hospitality and Tourism.* London: Cassell.

Yeoman, I. and Watson, S. (1996) 'Yield management: a human activity system'. In Proceedings of the First Annual Yield Management Conference, Walton Hall, Warwickshire, September.

10

Computerized Yield Management Systems: Lessons from the Airline Industry

Nick Johns

INTRODUCTION

The day-to-day capacity of many commercial services is strictly limited. This is especially true of airlines and hotels, because there are just so many seats on a particular flight or rooms in a given hotel on a particular night. As business competition intensifies, it becomes increasingly important to ensure that all of those seats or rooms are full, and that the occupiers have paid the maximum price that can be asked for them. This activity, called yield management, broadly exploits market forces. When demand fails to fill the available seats or rooms, the price must be lowered, to make them more attractive. In a situation of over-demand the price must be raised, to get the maximum revenue from the limited resource. Hence yield management has been summed up by Kimes (1989a, 1989b) as a technique which 'can help a firm sell the right inventory unit to the right type of customer, at the right time, and for the right price'.

This process is much more complicated than this simple analysis suggests, for a number of reasons.

- In order to balance booking status with available demand one needs to have an overview of booking status of all flights or hotel rooms, updated in real time and available at all the outlets where booking takes place.
- In order to make precise judgements about available demand one must also convert overall sales patterns into current demand in real time and make this information available at all booking outlets.
- The optimum mathematical solution to a yield management problem will be a point on a smooth continuum of possible seat or room prices, but in practice there have to be published tariffs of specified prices. It is possible to update these in response to demand, but only in the longer term (3–6 months).

140

● Different categories of guests expect different rights, depending upon the price they have paid. In principle, if a business flight passenger cancels, ideal yield management practice should be to replace him or her with another business class passenger, so that there is no loss of revenue. In practice, airlines only overbook seats with tourist class or saver fare passengers who are less likely to damage business if they are bounced off the plane. SAS recently guaranteed that members of its Eurobonus (frequent flier) Scheme who booked business class 48 hours ahead would get on the plane, even if only in economy class (Bray, 1999).

Thus it is easy to see the role that information and communications technology can play in yield management, in transmitting data between a central processing point and numerous sales and booking outlets. Nowhere has this been more important than for the airline industry, whose members commonly operate and book on a global scale, and have faced steadily mounting competition since the late 1970s.

The contribution that computerized yield management systems (CYMS) could make to capacity management has been recognized by a number of service industries, especially the hotel sector. Such systems have been hailed as a potential aid to all levels of personnel, providing organizations with consistent sales decisions and a reliable and robust tariff sttructure (Kasavana and Brooks, 1991; Jauncey *et al.*, 1995; Cho and Connolly, 1996; Sumner and Sellers, 1996).

Yield management has been described as a 'dark science' (Anon, 1990), suggesting a role somewhere between high technology and the black arts. Lucy (1995) classifies yield management problems as *semi-structured*, because they represent a mixture of mathematically accessible problems and intuitive decision-making. The basic parameters of a yield management problem can be quite easily identified, allowing them to be expressed and ultimately tackled in a structured way. Such rules relate to the inventory levels to be made available, the associated rates and cost factors and the market segments served. However, 'the' yield management problem actually changes continuously (in effect it changes as each new guest enters or leaves the system), making its solution a moving target. In addition, many human factors must be taken into account, including the actual setting of prices (which may depend partly on outside factors such as company policy) and the way real guests are handled (with respect to overbooking, 'perks' and so on). These issues destructure yield management problems, so that, on the one hand, they are too complicated to be accomplished manually by booking staff and, on the other, they are too sensitive to be left wholly to technology. For its most effective use, yield management requires a balanced interaction between machine and operator.

Here too the airlines have important experience to impart, since they have often had to achieve this balance with personnel over whom they have no control (travel agents, etc.). One solution to this has been to centralize yield management, and link it to a master database (e.g. a central reservation system, discussed below). However, this solution is less effective for hotels, which frequently have to make both centralized and local decisions. In order to do this it is necessary to offer a centralized, suggested yield management solution, which can, if necessary, be overridden locally, by intuition or by locally based yield management software.

This chapter reviews the development and application of CYMS in the airline industry and discusses the role and function of such systems in hotel organizations. In most cases, yield management is achieved by modular software, integrated with the large databases from which the information for calculations is derived. Thus the initial

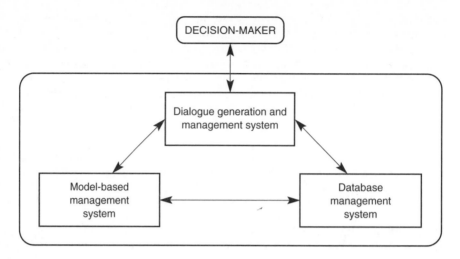

Figure 10.1 The main components of a DSS

section describes such software (known as decision support systems) and discusses how it can contribute to operational management decisions on a day-to-day basis.

DECISION SUPPORT SYSTEMS

Most CYMS are achieved through modular computer programs, which work in a concerted way with the large databases in which market and capacity information is stored. These program modules are classed as decision support systems (DSSs). Their task is to apply algebraic and statistical techniques to the analysis of information. Keen and Scott-Morton (1978) define a DSS as 'a coherent system of computer-based technology (hardware, software, and supporting documentation) used by managers as an aid to their decision making'. DSSs have three primary objectives:

- to assist managers in the making of decisions to solve semi-structured problems;
- to support managers' judgement, rather than try to replace it;
- to improve managers' decision-making effectiveness, rather than its efficiency.

DSSs deal with the structured aspects of a semi-structured problem and rely upon human input in the form of individual or collective judgements to address unstructured aspects and provide a final, workable solution. To deal with the structured aspects of a decision, a DSS needs three fundamental components:

- A dialogue generation and management system (DGMS) that enables the user to interact with the DSS.
- A model base management system (MBMS) that enables the system user to explore the decision situation and the range of alternative solutions to the problem. This is achieved through the use of a model based on algorithmic mathematics aligned to a range of procedures and management protocols.

Figure 10.2   Optimization model and variables

- Database management systems (DBMS) that enable the DSS to draw upon data contained within either an interfaced or integrated database and to make available these data to the user of the systems who may require it in order to inform the decision situation. Within an airline, this database is normally the central reservation system (CRS, discussed below). In hotels it is usually the property management system (PMS), linked to the front office software. The database collects, stores and maintains information about inventory levels, availability and the range of prices to be considered. It usually holds vast banks of historical data about previous demand patterns.

These three components of the DSS interact with one another as shown in Figure 10.1, the DNMS accessing the data, the MDBS analysing it, while users interact with it via the DGMS. The DSS provides the user either with a series of questions and answers or with numerical or graphical outputs that are directly related to the problem under interrogation.

The MBMS allows the user to explore the decision situation, by way of a simulation model that aims to mimic the real world situation. It can recalculate the data on an interactive basis, in a 'what-if' analysis which gives rise to a series of scenarios. From these can be derived a likely set of outcomes or likely results from the implementation of each possible decision. As this occurs, the DBMS feeds into the MBMS the variables it needs to respond to the user's queries. Generally speaking these can be classified as in Figure 10.2.

Thus yield management optimization models use much the same type of information that a human decision-maker would need to set room rates on a scientific basis. This information includes levels of forecast demand, cancellation information, no-shows, rules for restricting the sale of discounted rooms, estimations of revenue, displacement of transient demand caused by group demand, recommendation and control reservation availability on the basis of length of stay and daily rates and so on. The difference between computerized and manual calculation is simply the volume and speed with which the data can be handled.

CYMS cannot replace human decision-makers. Their role is to enable busy managers to cope with the vast quantities of information needed to make accurate predictions of supply and demand. Because they can model outcomes, CYMS allow users to explore complex decisions using real data. Used in this way, a DSS can often build users' confidence, allowing them to justify their own intuitive judgement, but at the same time reducing the risk and uncertainty normally associated with decision-making. In time this can improve a user's decision-making skills.

CYMS IN THE AIRLINE INDUSTRY

Many of the developments, both in yield management theory and in its practical application through computerized systems, have come about in the airline industry. Yield management (or capacity management as it is often referred to in this industry) has risen rapidly in importance since the late 1970s and today is absolutely essential for profitable operation of most of the world's airlines. Historically, adoption of yield management in the airline industry has been driven by the following factors:

1. Deregulation of many airlines and routes, which began in the late 1970s in the USA and has subsequently spread to the rest of the world, producing a rapid increase in the numbers of airline operators and routes serviced. This expansion intensified competition, bringing a need to manage the revenue yield from an ever-growing stock of seats in an increasingly hostile market environment.
2. The 1991 Gulf War drastically reduced the number of US passengers flying to the rest of the world, and its knock-on effects were felt by all airlines (it also had a very damaging effect on other travel-related markets, such as the hotel industry).
3. Low cost carriers appeared in the wake of deregulation, first in the US domestic market and later (coinciding with the end of the Gulf War) among the international airlines. They drove down prices at the lower end of the market, making it necessary for all airlines to introduce saver flight fares. Thus airlines had to manage not only more routes and seats, but also a widening range of fare tariffs, offered to different market segments, that were often travelling on the same aircraft.
4. The development of central reservation systems (CRS), which can manage bookings on a centralized basis, allowed airlines to assume greater control over the total reservation process, which had previously been decentralized. From the outset, CRS grew rapidly, ultimately developing into a handful of 'global distribution systems' (GDS). They permit an ongoing overview of real-time capacity and demand, and are therefore a major enabling factor in the management of airline capacity, and hence yield.

The development of airline-owned CRS can be traced back to the 1950s, when the first prototypes were introduced to automate the traditionally manual management of flight reservations. The first such CRS to go into commercial use was SABRE (Semi Automated Business Research Environment), which was developed by American Airlines in conjunction with International Business Machines (IBM). The initial function of this database was to enable the airline to keep track of its reservations in a central location. This objective was achieved successfully and was followed by the rapid introduction of more terminals, through which travel agents could access the system from remote sites, and gain direct access to inventory information. These terminals allowed travel agents to reserve airline seats more efficiently, because they no longer had to rely upon person to person telephone calls.

Today SABRE is a truly global system, with international accessibility, offering a wide range of products. Some 20,000 travel agents in 54 countries use the system, which is estimated to serve more than 130,000 terminals (Smith *et al.*, 1992). Each day SABRE takes 1.6 billion bookings for 740 airlines, and deals with 20 times this number of enquires about other travel-related products. The importance of SABRE to American Airlines was felt as long ago as the 1980s, when the owner company realized that it was making more money from operating the reservation system than from flying aeroplanes.

SABRE has been considerably extended beyond its original function of reservations management. It can now generate flight plans, schedule crews, track and monitor spare parts, manage cargo and integrate with a variety of DSSs to provide management information to several different travel-related industries. Many of the benefits from SABRE come from the creative way the company has used its information. The system is increasingly exploited by American Airlines to develop the decision-making capabilities of route inventory personnel.

The decision support capabilities of SABRE have been further aided by the formation of a dedicated team of professionals, known as the American Airlines Decision Technologies Team (AADT), who focus on developing and exploiting the system's information capabilities. The team have built innovative DSS software into the CRS, which they have called DINAMO (dynamic inventory and maintenance optimizer). DINAMO is a management support tool with which route inventory personnel can maximise daily revenue on each flight. It can access all the variables required for calculating yield management in an airline operation, including passenger demand, cancellations, no-show details and other characteristics of passenger behaviour. DINAMO itself is a complex optimization model that aims to replicate realistically the real world situation at any point in time given a specified set of operating conditions. This model allows the airline's route inventory management team to forecast expected yield on any particular flight with some degree of accuracy, in relation to current demand patterns. This information allows the relevant personnel to identify the most appropriate pricing strategies to be used in relation to the various market segments. Similar techniques are used by many of the world's airlines for managing inventory, and many airlines also rely upon the innovations of the AADT team to keep them up to date with technological advance and market fluctuations.

CYMS IN THE HOTEL INDUSTRY

Larger hotel operators are well aware of the principles of yield management and often use differential pricing to stimulate demand for their products. Typically, however, managers rely on their own wealth of local market knowledge in deciding whether or not to book out a room on a given night at a particular rate. Notwithstanding this, CYMS are increasingly being deployed by larger operators as a sales tool, providing valuable decision-support aid to managers within this task area.

A hotel-based CYMS needs to draw upon a vast quantity of information, much of which is stored within automated front office systems, in order to identify demand levels and booking patterns for the hotel's room stock. This information is both current and historical in nature but within a CYMS it becomes the basis for predictions of expected future demand. The system uses this information to match room supply to demand and then to a particular pricing strategy, in accordance with the hotel's yield management policy.

A sophisticated CYMS can track the sale of rooms for a particular night over a 60-day lead-in period. This process typically involves calculating and recalculating future booking demands and applicable rates for a given room on a daily basis as the situation changes. To track a 60-day lead-in, CYMS require a complex optimization model, similar in principle to those used by the airline industry. Kasavana and Brooks (1991) list a number of advantages of CYMS for hoteliers, which are summarized below.

Continuous monitoring of the booking situation is achieved via direct access to the information in the hotel's PMS. The CYMS tracks the actual level of booking in real time on a 24-hour, seven days a week basis. This historical and updated information can then be compared with expected and actual levels of business, producing a continuously updated forecast, which can be used by managers to reassess the situation if it so warrants.

Consistency of decisions in changing conditions is achieved with CYMS, which can exploit historical information to provide forecasts of future demand patterns. This can be used by reservations staff to identify likely levels of demand and appropriate rates to charge in accordance with pricing and yield management policy. This information helps to eliminate much of the guesswork normally associated with rate-setting, producing consistency among the decisions of different personnel within the organization.

Regarding information availability, the CYMS is able to draw upon vast quantities of information stored within itself and in the hotel PMS and report this in a variety of different preset or customizable styles. This may be used at both unit and head office level to inform management decisions on hotel policy and strategy. The reports can be classified as follows:

- *Market segment reports*. These provide information on customer mixes, with information provided to forecast demand patterns of particular market segments.
- *Calendar/booking graphs*. These graphic outputs present demand patterns of rooms based on particular nights and the volume of reservations achieved.
- *Future arrival dates and status reports*. These produce demand information on a daily basis. and contain information on a variety of forecasting information that can then be used by management to monitor and track the booking situation effectively.
- *Single arrival date history reports*. These reports indicate the hotel's actual trends in relation to daily reservation uptakes.
- *Weekly recap reports*. Contain information on the selling of rooms and the particular rates achieved on a weekly basis.
- *Room statistics tracking sheets*. These reports track the levels and numbers of no-shows, cancellations, turn a ways and walk-outs and can be used to enhance further the forecasting capabilities of the yield management personnel and the CYMS.
- *Performance tracking*. Trends, based on the historical and actual demand data contained within the PMS business trends, can be reported regularly from management use. This allows an organization to track its business and monitor the success of its yield management policy.

Thus CYMS offer hoteliers a unique opportunity to enhance revenue maximization capabilities, in much the same way as has occurred in the airline industry. As such, hoteliers should view CYMS as a useful addition to the growing array of technological tools that they now have at their disposal to help in the management of their businesses.

CONCLUSION

The advent of CYMS has enabled many operators to benefit from the application of yield management to their fixed inventory products in order to maximize revenue. As has happened in the airline industry, CYMS are set to become indispensable management tools for hotel operators, as the business becomes increasingly competitive and more dependent upon the maximization of revenue and profit. Within this context it is likely that CYMS will evolve to take a central role and will develop along ever more sophisticated lines, as they are already doing in the airline industry. The new systems will have more finely tuned optimization models, embodied within increasingly sophisticated DSS. Software will become increasingly sensitive to the industry's norms, the market segments served and the information needs of managers, as they seek optimum decisions for the way ahead. Growth in the use of CYMS will occur through greater integration of DSS with PMS and CRS and a greater degree of interfacing with global distribution systems and destination marketing systems. Undoubtedly the future will also bring integration with national tourism intranets and with the public domain, through the World Wide Web, which is currently growing in importance as a distribution channel for the travel and lodging market.

REFERENCES

Anon (1990) 'Yield management. Leaders shed light on the "dark science" '. *Hotel and Motel Management*, **85**, 88.

Bradley, A. and Ingold, A. (1993) 'An investigation of yield management in Birmingham hotels'. *International Journal of Contemporary Hospitality Management*, **5** (1), 13–16.

Bray, R. (1999) 'Mileage is worth collecting'. *Financial Times*, 6 May, 3.

Brotherton, B. and Mooney, S. (1992) 'Yield management progress and prospects'. *International Journal of Contemporary Hospitality Management*, **11** (1), 23–32.

Cho, W. and Connolly, D. J. (1996) 'The impact of information technology as an enabler on the hospitality industry'. *International Journal of Contemporary Hospitality Management*, **8** (1), 33–5.

Hank, R. D. *et al.* (1992) 'Discounting in the hotel industry: a new approach', *Cornell Hotel and Restaurant Administration Quarterly*, **31** (1), 15–23.

Jauncey, S., Mitchell, T. and Slamet, P. (1995) 'The meaning and management of yield in hotels'. *International Journal of Contemporary Hospitality Management*, **7** (4), 23–6.

Kasavana, M. L. and Brooks, R. M. (1998) *Managing Front Office Operations*, 5th edn. Lansing, Mich: Educational Institute of the American Hotel and Motel Association.

Keen, P and Scott-Morton, M. S. (1978) *Decision Support Systems*. Reading, MA: Addison-Wesley.

Kimes, S. (1989a) 'Yield Management: a tool for capacity constrained service firms'. *Journal of Operations Management*, **8** (1), 349–50.

Kimes, S.E. (1989b) 'The basics of yield management'. *Cornell Hotel and Restaurant Administration Quarterly*, **30** (2), 14–19.

Lucy, T. (1995) *Management Information Systems*, 7th edn. DP Publications. London: Edward Arnold.

MacVicar, A. and Rodger, J. (1995) 'Computerised yield management systems: a comparative analysis of the human resource management implications'. Paper presented to the Hospitality and Tourism Educators Conference, University of Gothenburg, Sweden, October.

Mcleod, R. (1993) *Management Information Systems*, 5th edn. New York: Macmillan Publishing Company.

Orkin, E. B. (1988) 'Boosting your bottom line with yield management'. *Cornell Hotel and Restaurant Administration Quarterly*, **27** (1), 52–6.

Peacock, M. (1994) Hospitality managers who love computers too little? An investigation into the relationship between management and advanced technological change. Paper presented to the Third Annual CHME Research Conference Proceedings, April, Napier University, Edinburgh, April.

Smith, B. C., Leimkuhter, J. F. and Darrow, R. M. (1992) 'Yield management at American Airlines'. *Interfaces*, **22**, 8–31.

Sumner, J. R. and Sellers, T. (1996) 'Hotel computer systems: valuable tool or missed opportunity?' *International Journal of Contemporary Hospitality Management*, **8**, (2), 36–9.

11

Revenue Management over the Internet: A Study of the Irish Hotel Industry

Breffni Noone and Neil Andrews

INTRODUCTION

Revenue management is the application of disciplined tactics that predict consumer behaviour at the micro-market level and that optimize product availability and price to maximize revenue growth (Cross, 1997). According to Cross (1997), companies can achieve substantial revenue gains by adopting a revenue-driven attitude and applying the seven core concepts of revenue management. One of the core concepts identified by Cross (1997) is to 'continually re-evaluate revenue opportunities'. In the context of hotel organizations, information technology (IT) provides a valuable opportunity to optimize revenue. One key area in which technology has enhanced hotels' ability to manage their revenue is the application of yield management systems (Mandelbaum, 1997). IT has also had, in recent years, a dramatic impact on the channels of distribution that are used to make the hotel product available to the consumer. While many of the advances have centred upon the development of, and connectivity with, airline global distribution systems (Emmer et al., 1993), the emergence of the Internet, and in particular the World Wide Web (WWW), has opened a new channel of distribution for hotel organizations. Not only does the WWW provide hotels with the opportunity to target their existing client base, it also opens a new market place and revenue enhancement opportunities. As stated by Murphy et al. (1996), the Internet and the WWW have begun to revolutionize the way in which consumers choose and reserve hotel accommodation.

While the Internet serves many purposes, including exposure of hotel properties at a global level, marketing and advertising, faster and better communications, a source of information on other hotels, clients and the industry in general (Van Hoof and Combrink, 1998), less attention has been focused on the use of the Internet as a distribution channel in the revenue maximization process. This chapter begins with a review of current literature relating to how the Internet can be, and is being, used for the purposes of revenue maximization and continues with an examination of how Irish hotels are employing the Internet for revenue maximization.

Given that the majority of hotels in Ireland are small and medium-sized organizations (SMHOs), the chapter also examines whether presence on the WWW bridges the gap between SMHOs and larger hotels in terms of access to the revenue opportunities afforded by representation in the global market place. For the purpose of the chapter, SMHOs are defined as those properties with fewer than 50 rooms.

CURRENT INTERNET USAGE

In 1995, 37 million people were estimated to have access to the Internet (Nielsen, 1995). In 1998, Smith and Jenner (1998) estimated the total number of Internet users to be 90 million, with Americans signing up to the Internet at a rate of more than one million per month. The latest NUA Internet Survey we have, distributed to subscribers by e-mail on 16 February 1999, puts the number on-line at 153.25 million, 87 million of those in the USA and 33.39 million in Europe. Usage is predominantly from the USA, although significant growth has been noted in Europe (especially the UK) and Asia (Connell and Reynolds, 1999).

A wide variety of studies have broadly agreed about the demographic characteristics of Internet users. According to Baker *et al.* (1999), more males than females, people with a higher economic status, those with a college education and whites are all more likely to use the Internet. They conclude that the profile of the typical Internet user matches extremely well with the business hotel's target market. Surveys also indicate that there has been an increase in Internet access from the home, particularly in the USA. Statistics from TravelWeb, for example, indicate that 68.5 per cent of people booking accommodation via its site use TravelWeb from home (*Hotels*, 1997). From a hotel marketer's point of view, this move towards accessing the Internet from home could represent an increase in potential leisure customers, as one of the predominant objectives when accessing from home is for entertainment, leisure and data gathering – the information a hotel provides via the WWW fits well into all three categories (Baker *et al.*, 1999). Hoffmann and Novak (1996) suggest that the demographics of Internet users are shifting over time, with the result that the Internet appears to be going more mainstream in its demographic make-up. This trend is likely to continue as the Internet moves towards critical mass as a commercial medium.

THE INTERNET AS A HOTEL DISTRIBUTION CHANNEL

A plethora of websites with travel information exists and the number is increasing (Connell and Reynolds, 1999). Hundreds of hotel companies have established themselves on the Web with their own websites or via a link from a third party such as TravelWeb (http://www.travelWeb.com) (Gilbert *et al.*, 1999). As of November 1996, 20 of the world's top 25 hotel chains had established websites (Hird, 1997). Hilton Hotels booked over $1 million in rooms in its first three months of on-line booking. Marriott also reported more than $1 million in Internet bookings in the first several months of offering an on-line booking capability (Hird, 1997).

The nature of the hospitality product makes it a prime candidate for marketing over the Internet (Baker *et al.*, 1999). As stated by Connelly *et al.* (1998), 'booking travel accommodations is a good fit for the Internet because travel is an information-based product and the Internet is full of information'. In fact, the first home pages were little more than electronic brochures, now referred to as 'brochureware'. Since that tentative start, businesses in all industries have embraced the Internet as a way to reach consumers and transact business (Connelly *et al.*, 1998).

The WWW offers the hotel industry a distribution channel that enables customers worldwide to book hotel rooms. The Internet as a distribution tool is open 24 hours a day, 365 days a year, it can provide multilingual sites and its speed of data transfer can be up to 100 times faster than viewdata (Richer, 1996; Gilbert *et al.*, 1999).

A number of surveys have reported a strong preference for the Web as a hotel information source and as a hotel booking medium. A survey by Yankelovich Partners suggests that hotel reservations are among the most attractive items for on-line purchases among people who have yet to purchase items on-line, followed closely by computer software, airline tickets and CDs and videos (Weber, 1997). Smith and Jenner (1998) state that although purchases of travel products currently represent a small proportion of overall Internet sales – around 6 per cent according to one estimate, or just 0.5 per cent of all travel and tourism spending according to another – the potential for the travel and tourism sector, more than many others, appears excellent. It is important to take into account that not all shoppers use the Internet for the actual purchase of a product or service, even though information obtained on the Web may have been the influencing factor. CyberAtlas reported the findings of a joint CommerceNet–Nielsen survey that found that 53 per cent of Internet users used the WWW to reach a purchase decision, but only 15 per cent of those surveyed completed their purchase on-line. This behaviour is typical of what has been observed in the hotel industry, where a significant number of consumers use the Internet to learn more about individual hotels and destinations and to conduct comparison shopping but make their booking through conventional channels (Connelly *et al.*, 1998). According to Wardell (1998), the number of people actually purchasing travel services via the Web is expected to increase more than tenfold over the next five years. Gilbert *et al.* (1999) state that the growth rate of the Web is estimated at about 50 per cent per month, with the number of sales doubling every 53 days. In recognition of this, the Hotel Industry Marketing Group (HMG) has warned that 'hotels must not ignore the Internet as a key source of business in the future' (*Caterer and Hotelkeeper*, 1996).

Marcussen (1997) highlights the fact that unlike hotel chain computerized reservation systems (CRSs) and the airline global distribution systems (GDSs), the WWW, in the context of hotel organizations, is so far mainly an information channel and to a lesser extent a sales channel. He attributes this primarily to 'issues in connection with payment for the services which are being sold or booked via the WWW [that] still have not been solved satisfactorily'. It is important that the customer is comfortable with electronic shopping if people are going to book hotel rooms via the Internet. Studies have indicated that the key concern that both hoteliers (Connelly *et al.*, 1998) and consumers (Connell and Reynolds, 1999) share in relation to the Internet is the issue of security. Consumers have been reluctant to supply credit card details over the Internet as they judge it to be risky and have a fear of breach of security (Graphics, Visualisation and Usability Centre's 1996 Consumer Survey of WWW users). However, Richer has suggested that it is easier for hackers to obtain credit card details passed over a cordless or mobile telephone (Gilbert *et al.*, 1999). Popular Web browsers, such as Netscape and Microsoft Explorer, have now incorporated secure payment encryption algorithms. Electronic cash has also been developed by Digicash (http://www.digicash.com) for secure payments over the Internet without having to transmit credit card details (Gilbert *et al.*, 1999).

According to Jupiter Communications (1997), as secure electronic transactions protocols are implemented, and as other aspects of the on-line payment infrastructure are developed, such as the proliferation of smart-card readers in households, consumer comfort levels with purchasing on-line will rise. They state that the revenues generated from on-line travel are increasing exponentially each year and predict that, by the end of the year 2002, $8.9 billion will be generated in online travel revenues, consisting of airline bookings revenues, non-air bookings and advertising revenues from travel sites. Non-air revenues, consisting mainly of hotel reservations and car rentals, are projected to grow from $31 million in 1996 to $938 million in 2000 and to $2.1 billion by the end of 2002. Forrester Research predicts that lodging revenues alone will grow from $345 million in 1997 to $2.9 billion by the year 2001 (Wada, 1997). Reinders and Baker (1997) predict that around a half of business travel and up to a third of single component leisure travel will be booked on-line by the year 2005.

From a marketing perspective the major benefit accruing to hotel organizations of presence on the Internet is the greater degree of interactivity that it affords than other communication media (Gilbert *et al.*, 1999). Organizations are embracing the opportunity to benefit from on-line direct-to-consumer distribution (French, 1998). This direct link to customers affords hotel organizations the opportunity to improve customer relations and contribute towards the building of customer loyalty. It provides a useful tool in their adoption of micro-marketing, a key facet of revenue management (Cross, 1997).

While it is between five and ten times as expensive to win a new customer as it is to retain an existing one (Rosenburg and Czepiel, 1984; Liswood, 1989; Barnes and Cumby, 1993), hotel organizations must endeavour to exploit the new market potential of the Internet – the potential for incremental revenue. In a study conducted by Connelly *et al.* (1998), many of the hotel executives that were interviewed observed how different their client profiles are from those of typical Internet users. Nevertheless, they noted a growing trend in rooms booked via the Internet. Assuming that these bookings are not from their existing customer base (which is what executives themselves concluded), the bookings may well represent incremental room-nights from travellers who would alternatively select other products or perhaps not travel at all.

Hotels are now facing the same kind of increased distribution costs that the airlines have been exposed to for several years. If they are to continue operating profitably they must leverage IT and reduce distribution costs by exploiting the new reservations opportunities provided by the Internet. According to McCormack (1996), 'To airlines, hoteliers, package operators and tourist authorities, the Internet is a golden chance to bypass the travel agent. No more commissions to be paid, brochures to produce, no chance of an amateur outfit mis-selling your wares.' Baker *et al.* (1999) state that the cost of selling over the Internet is far cheaper per transaction than a GDS linked to a hotel's CRS. On TravelWeb, the cost is approximately 15 pence, with such cost savings being passed on to consumers in the form of reduced prices, typically 10–15 per cent. Even when compared with commission-free distribution channels – for example, a toll-free number access to a hotel's CRS – the costs associated with sales over the Internet are lower. According to Frook (1996), the industry-average cost for every minute of talk or hold time on a toll-free number is $1. Using Thyfault's average of seven minutes of talk time per reservation, each room booked via a toll-free line costs the hotel $7 (Thyfault, 1997). This does not take into account the cost of information enquiries, cancellations or commissions.

SMHOs, REVENUE OPPORTUNITIES AND THE INTERNET?

The Internet/WWW has improved the accessibility of all types of hotels. Berthon *et al.* (1996) suggest that the Internet provides 'a more or less level playing field for all [hotels]'. According to Jupiter Communications (1997), SMHOs will not be left out of the new market place on the Web:

> with its global reach, the medium will serve as somewhat of an equaliser for small hotels, for example. People around the world can just as easily seek out small inns or bed and breakfast lodging as they can expensive three – and four – star lodging in major chains.

In a similar fashion, additional sources concur that the Internet provides, essentially, an equal opportunity to all types and size of hotels to access the market, as entry costs are relatively low (Jolley, 1996; Gilbert *et al.*, 1999). However, estimates for the cost of developing a commercial website vary considerably – anywhere from a few thousand dollars to a few million depending on the type of site and its capabilities (Connelly *et al.*, 1998). Forrester Research estimates the average cost of developing and maintaining a website at $300,000 (Connelly *et al.*, 1998). According to Ted Julian, director of Internet research at International Data Corporation, development costs for sites capable of electronic booking average between $840,000 and $1.3 million, with a significant portion going to staffing costs (Kay, 1997). Other large expenses include investments in the technology and in ongoing enhancements and maintenance – costs that are difficult to project (Connelly *et al.*, 1998).

The high level of investment required to develop a website with full on-line reservations capabilities inevitably raises the following question. When the only or main electronic distribution channel for hotels was through CRS, SMHOs were at a disadvantage compared with chain hotels – does this difference still exist 'after WWW'? According to Marcussen (1997), yes it does. The hotels which are members of a hotel chain or a consortium, such as Best Western, or which are represented by a hotel representation firm, such as Utell International, are still at an advantage.

At present, both the variety and the complexity of Web distribution channels are continuing to evolve, with most companies using multiple routes to get their product to the consumer (Castleberry *et al.*, 1998). For example, in addition to being able to provide direct reservation capabilities on a hotel representative, consortium or hotel chain website, many hotel chains and those represented by consortia and hotel representative companies also distribute through intermediaries such as TravelWeb. Travellers booking reservations via TravelWeb query hotel reservation systems directly rather than indirectly through an airline GDS. This bypass helps to reduce the overall booking costs incurred by hotels. According to company statistics, TravelWeb has as members more than 80 chains, including 18 of the top 20 hotel chains worldwide. In total, TravelWeb's portfolio features more than 17,000 hotels. The number of TravelWeb visitors is estimated to be around 16,000 per day, extending to over 110 different countries. The company claims that: 'consumers booked approximately $20 million worth of hotel rooms through TravelWeb during the first half of 1998' (Pegasus, 1999).

Pegasus, the parent company of both THISCO and TravelWeb, has recently formed alliances with Expedia, Preview Travel and Internet Travel Network, allowing them access to its Switch technology to connect directly to hotels' CRSs, for travel reservations. This should, in turn, have a positive effect on hotel bookings and overall revenue gains from the Web. Not only is TravelWeb witnessing a good performance in terms of gross bookings, but also the cancellation rate has significantly decreased. For example, in January 1996 TravelWeb reported a cancellation rate of 32 per cent, but by November 1996 that rate had dropped to 19 per cent (Connelly *et al.*, 1998). This could signify either an increase in perceived security of the WWW or that users trust TravelWeb more (Baker *et al.*, 1999).

Many properties are also available on travel mega-sites such as Travelocity, as a result of their link with the GDSs. Another benefit of being affiliated with GDSs is that hotels have the opportunity of selling accommodation through Priceline.com (http://www.priceline.com). Bulberg (1999) of Priceline.com refers to the company not as a distribution system, but as a demand collection system for revenue management. The essence of the system is that it collects offers to buy from consumers, the objective being that hotels will get incremental revenues from customers 'without revenue being left on the table or empty rooms' (Bulberg, 1999). On the Priceline.com website the customer enters a bid price for his or her specific accommodation requirements at a particular location and the priceline.com database is searched to find a suitable hotel willing to sell at the bid price. The sale (non-changeable and non-refundable) is then processed through the Worldspan GDS. Priceline.com currently represents hotels in the USA and was due to enter the European market during the third quarter of 1999. When bidding, customers are not made aware of the hotel companies represented by Priceline.com and therefore cannot specify any brand preference when making a bid. As such, heavily branded chain hotels do not have an advantage over other less branded hotels represented by Priceline.com. However, as bookings are channelled through a GDS, only hotels affiliated with the GDS are suitable for representation on Priceline.com. According to Bulberg (1999), approximately 2,000 hotel rooms are sold per day through Priceline.com. The long-term objective of the company is to 'increase the profitability of the hotel industry' (Bulberg, 1999) by enabling hotel organizations willing to quote rates aggressively to benefit from their services.

While members of hotel chains and consortia, and hotels affiliated with a hotel representative company, benefit from both dual distribution through GDSs and the WWW and, more recently, the ability to sell through Priceline.com, the level of connectivity which stand-alone SMHOs are able to offer the Internet user cannot match that of hotel chains. Stand-alone SMHOs can make themselves present on the Web – that is, show their products and offer slow off-line booking functions, either by e-mail or by fax – but they cannot offer real-time availability information and booking facilities. They do not have the electronic means by which to make their database of availability accessible on the Web.

Jupiter Communications (1997) suggests that small suppliers can easily develop on-line store fronts, but will not draw the traffic, booking and advertising needed to survive as stand-alone sites. The company suggests that small hotels should look to supplier aggregators such as Inns and Outs, which has created a database of inns and bed and breakfast (B&B) operations. Because the B&B market does not offer a CRS that can be easily adapted to the Internet, Inns and Outs (http://www.innsandouts.com) does not offer on-line booking. Competitors such as WorldRes, however, have already made this a possibility for small, independent hotels. WorldRes developed Places to Stay (http://www.placestostay.com), a database of 1,000 hotels worldwide with booking capabilities (Jupiter Communications, 1997).

Jupiter Communications (1997) also suggests that regional and local tourism boards, most of which have created brochure-like content on their websites, will become increasingly more important in the destination marketing arena on-line. It is indicated that 'tourism boards [will] bring booking to their sites enabling small players with no CRS to receive reservations electronically' (Jupiter Communications, 1997). Examples of the development of electronic tourism destination systems is taking place worldwide, including Swedline in Sweden, Dandata in Denmark, Tirol Information system and Gulliver, the Irish tourism information and reservations system (Beaver, 1995).

In 1990, Bord Failte (the Irish Tourist Board) and the Northern Ireland Tourist Board, in a joint project, began the development of Gulliver. In 1997, the Boards sold off a majority stake in Gulliver (74 per cent) to FEXCO following recommendations from consultants that the Gulliver system would best be run as a stand-alone commercial operation. There are 11,000 Bord Failte and Northern Irish Tourist Board approved premises on the Gulliver database. The system is installed in all major Tourist Information Offices and also in the Gulliver International Call Centre. It also provides the information for the official Bord Failte Tourism Brand Ireland website at http://www.ireland.travel.ie. At the time of writing there is no facility for on-line bookings through the website. However, from mid-1999 on-line bookings should be available through the website.

IRISH HOTELS AND THE INTERNET: A MISSED REVENUE OPPORTUNITY?

Background

The Irish hotel sector has witnessed phenomenal growth in recent years. Between 1996 and 1998 the number of hotel properties increased by 12 per cent, resulting in a total bedroom inventory of over 30,000. Dublin supplies 26 per cent of total bedroom inventory, followed by the South West which supplies 23 per cent. This growth has created employment for over 50,000 people, an increase of 20 per cent in two years. Such development is set against the background of a thriving economy where tourism has become recognized as a significant economic sector and contributor to exchequer funding. Irish earnings from tourism have grown at over 10 per cent a year, the fastest growth recorded by any of the 15 prime European tourist destinations. Between 1988 and 1998, the number of tourists visiting Ireland from overseas increased by 127 per cent to 5.5 million, while overseas tourist revenues increased by 171 per cent to £2,281 million. The Irish tourism industry generates approximately 6.2 per cent of Ireland's national output.

In mid-1999 a survey was conducted, which drew a sample based on a total population of 771 hotels in the Republic of Ireland. A random sample of 500 hotels was taken, based on geographic area, number of hotel rooms and hotel grading. The market was defined in terms of size, with hotels with 1 to 49 rooms defined as SMHOs and those with 50 rooms or more defined as large enterprises. The sample size chosen was based on a 99 per cent confidence level, a confidence interval of 4.32 from the total population of 771.

For the purpose of the survey a questionnaire was developed. It was divided into three sections and composed of 24 questions. The first section contained questions that identified the hotel type, size, grade, average rate, occupancy and yield, and primary target markets. The second addressed the WWW presence of the hotel, including the type of website the organization is present on, the rates promoted through the Internet, on-line and e-mail reservations facilities. The final section of the questionnaire related to the distribution channels used by the organization and the volume and geographic source of business generated through those channels. In order to encourage a higher response rate, the questions posed were a combination of yes/no and short answers. The questionnaire was sent to revenue managers, general managers, managing directors and proprietors, depending on the size and management structure of the individual properties surveyed. The questionnaire was piloted before full-scale administration.

Profile of Respondents

Of the 500 questionnaires sent out to the hotel sample, a response rate of 173 (35 per cent) was achieved, with 48 per cent of the respondents being SMHOs and the remaining 52 per cent large hotel organizations. Of the SMHOs, 37 per cent are members of a hotel chain or consortium and/or affiliated with a hotel representative company. Sixty-eight per cent of the large hotels are members of a hotel chain or consortium and/or are affiliated with a hotel representative company. The main market segments for the large hotels are the corporate, group and weekend break sectors. Key sources of business, in geographical terms, are derived from Ireland and the UK, with mainland Europe and the USA also being important sources of business. Similar geographical sources of business and market segments were reported by the SMHOs, with the exception of one market segment, leisure business, which was rated more significant in terms of volume by the SMHOs. The average occupancy rate of the hotels surveyed is 64 per cent, with an average daily rate of £62.

Findings

Internet Presence

In our findings, 77 per cent of respondents, 39 per cent of which were SMHOs, stated that they have a Web presence. The authors, in a follow-up WWW investigation, discovered that all the respondent hotels actually have a WWW presence on one or multiple sites, most notably the Irish Tourist Board/Gulliver website (http://www.ireland.travel.ie). Seventy-three per cent of respondents (70 per cent of SHMOs and 76 per cent of large hotels) claimed an affiliation with Gulliver. However, only 23 per cent of respondents (22 per cent of SMHOs and 24 per cent of large hotels) claimed a presence on the Irish Tourist Board/Gulliver website. According to FEXCO, all hotels registered with Bord Failte are automatically featured on the Irish Tourist Board/Gulliver website – 98 per cent of the respondent hotels are registered with Bord Failte.

These findings indicate that almost all Irish hotels have an Internet presence. From a positive viewpoint, it may be observed that the findings of the study appear to support the claims of Berthon *et al.* (1996) and Jupiter Communications (1997) that SMHOs, in terms of presence, are on a level playing field with larger hotels.

Reservations Capabilities

In terms of reservations capabilities, 71 per cent of respondents said that they use e-mail to facilitate reservations, with 61 per cent of SMHOs and 79 per cent of large hotels providing e-mail based reservations capabilities. It was reported that the average time taken by hotels to process an e-mail is approximately one day. Thirty per cent of respondents (30 per cent of SMHOs and 29 per cent of large hotels) claimed that reservations for their property could be processed on-line. The authors, during their WWW investigation, discovered that on-line reservations can be processed for 46 per cent of the respondent properties. It was found that 37 per cent of SMHOs and 54 per cent of larger hotels have on-line reservation capabilities. A large proportion of the SMHOs providing on-line reservations facilities are represented by a hotel representative company (primarily Utell International) or consortium (primarily Best Western), thereby facilitating reservations to be made directly through these websites or through intermediaries, including TravelWeb, and travel mega-sites, including Travelocity. A small percentage used WorldRes to process on-line reservations. Similar findings were revealed for the larger hotels providing seamless on-line reservations. Additional third parties used to process reservations for large hotels included Lexington and Leading Hotels of the World. Fewer than 10 per cent of the large hotel properties used an in-house reservation system for real-time processing of reservations.

The findings also indicate that all properties that provided an on-line reservation facility, enabling the completion of reservations in a single seamless process, also provided the facility to check availability interactively, quote rates and accept a credit card to guarantee a booking.

The findings of the study, in terms of reservations facilities, compare favourably with the findings of a survey of the top 150 hotel websites conducted by O'Connor and Horan (1999). In that survey it was found that 79 per cent of the sites surveyed allowed users to make a reservation in some way, with 50 per cent of the sites providing the facility for the customer to complete the reservations process in a single seamless process. The findings also correspond with those of the *Hotels* magazine technology survey, which found that 51 per cent of US hotel chains accepted Web reservations (Hensdill, 1998). O'Connor and Horan (1999) also report similarities in the IT infrastructure utilized to process on-line reservation: 'Where on-line reservations facilities were provided, a noticeable trend was the use of third parties to actually process the reservation ... leaving just 28 per cent of companies using an in-house system.'

It appears that those SMHOs that are members of a hotel chain or are represented by a hotel representation firm are at a distinct advantage over other SMHOs in terms of on-line reservation capabilities – a characteristic also highlighted by Marcussen (1997). They are also at an advantage over large, stand-alone hotels in this respect.

As against this, one may contend that this ability to provide on-line reservation capabilities is totally mitigated by the fact that, in some cases, hotel managers do not seem to understand fully either their Internet presence or their reservation capability. Many of the respondent hotels do not appear to understand the technological infrastructure of their own distribution systems. For example, a significant number of organizations, both SMHOs and large hotels, did not appear aware of the presence of their third party representatives, most notably Utell, on the Web and the reservation capabilities afforded to them as a result. While many of these hotels offer e-mail reservation facilities to the user, their own sites are not linked, and do not make any reference to these reservation portals. Without this option, users of the property-based site may opt to use a different property-based site that will enable an availability check and the immediate generation of a confirmation number upon reservation. This lost opportunity represents, for hotels, excess capacity and lower overall revenues. Most significantly, it would be difficult to conclude from these findings that the afore-mentioned properties are using the Internet to maximize revenues or to gain market share when they are unaware of the opportunities afforded to them as a result of their presence on third party websites.

Rates Advertised and Achieved Over the Internet

In terms of the rates promoted on the Internet, 60 per cent of respondents (58 per cent of all SMHOs and 61 per cent of the large hotels) stated that they promoted rack rates via the Internet. With regard to the promotion of special and promotional rates on their websites, only 44 per cent of respondents (40 per cent of all SMHOs and 48 per cent of large hotels) promote such rates.

Hotel representatives interviewed by Connelly *et al.* (1998) suggested that the average daily rate for Internet bookings is higher than for reservations booked through other channels. Connelly *et al.* (1998) stated that while no hard evidence could be provided to explain this observation, respondents suggested that the higher rates could be the result of relatively sophisticated shoppers looking for upgraded accommoda-tions, or that hotels might be posting only their high rate rooms. The survey findings seem to support the later hypothesis, with Irish hotels being more likely to promote rack rates rather than discounted rates over the Internet. As the number of Internet users increases and the likelihood of leisure customers using the Internet to make reservations increases, it is feasible to suggest that the Internet would be well config-ured as a tool for hotels to promote reduced and discounted rates to stimulate demand during periods of low demand.

Only 4 per cent of respondents (equally represented by SMHOs and large hotels) offered a specific incentive (in the form of discounts or special Internet rates) to make a booking on-line.

The Internet as a Source of Business

Twenty per cent of respondents indicated that they are unable to identify the propor-tion of business generated by the individual channels of distribution utilized by them. Of the remaining 80 per cent of respondents, all hotels reported that they receive reservations through direct contact, i.e. by telephone or fax. Ninety-two per cent of the large hotels stated that they receive reservations in this way. Of those, 67 per cent receive 75 per cent or more of their reservations in this manner. Sixty-nine per cent of the SMHO respondents identified that they receive reservations through direct contact. Of those, 66 per cent receive 75 per cent or more of their reservations in this manner. The vast majority of the respondents (74 per cent) were not able to quantify the volume of business generated by any other distribution channel. Larger hotels identified hotel chain and hotel representative reservation systems as key channels of distribution for their properties. Gulliver appears to be a relatively more important source of business for SMHOs, non-affiliated hotels in particular, than it is for larger hotels. In terms of reservations generated through individual property-based websites, a response rate of 25 per cent was achieved. Of these, 55 per cent were large hotel properties, and the remaining 45 per cent were SMHOs, with both classifications claiming that, on average,

2.5 per cent of reservations are generated for their properties through that channel. Eleven per cent of respondents also stated that reservations are generated through hotel group websites; 4 per cent of respondents identified consortium/hotel representative websites as generators of reservations (SMHOs, 63 per cent; large hotels, 37 per cent) and 13 per cent identified other third party websites as generators of reservations (SMHOs, 59 per cent; large hotels, 41 per cent). Of those reservations generated on the Web, in the case of large hotels, the USA, Ireland and the UK generate an equal volume of Web-based reservations, with a relatively smaller proportion of reservations being generated by mainland Europe. For SMHOs, the greatest volume of Web-based reservations are generated by the USA, followed closely by the UK, Ireland and, to a lesser extent, mainland Europe. For both large and SMHOs, the volume of Web-based business generated by Asia is, at present, negligible.

The observation must be made that the above results may not reflect the true volume of business being generated over the Web for Irish hotels. Given that a significant proportion of hotels are not aware of their own presence on third party websites, they are without doubt not tracking the number of reservations made on the Web via those channels. If they are not aware of the exposure that affiliation with third parties is giving organizations to a global market place via the Internet, they are most likely not taking this factor into account when deciding upon allocations or number of rooms to make available through these channels. As a result, they may be losing out on potential revenues.

Conclusion

According to Baker *et al.* (1999), the Internet, despite its colossal growth, is still in its infancy as a product distribution tool. The cost of Internet access is expected to fall quickly due to the deregulation of the telecommunication market and the continuing drop in the price of computer hardware. These factors will open up the Internet to a far wider audience. Surveys already indicate that the demographic profile of users is extending beyond the business traveller to leisure travellers. Given the strong potential for the travel and tourism sector in terms of on-line purchases and the advances in facilities for secure payment over the Internet, hotels that fail to keep up with the new technological developments, particularly those trying to attract an international market, are likely to lose out on the revenue generating potential of the Internet.

Survey findings indicate that Irish hotel organizations are not fully harnessing the capabilities afforded to them by the Internet. It is vital that hotel operators familiarize themselves with, and take advantage of, the potential of the Internet in terms of facilitating direct interaction with customers, both to improve customer relations and to build customer loyalty. It is also imperative that hotel managers understand how the Internet is changing the ways in which third party representative bodies make hotel inventory available in the market place.

The development of a website with full on-line reservation capabilities is viable for large hotel organizations. However, given the significant investment required to achieve this, SMHOs should attempt to affiliate themselves with aggregated sites such as WorldRes or a hotel representative organization in order to acquire an on-line reservation capability. On-line capabilities are currently being developed for the Irish Tourist Board/Gulliver website. When this reservation facility is fully functional it will provide Irish hotels, in particular non-affiliated hotels, both large and SMHOs, with an additional channel of distribution and the opportunity to increase revenues. The significance of these developments is that they will place the non-affiliated hotels on an equal footing with their affiliated SMHO and larger counterparts. Priceline.com, when it enters the European market, will also provide a mechanism for GDS affiliated hotels to sell excess capacity if the bid price is right.

At present the hotel industry in Ireland is a booming sector of the economy. As a result, a key factor contributing to the lack of awareness of, or attention to, the revenue opportunities that the Internet provides may be the high average occupancies and average daily rates that Irish hotels, in general, are currently enjoying. However, as indicated by the Horwath (1999) survey, the hotel industry in Ireland is facing a period of increased competitiveness, likely to be reflected in declining occupancies and an erosion in average room rates. In the light of their hotel's particular target markets, distribution channels and associated distribution costs, hotel operators should review the channels of distribution currently used and the amount of inventory released for sale through each of the various channels. They should investigate the potential of the Internet as a channel of distribution for their organization and, if they consider that the Internet will provide revenue opportunities for their organization in the future, they must develop and implement a strategy to ensure that these opportunities are realized.

REFERENCES

Baker, M., Cossey, A. and Sussmann, S. (1999) 'The World Wide Web and the hotel: on-line or off course?' In Proceedings of the CHME Hospitality Research Conference, University of Surrey, Vol. 2.

Beaver, A. (1995) 'Lack of CRS accessibility may be strangling small hoteliers.' *Tourism Economics*, **1**(4), 341–55.

Berthon, P., Pitt, L. F. and Watson, R. T. (1996) 'The World Wide Web as an advertising medium: towards an understanding of conversion efficiency'. *Journal of Advertising Research*, January/February, 43–54.

Bulberg, G. (1999) 'Personal interview, 3 July.

Castleberry, J., Hempell, C. and Kaufman, G. (1998) 'The battle for electronic shelf space on the global distribution network.' *Hospitality and Leisure Executive Report*, **5**(2), 19–24.

Caterer and Hotelkeeper (1996) 'Hoteliers told of net assets'. *Caterer and Hotelkeeper*, April.

Connell, J. and Reynolds, P. (1999) 'The implications of technological developments on tourist information centres'. *Tourism Management*, **20**(4), 501–9.

Connelly, D. J., Olsen, M. D. and Moore, R. G. (1998) 'The Internet as a distribution channel'. *Cornell Hotel and Restaurant Administration Quarterly*, **39**(3), 42–54.

Cross, R. G. (1997) 'Launching the revenue rocket'. *Cornell Hotel and Restaurant Administration Quarterly*, **38**(2), 32–43.

Emmer, R. M., Tauck, C., Wilkinson, S. and Moore, R. G. (1993) 'Marketing hotels using global distribution systems'. *Cornell Hotel and Restaurant Administration Quarterly*, **34**(4), 80–9.

French, T. (1998) 'The future of global distribution systems'. *Travel and Tourism Analyst*, **3**, 1–17.

Frook, J. E. (1996) 'The ABCs of one-to-one marketing'. *Communications Week*, 16 September (628), 63.

Gilbert, D., Powell-Perry, J. and Widijoso, S. (1999) 'Hotels, relationship marketing and the Web: searching for a strategy'. In Proceedings of the CHME Hospitality Research Conference, University of Surrey, Vol. 2.

Hensdill, C. (1998) 'Hotels technology survey'. *Hotels*, February, 51–76.

Hird, S. A. (1997) 'Hoteliers find initial success on the Web'. *Hotels*, February, 64.

Hoffmann, D. and Novak, T. P. (1996) 'A new paradigm for electronic commerce'. http://www2000.ogsm.vanderbilt.edu/novak/new.marketing.paradigm.html

Horwath, A. S. M. (1999) *Ireland and Northern Ireland Hotel Industry Survey*. Belfast: Horwath Consulting.

Hotels (1997) 'TravelWeb booking data'. *Hotels*, February, 22.

Jolley, R. (1996) 'Internet offers users direct access to hotel chains'. *TTG UK & Ireland*, June, 12.

Jupiter Communications (1997) 'Travel and interactive technology: a five year outlook'. A special report commissioned by the Travel Industry Association of America.

Kay, E. (1997) 'What's the Web gonna cost you? Internet sticker shock: electronic commerce isn't cheap'. *Information Week*, 7 April.

Liswood, L. A. (1989) 'A new system for rating service quality'. *Journal of Business Strategy*, July/August, 42–5.

McCormack, M. (1996) 'Free agents make the world their oyster'. *Daily Telegraph: Connected*, 10 September, 8–9.

Mandelbaum, R. (1997) 'Hotel sales-and-marketing management'. *Cornell Hotel and Restaurant Administration Quarterly*, 38(4), 46–51.

Marcussen, C. (1997) 'Electronic distribution of holiday and business hotels'. In Proceedings of the ENTER '97 Conference, Edinburgh, 23 January.

Murphy, J., Forrest, E. J. and Wotring, C. (1996) 'Restaurant marketing on the World Wide Web'. *Cornell Hotel and Restaurant Administration Quarterly*, 37(1), 61–71.

Nielsen, J. (1995) *Multimedia and Hypertext: the Internet and Beyond*. Boston: AP Professional.

O'Connor, P. and Horan, P. (1999) 'Failing to make the connection? An analysis of Web reservations facilities in the top fifty international hotel chains'. In Proceedings of the HITA '97 Conference, Edinburgh.

Pegasus (1999) http://www.pegsinc.com

Reinders, J. and Baker, M. G. (1997) 'The future for direct retailing of travel and tourism products: the influence of information technology'. In Proceedings of the ENTER '97 Conference, Edinburgh, 23 January.

Richer, P. (1996) 'Beyond viewdata'. *Electronic Markets*, 6(1), 7.

Rosenburg, L. J. and Czepiel, J. A. (1984) 'A marketing approach to customer retention'. *Journal of Consumer Marketing*, 1, 45–51.

Smith, C. and Jenner, P. (1998) 'Tourism and the Internet'. *Travel and Tourism Analyst*, 1, 67–81.

Thyfault, M. E. (1997) 'Voice recognition enters the mainstream'. *Information Week*, 14 July, 146.

Van Hoof, H. B. and Combrink, T. E. (1998) 'US lodging managers and the Internet'. *Cornell Hotel and Restaurant Administration Quarterly*, 39(2), 46–54.

Wada, I. (1997) 'Research firm: online caps will backfire on carriers'. *Travel Weekly*, 7 July, 41.

Wardell, D. (1998) 'The impact of electronic distribution on travel agents'. *Travel and Tourism Analyst*, 2, 41–55.

Weber, T. E. (1997) 'A closer look: who's buying – and what'. *Wall Street Journal*, 27 March, B6.

12

The Use of Marketing Information Systems and Yield Management in the Hospitality Industry

Hilary Main

INTRODUCTION

In this chapter marketing is examined with the concepts of yield management. It is clear that there are key areas of overlap in terms of segmentation, the marketing mix, particularly optimal price and the product life cycle. The focus of this chapter is on the area of information flows common to yield and marketing management and information systems. The methodology and context is by survey of small and medium-sized hospitality enterprises (SMHEs), a case study of a medium-sized UK hotel and review of a larger survey executed in Germany.

SMHES

The hospitality industry is dominated by small and medium-sized enterprises. In fact the vast majority of accommodation establishments around the globe are small, independent, belong to local entrepreneurs and employ predominately members of the host society. They are generally flexible, seasonal and family managed (Shaw and Williams, 1990; Sheldon, 1993). This is evident in several countries, such as the UK, Switzerland, France, Greece and the USA (Cooper and Buhalis, 1992). Small/medium hotels contribute 60 per cent of all hotel capacity in the UK and 96 per cent of all hotel properties, while creating the dominant image of hotels in the mind of the public.

Some hotels are currently threatened in a number of areas, there is pressure to join consortia, they are for the most part missing a presence in the electronic market place and they lack the economies of scale available to large affiliated hotels. This affects external links in the purchasing and marketing functions and internally in economies and diversity of resource management. There are, however, opportunities available to the SMHEs (Medlik, 1994). They can present a unique lodging experience for the visitor, they can be flexible and appeal to unique niche market segments by being able to alter immediately their portfolio of characteristics and their market mix. They contribute greatly to the local economy of the destination via the secondary spend of the guests and the consequent multiplier effect.

THE MARKETING OF HOSPITALITY ENTERPRISES

There are some important differences in the way that large and small hotels seek to match their markets and product offerings. Large, usually chain, hotel operators are increasingly assessing their markets and setting out to sell their hotel products to identified market segments, e.g. the business traveller (Morrison, 1995). Smaller hotels tend to approach their markets less formally and more intuitively from their detailed, close contact with their guests and their requirements. Importantly, hotel accommodation is increasingly part of the total tourist product and this has important implications for hotel marketing, where channels of distribution and interconnectivity become important elements in the marketing mix and marketing activities.

The investment generally in the UK hospitality sector in marketing activities and indeed in Europe is considerably less than in the USA, Canada, Australia and Pacific rim countries (Worldwide Hotel Industry, 1993). There is evidence (Main, 1994; Buhalis, 1995) that SMHEs fail to focus on strategic issues, such as marketing planning and intelligence gathering, as they are preoccupied with the tactical and operational running of their hotels.

In the hospitality industry, marketing is a term frequently used when referring to selling and advertising (Morrison, 1995). A broader approach to marketing is required. Effective marketing requires planning from the initial conception of a product (aided by relevant market intelligence information) right through to its delivery to the customer and thereafter to the retention of the customer.

Yield Management in SMHEs in the European Union

To practice yield management effectively, a business must be able to measure demand and respond to it in a timely and dynamic fashion. Management must be able to identify and cultivate market segments and to communicate changes in price and availability, as well as special offers. An effective flow of information between an enterprise and its customers, in both directions, is needed, similar to an effective marketing information system.

Where inventory management is not clearly assigned at a high level in the organization, the conflicting interests of different departments may lead to sub-optimal capacity use. Many hotels that have been successful with yield management have assigned overall responsibility for rooms' inventory to one person. An explicit organizational emphasis on yield should be reflected in the ways performance is measured. The effectiveness of yield management can be undermined, for example, if managers are rewarded on the basis of volume alone, without consideration of price.

In small businesses, an entrepreneurial spirit and an interest in yield management on the part of the owner may be the key to establishing the appropriate organizational atmosphere. One vendor noted that successful results are often achieved when an owner makes yield management a personal 'hobby'.

It is no coincidence that yield management tends to be most prevalent in those countries where market information is most widely available. This information may take the form of official tourism statistics or business performance data published by chambers of commerce, trade associations or independent consultants. Here it is evident that the information flows are similar to those required by an effective marketing information system (see Figure 12.1).

When considering SMHEs, it is necessary to distinguish between yield management concepts and yield management technology. Many small businesses for which computerized yield management technology is too expensive can and do benefit considerably from the systematic 'manual' application of yield management concepts. Andersen Consultants' (1997) Dr Scot Hornick has identified five 'functional aspects' of yield management, as follows:

- *Market segmentation.* Identifying distinct groups of customers which behave differently from one another, and which are relevant to a company's marketing activities, pricing and other business decisions.
- *Price management.* Systematically offering different prices to different customer segments, in response to changes in demand.
- *Demand forecasting.* Forecasting future demand on the basis that a business can more rationally and accurately anticipate the size of different market segments and the prices that each segment will accept.
- *Availability and/or capacity management.* Limiting or shifting the availability of certain products or services according to customer demand.
- *Reservation negotiation.* It is in the reservation or sale processes that management must implement its decisions about pricing and availability. Where the opportunity to negotiate exists, 'up-selling' to a more expensive product or 'cross-selling' to an alternative product may be attempted.

Yield management is already used in many areas of the hospitality sector. In many other areas, it could be applied, but has received little attention. In general, yield management is applicable and of interest to businesses with the following characteristics:

1. *Perishable inventory and/or seasonal demand*, so that the timing of a sale is important.
2. *High fixed or sunk costs, and relatively low* marginal costs of selling an additional unit.
3. *Fixed capacity*, either overall or in the short term.
4. *Advance purchase* (or, at least, reservation) of products or services.

The hotel industry, at both chain and SMHE level, meets all these criteria. Levels of yield management within each industry area and in the different countries of the European Union vary in the extent to which yield management concepts are being applied and to which yield management technology has been developed greatly from one hospitality business to another. As a framework, four basic categories or levels of yield management are in use among those enterprises which *could* use yield management. At a low level a small bed and breakfast charges a single fixed price per person during the summer months. It is closed during the rest of the year. In this case no real yield management is in use. At the next level a hotel enforces a two or three day minimum stay requirement during large trade fairs, festivals and other major scheduled events. Here we could say that some formal, intuitive use of yield management concepts is applied. The next level is where a hotel manager sets limits on the number of rooms that can be booked by groups (i.e. at lower group rates) on any given day, using computer generated sales reports and 'manually' produced forecasts. In this case we could say that there is some systematic use of management information though no computerized optimization. At a very high level of fully computerized yield management system we would see a hotel chain using its yield management system to determine the contribution to income made by different groups of guests and viability of capacity for each group is adjusted accordingly.

In the hotel industry, awareness and use vary across a broad range, from the small guesthouse operator who believes his rooms have an inherent value (usually based on cost), to the large, international chain using state-of-the-art yield management technology. For the SMHE, awareness is low, but intuitive applications exist. Many make use of yield management concepts on an informal, intuitive basis. The majority of European SMHEs practice at least limited price differentiation. Discounting and overbooking are generally becoming more common. Pricing is a 'hot topic' in most areas of hotel management, for SMHEs as well as large enterprises. Consolidation is seen as giving price advantages to large enterprises, at the expense of smaller service providers.

Yield Management and the Large Affiliated Hotels

At the upper end of the sophistication range, automated yield management is really used only by a few large, chain-affiliated hotels. This includes simple implementations on both chain-wide and single-hotel base. To date, Marriott appears to be the front-runner in terms of centralized, chain-wide yield management implementation. Most of Marriott's full-service hotels are connected to a centralized yield management system, in which is the hotel-specific Marriott's central reservations system, through which all bookings flow. Pricing and availability decisions are ultimately taken at the property level, where local factors can be taken into account. Holiday Inn is another chain with top-level yield management expertise. The Holiday Inn Revenue Optimization system – HIRO – is intended to be implemented throughout the chain in the next several years, first in North America and then in Europe. The implementation of automated yield management packages by single hotels in Europe is also concentrated among chain-affiliated hotels. Overall, the pattern of implementation reflects the supposition that yield management works best in markets with strong transient demand and for larger hotels.

MANAGEMENT INFORMATION SYSTEMS AND MARKETING INFORMATION SYSTEMS

In a constantly changing market place, external and internal information is required to support strategic, tactical and operational marketing decisions and provide a competitive advantage. Thierauf (1997) describes an effective management information system (MIS) as one that allows the decision-maker (i.e. the manager) to combine his or her subjective expertise with computerized objective output to produce meaningful information for decision-making. The ability to use MISs effectively is essential to the successful operations of most organizations (Reynolds, 1992) Information is now considered to be a sixth major resource for most businesses (Thierauf, 1987), and in this information age could be described as the most important resource for some industries. These MISs tend to have subsystems which relate to traditional functional areas of the business, i.e. corporate planning, manufacturing, accounting and finance, personnel and marketing subsystems. A marketing subsystem would have further subdivisions, i.e. sales forecasting, marketing research, advertising, sales order processing and physical distribution.

These systems and subsystems would not be appropriate for all industry sectors and the model may be too complex to be of use to the SMHE manager. A simpler system which concentrates on continuous and dynamic data, information and intelligence flow to support marketing decisions may be more relevant (Majaro, 1993).

It is evident that marketing efforts can be enriched through the introduction of a system that ensures personnel are motivated and stimulated to communicate their impressions, opinions, factual observation providing bits of intelligence which gives insight into the market. There is evidence (Braham, 1988) that the larger, usually affiliated, hotels have implemented MISs or Marketing Information Systems (MKISs), e.g. the Delphi system used by Hilton, but there is little evidence to suggest that SMHEs are utilizing MKISs.

'Sound marketing information is an effective prerequisite for sound marketing decisions' (Brassington and Pettitt, 1997). Early evidence (Main *et al.*, 1996) suggests that SMHEs do not collect or use information gained internally on market segments and rarely access external sources of information. Not only do they not know their customers but they do not know their market environment. External information is crucial for effective information systems. The demand for accommodation may change for reasons of government action, weather, business booms and busts, tourism fashions, special events, festivals, building projects or simply increased disposable income. Economic, political and environmental changes can quickly affect this volatile industry. A small hotel, particularly, has to fit as a whole entity into the physical and social ambiance of a city or local community. It has to have the relevant information to make wise marketing decisions in terms of positioning, market mix variable, segmentation and targeting. Definitions are available from respected marketing authors. Teare *et al.* (1994) stated: 'An MKIS is the framework for the day-to-day management and structuring of information gathered regularly from inside and outside the organisation.' Dibb *et al.* (1991) defined MKIS as: 'A formalised set of procedures for generating, analysing, storing and distributing information from internal and external, to marketing decision makers on an ongoing basis.'

O'Brien (1990) makes the point that smaller organisations, in other business sectors, have more advanced information systems than those that even the largest companies had ten years ago. The use of CD-ROM and easy to use databases has put more information at the marketing managers' fingertips.

Martell (1988) and Mitchell (1988) state that MKISs enhance a products range and customer services and provide a comparative advantage. Pottruck (1988) maintains that information is a strategic marketing offensive weapon. Therefore there is substantial evidence of the need for MKISs, though the form they may take, in the form of an MKIS model, the nature of the inputs, processes and outputs, is still subject to debate.

MKIS Models

Some industries have been extremely successful in implementing successful MKISs, e.g. banking and charities and possibly lessons could be learnt from their experiences. Other studies (Li *et al.*, 1993) would suggest there has been a tendency to keep MKISs separate from other information systems (ISs) as decision support systems evolved in the 1980s to support functional business activities and marketers jumped on the bandwagon of keeping MKISs separate from integrated ISs. (Li *et al.*, 1993) maintain that an MKIS is a conceptual model and was never intended to operate in a stand-alone manner, as marketing must integrate its data from other subsystems and vice versa. Mitchell (1992) suggests that MKIS should be a 'natural' element and utilized for a more 'sensory information' approach to collecting information and promoting a wider degree of information sharing.

Though there is some published academic research on MKIS and large hospitality organizations there are few or no published data on the use or utility of MKISs to SMHEs. Much of the current published information concentrates on the affiliated sector of the market and focuses on the US market sector (Kotler *et al.*, 1996). Recent research (Ingold *et al.*, 1996) and anecdotal evidence suggests that current marketing decisions are made without reference to data, internal and external, and that marketing plans are rarely used.

Morrison's (1995) model is based on data types from the macro and micro environment, system type (accounting and marketing) and purpose, i.e. planning, executing or controlling was proposed specifically for the hospitality industry. There are obviously several models, with appropriate inputs, processes and outputs, that have to be considered in the development of a MKIS and perhaps the best model appropriate to the SMHEs would incorporate the best features and practices of these different epistemologies.

Buttery and Buttery (1991) suggest there are three main models for MKISs in general use, and these are prescriptive, positivist and phenomenological. Other simpler models exist, e.g Kinnear *et al.*'s (1995) model is based on inputs from competitors, government statistics, market research findings, industry data and accounting and sales reports into the system. Li *et al.*'s (1993) model is based on a framework of the 4Ps (product, price, place and promotion) but linked into other subsystems within the business. Brassington and Pettitt (1997) suggest a similar model with internal and external inputs.

There are obviously barriers which hinder the implementation of MKIS. Anecdotally these are the hotel manager, his or her level of education and the lack of available financial resources (if an IT solution is considered) and sources of reliable, external hospitality data that are timely, accurate, dependable and economic.

Figure 12.1 was consequently extracted and developed as a MKIS model for SMHEs in order to summarize and review the utilization of current marketing data.

RESEARCH AND METHODOLOGIES

Several research methodologies were used for this chapter. First, a broad review of the secondary literature was conducted to form a foundation to the study. An attempt was made to ensure that all relevant literature which might relate to the project was scanned. The literature abstracted and cited in the report is only that which relates

	INPUTS	PROCESS	OUTPUTS

External		**Marketing Mix (7 Ps)**
Published Research		Price
Market Research Reports		Place
Government Statistics		Promotion
Press and Media		Product
Trade Associations		Physical Evidence
Tourism Boards		Process
Competitors		People
	Marketing Information Database	
Internal		**Decision Support System**
Sales Records		Personnel
Customer Records		Finance
Communications		Stock Control
Commissioned Studies		Yield Management
Internal Customer Feedback		Inventory Control
(Staff) Motivation		

Figure 12.1   Marketing Information System for SMHEs

directly to this study and does not include the broader work relating to the large-scale study of which this report forms a part.

The second research methodology utilized was a telephone questionnaire administered to a selection (14) of SMHEs in England and Wales. These were chosen from the English and Welsh Tourist Board publications for 1996 using a randomization process. The questionnaire was designed to discover what internal and external information was collected by the participant hotels, how it was processed and how it was used.

The third methodology for this research was a case study of a SMHE located in the West Midlands region of England and one from from Germany. A review of MKIS models and yield management sytems was undertaken. The use of information by the case study hotels was then reviewed in the light of these models and analysed on the basis of the use or potential use of the information for marketing and revenue optimization. In addition a survey is reproduced here that was carried out by DE-HOGA in Germany on 85 hotels that had between 50 and 100 rooms to determine their use of yield management and marketing information.

Questionnaires

To the extent that our small sample reflects the SMHE sector these hotels seem to be information-rich or information-poor, with little in between. The data collected from internal sources mainly consisted of guest records and accounting information, including data kept for taxation and other legal purposes. None of the hotels produced any in-depth statistical analysis; instead the data tend to be lists and counts, e.g. number of meals served. Customer information was retained when collected, usually at time of check-in; some useful information is collected informally but seldom utilized. Many identified what data would be useful to collect and perceived a gap in their marketing data. Hotels used little or no external information, though some were members of professional bodies and associations but found them inadequate as sources of market intelligence.

The Case Study

The hotel in the West Midlands has 70 bedrooms, a 100 cover restaurant, 7 conference rooms of assorted sizes and parking for 100 cars (important in the area). The hotel is privately owned and has previously been a member of a consortium, but the proprietor/manager decided that this was not cost-effective, so the hotel is now completely independent.

There are few links with the local tourist board and the hotel makes little use of external information other than making pricing decisions based on those seen as local competitors. The proprietor is entrepreneurial and makes 'seat of the pants' decisions which he (rightly) sees as having carried him through recent periods of recession in the UK.

Staffing in the hotel is based around a very few key full-time permanent personnel, with a large number of part-time workers from the tertiary labour force. Although the owner is autocratic, he will take some account of his employees' ideas, but there is little obvious empowerment of employees.

The owner, and indeed the key personnel, tend to confuse marketing with advertising. Little use is made of any marketing methodologies. Most use of external agencies is for advertising purposes and these are assessed in terms of short-term payback. The proprietor does target a market segment, largely the business market, but does no market research to find out what his customers require.

The hotel has a front-of-house/reservations system which is rich in information. Interrogation of the system shows that a wide variety of business segments are identified as using the hotel. Although the hotel information system is seen as information-rich, with historical data being available in archives dating back five years, these data relate only to numbers of customers. However, information on trends in bookings was available for the previous three years.

The hotel had rack rates which were set on prices of their perceived competitors. Pricing took no account of any actual fixed or variable costs relating to hotel rooms. Indeed, approximations of costings were often worked backwards from the selling price. It is thus a matter of some luck that the hotel has proven profitable, this together with some optimistic vision of the actual position of the hotel in the market place.

Rack rates were seldom adhered to, discounts being offered to business clients as a matter of course. The hotel reservation system showed that more than 150 different rates had been offered in the four months preceding February 1997.

Conclusion

From the *questionnaire* it is clear that the hotels collect valuable information both formally and informally but cannot either extract it from their software package or shape it in manual form to meaningful, usable information.

Frequently marketing intelligence from external sources is no more than monitoring and matching competitors' activities. There is little use of external sources of data, consultancies, trade associations or tourist boards. They make little use of loyalty schemes to encourage repeat business and there seems to be no effective measurement in terms of cost-effectiveness of marketing activities. They are 'too busy being busy'.

If the hotel, in the *case study*, is to operate a yield management system which could optimize revenue, make best use of resources and compete in its market niche, then it needs to take account of a number of factors. It must develop its computerized decision support system, develop an effective internal communication system, from management to staff to customer, and the reverse, and it must undertake market research to understand fully the market environment it is operating in, keeping up to date. It should also be aware of the broader economic environment and the hotel team should keep abreast of external information for this awareness.

If the hotel takes due cognizance of these factors then it should begin to develop a realistic understanding of the importance of the marketing mix.

The manager must be willing to share with his key personnel all the information he has from the decision support system, together with his vision for the future of the organization. Instead of the role of gatekeeper of information, he must become the team leader, developing the sharing of ideas and information.

The staff will need to be educated to take responsibility for decisions which may be seen to be high risk in strategy in the knowledge that the manager will support them. Staff must understand that lower rates can only be offered if costs are reduced; thus inclusive cheap packages cannot be offered as a matter of course. Closing out strategies will need to be adhered to. The hotel will need to understand what information is important and needs to be collected. Information on go-shows and no-shows, for example, will need to be retained and used to develop an overbooking policy.

The information collected and analysed in this case study demonstrates how one SMHE could move to a position whereby it could use a MKIS effectively to move to a situation of improved profitability and stability in a dynamic operating environment. Future research will follow the changes that are implemented in this hotel in order to take a more market-orientated approach to revenue optimization and customer focus.

Review of Survey of Hotels in Germany

The results of a survey carried out by Arthur Andersen and DEHOGA, the German hotel and restaurant association in Germany help to illustrate the range of sophistication with which many European hotels – especially medium-sized enterprises – apply yield management concepts. Eighty-five hotels responded to the survey questionnaire. All had at least 50 beds, and most had fewer than 100 rooms. Only 6 of the 85 respondents reported having made an investment in yield management technology or know-how.

One of the six had purchased an automated yield management system. However, 67 per cent stated that they use yield management. Still larger numbers indicated they use specific tactics related to yield management:

- 82 per cent reported offering special packages or discounts aimed at particular market segments;
- 73 per cent indicated they vary prices according to time of year;
- 69 per cent stated they conduct demand forecasting;
- 72 per cent said that they vary the availability of special offers according to the overall demand situation.

Several hotels' pricing policies were based on cost and/or the idea of an 'inherent value', independent of changing demand patterns. These were the exception rather than the rule, however, suggesting that the importance of the supply–demand relationship in determining price is now broadly accepted in the industry. What is most frequently lacking is a degree of systematization and precision in the management of prices and capacity, as illustrated by the following observations.

While 69 per cent of respondents said they practise demand forecasting, only 34 per cent reported using a computer to make forecasts. Only 56 per cent had calculated the variable or marginal cost of selling an additional room. While 82 per cent of the hotels said they track actual demand (i.e. rooms sold), only 46 per cent reported keeping track of cancellations or no-shows and only 33 per cent of 'turnaways' (i.e. would-be guests who cannot be accepted because the hotel is fully booked).

CONCLUSION

The obstacles and success factors noted above may pertain to businesses of all sizes. In the course of the research a number of points were identified of specific relevance to SMHEs, with respect to the practice of yield management: SMHEs are not homogeneous. The definition of an SMHE is quite broad, encompassing the majority of businesses in some sectors (such as hotels), and there is often a need to distinguish between 'small' and 'medium' or between 'small' and 'very small'. In some of the countries researched, 'medium' would actually be considered 'large'.

In general, medium-sized enterprises are better positioned than the small or very small to implement relatively sophisticated yield management techniques – in some cases even automated forecasting and automated yield management. They are more likely to have an intuitive grasp of yield management concepts, more likely to have skilled personnel and more likely to have some information systems (whether electronic or not) already in place. They are also more likely to be active members of trade associations through which they could learn about new management techniques and technology.

Many truly small enterprises require more basic marketing and financial management skills, before any more than the rudiments of yield management could be effectively applied. Unfortunately, small enterprises are least likely to belong to trade or other professional organizations through which marketing and yield management know-how might be derived.

SMHEs often lack highly skilled personnel. SMHEs often lack the human resources (in terms of skill and time available) to carry out complex, systematic pricing and capacity management strategies. Their own business data may be too limited to reflect an accurate picture, whereas large businesses in dynamic markets have a particular advantage in that their own experience is likely to be generally indicative of the market as a whole.

For a large city hotel, for example, diligently counting turnaways, cancellations and no-shows as well as actual sales will give a reasonably good picture of overall demand patterns. For smaller enterprises, it may be much more difficult to gain an adequate understanding of total demand in the market. Moreover, small businesses are less likely to be involved in the kinds of benchmarking exercises, surveys and information exchanges that provide many larger enterprises with an overview of the markets in which they compete. Adopting forecasting and other yield management techniques without understanding total demand can result in the reinforcement of historical, sub-optimal sales patterns.

Where past practices and background data have not been adequately documented (as is likely for many small businesses), measuring the specific benefits of new policies may be impossible. Similarly, the lack of formalization of procedures that is common in independent businesses may make the results of particular actions difficult to isolate and measure.

SMHEs frequently do not have the same access to capital enjoyed by larger firms. This makes the development or purchase of expensive, automated forecasting and yield management technology unworkable for many. The smaller a business's capacity is, the less flexibility management has to manage that capacity in a sophisticated way. Clearly, this factor restricts many small enterprises.

IN SUMMARY

The constructive use of information is pivotal to support effective management. It is therefore evident that successful management of these two areas is crucial to SMHEs. A MKIS would provide the necessary information system to build up a database of external and internal information where predictive modelling and the analysis of historical data would enhance the decision-making of the SMHE operator. Evidence suggests (Main *et al.*, 1996) that current yield and marketing decision-making is made without reference to marketing intelligence data and many firms do not link their marketing plans with company-wide information systems. These MKISs and YM systems can be manual or computer-based, though recently re-engineering of business processes has come to be associated with computerization and technology has provided useful tools for marketing communications with customers, suppliers and colleagues. In a technology-driven environment IT has become one of the most vital elements of effective information flow as it can collect, process and distribute data and information rapidly.

In this era marketing and revenue management can no longer be an area of a few specialists; everyone within an organization should be involved. Many firms do not link their marketing plans with company-wide information systems and consequently crucial access is denied to important decision-makers. Automated, centralized, accessible information systems make that crucial information available to all relevant decision-makers. In an increasingly competitive market place, locally and globally, an effective system would provide the SMHE operator with the necessary tools to support the marketing mix and revenue forecasts to formulate a vital competitive edge for survival.

Automated yield management is several steps away for most SMHEs. No more than a handful of SMHEs are using automated yield management technology, and, for most, the implementation of such technology is not immediately feasible. Even if the price of computerized technology could be overcome, most SMHEs would still lack the necessary training, information and organizational focus on yield to use that technology successfully. As a result, the immediate need is for a greater degree of logic and precision in the pricing and capacity management process. In most cases, this could be achieved through intermediate steps, such as the introduction of basic information systems, or the implementation of computerized forecasting.

Appropriate technology is not readily available. The developers and vendors of yield management technology have not had an economic incentive to develop automated systems for small businesses. Worldwide, there is still sufficient demand for yield management technology and services among large enterprises to support the rather small pool of true yield *management* experts.

Immediate opportunities are for greater 'low-tech' yield management. The immediate opportunity among SMHEs is for greater, more systematic 'manual' application of yield management concepts, through training and the improvement of informational tools and analytical skills. In some cases, the training needs are quite basic: small businesses are often run by professional hosts, enthusiasts, etc., rather than by professional, skilled business managers.

The business environment blocks even low-tech yield management in some locations. The most frequent problems are the lack of sufficient transport and tourism infrastructure to support market segmentation and price differentiation efforts by individual businesses, and the reliance of individual SMHEs on tour operators and other contractors, which essentially take over control (and the associated risk) of the SMHEs' inventory.

The hotel industry is probably the single most important area of tourism in terms of the potential for further utilization of yield management concepts and technology. The industry is both large and highly fragmented, with enterprises spread across the broadest possible range of sizes and levels of sophistication. Increased competition is a common feature across Europe, making pricing a topic of great interest. Awareness of the term 'yield management' and of yield management as a formal discipline varies greatly among countries and different types of hotel.

Awareness seems largely to be related to the overall level of information system vendors have in the different markets, the penetration of local markets by international hotel chains and the propensity of hoteliers to read national and international trade journals and generally to follow business management and technological trends. The lack of local-language discussions of yield management almost certainly contributes to the very low awareness levels.

REFERENCES

Arthur Andersen (1997) *Yield Management in Small and Medium Sized Enterprises in the Tourist Industry*. Brussels: Directorate General XXIII.

Birks, D. F. and Southam, J. M. (1990) 'The potential of marketing information systems'. *Marketing Intelligence Planning*, **8**(4), 15–21.

Braham, B. (1988) *Computer Systems in the Hotel and Catering Industry*. London: Cassell.

Brassington, F. and Pettitt, S. (1997) *Principles of Marketing*. London: Pitman.

Buhalis, D. (1995) 'The impact of information technologies on tourism distribution channels: implications for the small and medium sized enterprises' strategic management and marketing'. PhD Thesis, University of Surrey, Guildford.

Buttery, E. A. and Buttery E. M. (1991) 'Design of a marketing information system'. *European Journal of Marketing*, **25**(191), 26–40.

Cooper, C. and Buhalis D. (1992) 'Competition or co-operation: the needs of small and medium sized tourism enterprises at a destination level'. In E. Laws (ed.), *Tourism Destination Management*. London: Routledge.

Dibb, S., Simkin, L., Pride, W. M. and Ferrell, O. C. (1991) *Marketing Concepts and Strategies*. London: Houghton Miffin.

Douglass, D. P. (1990) 'Building marketing information systems'. *I/S Analyser*, **28**(4), 1–16.

Fletcher, K., Buttery, A. and Deans, K. (1988) 'The structure and content of the marketing information sytstem: a guide for management'. *Marketing Intelligence and Planning*, **6**(4), 27–35.

Heintzeman, S. B. (1994) 'Marketing with technology: bringing buyer and seller together'. *Bottomline*, **9**(3), 28–32.

Higby, M. A. and Farah, B. N. (1991) 'The status of marketing information sytems, decision support sytems and expert sytems in the marketing function of US firms'. *Information and Management*, **20**(1), 29–35.

Ingold, A., Main, H. and Chung, M. (1996) 'A preliminary study on data utilisation by small to medium sized hotels'. Proceedings of the First International Yield Management Conference, Walton Hall, Birmingham.

Kinnear, T. *et al.* (1995) *Principles of Marketing*. New York: HarperCollins.

Kotler, P., Bares, J. and Mahens, J. (1996) *Marketing for Hospitality and Tourism*. London: Prentice Hall.

Knutson, B., Malik, M. and Schmidgall, R. S. (1995) 'When it is smart to turn away business'. *Cornell Hotel and Restaurant Quarterly*, **36**(6), 56–61.

Li, E. Y., McLeod, R. and Rogers, J. C. (1993) 'Marketing information systems in the Fortune 500 companies: past present and future'. *Journal of Management Information Systems*, **10**(1), 65–193.

Main, H. (1994) 'The application of information technology in the independent hotel'. MPhil Thesis, University of Wales.

Main, H., Chung, M. and Ingold, A. (1996) 'A preliminary study on data utilisation by small to medium sized hotels'. Paper presented to the Yield Management Conference, Birmingham, September.

Majaro, S. (1993) *The Essence of Marketing*. London: Prentice Hall.

Martell, D. (1988) 'Marketing and information technology'. *European Journal of Marketing*, **22**(9), 16–25.

Medlik, S. (1994) *The Business of Hotels*, 3rd edn. Oxford: Butterworth-Heinemann.

Mitchell, V. W. (1992) 'The human face of MKIS'. *Marketing Intelligence and Planning*, **9**(191), 19–27.

Mitchell, J. W. and Sparks, L. (1988) 'Marketing information systems in the major UK banks'. *International Journal of Bank Marketing*, **6**(5), 14–29.

Morrison, A. (1995) *Hospitality Marketing*. Oxford: Hospitality Press.

O'Brien, T. (1990) 'Decision support system'. *Marketing Research*, December, 51–5.

Pottruck, D. S. (1988) 'Turning information into a strategic marketing weapon'. *International Journal of Bank Marketing*, **6**(5), 9949–57.

Reynolds, G. (1992) *Information Systems for Managers*, 2nd edn. Columbus, OH: West.

Shaw, G. and Williams, A. M. (1990) 'Tourism economic development and the role of entrepreneurial activity'. In C. Cooper (ed.), *Progress in Tourism Recreation and Hospitality Management, Volume 2*. London: Belhaven Press.

Sheldon, P. (1993) 'Destination information systems'. *Annals of Tourism Research*, **20**(4), 633–49.

Teare, R., Calver, S. and Costa, J. (1994) *Marketing Management: A Resource Based Approach for the Hospitality and Tourism Industry*. London: Cassell.

Thierauf, R. (1987) *Effective Management Information Systems*. Ohio: Merrill Publishing.

Worldwide Hotel Industry (1991, 1992, 1993) Worldwide Industry Reports, London.

PART IV
SERVICE SECTOR STUDIES

13

Yield Management and the Airline Industry

Anthony Ingold and Jeremy R. Huyton

INTRODUCTION

The history of civil aviation can be traced back to the early 1920s, when air postal systems were set up in the USA and Europe. These air mail flights were far more influential on development of aviation in this early period than carriage of passengers, which was seen as a secondary (and hazardous) activity. In the 1930s the early, pioneer passenger services began to emerge, with such players as KLM, Air France and Imperial Airways becoming established. This phase of development was interrupted by the Second World War in 1939.

The war proved to be a turning point for the airline industry, giving a huge boost to the production of larger, more powerful and more reliable aircraft. Following the cessation of the conflict in 1945, aircraft manufacturers turned their energy to modifying their machines of war as domestic carriers. Examples are the civilianized Lancaster bomber having a modest success with British Overseas Airways Corporation (BOAC). In the USA, an all-aluminium wartime utility aircraft, the Douglas Dakota DC3, and variants were produced in their thousands, with many still in use today (a US Federal Aviation Authority Air Directive stated of the Dakota 'good till worn out'!). According to Lyth (1993), the Dakota was the first aircraft that allowed airlines to make a profit from the carriage of passengers alone. Developments continued apace, with a long lineage of technical achievement by manufacturers, now household names, such as Airbus Industrie, Boeing and British Aerospace, producing ever larger, faster, more efficient and now quieter and less polluting aircraft. This has led to the familiar fleets of jet and turboprop aircraft in variants to cope with short haul business flights (DeHaviland Dash 8), tightly packed package holiday flights (Boeing 737) and long haul journeys, non-stop half way around the world (Airbus A300 series). Thus the modern airline industry has all the aircraft variants it needs to operate, but it must do this in a highly competitive open market, and this is the focus of this chapter.

Airline seats are the ultimate perishable commodity. Once an aircraft has departed, the revenue from the unfilled seats will never be recouped. It is therefore perhaps unsurprising that airlines were the birthplace of yield management. Indeed, airlines were well placed technically to introduce statistical tools, with their large operational research units and use of sophisticated computerized booking systems from an early date. The purpose of this chapter is not to outline how yield management works, which is described elsewhere, but to examine the application and effects of yield management on the airline industry and the associated sectors of the travel trade. In an earlier study, Ingold and Huyton (1990) noted that prior to the introduction of yield management, QANTAS and probably other airlines used break-even analysis to analyse yield. This method is notably unreliable, in that it cannot be used to predict yield. Indeed, some airlines found that they needed a 90 per cent load capacity just to break even!

Prior to the introduction of yield management, discounted fare systems such as APEX and Super APEX were introduced in the 1960s. These would provide discounts for customers who were willing to book in advance. However, there was no provision for maximizing revenue from those who were willing to pay top fares, other than the traditional first class section, and this was relatively inflexible. The introduction of yield management is generally credited to American Airlines, around the late 1970s (Cross, 1997). According to Smith *et al.* (1992), American began its studies into operations research modelling in the early 1960s. It soon realized that managing revenue using data from its reservations inventory was a huge task given the technology available at that time, so it reduced the large problem into three manageable sub-problems. These were the now familiar overbooking, discounting practice and traffic management. American then used yield management to determine flight schedules and fares. These are open to the public via the reservations system SABRE (semi-automatic business research environment), now updated to Super-SABRE. All sales must pass through this system, which updates availability and prices for all flights continuously. Reservations are only accepted if the yield management programme allows. Most airlines have since followed suit in introducing revenue management systems. These CRSs (computerized reservation systems) are a key to the operation of yield management for the airlines.

The deregulation of airlines in the USA in 1979 was the cause of major upheaval in the early 1980s, with airlines facing heavy competition. This competition lead to a price-cutting war, which is considered in more detail below. Some airlines cut prices to suicidal levels, several going out of business (e.g. PanAm could not survive without its state subsidy), and many others filed for Chapter 11 bankruptcy (e.g. TWA was protected in this way and is now seemingly viable again).

A second factor which was to upset the competitive balance was globalization and the development of hub and spoke networks. Hubs were also developed as a result of deregulation, as airlines were allowed more freedom to develop their routes and schedules. The underlying idea is that a number of regional airports will feed into a hub airport using small aircraft (KLMUK and American Eagle are examples). Thus a large number of passengers can be concentrated in the hub airport and the carrier can fill a large aircraft (e.g. Boeing 747) for an onward intercontinental journey. This is obviously more cost-effective, but provides a larger logistical problem for the airlines in managing flights, revenue and thus yield. These issues are not explored further in this chapter as they are not core to the concept of yield management itself. The reader is referred to Graham (1995) for further reading of the broad issues of geographical and political change with respect to the airline industry. A new competitive feature was introduced into the airline industry in the late 1980s (USA) and early 1990s (Europe) with the low-cost start-up airlines such as easyJet. These are discussed in the next chapter.

THE INTRODUCTION AND APPLICATION OF YIELD MANAGEMENT: A CASE STUDY OF BRITISH MIDLAND AIRWAYS

The authors visited British Midland Airways in 1992, during the course of a wide-ranging study on the use of yield management in the United Kingdom (unpublished results). At that time the airline was relatively small, had just introduced yield management and was operating a manual system, albeit quite innovative for an airline of its size. However, such a manual system has many drawbacks, which were readily admitted to. These mainly relate to lack of sensitivity of the system due to the necessity of working with restricted amounts of data manually. These restrictions thus allowed only a limited forecasting of future demand, few passenger price categories could be coped with and there was a difficulty in predicting necessary overbooking rates. Nevertheless, history has proven that the system helped to give British Midland some competitive edge over aggressive competitors, some of which were (and probably still are) receiving subsidies from their respective states. It is difficult to quantify the exact contribution of yield management to the success, however, as the company is innovative in a number of ways and thus has attracted customer loyalty for a variety of reasons.

The authors subsequently paid a more recent visit to British Midland, in 1995, to discover how it had progressed, to review its current ideas and to discover how it views the future for yield management for themselves and for the industry.

The airline industry, in its early and highly profitable days, had very little use for revenue maximization. Flights tended to be full and fares were rarely discounted. Flying was for the rich, the famous and the businessman. However, as aircraft and airports became more efficient, fuel prices fell, the travelling public grew and the number of airlines expanded extensively, the aircraft load factors (the numbers of passengers per flight) got worse. It was not a rare occurrence to find an aeroplane with less than a 50 per cent load factor. It was at this point that airlines looked at how to attract a greater market share. By the mid-1960s fares were being reduced, discounts given and a price war was in the offing. The airlines realized that this would happen and set about trying to regulate themselves through the International Airline Transport Association (IATA). All agreed that full-fare prices were still high but felt that they were acceptable for the businessman, but for the tourist or occasional traveller they were too high. Thus air fare deregulation came into operation, overseen by IATA, and an overall discounting policy was agreed upon, and while its implementation was not mandatory, most airlines accepted the new APEX (Advance Passenger EXcursion) fare that came into operation.

This style of fare meant passengers got reduced fares on certain flights but were bounded by a variety of flight restrictions, such as times of flights, duration of stay outside of the departing country and length of time the seat has to be booked and paid for prior to departure. This type of fare was even more finely tuned and other fares, such as the 'Super APEX', came on to the market. This meant that airline reservations clerks tended to sell seats by stating that 'yes they did have seats' and 'they start from "n = low" dollars or pounds'. They filled the aeroplane on a first come first serve basis, which tended to mean that the cheaper seats filled first. Not a good ploy to optimize revenue!

This method of filling an aircraft remained very much the same for the next 10–12 years until the US airlines reappraised the whole process of filling an aeroplane. While they agreed that there have to be APEX, Super APEX and the plethora of other cheap fares which then existed, they did not have to fill their entire aeroplane with them. They started to restrict the numbers of cheap seats, and within the passenger bands of first class, business class and economy they had price classes. Thus we now find that, for example, a Boeing 747 which had three classes, first, business and economy, may now have all of its seats in first class at the same price, but business now may have full fare seats and other seats discounted, perhaps as a corporate rate offer. Then in economy there could be full fares, APEX fares, discounted fares, group fares and so on, but all with a finite number of seats at each price category.

It was at this point that the airlines decided that to be able to control such a variety of prices a computer should be utilized and the birth of computerized yield management occurred. Yield management for the airline industry is the maximization of revenue on each flight. The controlling of the numbers of seats sold at different price categories was to ensure that a person who books at the last minute for a flight is not turned away because the flight is full of APEX or group passengers who are paying a considerably reduced rate.

While the early days of manually restricting price classes worked well, and represented in fact the first simple yield management system, to capitalize fully on a yield management system requires information, and a great deal of it. Data on past flights, their utilization and passenger class breakdown, as well as projections on forthcoming world or local events and times of the year which would cause flight capacities to be affected, were also required. Such major events include the Olympic Games in Sydney, local events like the Edinburgh Festival in Britain or the Oshkosh aviation rally in the United States and holiday seasons like Christmas or Easter. In order to analyse fully all the potential and actual information which could be accrued and to do so accurately and swiftly a computerized yield management system is certainly needed.

HOW DOES AN AIRLINE YIELD MANAGEMENT SYSTEM WORK

Once all the data regarding all of an airline's flights are collected and input into the system, they are used to give a flight analyst the best opportunity of making an accurate decision as to what categories of passenger to take. On a daily basis the computer will give the analyst a consolidated breakdown of the capacities of all the flights which it is handling, all the seats booked and the availability. This is for every flight for every day and well into the future. Dependent on the size of the system the future can be anything from two to six months. With this information the analyst can now look at each flight and make an educated decision as to which categories to close out and which to open. For example, a mid-summer flight to Paris may have long ago been closed out to group or cheap fares because the allocated number of seats for these fare classes have been used. However, with only two days to go before the flight leaves the expected number of full fares have not materialized. This being the case, the analyst could decide that it will be financially beneficial to this flight to open up the cheaper fares to try to fill the aircraft, while at the same time keeping the group or party fares still closed. All of this achieves an optimum revenue by taking all the influencing factors into account.

So that the maximum benefits can be achieved for an airline with regard to filling each aircraft and at the same time gaining the best revenue from each flight, forecasting is essential. According to the senior flight analyst of British Midland Airways, 'Everything is only as good as the demand forecast.'

What then are the overall benefits of implementing a yield management system? Apart from the obvious aspect of maximization of revenue, it allows an airline the chance to operate a large variety of fares so as to enhance the attractiveness of that airline to the consumer. However, the computerized system gives the analyst far more information, far more quickly than could have been achieved through a manual system. This in turn not only allows the flight analyst to look at load factors and revenue on a seasonal or weekly basis, but permits fine tuning for flights on a daily and even hourly base. British Midland gave the example of a flight leaving Paris for London, with a seating configuration of 30 first class seats and 102 in economy. On a late afternoon flight there may be only 24 in first class and 80 in economy, yet only 50 minutes later the flight could have over 90 requiring first class and 130 for economy. In this case the computer will analyse the flight for revenue optimization and give its best prediction to the flight analyst, who could go with that prediction or personally fine tune the suggestion so as to achieve an even better revenue.

Yield management would bring attention to the fact that there is a great demand for first class seats for the late Paris–London flight. Accordingly the airline can fly a larger capacity aircraft, or possibly alter the seating configuration so as to enlarge the business/first class section of the aeroplane. Sometimes a flight may be comprised of business class only.

The sales and marketing department of an airline can also use yield management as a sales tool. For example, an airline may have three classes within the business segment of the aircraft. Class A is for full fare paying passengers and will remain open at all times. Class B could be for passengers with a 5 per cent discount and would be closed out only when all the class A seats have been taken. Class C could be for business passengers with 10 per cent or more discount and would be the first to be closed out as the business segment of the aircraft filled. All the opening and closing of classes would be monitored by the flight analyst. However, the sales department may have reached a particularly good deal with a company and offers it 12 per cent discount. While the discount in itself may be a good offer, a further inducement could be to categorize all corporate staff as class B passengers. This would mean that although class C is the first to be closed out, this company's passengers could still get a flight. It could be extended even further by offering senior managers within the company class A status and thus they would always be ensured a seat even with a 12 per cent discount.

The following quotes from the flight analyst staff of British Midland Airways aptly summarize the attitude of the airline industry towards yield management:

> Yield Management allows you to sell any class at any rate at any number you want.

> It [yield management] gives you the scope to match whatever the market is out there.

> YM helps you to find what fare within each class is being sold. You can see what load factors at what fare are coming in. You can then control that demand.

> You can't monitor the demand and play with it without a computer.

YIELD MANAGEMENT AND THE MARKETING MANAGER: THE PERSPECTIVE OF A LARGE AIRLINE

The principal information which a sales and marketing team requires in order to be effective in fully utilizing an aircraft is:

- How many seats are available?
- What price are those seats?
- What is the time of day of that flight?

A computerized yield management system can give teams this information, both current and historical, swiftly and accurately. They are then able to ascertain the shortfalls in both seat capacity and revenue, and from that to devise the necessary strategies to counteract the problems.

For airlines already operating yield management systems the role of the marketing manager is to improve the yield of the various aeroplane routes. To do this he or she has to improve the mix of seats by creating a series of 'yield buckets'; that is, a series of market segments to suit the flight route. All flights should make a marginal contribution to the overall profit of the airline and to ensure this all flights should earn sufficient revenue at least to cover all the variable costs. In this context these are costs closely associated with the actual flight, its departure, flight path and destination. These variable expenses could include airport security, traffic handling, landing and parking fees, fuel costs, in-flight catering, air-traffic control, crew allowances, commissions and more. Added to these is a further category called semi-variable costs, which would include such things as passenger service charges. These are a fixed charge per passenger, but the overall cost per flight will obviously vary according to the number of passengers on each flight. Once all these expenses have been covered the revenues from that flight should also try to cover all fixed costs: expenses such as engineering, aircraft leasing costs and cabin and flight crew expenditure. Given all these expenses the marketing departments are then in a position to establish firmly the 'return on sale' for each flight. This means that they are able to work out how much profit has been made from every unit of revenue.

Figure 13.1 shows a spread of flights of one airline from a UK regional airport to destinations around Europe and to the USA. By using a basic yield management package the computer can print out a profitability status report of all the various flights from the airport, on a cumulative basis.

From Figure 13.1 it can be seen that the seat factor percentage (*x*-axis) ranges from 20 to 100 per cent, which indicates how many seats have been taken (load factor) for the various flights. The *y*-axis shows the percentage score for the marginal contribution which each flight makes. Thus it can be seen that while the Reykjavik flight is approximately 65 per cent full it is in a negative situation being some 35 per cent below break-even. This is highlighted even more with the UK regional to Dublin flight, which appears not to be as bad as the Reykjavik flight by being only 25 per cent below break-even. However, what makes this flight worse overall is the fact that in addition to making no marginal contribution it has a load factor of nearly 80 per cent!

This information, particularly in such a graphic format, enables the management to examine the future of poorly operating flight routes and decide whether or not to continue. On the other hand, it can be seen that the New Orleans flights have an average load factor of some 73 per cent and provide the best marginal contribution of

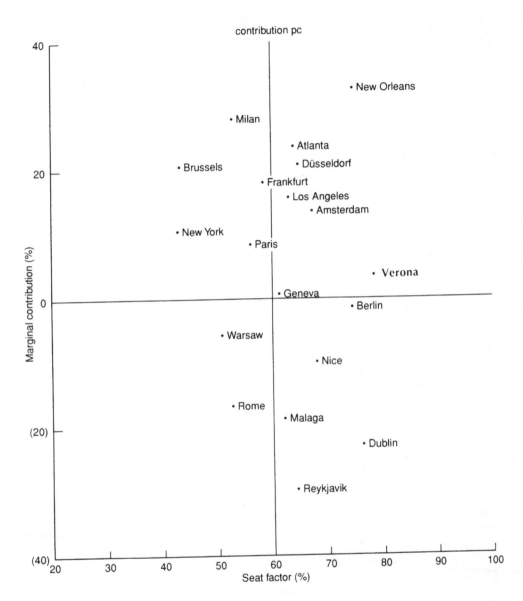

Figure 13.1 Marginal contribution analysis for a UK regional airline

approximately +30 per cent. Obviously a successful route in terms of both passenger utilization and maximization of revenue.

To formulate these figures accurately, operational expenses are calculated for each flight and then divided by the number of available seats on that flight. This means that each seat has a fixed cost associated with it. To make this figure even more meaningful that cost is then broken down to cost per kilometre. Therefore, each flight has an available seat kilometre (ASK), which is computed by multiplying the number of seats on the aeroplane by the distance of the flight. For example, if a Boeing 747 with 400 seats flies from London to Johannesburg, a distance of around 10,000 kilometres, the ASK for that flight will be 4 million. And if the full cost of that flight is £210,000, then the actual cost per ASK will be £210,000 divided by 4 million, i.e. a flight cost of 5.25 pence per seat per kilometre.

To find out if the yield on revenue of that same flight has been good, bad or indifferent, a further calculation is required. The marketing team needs to know the revenue per passenger kilometre (RPK) of each flight. This is quite simply calculated by taking the operating cost of the flight and dividing that by the revenue achieved from all the fare paying passengers on that flight, irrespective of the amount which they paid. Using the same flight and costs as before, the RPK would be worked out as follows:

Flight from Edinburgh to Johannesburg via Nairobi

380 passengers Edinburgh to Johannesburg: total revenue £247,500

Total passenger kilometres = 380 × 10,000 = 3,800,000

Thus RPK = 6.5p, which gives a yield of 23.8 per cent over the ASK

It can be seen, therefore, how marginal airline operations are, since factors as low as a fraction of one penny can adversely or positively affect the revenue yield of a flight, and it is by the use of yield management data that the marketing team can react to the varying yield from the different flights. This does not mean that airfares are altered on a daily or even monthly basis. What it does mean is that it gives the sales and marketing staff an indication of trends, and 'forewarned is forearmed'. This may mean that flights with low or negative yields need to have more yield buckets opened up, to encourage more passengers in the different classes. On the other hand, on a heavily subscribed flight it may be decided to reduce the number of yield buckets by removing the cheaper fare categories.

Yield management also takes into account the currency differentials of the various departure points around the world. In some countries the local currency may be non-negotiable; that is, it cannot be traded outside its own borders. This means that for any airline selling seats in that country and being paid in the local currency it is unable to remit that currency back to its bank in another country. Thus an airline may amass quite a sizeable amount of money in a country and be unable to use it outside that country. In a case such as this yield management is used to control the number of seats which are sold in the local currency. For example, a Russian airline may operate into and out of Lagos, Nigeria, where the local currency is not allowed to be transferred. If the aircraft fills with local paying people then the airline has a full load but the revenue it has generated is worthless, in as much as it cannot be transmitted back to the operating country and therefore cannot be used to help to offset central operating expenses. By using YM the airline can open a price bucket which could be entitled 'local paid'. This would enable a number of local passengers to be able to use the airline even if they are unable to pay with another currency, but at the same time ensuring that the airline can achieve some marginal contribution towards overall costs. Should the requirement for seats being paid by currencies other than Nigerian decrease, then the 'local paid' bucket can be re-opened, so as to ensure a full flight which is earning some form of money. One airline to which the authors spoke operates four classes within its first class fare structure on the Nigeria to Russia route. They are:

Full first class (F).

Discounted first class (E).

Complimentary first class (O).

First class from Nigeria paid in local currency (G).

The reverse of the suggested Nigeria case is, for example, flights from Germany to England. For example, the cost of a flight from Dusseldorf to London costs more than a flight from London to Dusseldorf. Thus yield management is used here to establish the number of seats that will be open to UK–Dusseldorf–UK, where the revenue earned would be less than a Dusseldorf–UK–Dusseldorf flight. However, things are not that simple because the system has to take into account not only the price variance between the two countries but also whether or not the tickets purchased are for a single journey or return.

A final element in which yield management plays a large part is the control of the aeroplane's load factor. Apart from maximizing revenue, it is also used to fill the aircraft with passengers. YM systems help to monitor 'go-shows'; that is people who just arrive at the departure counter to get on a flight. These are passengers who know that they will have to pay the full fare. There are also a regular percentage of 'no-shows': passengers who have booked flights but just do not arrive to catch the flight. To ensure that the aircraft leaves full it is normally necessary to overbook (to sell more seats than are available). However, to enable the airline management to overbook with greater accuracy, all the historical data for that flight are taken into account by both the computer and the flight manager. Such elements of information as go-shows, no-shows and last minute cancellations for that particular flight, or for all flights from that destination at that time or that day, are extracted from the computer so that the aeroplane will leave with all seats occupied, but leaving no one behind.

The benefit of a yield management system to the marketing departments of airlines is in its ability to produce information for management speedily and accurately. It is simply a tool to facilitate the making of both short- and long-term decisions as to the best ways to maximize revenue and load factors for either an individual flight or a series of flights to the same or similar destinations.

The pilot also has a role to play with respect to yield management, as he or she is the final arbiter of the load carried. The pilot in command is totally responsible for the safety of the aircraft, its crew, cargo and passengers. An interview with a pilot working for a small independent UK-based passenger airline told the authors that:

> The airline managers may specify the load for the aircraft, but in the final analysis, the pilot in command is responsible for the weight and balance calculations, fuel including diversions and so on. The pilot in command has the final 'go–no go' decision on any flight.

TRAVEL AGENTS

To discover how yield management impinges on travel agencies, an independent travel agent was consulted. Yield management is basically known in the travel trade as price consolidation. While it does not generally cause major problems, it is viewed as something of a nuisance. This is because the general public are largely unaware of the concept of yield management, presume that when they book a flight they will get the lowest price for that flight and cannot fully appreciate that lead time to aircraft departure is very important.

At counter contact, potential customers tend to accept the information and prices given. However, once they have booked and fly then problems may arise. This is primarily from the passengers of the scheduled flight sector, who chat during their flight to the passengers next to themselves. Often they ascertain that they have paid more for the flight than they feel they need to have done, sometimes considerably more. Consequently, upon their return they complain to the travel agency. As a consequence the trust they may have for their travel agency may be lessened. Travel agents very rarely have any complaint from passengers on charter packages. This is because in most cases they do not know the actual cost of the flight, which is usually extremely low anyway.

At present there are some 24 fare options for most scheduled flights: full fare and discount for first and business class, but anything up to 20 fares for economy class. In the words of the travel agent, life in the travel industry has become an 'air fare jungle'. In an effort to cope with these various fares staff are well trained, but with so many variations available there may well be errors and problems arising.

Today's travel agent has to know not only as many of the seat prices as possible but also the variety of routings which can account for any disparity in prices. For example, because most businessmen want to travel from London Heathrow to Johannesburg, for example, as quickly as possible, they choose direct routings and flights. However, if a potential flier has the time to spare then a flight with Gulf Air via Bahrain will work out considerably cheaper. This is because many airlines fly to the standard destinations but have to, or choose to, get there via their home hub, for operational reasons mentioned earlier.

Another problem for travel agents is the need for airlines continually to promote new routes. For example, Emirates flies London Heathrow to Dubai. This is a busy and successful route. It also flies Dubai to Hong Kong. This route is not as popular because it takes 3–4 hours longer to get from Hong Kong to London than the non-stop direct route. On a recent trip one person paid £658 for a London/Dubai/London flight, whereas his colleague flew London/Dubai/Hong Kong/Dubai/London for only £654. This was because he was able to use the special rates which applied to the Dubai/Hong Kong sector. As previously mentioned, because of so many variations it is sometime impossible for a travel clerk to be able to keep abreast of all the fares and fare structures at all times.

Finally, yield management is used to attempt to reduce the amount of arbitrage which businessmen use. In their attempts to maximize seating capacity and sell special deals, the airlines have been somewhat self-defeating. An example given by the travel agent is the fact that an airfare from London Heathrow to Los Angeles is more expensive than an airfare from London to Las Vegas, and this flight has to land in Los Angeles where the passengers for Las Vegas change planes. Thus the travel agents are selling the London Heathrow to Las Vegas flights to passengers who only want to go to LA, telling then to just not use the Las Vegas portion of their tickets. This is called 'hidden city ticketing'. However, the airlines have now picked up on this and are suggesting that customers and, by implication, travel agencies who use this practice are, in the words of *Air Transport World* (Feldman, 1994), 'illegal, certainly unethical, immoral and probably fattening'. But is it? Are they? The Official Airline Guide records that on any day more than 700,000 changes are made to airline fares.

Nelms (1994) has suggested that it is this plethora of restrictions and conditions that cause this vast diversity of fares that are being used against the airlines to avoid passengers paying the more expensive fares. Obviously, from the viewpoint of airline revenue optimization managers, this practice goes against all their elaborate efforts to fill all seats with the highest paying passengers possible. It is possible to construe such avoidance as fraud, the IATA definition of fraud being 'any action that deprives a carrier of the normal revenue to which it is entitled, undertaken without the carrier's knowledge or consent'. The most common avoidance practice in the USA is reported by Feldman (1994) as being 'back-to-back ticketing'. She describes it thus:

> The traveller simply buys two sets of tickets – one a round trip from city A to city B and the other from city B to city A – with each having a Saturday night stay over. Bought so that the first leg of each ticket is in the same week, the tickets allow the traveller to fly out on the first leg of ticket A and back the same week on the first leg of ticket B.
>
> If each discount ticket costs less than half the full unrestricted fare, the user can discard the unused portions and still come out ahead. Or if the traveller needs to return to the same city, he may use the two remaining portions for the next journey.

But is this practice illegal? It is obviously in the interests of the airlines to propose that it is. The truth is that no one actually knows, and it is interesting that no airlines have actually contested the practice in the courts. It is probable that none of the airlines wishes to be first to be seen to take punitive action against its customers, so they turn a 'blind eye' to the practice.

How do the travel agents fit into the picture? The agents see the passenger as the customer, which may be anomalous, since it is the airlines that actually provide them with their income. It is interesting that Delta has actually accepted the practice. It seems to consider that if consumers are willing to go to the lengths needed to resort to multi-ticketing, then it is the airline's own fault for making the process so complex.

DEVELOPMENTS THROUGH THE 1990S

This section discusses the changes that have occurred in the recent past. The story begins with the fierce competition for passengers that was at its worst in the early 1990s and was very destructive to airlines worldwide. According to *Air Transport World*: 'The losses from, and government interest in, the Great US. Price Wars of 1992 ensure them a permanent place in the history of business. The question is: What lessons did airlines learn from the experience? And did they do any good?' (Anon., 1993).

During the period from 1991 to 1993, pricing was very unstable despite two attempts by the major airlines to raise business fares in the last quarter of 1992. In fact some airlines, e.g. USAir, found that they actually had to reduce their business fare to retain market share. Research by the Topaz organization showed that there was an annual fare pattern developing consistently. The fares started relatively high in each year from 1991 to 1993, then headed down rapidly, bottomed out in the spring months, flattened out, then began a slow recovery in the autumn. In 1992 the pattern was extreme, and the airline reactions were also bizarre. For example, Northwest introduced a 'Kids Fly Free' promotion and in response American Airlines introduced a ten-day, 50 per cent off promotion. According to *Air Transport World* (Anon., 1993), a former member of American Airlines staff described the response as purely 'emotional'. The response was particularly unexpected from American, which had been perceived as rational and responsible, basing its decisions on an industry-leading yield management system and a highly computerized decision process. Such reactions have turned out to be disastrous for the industry in general and often worse for the initiating company than for its competition. Such promotions are exactly opposite to the aims and rationale of the yield management and revenue optimization departments of the airlines.

There is a tendency for the airlines to blame their problems on unfair competition from airlines in Chapter 11 bankruptcy. However, this is a simplistic response, as pointed out by Peter Belobaba of Massachusetts Institute of Technology: 'As important as revenue management is to the airlines, even the "best applied" revenue maximization techniques cannot make up for poor management decisions, poor scheduling, irrational pricing or overall cost efficiency.'

It would appear that airlines need to take an integrated approach which matches the objectives and decisions proposed by the yield and revenue management departments and the sales staff when negotiating fares. However, Stephen Regulinski, United Airlines' vice president for financial planning and analysis, says that rational pricing is not the real problem that the airlines face. He suggests that their real problem is that they cannot afford to offer lower prices. He asserts: 'What's going on is structural change, which is quite independent of yield and pricing. That has to do with costs. And that will have a larger impact than price changes.'

By 1994, the airlines were, in general, heading back into profit after the period of low-cost competition. Trans World Airlines was still in Chapter 11 bankruptcy, so the restructuring that had been going on in the airlines was not, for TWA, complete. At the height of the competition 'mania', yield was down to as little as US¢7 per revenue passenger kilometre (RPK). During the period of uncontrolled competition to fill seats at any price, one of the main instigators of the price wars was said to be South West Airlines, which itself suffered severely from the fierce price cutting.

Airlines had by now realized that they did have to restructure to reduce costs, and Delta, for example, aimed to cut costs down to US¢4.66 RPK. Delta is now heading towards being one of the most profitable of the US airlines.

In Europe, one of the success stories has been Scandinavian (SAS), which has shown a 10 per cent growth in sales, with an accompanied 1 per cent drop in passenger traffic. Even better for SAS is that the 1 per cent drop in traffic was mainly in the economy class seats, while at the same time there was a 5–8 per cent increase in premium passengers. In Europe, over-capacity is now declining rapidly and the International Air Travel Association (IATA) is estimating that member airlines are on course to achieve a US$1.8 billion net profit on international operations in 1994. This was to be the first positive result for five years. In 1995, profits topped $5.5 billion. However, investors still considered this a low return on their investment (O'Toole, 1995a).

Recent developments in pilot recruitment has also reinforced the evidence for the upturn in airline activity. In an editorial, *Flyer* (1995) reported that British Airways were expected to resume their cadet training scheme, with up to 100 cadets being trained in each of the next two years. This is a reversal of the situation that existed for the past several years, with an over-supply of qualified pilots looking for employment. The shortfall is ongoing into 2000.

In 1995, Flight International carried out its latest rating of airline profitability and this is shown in Table 13.1

Table 13.1 Airline profitability for 1994

Top three	US$ million profit	Bottom three	US$ million loss
Singapore Airlines	601	US Air	685
British Airlines	376	Continental	613
Cathay Pacific	309	TWA	436

Source: O'Toole (1995b, p. 38)

The situation would seem to be improving, with only one-third of airlines showing a loss in 1994, compared to one-half showing a loss in 1993. Even better news is that four out of five airlines are now showing profits at an operating level. By 1999 the global industry was in the black.

There are a variety of reasons for this brighter outlook for the airlines. First is the more buoyant world economy, which has led to a 4.7 per cent increase in airline traffic in 2000. The American market, which is considered mature, has shown only a modest improvement, and Europe has shown a considerable boom. There has been a similar increase in business in the Asia-Pacific region. However, even given these optimistic forecasts for an improving market, yields are still expected to decline slightly in future years and so airlines will need to continue with their cost reduction programmes to match. The effect of rising fuel prices also has yet to take effect.

The effective application of yield management can be seen by perusing the operating figures for some European airlines. Table 13.2 shows the data for scheduled passenger traffic for four airlines for 1994.

Table 13.2 compares two large airlines (British Airways and Air France) and two medium-sized airlines (SAS and Swissair) It clearly shows two developmental patterns, in that the two successful airlines have similar load factors to the less successful competitors and all have shown an increase in RPK. However, British Airways and SAS produced a positive increase in yield, quite substantial in the case of SAS, whereas Air France and Swissair showed a considerable reduction in yield. This suggests that in addition to restructuring to reduce costs, the latter two airlines are taking too many economy or reduced fare passengers at the expense of business class passengers. This factor could be remedied, at least in part, by operating an effective yield management strategy, as aggressively applied by both British Airways and SAS. The Association of European Airlines recognizes that if the industry cannot produce a reasonable profit with the aircraft fuller than they have ever been, then there is little option but to reduce costs drastically and/or raise yields. Although yields did rise by 3 per cent in 1994, forecasts suggest that in the long term there will be a gradual decline, so cost cutting will be required. British Airways have led the field in this, not without a little trauma on the

Table 13.2 Some operating factors for four European airlines

Airline	Traffic (RPK) in millions (and % change)	Capacity change 1994 (%)	Load factor (and % change)	Yield change (%)
British Airways	86,232 (+7.3)	+5.9	71.1 (+1.2)	+0.6
SAS	18,466 (+1.8)	−1.5	65.6 (+2.1)	+6.6
Air France	50,199 (+15.1)	+6.8	73.0 (+1.9)	−9.9
Swissair	18,403 (+7.4)	+4.2	63.4 (+1.9)	−10.5

Source: O'Toole (1995b, p. 39)

way. The airline has achieved annual cost reductions of $200 million, with a total saving since 1991 of $1 billion. Smaller independent airlines, such as British Midland have also shown that it is possible to cut costs, while at the same time providing a value added business class service which fills up the aircraft with premium passengers by adept use of yield management.

In the Asia-Pacific region, the cost effect is again cutting into airline profits, despite the high growth in air traffic. Even the successful airlines, Singapore Airlines and Cathay Pacific, are faced with the dilemma of increasing costs and falling revenue. In this region, as in Europe and America, stiff competition and high capacity growth are impeding a return to good profitability. O'Toole (1995b) suggested that 'Battles for market share are no substitute for good housekeeping.' The authors would suggest that prudent application of yield management should continue to form a major plank in the implementation of that good housekeeping.

YIELD MANAGEMENT AND AIRLINE ALLIANCES?

Airline alliances are groupings of airlines that come together in an attempt to gain competitive advantage. These alliances may be long-lasting, as in the case of KLM and NorthWest, which have stayed together for ten years. However, some alliances may be less stable, with partners shifting between groups as they see advantage changing. Because alliances are seen to provide considerable advantages, sometimes the regroupings are contentious and hard-fought. Major alliances include Star (Air Canada, Air New Zealand, All Nippon Airways, Ansett Australia, Lufthansa, Mexicana, SAS, Thai International, United Airlines, Varig), One World (American Airlines, British Airways), NorthWest/KLM/Alitalia (soon to incorporate Continental and relaunch as Wings) and Delta Airlines/Air France, which is just forming and enlisting new members. The level of integration between these alliances varies greatly and often begins with codesharing operations on complementary routes.

In theory, alliance partners need to trust each other enough to share information. One key area in which alliances could gain competitive advantage, which is presumably why they were formed, would be to amalgamate their revenue management systems. Alternatively they could create, *de novo*, a system that integrated the member's yield management operations right across the alliance partner's networks. In practice life is not so simple, as airlines are notoriously wary of sharing their closely guarded data and research with anyone. To compound this, the sometimes ephemeral nature of alliance partnerships makes airlines even more wary of committing their specialist knowledge to the alliance pool.

In circumstances where two powerful airlines may consider an alliance partnership, a question is likely to arise over whose revenue management system to adopt. Even if the two systems could be merged, this is extremely unlikely to occur because no powerful airline wishes to give over any control of its cost and price structure to a partner, which may tomorrow be a competitor! In an alliance between large and small partners, there may be pressure on the weaker partner to adopt the yield management system of its larger partner. This may provide additional revenue to the vendor, with sale, installation and training costs being paid by the smaller partner. This may be resented or resisted by the smaller partner. Compounding this, there are cases where a smaller partner has the most sophisticated system. This is exemplified in the Star

Alliance, where SAS has a highly sophisticated yield management system, although it is a relatively junior partner as rated by size. SAS would be highly unlikely to be willing to forgo its system for a less sophisticated system from one of its larger partners. Equally, it would probably be unwilling to share its expertise, gained from expensive operational research, with its Star partners.

Star alliance also exemplifies another potential problem for alliance partners trying to integrate their yield management operations. This is that yield management systems developed for US or European operations and markets may well not be suitable for Thai Airlines, which operates in the Asian market.

Even time does not seem to help in the integration process. Feldman (1999) cites the case of NorthWest and KLM, whose alliance was created ten years ago. These airlines have anti-trust immunity, so that they are legally empowered to combine their yield management systems without judicial scrutiny. However, Feldman notes that, in ten years, the airlines have not even got to the point of creating compatible software systems for revenue accounting, let alone revenue management. She cites Ron Stewart of Andersen Consulting: 'They're chopping away at it', but not very quickly. 'We talk about e-speed; then there's alliance speed.'

One way in which things may move forward on the yield management integration front is that third party developers are becoming involved in developing IT systems for alliances. The way forward on this road could be for airlines to retain their separate systems and their valued key data, but to share some agreed data via a neutral core system. This will also need a bid price system (setting minimum seat values) to enable purchase of seats across members and the network. Airlines need to develop bid price systems anyway if they are to sell seats profitably on the Internet. The downside of this is that each airline will need to trust its partners not to dump low yield seats on it. Even when this is achieved it is likely that airlines will be looking over their shoulders for an escape route with minimum loss should an alliance fail.

Another potentially contentious issue is the equitable sharing of the additional revenue derived from adoption across an alliance network. This is no simple matter, and the provision of a suitable algorithm, taking account of all the factors, to suit all the partners, is no trivial task. Given all the foregoing considerations, and the extremely competitive and unpredictable nature of the airline market environment, it is perhaps not surprising that alliances have so far failed to make real advances in integrating their revenue optimization systems. Perhaps at the end, the will to do so is not there.

YIELDING CARGO

While most, if not all, airlines make use of yield management in their passenger operations, few to date appear to have overtly turned their attention to the issue of yielding their freight operations. This may have something to do with the multifactoral complexity of the space and weight algorithms that need to be developed to address the problem. However, airlines already have excellent information management systems in place, a good knowledge of their markets and customers and a high level of knowledge of their cost structures. Given that airlines are beginning once again, in 2000, to struggle with over-capacity, they surely cannot afford to ignore a market in freight that was valued at $40 billion (Philipson, 1998).

This is also a market that is predicted to grow considerably in the near future:

| 1998 | 1,453 |
| 2018 | 3,442 (predicted) |

Source: Airbus Industrie

Information technology is transforming many aspects of the business world, with consumers internationally expecting quality products to be delivered ever faster. To cope with this, manufacturers and distributors are reducing stock levels (just in time) while at the same time gearing up for faster development cycles. Alongside this is a requirement for more frequent and often smaller shipments. Freight transport is now seen by many as a value-added part of the logistics chain. The two major concerns of shippers are now seen to be cost and reliability of service. Reliability is stated as time defined and accurately tracked delivery. To respond to this, many freight and carrier companies have begun to develop integrated and seamless delivery systems. To compete, airlines need to form new alliances and partnerships to take advantage of this. While there are freight operators such as FedEx, which already integrates its own air transport operations into its logistics process, there is still great scope for the passenger carriers to augment their passenger revenues with freight services. They can do this by concentrating on high-value and high-yield business.

One way in which airlines can begin the process of yielding freight is to differentiate value as a priority by using a class system. At its simplest this might be three classes:

A   High value – must ship.
B   Medium value – should ship.
C   Low value – will ship when space is available.

Such a system could then be linked to an overbooking system. Class A goods (first class) will never be overbooked. Class B goods (business class) may exceptionally be overbooked. Class C (economy) can always be overbooked and held on standby.

Cargo forecasters need to have information available from the passenger yield management system, so that they can calculate weight and volume available for freight. Alongside this, the freight manager will need the yield management information for freight and the forecasting system will need to be continually updated.

As has been mentioned, freight is a multidimensional problem, with both weight and volume being highly variable. Evidence suggests that aircraft holds usually hit volume limits before they hit weight limits for freight. This means that some measure or estimate of freight density needs to be added to the algorithm.

One area of flexibility that airlines have with freight that they do not have with passengers is routing. In general, it does not matter which route the freight takes to get to its destination, or how many transfers there are, as long as the freight arrives on time. However, this flexibility again adds to the complexity of the algorithm for yielding freight, since some sort of matrix/network calculation will need to be integrated into the calculation for time and route planning. Nelms (1999) notes that complexity can compound errors. He cites an example of a shipment of freight from the USA that was bound for England. The paperwork was put on a flight to England, but the freight was sent to China. Because the freight was in China with no paperwork, it sat in China for six months before the link was made with the paperwork in England. In terms of customer relationships, there may have to be some trade-off of yield, according to gross customer value. This is similar to the corporate customer decisions that have to be made by hoteliers. This would mean that customer-weighting values that will vary over time would need to be built into the yield algorithm.

Overall, it can be seen that building a yield management system for cargo is a complex operation, but airlines and freight carriers have begun to address this issue.

STATE OF YIELD MANAGEMENT CARGO SYSTEMS AS AT 1999–2000

Current systems can be seen to have many limitations and none are truly yield management systems. Systems are based upon and adapted from passenger-orientated systems and have not been designed *de novo* as freight systems. Moreover, systems have, not surprisingly, been developed in the main by individual airlines, which means that they are difficult to integrate, for example, across alliances. There is also a problem within airlines that have more than one IT system in use. For example, SAS has problems with linking a software system that was 25 years old with a new system developed specifically for its new freight terminal at Copenhagen. One of the best systems, not surprisingly developed by American Airlines for its freight operation American Cargo, is called QIK. However, this sits on top of SABRE. It does not currently forecast capacity, it cannot totally fulfil the revenue optimizing role and it does not help with decisions as to which freight to carry or which to leave for any given flight. However, Scott Hyden, Vice President Cargo, Finance and IT at American, states that American Cargo 'is in the process of making a decision on some newer technologies which would forecast capacity, aid in revenue management and help make decisions on what freight to take or not.' United Airlines also realizes that important decisions need to be taken urgently. James Hartigan, Vice President Cargo, has said: 'For the most part we are doing business today as we did 30 years ago . . . This isn't going to work in 2000 and beyond.' Possibly the most complete system in place today is that produced by Cargolux, called 'cargo handling and management planning' system (CHAMP), which has been taken up by 22 companies (see Figure 13.2).

However, even CHAMP has no yield management capability, although it is a decision support system. According to John Goldberg, a management consultant for CHAMP, it will be another four years before CHAMP has the yield management capabilities of a passenger system.

FUTURE POTENTIAL

It is likely that, in the future, more factors will need to be taken into account in pricing decisions than have been used for yield management in the past. Since yield management is based upon historical data it will provide best results in a stable market situation, and in the case of airlines, when the percentage of filled seats is high. Although excess capacity is gradually reducing, the market situation certainly cannot be said to be stable.

In the past ten years, one of the main problems has been over-capacity and it has been calculated (Feldman, 1994) that this has forced US airline yields down by as much as 25 per cent. On the other hand, it is considered that where yield management is used it will boost revenues by only a maximum of 10 per cent.

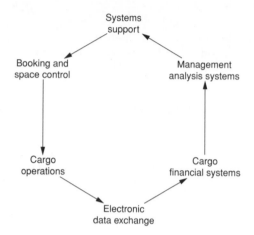

Figure 13.2 CHAMP
Source: *Air Transport World* (1999)

The types of problem that occur with yield management are that the decisions may be applied within too rigid a framework, leaving no room for the sales staff to manoeuvre in unexpected scenarios. Alternatively, the sales and revenue management staff might be allowed too much flexibility to override the system, use intuition to make decisions and generally interfere with what may be a well structured system. Probably the worst thing that can happen to a revenue manager, trying to control seating sectors with yield management, is executive interference. Ron Woestermeyer, President of Seabrook, has said that 'airlines are managing everything except the business'.

Feldman (1994) suggests that the new way forward may be fully automated pricing. Aeronomics Inc. of Atlanta, GA, USA, has already produced a system which is based upon use of 'readily available information, including the airlines' own information, central reservation systems, US Department of Transport, schedules, filed fares and fare changes, to name some'. The idea of the system is to use dynamic data to produce reports which are based on current information as well as the airlines' own historical records, providing managers with a potentially proactive toolkit. Aeronomics posits that consumer behaviour does not change radically, but situations in the real world do.

Delta has added a form of competitive benchmarking to this, a system called Quality Service Index. This index allows Delta to compare its own service with that of its competitors in a whole range of areas, including flight frequency, departure times, non-stop flights, frequent flier programmes and meal provision and service. On the basis of these factors Delta can decide its pricing policy for fares in relation to its competitors.

The future looks to be one of continuing turbulence and instability, where airlines will have to continue to become leaner, meaner and more prepared for competition. They will need to invest and make best use of the new super jumbo jets for long haul flights and the more efficient small jets for links to their hubs. They must look to their cost base for savings. They will have to cope with ever increasing regulation for safety and environmental concern. They will have a consumer base who will increasingly expect value for money.

The critical success factors may well be the efficient and effective airline, ready to innovate, that is consumer aware but willing to hold out for an effective cost base by continuing to implement a state-of-the-art revenue optimization system.

And then there is the Internet . . .

ACKNOWLEDGEMENTS

Our thanks are due to the Revenue Optimisation Team at British Midland Airways, whose information and assistance was invaluable.

REFERENCES

Anon. (1993) 'What's a revenue manager to do?' *Air Transport World*, August, 78–9.

Feldman, J. M. (1994) 'Getting serious on pricing'. *Air Transport World*, October, 56–60.

Feldman, J. M. (1999) 'This is progress?' *Air Transport World*, December, 46.

Flyer Airline News (1995) 'British Airways looking for new pilots'. *Flyer*, October, 14.

Graham, B. (1995) *Geography and Air Transport*. Chichester: Wiley.

Huyton, J. R. and Ingold, A. (1990) 'To yield or not to yield, that is the question'. Paper presented to the Conference of International Journal of Contemporary Hospitality Management, University of Surrey.

Lyth, P. J. (1993) 'The history of commercial air transport: a progress report, 1953–1993'. *Journal of Transport History*, 3rd series, **14**.

Nelms, D. W. (1994) 'Getting around airline fares'. *Air Transport World*, November, 108–11.

Nelms, D. W. (1999) 'Close but no cigar'. *Air Transport World*, September, 75.

O'Toole, K. (1995a) 'IATA forecasts record airline profits'. *Flight International*, 28 June, 5.

O'Toole, K. (1995b) 'Back to break-even'. *Flight International*, 28 June, 38–42.

O'Toole, K. (1995c) 'Has ValuJet broken the mould?' *Flight International*, 5 July, 24–5.

Smith, B. C., Leimkuhler, J. F. and Darrow, R. M. (1992) 'Yield management at American Airlines'. *Interfaces*, **22**.

14

Yield Management in Budget Airlines

Gerald L. Barlow

INTRODUCTION

The budget sector of the airline industry in both the UK and USA dates back to the 1950s and growth in demand for new holiday destinations, and the growth in air transportation. Initial budget airlines concentrated on the holiday market, offering charter flights. In Europe this meant Spain, France, Greece and the Balearic Islands in the summer and European ski resorts in the winter. Although this market still exists with specialist companies in the UK like Britannia Air, the start of low-cost flights began with 'the battle for the transatlantic business' as seen by Freddy Laker, with Laker Airways and The People's Express. The true budget airlines, however, took shape with deregulation in the United States. The most successful budget airline to develop in America was SouthWestern Airlines, while the main player in recent years in the UK has become easyJet. easyJet is probably following the SouthWestern formula in its operations and development of service and routes. The earliest European low-cost or budget airline still operating with significant passenger numbers and routes in the European market is the Irish carrier Ryan Air. The basic premise of business in the budget airlines is of course similar to that of the major inter-continental air carriers. There are, however, major differences between the inter-continental carriers and the budget airlines in both the United States and Europe, which have knock-on effects throughout the budget airline operations. The major differences between the operating processes and cost base of both types of carriers, are outlined in Figure 14.1. To be effective easyJet operates from low-cost airports (Luton and Liverpool) and flies to low-cost airports, (the costs charged to the airline operators are lower at airports like Luton than major international centres like Heathrow or Gatwick). Additionally, it operates only one type of plane, the Boeing 737–500, which again helps to reduce operating and running costs. This has benefits for yield management as it means only one type of capacity, consisting of 159 seats or units, is available.

Yield management within the airline industry may be a prerequisite, but in the budget airline sector it is still developing. Whether it is called yield management,

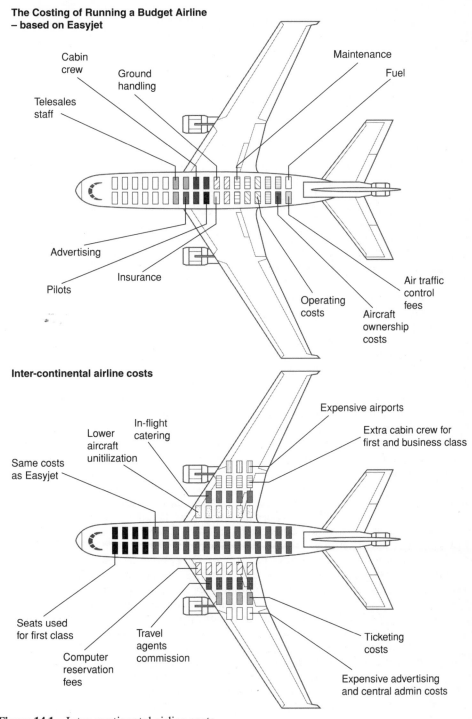

Figure 14.1 Inter-continental airline costs

revenue management or revenue maximization its aim or purpose is clear: to achieve the highest possible income from every single flight within an airline's portfolio of flights and routes. To investigate how budget airlines use and gain competitive advantage from this technique, easyJet is used as an example.

EASYJET

easyJet began in November 1995, with two aircraft operating a three flights a day programme between Glasgow, Edinburgh and its base at Luton. Business was brisk and turnover rose from £25 million in 1996 to over £50 million by the end of 1997. Routes began to expand and by 1998 these included Aberdeen, Edinburgh, Glasgow, Inverness and Belfast, complemented by Holland, Switzerland, Spain, France and Greece on mainland Europe, and adding Liverpool as a second English base. The company was conceived and run by a charismatic chairman, Stelios Haji-Ioannou, then a 31-year-old Greek graduate of the London School of Economics, who admits the idea came as a result of Virgin Airlines' first attempt to operate a franchise on the Athens to London route.

The company operates a no frills airline, based on short haul flights, aiming at maintaining a low-cost strategy and providing a quality low-price flight. In the autumn of 1997 Haji-Ioannou signed a $500 million order for a number of brand new Boeing 737–500 planes, due to enter service by the end of 1999, to provide the needed capacity for the company's expansion up to six million passengers. Haji-Ioannou's declared ambition is for easyJet to be the 'McDonalds' of flying, and he is perhaps on course for this aim. The image easyJet is creating is one of simple efficient service, for quick easy use. From the attractively simple but functional black trousers or skirts with orange shirts of the in-flight crew, to the very effective and efficient on-line Internet booking system which offers you a simple quick way to book your tickets (thus also providing a good view of a yield management system working minute by minute), easyJet has developed an effective and efficient operation, a single positive brand image and a successful marketing strategy. easyJet and Haji-Ioannou's commitment to Luton has probably done more in its first two years for Luton airport than any other single company or person, including Lorraine Chase and Campari! Future development plans for easyJet, to allow it to achieve its growth potential and fill the capacity created by the new plane acquisitions, include considering additional destinations, such as Munich, Copenhagen, Oslo, Hamburg, Berlin and Stockholm, along with plans to develop further the facilities at Luton Airport. Complementary company developments include a chain of Internet cafes and a low-cost car hire operation, both of which have implications for the use of yield management. Has easyJet been successful in its aims and objectives to date? By most methods of judgement, the answer must be yes. But perhaps British Airways' attitude is the best measure. In 1996, it described easyJet as the 'peanut airline' at the time of its launch, but just two short years later British Airways had announced the launch of its own low-cost airline, GO. Imitation, it is said, is the greatest of compliments. If you are uncertain of the success of easyJet the best answer is to try it for yourself. easyJet has seen an opportunity to develop direct marketing and sales of short haul European flights and has used all the operational tools necessary to ensure its success, one of the main tools being the development of its own dedicated yield management programme.

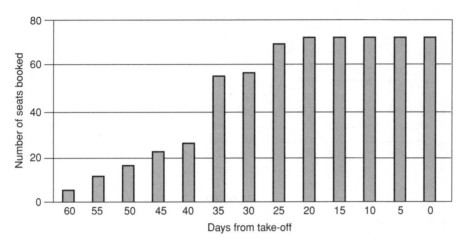

Figure 14.2 Airline booking patterns – leisure segments

YIELD MANAGEMENT AT EASYJET

easyJet uses an automated yield management system based around maximizing the revenue on each flight, every day. The easyJet reservation system is somewhat different from those of most of its competitors in that all its booking must be made directly with the airline reservations staff, via either the phone system or the Internet, as no agency bookings are accepted. The yield management system, managed by the revenue manager, is one specifically developed for and by easyJet, and is modified on a regular basis and adjusted as operations mature. easyJet has developed the model to cover each flight route, for every flight and every day. The principal aim is maximization of revenue, while ensuring that the appropriate balance of passengers is met.

easyJet does not segment its customers. However, it does segment its flights into the following categories:

1. Destination/route
   – business;
   – leisure.
2. Flight time
   – morning and evening flights;
   – daytime flights.

easyjet considers that there are, in its sector, two kinds of destination. The first is business destinations, like Glasgow, where the highest percentage of passengers are usually going for a short stay for business reasons. The second destination type is a non-business or leisure destination, like Palma, where the greatest percentage of passengers are going for non-business reasons with a longer stay over. The second segmentation is that of flight time, where the early morning, early evening, weekday flights tend to be regarded as business sector, while the middle day, late evening and weekend flights are non-business or leisure. Each segment/sector has differing booking patterns.

Figures 14.2–14.7 show different patterns of bookings. Figure 14.2 shows non-business customers, and Figure 14.3 business customers, with Figure 14.4 combining

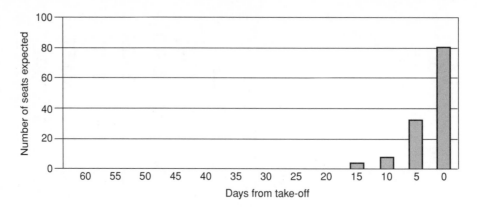

Figure 14.3 Airline booking pattern – business segment

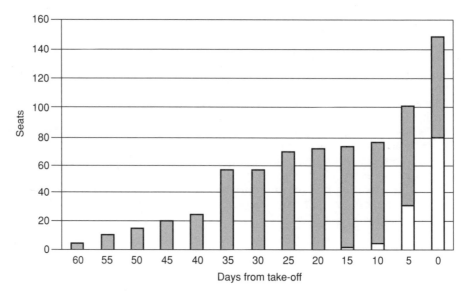

Figure 14.4 Combined booking pattern (date, time, destination)

them into a yield booking pattern. The prices can then be established around these expected patterns. The cheapest are available until, say, 25 seats are sold, then the next price bracket until 65, then 80, when the almost full price becomes available. The full price opens approximately ten days from take-off, when the majority of business segment fliers can be expected. Figure 14.5 shows actual bookings received as well as the yield plan.

Figures 14.6 and 14.7 indicate the yield plan for non-business/leisure flights, or weekend flights, together with an actual booking flow.

Figure 14.8 shows a flight yield pattern with the actual bookings received, along with the sales book-out price levels. This indicates that if the bookings received exceed 40 by or before 45 days from take-off, then the rate increases, and if it exceeds 60 seats sold

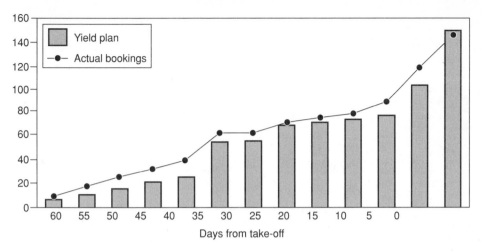

Figure 14.5   Booking plan showing yield forecast and actual (date, time, destination)

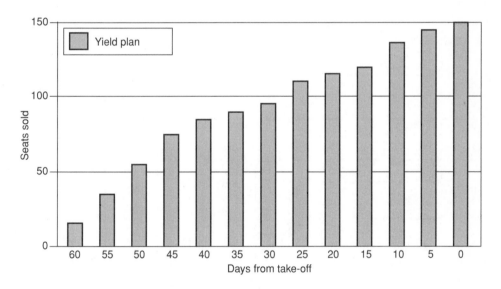

Figure 14.6   Yield plan for non-business destination

by or before 35 days before take-off, the price increases to the next level, and so on. Figure 14.9 highlights a similar booking pattern, but with late demand (business sector), and shows the price levels closing later and reopening again as the take-off date comes nearer, in the aim of increasing demand by offering a lower cost seat.

Why is yield so important to easyJet?

1. Unlike the major airlines, easyJet has a price structure with only a small degree of flexibility: the range in price available for any destination at easyJet is low. For example, Nice starts off at a low of £35 per seat, extending up to £129 depending upon level of bookings and number of days out from take-off. At BA, for a similar

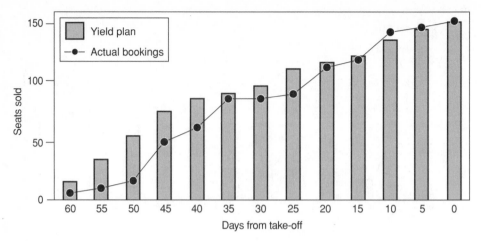

Figure 14.7   Actual booking chart – non-business destination (date, time, destination)

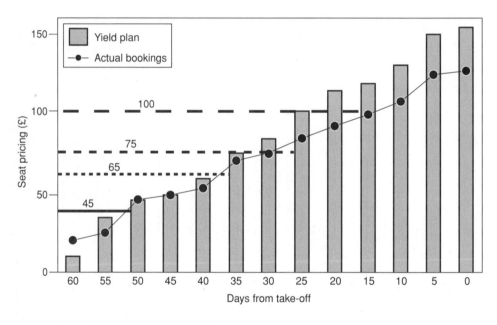

Figure 14.8   Yield pattern of actual bookings received and sales bookout price levels

flight, the price ranges from £284 standard fare, to £351 for business class, and the reduction can be very wide nearer take-off, depending upon source, e.g. bucket shop, travel agents' special late offers. This gives the major airlines a larger range of discounting opportunities, and more chance of a contribution to their fixed costs. (Both examples of prices are current at time of writing and one way.)

2. easyJet offers no agency bookings, and passengers can only book or inquire directly via the telephone sales staff and the Internet. Therefore it is essential to

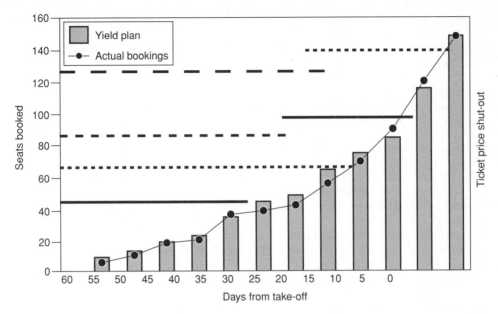

Figure 14.9 Booking pattern for late demand

have an easy and quick reservation system that shuts out and opens the various pricing levels as the take-off date nears, and the booking pattern becomes clearer. Any problems or delays within the computer yield management booking system could result in:

(a) staff giving different rates;
(b) lower rates than are necessary being given, and therefore loss of revenue;
(c) staff being able to differentiate prices as a personal choice;
(d) customers receiving unequal treatment, and thus becoming dissatisfied.

3. A system which instils confidence in the operation for management, sales staff and customers.
4. This system permits the staff to achieve a high level of operator efficiency, due to certainty, accuracy and simplicity, which is important to the company, and the operators who are paid on results (bookings achieved).
5. The easyJet Internet system is only possible with the use of a real-time yield management system. This system has proved so successful that during November 1999 it set a world record for airline bookings achieved via the net, 60 per cent of all bookings for a specific day.

How does this system vary from the traditional yield system operated by the major carriers?

1. The major carriers have inter-connecting flights, which means that yield management can be used to maximize the income over more than one flight. The use of low-cost flights encourages use of other flights, usually more profitable ones. easyJet does not have inter-connecting flights or arrangements with other carriers.

2.   easyJet does not have cancellations, whereas the major carriers offer this opportunity, with varying complexity.
3.   easyJet does not use travel agents, or any form of agency bookings, and this makes the reservations system easier and fully centralized.
4.   easyJet does not operate tickets, thus making last minute bookings easier to operate.
5.   easyJet operates from fewer airports, has only one central reservations base and has only a limited number of destinations.

Other major differences between easyJet and the majority of other airlines include:

1.   easyJet runs only one type of plane, the Boeing 737–500, which makes operations and reservations much simpler.
2.   easyJet offers few on board services, no duty free and only limited catering service, which is outsourced.
3.   easyJet operates without a ticket and has no actual boarding cards.
4.   easyJet runs with very few ground handling crew, and an extremely sales-orientated central head office.
5.   New plane purchases have been made and fit into the easyJet model, i.e. Boeing 737–500s.
6.   No external sales offices, or airport sales offices, are operated by easyJet. It has no linked or joint sales.
7.   Pricing is based strictly upon a revenue maximization process that matches the aims and objectives of yield management.

All these factors help the company to maintain a low variable cost, a key component in any successful yield management system, and provide an opportunity for leverage against its major competitors.

WHY DO AIRLINES PAY SO MUCH ATTENTION TO YIELD?

Airlines operate in a highly competitive market, and the low-cost operators, by the nature of this, are fiercely competitive. The environment in which they operate is one of high fixed costs, fixed capacity in the short term, a perishable product and seasonal variable demand. According to Arthur Andersen (1997), easyJet fulfils all the established criteria for the effective use of yield management. Dr Scot Hornick of Andersen Consulting has identified five 'functional aspects of yield management', as outlined below:

1.   *Market segmentation:* an area that easyJet feels is inappropriate, only segmenting by destination and flight time.
2.   *Price management:* systematically offering different prices to different customer segments in response to demand, the main issues for easyJet.
3.   *Demand forecasting:* forecasting future demand on the basis of past sales and known future events. Initially easyJet had obvious problems, as past history was short, and demand was increasing. It was through good forecasting of future events that yield management was successful. Now easyJet's historic records are becoming more useful, as it is becoming more established. But, with each new route easyJet opens, problems restart.

4. *Availability and/or capacity management:* limiting or shifting the availability of certain products or services according to customer demand. This is the main backbone of yield management in the airline sector. The capacity in terms of seats at easyJet is fixed, and is managed by good pricing to maximize the use of the limited seat capacity to obtain the maximum sales volume and to satisfy customer demand.
5. *Reservation negotiation:* in some sectors, management can achieve better yield with the management of price and availability, through the 'up-selling' of specific areas to higher more expensive products or 'cross-selling' to alternative products, so ensuring an even spread of sales. Here easyJet is restricted as it operates a single class product, and the pricing is fixed irrespective of the type or segment of customer. The price offered will be dictated by the yield management system, related to the seat availability and the closeness of take-off date.

Preconditions for yield management are:

1. *Perishable inventory/or seasonal demand:* seats on an aircraft are extremely perishable, for if easyJet fails to sell seats on say the 7.00 a.m. flight to Glasgow, those seats sales are lost for ever.
2. *High fixed costs or sunk costs:* thus resulting in a low or relatively low marginal cost of selling one extra unit. Here the cost of a Boeing 737–500 is a very high fixed cost, while easyJet's marginal cost of selling one extra seat on, for example, the 7.00 a.m. flight to Glasgow is very low.
3. *Fixed capacity either overall or in the short term:* easyJet operates a fixed seat capacity throughout the fleet, on all routes and flights.
4. *Advance purchase of service/product:* easyJet will only accept pre-booked flights.

The use of a yield management system has enabled easyJet to operate its low-price policy successfully from its conception. The main skills needed are developing a good forecasting plan and history to permit the yield system to be successfully developed. The differences between the levels of yield management within the industry are based upon the level of sophistication and actual understanding of the techniques and markets. Lack of systematization, improper use or lack of understanding of the system can lead to erroneous results and decisions. easyJet ensures successful operation through simple systematic operations, and constant modification of the system as the market continues to develop.

Obstacles and Success Factors

The barriers to the use of yield management in the airline industry are few, but the level of operation and sophistication will depend upon the complexity of the flight programmes and price structures. Table 14.1 summarizes them.

Kimes (1989a) identifies seven key techniques necessary for the success of a yield management system.

1. *Ability to segment:* easyJet has identified two major segments within its operations.
2. *Perishability of inventory:* clearly airline seats, like hotel rooms, are a highly perishable commodity.

Table 14.1 Barriers to yield management

Business-internal (Features of the business itself which interfere with yield management)		Environmental (Features of the environment in which the business operates)	
Attitudinal (Features of business philosophy, attitudes towards pricing, understanding of yield management)	Operational (Aspects of the way a business operates)	Infrastructural (Factors in the business environment which impede the effectiveness of yield management)	Regulatory (Governmental restrictions on a business's ability to practice yield management)
No awareness of YM.	Cost of technology.	Insufficient supporting infrastructure.	Governmental price restrictions.
Insufficient management skills; incompatible business philosophy.	Dependence on contract business with fixed prices.	Appropriate off-the-shelf computer YM technology not readily available.	
Resistance to formalizing information.	Insufficient information.	Rigid seasonality of demand.	
	High staff turnover.		
Negative misperceptions or scepticism towards YM.	Undifferentiated commodity product.		
No clear profit motive.	Capacity too small.		
As applied to easyJet			
Clearly fully aware.	Developed own technology; cost low compared to start-up costs.	New operation real issue.	High risk of governmental restrictions removed, thus opening way for easyJet type operations.
Management skills acquired.		High cost, so developed own model.	
New organization and staff, so no problems.	Lack of information a clear early problem.		
Very clear profit and financial incentives.	Staff new, constant training, ease of operations.		

Source: Arthur Andersen (1997)

3. *Product sold in advance of use:* easyJet, more than most airlines, insists on 100 per cent sales and payment in advance, and offers no in-airport sales desks.

4. *Fluctuation in demand:* clearly with a number of destinations and a number of flights at different times per day each day of the week, the demand for the product is subject to considerable variation.
5. *High fixed costs:* again, the cost of a 737–500 airline is relatively high compared to the ticket price.
6. *Low marginal sales costs:* here easyJet has a competitive advantage over most of its competitors, having very low variable costs.
7. *High marginal production:* here all airlines have a high marginal production cost. If the plane is full, and an extra seat is required for a customer, they are unable simply to produce one more seat and must decline, upgrade, provide an additional plane or compensate. It is here that easyJet, which operates a full-plane policy, with no standby, and no inter-connecting flights that can cause problems, has a cost advantage.

Kimes (1989b) also identifies five core requirements for the operation of a yield management system.

1. *Booking patterns:* yield management systems require information on how the reservations are made for a specific date. It is from this information that the system tracks and creates a picture of the booking process in the future, and from the past for the future. It is through this process that easyJet is able to: (a) operate its on-line live reservation system, and (b) create the necessary historic bookings profiles.
2. *Knowledge of the demand patterns by market segments:* as stated above, easyJet has identified, and operates with, two specific flight segments.
3. *An overbooking policy:* most airlines operate an overbooking policy, which when it goes wrong results in upgrades and stand-down discounts. easyJet works with very tight margins, without the back-up of business or first class upgrades to cover this situation, hence it operates to a pre-booked full seat capacity.
4. *Knowledge of the effect of price changes:* the team in charge of yield management need to know how changes in price will affect their customers, their occupancy and profitability. The major airlines change prices thousands of times a day, mainly in response to competitive pressure (Kimes, 1989b). Clearly this level of yield management system is sophisticated beyond the current needs of easyJet.
5. *A good information system:* to match all the requirements of a successful yield management system, the operator requires a great deal of accurate information. It is in this area that the company has its greatest problem, since it is very young, and therefore lacks the in-depth history of a company like British Airways. Additionally, the capturing of such data is very costly, in terms of both the methods used and staff time. This has resulted in easyJet only capturing information on actual bookings. The history on denied bookings is not recorded, an item which most writers (e.g. Orkin, 1988; Kimes, 1989a, b; Jones and Hamilton, 1992; Leiberman, 1993) suggest is a prerequisite for successful yield management. However, it is an area, in which the company acknowledges information is desirable, and hence this is more a question of the cost of collection and the time involved. The collection would need to be undertaken by sales staff, whose job is designed to be as time efficient as possible to help to maximize both the company's and the employees' income.

How Does This System Fit in with Senior Management Plans?

Clearly easyJet is focusing on Michael Porter's (1985) low-cost strategy, and its version of yield management helps it along this path. However, without top management commitment the process would fail. To this end, one person, the revenue manager, has full responsibility for the development and management of the system. The system is designed to be user friendly, very simple in operation and adaptable to any changes brought about by internal or external factors.

CONCLUSION

Theoretically yield management as a management tool in the airline industry has an enormous potential to increase the financial performance of the airline. Sir Colin Marshall (1992) attributed BA's success to cost cutting and sophisticated yield management. However, for a newcomer and a low-price airline, it is not going to be easy. However, easyJet has created a successful system within a short time. It first flew in November 1995, and has seen its market share grow from 0 per cent in June 1996 to 29 per cent by December 1997 on the UK–Nice market (Nice Airport, 1997). There are many lessons that companies, not just in the airline sector, can learn from easyJet's dedication and belief in the systems, which were necessary if it was to become truly successful. The findings presented here show how with determination and belief companies operating in a number of sectors could create and use a yield management system, suited to their specific needs to help create more successful operations. The system developed by easyJet perhaps has more in common with some hotel operations than many of its airline competitors, and certainly a number of them could learn from the easyJet experience. As Porter (1985) has pointed out, success comes from innovative products and service, often introduced by a competitor new to the industry.

REFERENCES

Arthur Andersen (1997) *Yield Management in Small and Medium-sized Enterprises in the Tourist Industry*. Brussels: Directorate-General XXIII, European Commission.

Jones, P. and Hamilton, D. (1992) 'Yield management: putting people in the big picture'. *Cornell Hotel and Restaurant Administration Quarterly*, **33**(1), 88–95.

Kimes, S. E. (1989a) 'The basics of yield management'. *Cornell Hotel and Restaurant Administration Quarterly*, **30**(3), 14–19.

Kimes, S. E. (1989b) 'Yield management: a tool for capacity-constrained service firms'. *Journal of Operations Management*, **11**(4), 348–63.

Leiberman, W. H. (1993) 'Debunking the myths of yield management'. *Cornell Hotel and Restaurant Administration Quarterly*, **34**(1), 34–41.

Marshall, C. (1992) *BA Company Report*. London: British Airways.

Nice Airport (1997) Monthly flight data, January.

Orkin, E. B. (1988) 'Boosting your bottom line with yield management'. *Cornell Hotel and Restaurant Administration Quarterly*, **28**(4), 52–6.

Porter, M. E. (1985) *Competitive Advantage*. New York: Free Press.

15

Revenue Management in Scottish Visitor Attractions

Anna Leask, Alan Fyall and Philip Goulding

INTRODUCTION

The visitor attraction sector plays a significant role within British tourism, stimulating destination development, revenue generation and employment. While there is no lack of visitor statistics for the sector, much of this information uses differing definitions and often *ad hoc* surveys. This chapter starts with a background to the visitor attraction sector and a market analysis, in order that the issues pertaining to yield management and Scottish visitor attractions may be set in context.

While many definitions of a visitor attraction have been recorded, the most widely acknowledged in the United Kingdom context is that stated by the Visitor Attraction Advisory Committee of the British Tourist Authority (BTA):

> a permanently established excursion destination, a primary purpose of which is to allow public access for entertainment, interest or education, rather than being a primary retail outlet or a venue for sporting, theatrical or film performances. It must be open to the public without prior booking for published periods each year and capable of attracting day visitors or tourists as well as local residents. (English Tourist Board, 1997)

The above definition is adopted here given its use by the national tourist boards and other relevant bodies in the UK. The emphasis of this chapter is on those attractions charging for entry rather than on the total attractions market, as it is in paid attractions that the application of yield management principles is more clearly demonstrated.

Inskeep (1994) identified three main categories of visitor attractions:

1. Natural attractions based on features of the natural environment.
2. Cultural attractions based on human activity.
3. Special types that are artificially created.

These attractions range from single unit, individual sites to clearly defined small-scale geographical areas that people visit for a short, limited period. The attractions offer 'an experience', an intangible product, often composite in terms of the purchase (Markwell *et al.*, 1997), that customers participate in and add their own values to. It is the perishable nature of the product, in common with many other sectors of the hospitality and tourism industry, that creates some of the revenue generating issues. Of the 6,074 visitor attractions in the United Kingdom most are small businesses, with 75 per cent recording annual attendances of less than 50,000 and only 7 per cent recording over 200,000 (BTA, 1998). Many do not operate as viable commercial businesses, relying upon financial or voluntary assistance from local authorities or trusts. High profile ventures can attract large amounts of funding and may raise industry standards, while few attractions offer return on investments and therefore there is little opportunity for reinvestment. Standards vary enormously between properties in terms of facilities, access and management, although a number of organizations have been set up to monitor quality and develop best practice. In Britain these include the Association of Leading Visitor Attractions, the Association of Scottish Visitor Attractions (ASVA), the Historic Houses Association and the Independent Tourist Consortium. These organizations are mainly industry-led, although they do work in conjunction with area, regional and national tourist boards.

An alternative classification for visitor attractions is to divide them into natural and man-made attractions and to distinguish them according to the reason for building. Natural sites may attract substantial numbers of visitors for activity-based purposes or simply as site-seeing locations. Built attractions can be split into those built for reasons other than tourism, e.g. churches and industrial sites, and those built specifically for use by visitors, such as visitor centres and galleries. However, it is not always an easy task to place each type of attraction within one single category. Country parks, for example, are classified here as *natural* attractions, although the argument is compelling that they are in fact designated areas for specific purposes. Table 15.1 shows the authors' categorization, taking into account the resources available as the product base.

The range and number of Britain's visitor attractions have shown remarkable growth since the 1980s, outpacing other tourism sectors (Robinson, 1994). According to Smith (1998) it is commonly held that in Scotland there is an oversupply of visitor attractions. This growth in the UK as a whole may be attributed to several factors: increased disposable income, greater leisure time, increasing levels of education, technological developments, media interest and increased marketing activity. Development of the sector displays a variety of trends, in terms of attraction type and visitor numbers.

The growth of visitor attractions impacts upon other areas of tourism activity, particularly those with close operational links. They are central to the development of destination. Their objectives of increasing visitor stay and revenue generation within a wider destination area are illustrated by the Lomond Shores visitor centre currently under development at Loch Lomond. Visitor attractions and transport have a close relationship due to the need for access. Indeed, attractions may directly lead to the development of transport networks and services, as in the high speed rail line to Disneyland Paris. In some cases the form of transport may even become a key attraction, as seen with the cable cars in San Francisco. Tour operators also benefit from the growth in popularity of visitor attractions, gaining in increased excursion package opportunities and lengthened seasons if attractions stay open.

Overall, the positive impacts of growth in the visitor attraction sector are through increasing the visitor numbers to an area, leading to increased employment, local area multiplier effects and more funds for conservation and investment. Negative impacts

Table 15.1 Classification of visitor attractions

Natural	Mountain areas
	Sites of Special Scientific Interest (SSSIs)
	Country parks
	Forests
	Lochs/rivers
	Wildlife
	Cultural landscapes
Built for purposes other than tourism/adapted for tourism use	Castles
	Historic houses/stately homes
	Gardens
	Industrial heritage sites
	Archaeological sites and monuments
	Churches and cathedrals
	Historic transport
	Harbour developments
	Farms open to visitors
Purpose built for tourism use	Visitor centres
	Heritage centres
	Craft centres
	Retail outlets
	Wildlife parks
	Museums and galleries
	Entertainment complexes
	Theme parks
	Sport and leisure facilities

centre on the seasonal nature of the employment and economic activity, the lack of sensitive use of environmentally aware management and resulting socio-cultural problems.

Swarbrooke (1995) identified key trends within the UK attractions market, including the move towards more participative exhibitions involving hands-on experiences and virtual reality, e.g. Our Dynamic Earth, which opened in Edinburgh in 1999. The 1993 Industrial Heritage Year in the UK stimulated interest in visiting workplaces such as farms and workshops. Visitors are also developing sophisticated expectations, often the result of experiencing high standards abroad, and are demanding those at home too, shown in the growing popularity of hi-tech, interactive interpretation. The quest for learning has encouraged the development of computer-based attractions, often involving experts in the field as interpreters, such as in London's Science Museum. Consumer trends influence attraction products and merchandise, such as the provision of healthy eating menus and fair trade items, while the concern for animal welfare has impacted on visits to zoos. The 1980s saw the spread of waterfront developments such as the Albert Dock in Liverpool, open air museums and resort complexes like Center Parcs in the UK, while the 1990s witnessed a major surge of interest in museums, heritage attractions and farm-life attractions, reflecting urban dwellers' growing interest in the countryside.

MARKET ANALYSIS OF UK ATTRACTIONS

According to the National Tourist Boards there were 6,074 attractions operating within the UK, recording a total of 409 million visits (BTA, 1998). A large number have opened in recent years, though while 50 new attractions opened in 1997, 60 existing ones closed! Sixty per cent of these charged admission, with the average adult admission being £2.71, and £1.59 per child (BTA, 1998). The prices varied between the types of attractions. The average adult charge at museums and galleries was £2.03, while that at leisure parks stood at £7.16. The BTA survey takes a sample of attractions receiving over 10,000 visitors per annum. A Deloitte & Touche (D&T) survey in 1997 showed that entrance charges have continued to rise faster than inflation, with charges now over 20 per cent higher in real terms than in 1993 (D&T, 1998). The highest admission charge levels were recorded in the pleasure attractions, with 50 per cent charging over £10.50, a reflection of their site, operational complexity and often extensive product offering. In contrast, nearly 70 per cent of cultural attractions and 61 per cent of wildlife/outdoor sites charge less than £5.50 (D&T, 1998).

Revenue sources recorded at the attractions used in the Deloitte & Touche survey showed that 55 per cent came from admission charges, followed by retailing, catering and other sources (D&T, 1998). This reflects an increasing reliance on admissions revenue, particularly in the wildlife/outdoor sector. Most attractions now incorporate an in-house retail outlet to boost revenue, while many have catering outlets either contracted out or operated in-house.

Ownership of the visitor attractions impacts upon the operation and management of sites. Traditionally museums, galleries, historic buildings and country parks have fallen under public ownership and, viewed as public services, have free entry, while the higher revenue generating sectors of theme and leisure parks have been owned by the private sector. It is also usual to find heritage centres and historic houses to be within voluntary or trust ownership. In *Visits to Tourist Attractions 1998*, 60 per cent of the 2,225 attractions with over 10,000 visitors were privately owned, 29 per cent were local authority owned and the remaining 11 per cent fell under state control (BTA, 1999).

In Scotland, visitor attractions show slightly different patterns of charges and ownership, compared with the UK as a whole. The Scottish Tourist Board (STB) Strategic Plan cites the wide range of visitor attractions as a key strength of the Scottish tourism product (STB, 1995). The plan gives priority to upgrading and renewing existing sites, rather than providing new ones, with an emphasis on the adoption of new technological and interpretation techniques. *The 1998 Visitor Attraction Monitor* (STB, 1999) surveyed a sample base of 976 paid and free admission sites. Of those responding, 55 per cent charged admission, 83 per cent of which charged between £1.00 and £3.99. The average entrance charge in Scotland was £2.75; the highest sector average was pleasure cruise/boat trip, while museums and art galleries, industrial and craft premises and churches recorded the lowest.

Ownership patterns are also recorded in the STB *Visitor Attraction Monitor*, with 33 per cent of attractions being privately owned, 21 per cent local authority owned, 17 per cent owned by other trusts and 15 per cent owned by Historic Scotland and the National Trust for Scotland (STB, 1999). As the largest operator and owner of attractions, Historic Scotland maintains over 330 free and paid entry properties, while the National Trust for Scotland also plays a major ownership role, with 105 properties. The Deloitte & Touche (1998) report showed an 'erratic trend in terms of overall visitor numbers to attractions since 1993, with little growth registered in any sector'. In 1997 both free and charging attractions recorded a decline in visitor numbers, with charging attractions noting fewer visitors in 1997 than 1993, when the UK was still considered to be in recession. The only categories in this survey to show increases were wildlife/outdoor charging attractions and free cultural properties. These results are particularly disappointing in the light of high levels of investment over the previous two years.

Similarly, the BTA (1999) survey shows a decrease in visitor numbers to free and paid attractions between 1997 and 1998. Both categories fell by 2 per cent, with no sectors recording increases, though several recorded no change, including museums and galleries, wildlife attractions and farms. It is important, however, to view the figures in the long term, where an increase in visits to tourist attractions of 10.9 per cent can be seen in the UK between 1993 and 1997, though this reflects a decrease in the share of tourist time, with increased time spent undertaking leisure and retailing activities (Keynote, 1998).

Comparison of Scottish visitor attraction figures between 1997 and 1998 shows another overall decrease, of 1 per cent, with 13 of the top 20 paid attractions recording decreases (STB, 1999). In particular, historic heritage sites and historic houses appear to have suffered, while interpretation and visitor centres and museums and galleries have increased their numbers. The seasonal nature of the visits is clearly seen in some sectors, e.g. castles, where 84 per cent of visitors arrive in April–September.

Reasons for these recorded decreases are varied, with operators citing increased competition, the strength of the pound, poor weather and changes in government policies. What is apparent, however, is that these properties need to find ways to manage themselves more effectively if they are to have a viable future. A vicious circle of low visitor numbers and increasing reliance on admission charges will not assist in the development of quality visitor attractions.

THE ROLE OF PRICING IN TOURISM SERVICES

The role and nature of revenue generation varies significantly across different types of tourism service. It is indeed a key factor in the heterogeneity of the tourism 'industry'. Comparing the role of revenue generation in visitor attractions with other tourism service operations highlights this diversity. For example:

- No *airline*, in either private or state ownership, will subsidize passenger fares to the extent of providing free passage as an operational norm, apart from accompanied infants. A contribution to total revenue from every passenger is a commercial expectation for an airline, even when a route is clearly non-viable but designated as fulfilling a social need (as with many geographically peripheral areas). The same principle applies equally to other transport modes and operations. As has been noted above, a significant proportion of visitor attractions in Britain have free entry or access.
- Within the *lodging* sector, even non-profit establishments such as youth hostels and YMCAs price their services, usually adopting simple price structures, which are published and communicated to target markets through a variety of distribution channels.
- In *tourist information centres* (TICs) the core activity, i.e. information provision, is normally free of charge. The cost of producing leaflets, timetables, 'what to do' guides and other print material normally rests with the individual service supplier or the destination marketing organization. However, destination marketing is increasingly viewed as a commercial activity, with the effect that TICs are often designated revenue centres. Accordingly, emphasis is placed on

the sale of information in professionally published formats and on the provision of a wider range of priced services. In larger TICs such services include bureaux de change, merchandised goods, maps and literature, the sale of commission earning tickets for events, tours and attractions as well as accommodation reservations. A prime example of this type of development is Edinburgh and Lothian Tourist Board's visitor centre in the heart of Edinburgh. It serves as a 'gateway' visitor information centre for Scotland as a whole, in addition to its function in promoting the services of the board's 800 or so member businesses.

For the *visitor attractions sector* as a whole, the nature of revenue generation tends to be a more complex issue. This is for a variety of reasons.

It is not always feasible to provide a *visitor management presence* at the site of many attractions. This is particularly the case for historic monuments and relics in remote, rural or wilderness areas such as at some of the small Celtic remains in the Highlands and Islands of Scotland. In economic terms, they are akin to the 'public' or 'collective' goods status ascribed by Wanhill (1998) to natural resource endowments, i.e. where consumption occurs freely as it is unrealistic to deny public access. Most natural attractions and many adapted for tourist use (as identified in Table 15.1) have no direct revenue generating capability.

Some attractions have *free admission policies* derived from the behest of benefactors (e.g. Glasgow's Burrell Collection), local authorities (City of Glasgow) or the trusts that administer them. In the absence of a gate price, revenue generation may rely on donations or 'honesty boxes' at unstaffed sites. The three problems with this form of *voluntary pricing* are that: contributions may not reflect visitors' value for money perceptions of the attraction, and the contribution is often an act of clearing loose change from a pocket or purse; revenue yield does not mirror any definable market segments; income flows from donations are unreliable and less predictable than when a managed pricing policy is operated.

An attraction may *trade off revenue from admission charges against broader marketing objectives.* This is the case in many privately operated workplace-based attractions like whisky distilleries, crystal glass factories and potteries. The visitor experience typically includes viewing the production process in action, interpretation of the historical development of the firm and its core products and an opportunity to purchase the product(s) at the place of manufacture.

McBoyle (1994) found that visitor-orientated distilleries formulate their visitor experience towards achieving longer-term marketing goals rather than short-term revenue maximization. Their strategic goals include using the visit to build customer awareness of the core product, developing customer loyalty to the brands experienced during the visit and promoting a lasting image of quality. To this extent, the visitor centre is part of the augmented product and serves as a means of generating future income to the organization.

Some visitor attractions have *short-term variations in their product offering.* For instance, museums and galleries may house touring exhibitions of national or international repute; castles and stately homes often host events such as tournaments, vintage vehicle rallies, media events or live entertainment. In such cases, a short-term variation in pricing to match the extended product may not be easily communicated in advance to all visitor markets. This is especially so in the case of non-local day excursionist markets. Hence, often no price variation is undertaken. The commercial role of special events or exhibitions is a means of generating repeat visits to the attraction.

The *range of revenue sources* for attraction operators outside the private sector can be diverse. As previously stated, relatively few attractions beyond theme parks and amusement parks are inherently viable, especially those based on natural or historic resources. Multiple site operators in particular often seek alternative cost-effective ways of generating revenue.

Historic Scotland, a government-funded agency whose mission statement is 'safeguarding the Nation's built heritage and promoting its understanding and enjoyment' (Historic Scotland 1999), recorded gross income from properties of £11.9 million in the 1997/98 financial year. Receipts from visitor admission charges and subscriptions from Friends of Historic Scotland constituted over 65 per cent of this. Other income sources include turnover from retail sales, publication sales, functions, facility hire fees, conservation income, property rental, funding from the Scottish Museums Council and management fees.

The National Trust for Scotland's (NTS's) trading activities include corporate entertainment, special events, rental of holiday accommodation, retailing, catering and even sea cruise operations. In addition to direct admission receipts membership of the Trust is a major income source. The policy of free admission to properties for NTS members and for members of the National Trust in England and Wales (a separate organization) means in effect that the Trust's pricing policy for membership fees is a significant determinant of its income potential.

The role of revenue generation is influenced in large part by *the role(s) of the attraction* itself. More than any other sector of the tourism industry, visitor attractions have a wide portfolio of roles to perform. These typically include a mixture of education, preservation, conservation, enlightenment and entertainment. Contributing to the economic well-being of the community or destination area is a role that may be made explicit in the development funding or subsidy of an attraction. Some of these roles are, if not mutually exclusive, difficult to reconcile in terms of income maximization.

Some ecclesiastic buildings of national importance have imposed admission charges for visitors over a long period, Salisbury Cathedral and York Minster being cases in point. Both are strong pulls on the destination choice for non-local visitors. Both also epitomize the dilemma of requiring continual large-scale repair, restoration and upkeep funding without having an assured income generation base. The decision to impose admission charges for London museums in the mid-1980s was a response to a similar dilemma of mixed roles and funding deficits.

CAPACITY MANAGEMENT AND VISITOR ATTRACTIONS

The applicability of yield management to tourism service suppliers is only meaningful in terms of the concept of *capacity* in each type of operation. In the lodging and aviation sectors (where the application of yield management is most advanced in practice), the *unit of production* is clearly defined. The perishable nature of the hotel bed-night and the aircraft seat occupancy is an intrinsic determinant of capacity for each of these sectors. Accordingly, the *yield statistic* can be easily derived from an occupancy rate (Orkin, 1988) or a passenger load factor.

In contrast, the measurement of capacity and therefore yield in visitor attractions is less easily discernible. The perishable nature of the bed-night, flight departure or other transport departure has no obvious equivalent for visitor attractions. Middleton (1994) defined service production as the *capacity to produce* rather than the *quantity of products* resulting from a productive process. In tourism, capacity utilization is equated with the consumption of services, i.e. when customers are present on the premises of the producer. In this respect, the general concept of capacity can be seen as appropriate to visitor attractions, despite the fundamental difference between the *temporary* nature of the bed-night or flight departure and the *permanency* of the attraction.

In common with the lodging sector, the core product is static and permanent. However, unlike accommodation, recurrent costs are not generally attributed to an individual sales unit such as a room, a bed or a mini-bar. Large theme parks like Alton Towers and Blackpool Pleasure Beach are a clear exception here, insofar as the demand for individual rides can be monitored easily. Similarly, the individual rides can operate as separate cost centres. Despite this, many major theme park attractions in Britain have adopted a single charge pricing policy for admission, with the effect that yield potential per ride is not ascertained.

For visitor attractions, the unit of production most closely relates to the through-put of people within a defined operating period. *Effective visitor capacity* is defined by Middleton as the space in which visitors can move around an attraction in comfort. The *annual productive capacity* for a museum, gallery or similar type of attraction is thus determined by the optimum visitor numbers at any point in time, their average length of stay, the hours of opening per day and trading days per year. While, in theory, capacity may be calculated according to the above variables, in practice visitor attraction operators find it difficult to calculate *available* capacity with precision given the range of extraneous factors influencing demand patterns and consumption patterns on site. However, with the exception of the best known, highest profile establishments located in prime hub locations and typically attracting a wide range of market segments, few British visitor attractions achieve their optimum utilization levels on more than a handful of days in an operating season.

Figure 15.1 depicts a fairly standard pattern of demand for an attraction operating year round. The horizontal line shows the fixed capacity to produce (FCP). The peaks indicate daily variations, with weekends showing greater incidence of visitor numbers. The shaded area identifies where demand exceeds supply, and in consequence where revenue is forgone (for example, because of customer resistance to queuing or temporary suspension of further admissions to relieve crowding). The area in which the demand line (D) is below line FCP represents the degree of under-utilization or under-production of the attraction.

The discretionary nature of the market for visitor attractions, relative to those of airlines and lodging sectors, translates into less predictable visitor flow patterns in any given short-term period. Supply-side capacity determinants include (in addition to the physical size of the attraction):

- limitations of market access, such as public transport, signage or location;
- controlled and designated entry points;
- health, safety and fire regulation provisions, e.g. demarcation of space between visitors and dangerous production processes in work-based attractions, and capacity controls for 'white-knuckle' rides in theme parks;
- provision of parking for private cars and/or coaches parking;
- ability to cater for special needs markets and for young children;
- provision of non-core facilities such as catering and retail operations.

Bull (1995) suggests that visitor attractions use supply rationing methods to overcome capacity constraints (i.e. effective supply) particularly where there is a problem with

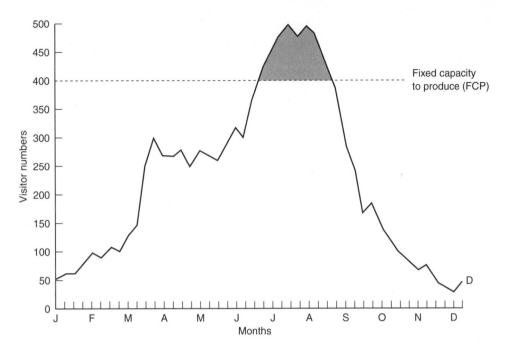

Figure 15.1 Pattern of demand for year-round attraction

excess demand at peak periods. Cordoning car parking, queue management and controlling the extent and level of provision of catering facilities are examples of supply rationing. In their study of cultural heritage sites, Carter and Grimwade (1997) assessed a range of strategies for adjusting capacity and site use by visitors.

HOW APPROPRIATE IS THE CONCEPT OF YIELD MANAGEMENT TO VISITOR ATTRACTIONS?

Kimes (1989) identified seven characteristics common to lodging and airline sectors that make them 'ideal candidates for yield management systems'. Table 15.2 summarizes each characteristic and its application to the visitor attraction sector.

As can be seen from Kimes's framework, the visitor attractions sector in its widest application does display some of the same economic, operational and market characteristics that pertain to airlines and accommodation. However, the diversity of visitor attractions in terms of both supply and demand characteristics, as outlined above, illustrates the difficulties in applying principles of revenue management to this sector. This has been discussed further by Yeoman and Leask (1999) with particular regard to heritage visitor attractions.

Visitor attractions' cost structures typically contain a significant element of fixed costs in relation to variable or operating costs (Yale, 1991; Middleton, 1994; Wanhill, 1998). Furthermore, capital costs for new attractions or for the extension or upgrading of existing sites tend to be high in relation to annual revenue potential for many attractions (Robinson, 1994).

Market-orientated pricing policies are therefore appropriate for attraction operators who have to meet the costs of servicing the investment on their attractions and their

Table 15.2 Yield management factors and visitor attraction characteristics

Characteristic	Visitor attraction application
Relatively fixed capacity	(a) Physical capacity fixed in short to medium term. (b) Concepts of capacity utilization and unit of production differ from airline and lodging sectors.
Ability to segment markets	(a) Demand is heavily geared towards leisure markets/discretionary demand; limited exploitation of corporate business opportunities. (b) Visitor attractions are able to segment leisure markets according to a range of variables – typically by age, affinity, place of origin, purpose, independent/group travel, etc. (c) Limited ability to segment according to time of utilization (in comparison to leisure centres) given generalized nature of demand. (d) Attractions use intermediaries such as coach tour operators, consortia and destination management organizations to segment markets.
Perishable inventory	(a) Element of permanency in the physical structure of attractions. (b) Perishability manifest when lack of demand results in underachievement of revenue potential. (c) Clearly defined inventory in revenue generating terms in some visitor attractions, e.g. preserved railways, theme park rides, special exhibitions. (d) Perishability of sales opportunities in non-core amenities, e.g. catering, retail, garden centre.
Product sold in advance	(a) Little relationship in practice between capacity and advance sales. (b) Promotional methods sometimes used to stimulate advance purchase of admission, e.g. discount vouchers, passport schemes, though these constitute a small proportion of sales. (c) Advance purchase largely confined to intermediary sales channels. (d) Independent visitors' decision to visit an attraction is usually discretionary within the destination choice and is not normally time specified.
Fluctuating demand	(a) High reliance on leisure markets causes unpredictability in demand patterns. (b) Performance of tourism in the destination area exerts a strong influence on visitor attraction demand. (c) Demand is influenced by leisure day trip patterns and activity. (d) Periodicity of demand (time of day, day of week) affects revenue flows.
Low marginal sales costs	(a) Marginal sales costs for visitor attractions vary according to size of attraction, level of admission charge, promotional spend and market base. (b) Lower for multiple attraction operators where economies of scope are realizable.
High marginal production costs	(a) High marginal cost of extending capacity beyond current full production limit, e.g. extending space. (b) Low marginal staff costs in voluntary sector attractions. (c) High marginal production costs in extending operating season at either end of season.

fixed costs of operation, i.e. where subsidies are not provided by public or voluntary bodies. In such cases, it is a function of pricing to optimize revenue yield through a variety of segmentation and promotional pricing techniques, in much the same way as airline and hotel operators do.

In the final analysis, the applicability of yield management comes down to a combination of two fundamental issues. On the one hand, the sector is at the mercy of a set of demand variables over which it has very little influence and even less control. On the other hand, there is the difficulty in solving the relationship between how visitor attractions define their capacity in sales volume terms and how they measure their unit of production.

MARKET DETERMINANTS OF PRICING POLICY FOR VISITOR ATTRACTIONS

The previous sections have discussed how operational and structural characteristics influence the role of revenue generation for visitor attractions. In considering what determines pricing policy, it is again apparent that visitor attractions are subject to a more complex interplay of factors than most other revenue generating tourism services. These include the following.

The Role of an Attraction within a Destination Area

An attraction can determine the existence of an area as a tourism destination in an international market arena. Major themed attractions such as Disney World and the Epcot Center in Florida and Legoland in Denmark epitomize this point, though the case is not confined to 'man-made' attractions. Managed historical/heritage attractions of world standing, such as Shakespeare's birthplace, the pyramids or the Lascaux cave paintings exert strong influence on visitor flows within countries or regions.

While in theory unique products may command a premium price policy commensurate with their status, in practice all monopolistic-based visitor attraction operators have to be sensitive to the complexities of the market place, whether international, domestic or localized. Even the least price sensitive world travellers will put a maximum market value on an attraction.

An attraction may project the identity and image of the destination (e.g. the Eiffel Tower, the Statue of Liberty). Most attractions, however, lack the element of competitive advantage inherent in having an international or national reputation and recognition, and in practice compete for visitors' preference with other attractions and other leisure activities in a destination area.

Price Levels of Competing Attractions

Competing attractions act as a barometer for price setting for most attraction operators. In a survey of Scottish visitor attractions conducted during the summer of 1999, in which the authors questioned attractions managers on the factors that influence the setting of admissions charges, 28 per cent of respondents cited admissions charge levels in competing attractions as a major pricing determinant. What is much less known is the extent and way in which other activities, such as entertainment, sporting and recreational pastimes, compete for visitors' time and expenditure, and their effect on pricing.

Value for Money and Price Sensitivity

Robinson (1994) found that visitor sensitivity to changes in admission price levels is relatively low at visitor attractions. This appears to be the case despite the fact that in Britain, visitor attraction admission charges have risen faster than the rate of inflation (Broom, 1990; D&T, 1998). Provided that an increase in admission charges is reasonable, Robinson noted, such an increase will tend not to act as a deterrent to entry at that time. However, pricing is relevant to perceptions of value for money and the potential of repeat visits.

On the other hand, the introduction of admission charges to attractions that were previously free is known to impact more on visitors. This is nowhere better illustrated than in the loss of trade suffered by the Science Museum and Natural History Museum in London in the late 1980s, following the introduction of charges for admission. It is likely that the major source of resistance to the imposition of charges on museums and galleries arises from local market segments that make multiple visits; for example, exhibition-orientated rather than facility-orientated visitors. Increasing admissions charges may, however, impact on potential secondary spend elsewhere within the attraction, such as catering and retail, with the effect that the average spend per visit increases less than proportionately to the increase in the admission charge.

Value for money perceptions and expenditure patterns at attractions are known to be influenced by the recreational context of the visit as well as by the different levels of visitors' interest. In his study of Isle of Man heritage attractions, Prentice (1993) found that visitors expressing a particular interest in heritage were more likely to make purchases at heritage attractions than were 'general interest' visitors. Various studies (Edwards, 1989; Johnson and Thomas, 1990; STB, 1991) have shown that tourists staying in an area have a higher on-site spend propensity in visitor attractions than do day trippers.

Seasonality

The seasonal and temporal nature of demand at many visitor attractions has been previously noted. For transport, accommodation and leisure site operators, seasonal or time differentiated pricing is an extensively used strategy, particularly in leisure-orientated markets and where intermediaries such as tour operators reformulate the core service. In contrast, seasonal pricing remains a very under-utilized pricing strategy for visitor attraction operators. This is all the more surprising given the high proportion of fixed costs of operation for most attractions and the consequent limited variation in attractions' seasonal costs. Wanhill (1998) suggests that the operators' resistance to seasonal pricing is influenced by customer value for money perceptions, given the relative uniformity of the product/visitor experience throughout the year. This view tends to mirror practice in most managed attractions in the UK. Where time differentiated pricing strategies are employed, the main objective of operators is often to shift demand away from peaks rather than to create additional demand.

The Degree to which the Product Can be Extended or Augmented

This may determine or influence price, i.e. according to the range of facilities and experience offered. In his study of Scottish whisky distilleries, McBoyle (1994) identified three levels of distillery differentiated by range of facilities and service provided for visitors. The primary level includes a tour, a dram of whisky and a shop selling a limited merchandise range. The secondary level includes a cafe and/or a more extensive shop, and at the tertiary level (e.g. Glenturret) the distillery includes corporate dining and conference facilities. Glenturret's pricing reflects its upmarket positioning and, as McBoyle states, the distillery claims to achieve high average spend per visitor.

PRICING AND REVENUE MANAGEMENT IN SCOTTISH VISITOR ATTRACTIONS

Across the whole spectrum of UK visitor attraction operations, the trend is towards greater reliance on commercially generated income sources. Attraction operators in the public and voluntary sectors are increasingly having to adopt the same kinds of business planning practices as their private sector counterparts. The phasing out of Section 4 development funding by the English Tourist Board in 1989 and the Scottish Tourist Board in 1994 played a significant part in heralding in a business culture for attraction operators. In Scotland this process has been furthered since 1994 by the transfer of the business development remit for tourism from the STB to the Enterprise Company networks. As Berry (1994) pointed out, potential financial sponsors of historic buildings now expect to see cash flow forecasts, revenue and out-turn, and other performance targets as a management norm before committing themselves to lend support. This sentiment applies equally to all types of visitor attraction.

One of the main organizations attempting to develop management skills and quality attractions is the Association of Scottish Visitor Attractions (ASVA), whose mission statement is 'to improve the quality and viability of visitor attractions in Scotland'. It is inevitable that the funding constraints on local authorities will encourage a greater emphasis on commercial revenue generation and concomitant management approaches in visitor attractions. The two largest multiple attraction operators in Scotland (Historic Scotland in the public sector and the National Trust for Scotland in the voluntary sector) both symbolize the move towards a more commercial bias in heritage/historic site management.

Historic Scotland

Sixty of the 330 ancient monuments, sites and historic buildings forming the Estate of Historic Scotland are income-generating attractions. These range from Edinburgh Castle, an attraction of international renown in a major tourist hub – which generated in excess of £7 million in 1998/9 – to castles, abbeys and industrial buildings in remote locations, which record fewer than 5,000 visitors and under £25,000 revenue per annum. The agency was reviewed in 1994, resulting in the setting of 'key performance targets' relating to visitor numbers, revenue generation and the primary objective of the conservation and presentation of Scotland's built heritage. Increasing income generation is specifically identified as an agency management objective. Commercial revenue objectives and opportunities are pursued via three principal means:

- through marketing initiatives with the travel trade (Historic Scotland has a Travel Trade Unit);
- development of on-site retail and catering facilities;
- the implementation of a central sophisticated information system which monitors costs, revenues and budgets on individual property, regional and estate basis.

Although visitor number and revenue targets are set centrally for individual revenue-generating monuments, the process involves regional teams and individual monument managers who have knowledge of the local tourist market. Revenue targets are subdivided into admission charge revenues and trading revenues which include retail sales, restaurants/tea rooms (gross of VAT) and events. Spend per visitor (SPV) analysis is undertaken on a monthly basis according to each trading component, so that the relationship between admission spend and other on-site spend can be evaluated and the trends monitored. Priorities are set with the regional teams on an annual basis for how to increase SPV at each revenue-generating site in their area.

Pricing policy and strategies are likewise determined collectively at the centre, with input from the agency's travel trade, marketing, events and retail management. Pricing strategy includes:

- *Price banding monuments* into five main adult price bands covering 56 of the 60 properties. Urquhart Castle (Loch Ness), Whithorn Priory (with access to the archaeological excavations), Stirling and Edinburgh Castles have each been designated higher price levels because of their national significance.
- *Streamlined market pricing.* Three standard admission charge levels per property: adult (including students); 'reduced' (including senior citizens and ES card holders (unemployed)); child rate (5–16 years), with free admission for accompanied under 5-year-olds.
- *Joint-entry tickets* for properties in close proximity, including all sites on Orkney.
- *Scottish Explorer Tickets* covering admission to all Historic Scotland properties, valid for either 7 or 14 days at adult reduced and family rates.
- *Group discounts.*
- *Voucher incentive scheme* offered to accredited tour operators.
- *Membership rates* for Friends of Historic Scotland, segmented into adult, senior citizen, student, family, cohabitees, corporate and life membership rates.
- Free entry for pre-booked *educational parties* in off-peak months.
- Participation in the *Great British Heritage Pass* scheme for overseas visitors.

A student rate trial period was undertaken in 1998 but failed owing to time-consuming complications in the student identity system. Negative aspects of visitor queuing were felt to outweigh the benefits of the discount and it was stopped.

Despite the considerable variation in seasonal operation across the estate's properties, seasonal pricing has not been adopted on a property-by-property basis. However, Historic Scotland is participating in the national Autumn Gold and Spring into Summer campaigns, giving reduced admission rates and extended opening hours for attractions throughout Scotland in these shoulder periods.

National Trust for Scotland (NTS)

The NTS is a voluntary organization with charity status, established by an Act of Parliament in 1931. Its remit includes the care and conservation of landscape, historic buildings and their contents, and promotion of public enjoyment of these attractions. The NTS had 228,000 members in 1998 (NTS, 1999a) and has a mutual free entry policy for members of the National Trust in England and Wales.

Of the NTS's 120 properties, 48 can be described as commercial (having a managed admission charge system) and a further eleven rely solely on 'honesty boxes' (voluntary pricing). The remainder either offer free entry or are not open to the public (e.g. tenanted cottages) (NTS, 1999b).

Although the ultimate decision-making body of the Trust (the Council) and the Executive Committee are voluntary committees, the organization's commercial objectives are carried out by a management group, including a managing director of the trading company and a commercial director. Budget and revenue targets are formulated at a regional level (individual property managers consult with and report to a regional director) and in turn are sent to the central management group for ratification. A formula approach is applied, based on performance scanning of local, regional and national tourism trends and forecasts and attainment of past budget targets.

The NTS thus has a broadly similar approach to Historic Scotland in the deployment of revenue-generating activities. Although each property is viewed as a cost centre, only the main commercial properties have individual revenue budgets.

Budget formulation includes all significant costs (160–170 items) and sources of income applicable to an individual property. Admissions revenue is thus considered one element among several for the assessment of overall yield potential. For example, gross profit on corporate entertainment is relatively important in relation to admission charges in Haddo House; Culzean Castle's revenue sources include holiday cottages, corporate hospitality, weddings, banquets and other special events.

As with Historic Scotland, a strategic rather than tactical pricing approach is generally adopted by the NTS. Short-term discounting, seasonal price variation and time differentiated pricing are not normally applied, except in the case of participation in the Spring into Summer campaign and, conversely, where a major event in a property prompts levying an extra charge on visitors. Properties are price banded, though in several of these split pricing is used (in addition to composite pricing) to promote visits to separate parts of the property. This applies particularly in larger attractions such as Culzean Castle and Country Park, Brodick Castle and Gardens, and Falkland Palace and Gardens. The NTS also rebands properties periodically, to take account of restoration costs or added facilities.

Price segmentation of admission charges is based on a percentage discount of the adult rate, e.g. the concessionary rate (including children) is 67 per cent of the adult rate, the pre-booked adult party rate is 80 per cent of the full adult rate and the family group rate calculated as two adults plus one child, though up to six children can accompany the adults.

Travel trade sales include Trust Touring Passes (in conjunction with the National Trust in England and Wales) for the domestic UK market (commissions to tour operators and other travel principals) and participation in the Great British Heritage Pass scheme. Utilization of these passes is monitored in individual attractions. Despite the opportunity cost of these pass schemes (i.e. the risk of reduced revenue yields from visitors who might otherwise have visited individual properties at full adult cost), Batchelor (1994) argues that for attraction operators and users alike, the benefits outweigh the disadvantages.

SCOTTISH VISITOR ATTRACTIONS SURVEY

In 1995 the authors identified a number of characteristics common to many visitor attractions across the United Kingdom, with a particular emphasis on those attractions located in Scotland. Both the number of public and voluntary sector attractions for whom the generation of profit was often not the primary goal and the large number of small private businesses with limited resources serving small markets were typical characteristics of the visitor attraction landscape of the mid-1990s (Goulding and

Leask, 1997). In addition, the pervasive adoption of a 'curatorial' rather than a 'commercial' management approach by attraction management, the limited use of comparative performance information and the habitual seasonality of many attractions were also accorded as 'typical' for many visitor attractions across the country at the time. In the light of these characteristics the *Scottish Visitor Attraction Survey*, which was conducted by two of the authors back in 1995, set out to determine the views of visitor attraction managers with regard to the applicability of revenue management to visitor attractions, as well as to assess the actual utilization of revenue or yield management practices within visitor attractions. The findings, which were reported in the first edition of this text, went a long way to support these initial characteristics and demonstrated that in the mid-1990s visitor attractions were relatively unsophisticated in their general management and pricing practices, despite the above average usage of yield management techniques.

With the passage of time and the numerous changes to the visitor attraction landscape in Scotland, as mentioned throughout this chapter, a further survey was conducted by the authors to compare and contrast the progress of the visitor attraction sector in Scotland since the previous study in 1995. In particular, the updated survey set out to revisit the views of managers with regard to the applicability of revenue management to visitor attractions and the actual utilization of revenue management practices within attractions. However, in view of the changing trading climate the survey sought to identify the views of visitor attraction managers in Scotland on a number of additional issues. The title of the survey, *Scottish Visitor Attractions: Revenue, Capacity and Sustainability*, alludes to the three distinct themes of the research, which was clearly much broader in remit than the original survey conducted by the authors.

The research approach chosen again entailed the construction of a questionnaire designed for posting to managers of visitor attractions which levy a charge for admission. Each had been personally identified and contacted by telephone to elicit their appropriateness and willingness to participate in the survey. In total the survey sample contained 510 paid entry visitor attractions in Scotland. The number and nature of attractions included is very close to those reported recently in the official visitor attraction survey conducted on behalf of the Scottish Tourist Board. In practice the 510 attractions included in the sample represent a census of all attractions which charge for visitor entry in Scotland. The survey methodology generated 301 usable responses, an overall response rate of 59 per cent and the basis for a very credible, reliable and noteworthy analysis.

The questionnaire sought to elicit four sets of information:

1. General operating and market-related information for the establishment (e.g. period of opening, visitor numbers, annual turnover, the standard adult charge for admission, sources of revenue generation and the extent to which they are either managed in-house or contracted out to a third party).
2. Pricing, promotional and other marketing-related activity relating specifically to the core attraction, such as seasonal pricing, price differentiation by market segment, promotional pricing methods and those factors deemed to be important and influential when setting entry prices.
3. Revenue management information. For example, who determines prices, management information activities, the extent to which computers are used as a basis for management decision-making, the relevance of revenue management to the visitor attraction and the extent to which the respondent felt that yield management is practised at their establishment.

4. Information relating to the degree to which their establishment was impacted by environmental concerns such as overcrowding, general wear and tear, traffic congestion, general visitor behaviour and the extent to which visitor management initiatives compromised the overall authenticity of the attraction.

As was the case with the original survey back in 1995, respondents were given the opportunity to provide further comments concerning some of the key issues raised in the survey, as well as being requested to provide, in their own words, what they thought makes a 'successful' visitor attraction. The key findings to the survey are summarized below and provide a comparative update to those findings presented in 1995.

Those numbers of attractions which open on a seasonal basis (normally April to September) still represent just under two-thirds of all responding attractions. Only a small minority of attractions (5.5 per cent) has sufficient commercial confidence and market attractiveness to exceed nine months of opening.

In terms of market size, the majority of visitor attractions in Scotland continue to have limited markets in volume terms. Well over half of responding attractions (63.3 per cent) report visitor attendance figures at 20,000 or less with only 20 per cent reporting visitor numbers of 50,000 or above. This compares unfavourably with the 1995 survey results, where one-quarter of all responding attractions recorded visitor figures in excess of 50,000.

The number of small-scale visitor attractions in Scotland has increased slightly whereby just under two-fifths of attractions now report turnover figures less than £25,000. However, there is a healthy representation of attractions that exceed the £100,000 barrier. Just under one-third report turnover above £100,000, while 6.9 per cent report turnover between £500,001 and £1 million, with a final 4.5 per cent of attractions (13 in total) that exceed the £1 million figure. As is the case with many other sectors of the tourism industry, the market for visitor attractions in Scotland is dominated by a few very large and lucrative players but consists mainly of a significant number of relatively small players surviving with limited resources and limited markets.

As before, the majority of attractions contain a wide selection mainly of on-site revenue-generating facilities and services. The most popular form of facility is the gift shop, whereby 77 per cent of respondents record either an in-house (74 per cent) or contracted out facility (3 per cent). These figures are almost identical to those reported in 1995 and indicate a state of maturity among visitor attractions in the inclusion of gift shops in their establishments. Other popular forms of revenue-generating facility continue to include guided tours around the attraction (51 per cent), cafes, restaurants and/or take-away outlets (43, 18 and 8 per cent respectively) and garden centres (9 per cent). Only a few properties contract facilities out to third party operators. A large percentage of respondents also indicate that 'ad hoc' (54 per cent) and 'other' (21 per cent) events now represent key items in their revenue-generating strategies. The rich myriad of events which respondents include under this banner include weddings, auctions, conferences and corporate functions, filming, exhibitions and numerous educational events.

The consistency with the research findings of 1995 continues, whereby neither seasonal admission pricing nor time, day and month differentiated pricing is practised to any great extent, with 94 per cent of respondents reporting no variation in prices. This reflects the exact percentage reported back in 1995. This would seem to suggest that only in a very small number of cases are admission charges being used as a vehicle to control, manage, limit and/or influence visitor behaviour at attractions. This is of particular significance to those attractions that experience problems of overcrowding.

The imaginative use of admission charges can, in some instances, alleviate problems of overcrowding and facilitate the more effective management of concentrated visitor numbers.

In contrast to the above, price differentiation of different visitor markets is widely practised. This is particularly the case for school parties (78 per cent), senior citizens (76 per cent), groups (67 per cent) and families (65 per cent). These results run parallel to those reported in 1995, as do the differential pricing rates for students (52 per cent) and business groupings (25 per cent). In addition to these, it is interesting to note that although only 8 per cent of all respondents claim not to vary their admission charges from the standard adult rate, there are a generous number of attractions which offer differential rates for disabled visitors (40 per cent) and members (54 per cent).

Promotional pricing techniques continue to be frequently employed by Scotland's attraction operators. For those who responded to the question, free or price reduction entry vouchers/tokens from media promotions are used by a significant 85 per cent of attractions. Likewise, 46 per cent use joint promotional vouchers in tandem with other attractions, tour buses and other collaborating partners. Again, for those who responded to the question, just over one-third of attractions are involved in some kind of marketing promotional consortium in an attempt to promote their visitor offering more efficiently and effectively.

A wide variety of factors appear to reflect the means by which admission charges are set at visitor attractions. Those two factors that respondents claim to be very/extremely important when setting prices are the maximization of end-of-year revenues (41 per cent) and the ability to charge what the market will bear (39 per cent). These two are closely followed by the need to achieve pre-set revenue targets (32 per cent) and the interesting finding that there exists a relatively strong moral obligation to keep admission charges as low as possible so that no one is excluded from visiting the attraction (31 per cent). The need to keep prices strictly in line with competition (30 per cent), the need to keep prices low in order to maximize the volume of admissions (29 per cent), the need to achieve break-even (28 per cent) and the need to maximise end-of-year surpluses (25 per cent) are also relatively influential in the price-setting equation. In contrast, the use of visitor feedback (24 per cent), the need to keep prices high in order to fund conservation programmes (19 per cent) and the need to keep prices high in order to keep visitor numbers down to reasonable levels (2 per cent) are accorded less importance and significance to the price-setting debate. Other factors mentioned as significant to the setting of prices include the need to create a perception of value for money, the link to the anticipated secondary spend while at the attraction and the average time spent at the attraction by the visitor. Local authority influence and the percentage of 'locals' anticipated as visiting the attraction are also mentioned. This said, it must be borne in mind that one-fifth of all respondents state that prices are set externally by others. In reality this reflects the pricing practices of Historic Scotland, the National Trust for Scotland and some of the locally owned properties.

When asked which single factor exerts the most influence on the pricing decision in their respective establishment, 'charging as much as the market was anticipated to bear' came out on top. This was closely followed by the fact that many respondents felt 'a moral duty to keep prices as low as possible', so as not to exclude any one from visiting their attraction.

The responsibility for setting prices 'in-house' again clearly reflects the management structure and ownership of an attraction. Of those who responded to the question, 18 per cent cited the general manager against 17 per cent before, although far fewer respondents accredited the marketing/sales and finance managers as having a significant role to play

(5 and 3 per cent respectively). In contrast, the owner clearly demonstrates the most influence as an individual (28 per cent), whereas the predominance of joint decision-making by trustees or by committee together account for just under one-third of all responses.

Attraction operators continue to differ in the extent to which they undertake management information tasks pertaining to revenue management. Omitting those who failed to respond to this question, 94 per cent of respondents claim to evaluate the pattern of admissions season-by-season (54 per cent manually, 36 per cent by computer and 4 per cent by both means). This closely mirrors the 93 per cent recorded in 1995. Although still widely practised, though to a much lesser degree, analysis of the revenue from various market segments (62 per cent), of group bookings (60 per cent) and of future sales forecasts (53 per cent) are all closely monitored. These results suggest a marked improvement in the adoption of management information activity since the previous survey. However, the analysis of group cancellations (27 per cent) continues to lag behind other areas, as does the measurement of the effectiveness of distribution channels (35 per cent) such as tour operators, consortium members and destination managers. There is, though, a noticeable improvement from four years ago. This would appear to suggest that the adoption of more purposeful analytical methods is slowly becoming the norm in the visitor attraction sector, although there are considerable gaps in some instances that suggest cause for concern. As a footnote, in practice centralized systems in the multiple attraction operators mean that revenue and market monitoring practices apply to a higher proportion of attractions than is apparent from the survey results.

Defined as 'a systematic approach to maximizing revenue from the sale of intangible tourist services and facilities through pricing, market segmentation and service enhancement', just under half of all respondents felt that yield/revenue management was undertaken at their establishment. This figure is disappointing in the sense that nearly 60 per cent of respondents from the previous survey acknowledged their usage of yield/revenue management. Although the negative response pattern among many attractions reflects the centralized nature of their management structures, it does also suggest that the benefits to be derived from such management techniques have been either poorly communicated or poorly misunderstood by the practising managers. There is also the option that visitor attraction managers are in fact practising yield/revenue management but merely fail to refer to it as such.

Unlike the previous study that concentrated on the issues of yield/revenue management alone, the current survey included a key section on environmental impacts with a deliberate reference to the issue of sustainability. The key findings are reported below. They are integral to the entire management of visitor attractions and frequently will overlap on many key decisions; not least the question of charging for admission, let alone how much.

The principal environmental concern that appears to be causing the greatest problem to operators of visitor attractions is the threat to the authenticity of the attraction by visitor management initiatives implemented by the operators themselves (51 per cent of respondents expressing that the issue is very/extremely important). Hence, in an attempt to control and manage the flow of visitor numbers, the operators may inadvertently damage the essence of the attraction visitors are in fact coming to enjoy. Fyall and Garrod (1998) identified this issue in a previous study where the problem was even more marked. Suggestions were made in this paper for the imaginative use of admission charges to alleviate some of these problems. However, there is little evidence of this to date with regard to visitor attractions in Scotland.

The second area of concern with regard to environmental issues reflects the behaviour of locals towards visitors (49 per cent of respondents regarding it as very/extremely important). Ironically, there would also seem to be a problem with the attitude of visitors to residents local to Scotland's many and varied visitor attractions (35 per cent of respondents expressing it as very/extremely important). Hence, although more obvious causes for concern such as overcrowding, traffic congestion and damage caused by graffiti and pilfering are issues for many, they do not pose such a worry and potentially negative impact on visitor attractions in Scotland as others. The nature of the relationship between visitors and locals and the threat to the authentication of the attraction product by well meaning operators represent by far and away the greatest threat to the sustainability of many visitor attractions in Scotland.

In many ways, the results from this survey do not differ significantly from those reported in 1995. This could mean one of many things. First of all, the similarity of results may be a consequence of the construction of the sample, or virtual census, of visitor attractions charging for visitor entry. The vast majority of attractions included in the original survey featured again in the updated survey, with many, it would appear, not experiencing or implementing significant change since 1995. The difficult trading conditions of the past couple of years certainly seem to have contributed to the static nature of many of the results, although the improved adoption of management information tasks pertaining to revenue management is to be commended. If anything, the results yet again confirm the particular characteristics of the Scottish visitor attraction landscape and demonstrate the opportunities and challenges to be faced in the new millennium.

To close, respondents were asked in an open format what in their opinion made a successful attraction. A wide range of opinions were offered, the most frequently repeated being: satisfied customers, value for money, stimulating, enjoyable, educational, memorable, quality product, uniqueness, seamless experience, as well as an attraction that keeps up with the pressures of time and at the same time meets its original aims and objectives.

CONCLUSION

This chapter has illustrated the diversity of the visitor attraction sector in terms of both supply and demand characteristics and has demonstrated the difficulties in applying some of the principles of revenue management to visitor attractions. Despite the numerous benefits that visitor attractions generate to the tourist economy, the volume, variety and scope of attractions across the UK make the standardized application of revenue management practices virtually impossible. Unlike airlines and hotels, which have a particularly good track record of the application of revenue management, visitor attractions continue to lag behind. Much of this can be attributed to the fact that the measurement of capacity and unit of production of visitor attractions is subject to wider interpretation than is the case for airlines and accommodation. For one, many attractions serve a far broader set of objectives than a purely commercial remit. In some instances, the relevance of revenue management is negligible and at times non-existent. This is particularly the case for many historic and heritage attractions, galleries and museums. However, the disappointing visitor levels recorded in many attractions across the country, coupled with the reported oversupply of attractions in a crowded tourist market, represent significant management challenges for the sector. In essence, the supply of visitor attractions, although outpacing the growth of other tourism sectors, has outpaced the growth in demand for such establishments. The challenge has thus been set whereby attractions need to find alternative ways to manage themselves more effectively if they are to have a viable future. Low or static visitor numbers, coupled with an ever growing reliance on admission charges for revenue purposes, does not necessarily represent a sustainable partnership for the development of a quality visitor attraction sector.

The above is particularly relevant in Scotland, where the visitor attraction sector is still predominantly characterized by small-scale operations in the voluntary and public sector domains. Key management activity often takes place away from the individual property. Despite this, there is sufficient evidence to suggest that the sector is beginning to recognize the commercial, rather than purely curatorial, aspects of managing visitor attractions. This said, there are still many attractions that fail to acknowledge that revenue-generating activities are important to the long-term well-being of their establishment. In part, this can be attributed to the quite unscientific approaches to pricing decisions in the sector and the relative lack of accurate, up-to-date and reliable market information upon which to base pricing decisions. Although many attractions appear to charge what they feel the market can bear, it can be argued that the paucity of relevant market data inhibits operators' ability to respond professionally to market conditions, which, in other tourism sectors, is vital to the successful implementation of yield management systems.

Visitor attractions are clearly moving in the right direction in terms of their ability to be considered as a serious, professional and commercially aware sector within tourism. However, the competitiveness for visitor spend is getting harder and harder, with competition continually emerging from within the attraction sector, the wider tourism industry and all other sources of competition eager for the discretionary leisure spend. Perhaps the time has arrived when acceptance and application of revenue management practices become the norm in the management of visitor attractions rather than a series of principles only relevant to the more commercial aspects of other tourism sectors.

REFERENCES

Batchelor, D. (1994) 'The Great British Heritage Pass'. *Insights*, July, C1–6.
Berry, S. (1994) 'Conservation, capacity and cashflows – tourism and historic building management'. In A. V. Seaton, C. L. Jenkins, R. C. Wood, P. Dieke, M. Bennett, L. R. Maclellan and R. Smith (eds), *Tourism: the State of the Art*. Chichester: Wiley.
British Tourist Authority (1998) *Sightseeing in the UK 1997*. London: BTA.
British Tourist Authority (1999) *Visits to Tourist Attractions 1998*. London: BTA.
Broom, G. (1990) 'Heritage attractions market'. *Insights*, November, B23–38.
Bull, A. (1995) *The Economics of Travel and Tourism*, 2nd edn. Melbourne: Longman.
Carter, B. and Grimwade, G. (1997) 'Balancing use and preservation in cultural heritage management'. *International Journal of Heritage Studies*, 3(1), 45–53.
Deloitte & Touche (1998) *UK Visitor Attractions Survey 1998*. London: Deloitte Touche Tohmatsu.
Edwards, J. (1989) 'Historic sites and their local environments'. In D. Herbert, R. Prentice and C. Thomas (eds), *Heritage Sites: Strategies for Marketing and Development*. Aldershot: Avery.
English Tourist Board (1997) *Visitors' Charter – National Code of Practice for Visitor Attractions*. London: ETB.
Fyall, A. and Garrod, B. (1998) 'Heritage tourism: at what price?' *Managing Leisure*, 3(4), 213–28.

Goulding P. and Leask A. (1997) 'Scottish visitor attractions: revenue versus capacity'. In I.
    Yeoman and A. Ingold (eds), *Yield Management: Strategies for the Service Industries*, 1st edn.
    London: Cassell.
Historic Scotland (1999) *Annual Report and Accounts 1998/99*. Edinburgh: Historic Scotland.
Inskeep, E. (1994) *Tourism Planning*. New York: Van Nostrand Reinholt.
Johnson, P. and Thomas, B. (1990) 'Measuring the local employment impact of a tourist
    attraction'. *Regional Studies*, **24**(5), 395–403.
Keynote (1998) *Tourist Attractions Market Report 1998*. London: Keynote Ltd.
Kimes, S. (1989) 'The basics of yield management'. *Cornell Hotel and Restaurant Administration
    Quarterly*, **30**(3), 14–16.
McBoyle, G. (1994) 'Industry's contribution to Scottish tourism: the example of malt whisky
    distilleries'. In A. V. Seaton, C. L. Jenkins, R. C. Wood, P. Dieke, M. Bennett, L. R. Maclellan
    and R. Smith (eds), *Tourism: the State of the Art*. Chichester: Wiley.
Markwell, S., Bennett, M. and Ravenscroft, N. (1997) 'The changing market for heritage tourism
    a case study of visits to historic houses in England'. *International Journal of Heritage Studies*,
    3(2).
Middleton, V. (1994) *Marketing in Travel and Tourism*. Oxford: Heinemann.
National Trust for Scotland (1998) *Travel Trade Manual 1999*. Edinburgh: NTS.
National Trust for Scotland (1999a) *68th Annual Report 1997/8*. Edinburgh: NTS.
National Trust for Scotland (1999b) *Guide to Scotland's Best*. Edinburgh: NTS.
Orkin, E. (1988) 'Boosting your bottom line with yield management'. *Cornell Hotel and
    Restaurant Administration Quarterly*, **28**(4), 52–6.
Prentice, R. (1993) *Tourism and Heritage Attractions*. London: Routledge.
Prentice, R., Witt, S. and Hamer C (1998) 'Tourism as experience: the case of heritage parks'.
    Annals of Tourism Research, **25**(1).
Relihan, W. J. (1989) 'The yield-management approach to hotel room pricing'. *Cornell Hotel and
    Restaurant Administration Quarterly*, **30**(1).
Robinson, K. (1994) 'Future for tourist attractions'. *Insights*, March, D29–40.
Scottish Tourist Board (1991) *Survey of Scottish Folk Festivals 1990*, Market Research Results
    RH4. Edinburgh: Scottish Tourist Board.
Scottish Tourist Board (1995) *Strategic Plan for Scottish Tourism*. Edinburgh: Scottish Tourist
    Board.
Scottish Tourist Board (1999) *The 1998 Visitor Attraction Monitor*. Edinburgh: Scottish Tourist
    Board.
Smith, R. (1994) 'Scotland's newest visitor attractions'. In A. V. Seaton *et al.* (eds), *Tourism: the
    State of the Art*. Chichester: Wiley.
Smith, R. (1998) 'Visitor attractions in Scotland'. In R. MacLennan and R. Smith (eds), *Tourism
    in Scotland*. London: International Thomson Press.
Swarbrooke, J. (1993) 'The future of heritage attractions'. *Insights*, January, D15–20.
Swarbrooke, J. (1995) *The Development and Management of Visitor Attractions*. Oxford:
    Butterworth-Heinemann.
Wanhill, S. (1998) 'Attractions'. In C. Cooper, J. Fletcher, D. Gilbert, S. Wanhill and Shepherd
    (eds.), *Tourism Principles and Practice*, 2nd edn. London: Pitman.
Yale, P. (1991) *From Tourist Attractions to Heritage Tourism*. Huntingdon: Elm.
Yeoman, I. and Leask, A. (1999) 'Yield management'. In A. Leask and I. Yeoman (eds), *Heritage
    Visitor Attractions – an Operations Management Perspective*. London: Cassell.

16

Yield Management Practices

Una McMahon-Beattie and Kevin Donaghy

INTRODUCTION

In an attempt to respond to the demands of a highly competitive market environment, excess capacity, a slow recovery from recession and high inflation, a number of major international hotel chains such as Hyatt, Marriott and Radisson began to adopt the management technique known as yield management (YM) (Fried, 1988; Koss-Feder, 1994) around the middle of the 1980s. In relation to hotels, YM is a revenue maximization tool which aims to increase net yield through the predicated allocation of available bedroom capacity to predetermined market segments at optimum price (Donaghy *et al.*, 1995). While the airline industry has been credited with the development and successful operation of YM (James, 1987; Carter, 1988; Larsen, 1988), it is currently being utilized by an increasing number of group and independently owned hotels in order to increase the effective use of their available bedroom capacity and improve financial success (McMahon-Beattie *et al.*, 1999).

It has been suggested that traditional accommodation management techniques and working practices are not that far removed from an organized YM system (Bradley and Ingold, 1993). The use of YM as a management tool is not entirely an innovation, as most hoteliers currently practise some form of YM, such as the adjustment of room rates to temper demand fluctuations between peak and off-peak seasons, midweek and weekend business. Despite this, previous studies have identified a low level of understanding of the concept and its precise function (Berkus, 1988; Salomon, 1990; Gamble; 1990; Donaghy *et al.*, 1994). The following text examines the results of two surveys into the accommodation management practices of hotel managers in Northern Ireland and the UK as a whole in relation to pricing and rooms inventory management, and identifies an increasing understanding of YM among hoteliers. Their strategies for increasing revenue and occupancy are examined in relation to a comprehensive framework for a formal YM system developed from the work of Orkin (1988, 1989a), Kimes (1989), Rowe (1989) and Jones and Hamilton (1992).

YM DEFINED

In relation to the airline industry, YM has been defined as 'the process by which discount fares are allocated to scheduled flights for the purposes of balancing demand and increasing revenues' (Pfeifer, 1989), while Belobaba (1987) considers YM to be the revenue per passenger mile, with yield a function of both the price the airline charges for differentiated service options (pricing) and the number of seats sold at each price (seat inventory control). Agreeing with these definitions, Larsen (1988) further crystallizes the meaning of YM in the airline context by dividing it into two distinct functions: overbooking and managing discounts. In its application within the hotel industry, YM is concerned with the market-sensitive pricing of fixed room capacity relative to a hotel's specific markets. As Kimes (1989, 1997) has stated, YM consists of two functions: rooms inventory management and pricing. The goal of YM is the formulation and profitable alignment of price, product and buyer. On a strategic level, Jones and Kewin (1997) have extended the definition of YM to incorporate historical performance, demand forecasting and decision-making to enable revenue optimization. This definition further highlights the differentiation between the strategic and tactical role that YM plays in managing capacity. Orkin (1986b) warns hoteliers that it may be dangerous for them to follow the practices of the airline industry and suggests that YM in the hotel industry should be considered as an 'integrated management technique' which 'includes all those systems and procedures designed to maximise revenues resulting from the sales of a product or service which has revenue producing ability and which perishes with the passage of time and is more or less fixed supply'. Lieberman (1993) proposes a broader definition which considers YM to be a management tool with the capacity to yield a net result of enhancing revenue and customer service capability through 'a melding of information systems, technology, probability, statistics, organizational theory and business experience and knowledge'. Despite some general debate, the common 'thread' in all these definitions is the potential of YM to enhance revenue generation.

YM AND THE HOTEL INDUSTRY

There is, however, some concern over the applicability of YM to the hotel industry. While both the airline and hotel industries operate with fixed capacity and perishable inventories, Kimes (1989) and Orkin (1989a) have identified some difficulties with the potential application of existing YM strategies:

1. *Multiple night stays.* Airline seats can be used on one day only and at one time only. Hotel guests, however, can arrive on a low rate day and stay through a number of high rate days. This leads to problems with rate determination.
2. *Multiplier effect.* By concentrating on the revenue that can be generated from the accommodation function, a hotelier may be ignoring the potential revenue which could be generated from other areas in the hotel; for example, restaurants, bar, banqueting suites, conference and leisure facilities.
3. *Lack of distinct rate structure.* It is well established that airlines have restrictions and barriers which, for example, prevent business travellers from securing a rate that has been structured for leisure travellers. Very few hotels have such restrictions.

4. *Decentralization of information.* Often within hotel groups the central reservation system is not integrated into the property management system. This may lead to the selling of rooms at too low a rate.

Kimes (1989) has stated that YM practices are applicable where the following six conditions exist:

- capacity is relatively fixed;
- demand can be separated into distinct markets;
- inventory is perishable;
- the product is sold well in advance of consumption;
- demand fluctuates substantially;
- marginal costs are low and marginal production costs are high.

Since these conditions predominate in both the airline and the hotel industries, it may be concluded that YM is applicable in some form in the lodging industry. Indeed, Kimes (1997) develops her ideas further by outlining a number of preconditions for the success of YM and has suggested a number of factors or ingredients which are prerequisites for the implementation of YM as a functioning, workable system. Therefore, it would appear that YM has been successfully adopted by hoteliers (Sieburgh, 1988, Donaghy *et al.*, 1998), though some modification in the approach used has been inevitable. Indeed, Hansen and Enringa (1997) cite evidence to show that YM within the hotel sector is distinct from YM within the airline industry but is successful in both.

Measurement

Traditional methods of performance measurements in hotels, such as average room rate and occupancy rate, have tended to focus on either the volume or value of accommodation sales. The problems associated with each of these have been well documented (Brotherton and Mooney, 1992; Donaghy *et al.*, 1995). Yield management aims to optimize both these variables simultaneously and this can easily be seen in Orkin's (1988) efficiency statistic:

$$\text{Yield} = \frac{\text{revenue realized}}{\text{revenue potential}}$$

In the definition by Orkin (1988) realized revenue is: 'actual sales receipts' and potential revenue is 'income that could be secured if 100 per cent of available rooms are sold at full rack rate'.

There are a number of drawbacks in using the yield efficiency statistic to compare the performance of hotels (Donaghy *et al.*, 1995). Primarily, rack rates are charged to one segment of the market; that is, walk-in or chance arrivals. For the many hotels which rely on discounted leisure and/or conference business, the use of the yield statistic would result in an unrealistic, low and totally misleading percentage. Second, where there is no uniformity in rack rate or pricing formulation, this may lead to inconsistent comparisons across hotels. Indeed, there are no industry-specific criteria for the establishment of rack rates. Third, the yield efficiency statistic focuses on revenue generated from accommodation in isolation from costs and other revenue-generating areas in the hotel. If YM is effectively to enhance yield then these should be taken into consideration. The market segment profit analysis (Dunn and Brooks, 1990) is one proposed technique which goes some way to encouraging a long-term pricing strategy based on maximizing profit through the accurate integration of the full costs in supporting specific markets.

An Age-old Practice

Boyce (1991) contended that most hoteliers practice some form of YM and aim to maximize their bottom-line revenue. Often, room rates are adjusted to temper fluctuations in demand between peak and off-peak periods, midweek and weekend business. As Lieberman (1993) has stated, 'Yield management does not try to accomplish anything different from what hoteliers have always tried to do: supply a quality product and be as profitable as possible in the long term.' Formal YM systems bring this process one step further. Breaking down the year by season, week and day, it determines in principle the exact level of demand by market segment. However, the 'frequency and scope of the decision-making process' (Relihan, 1989) are the features that make a YM system different from traditional accommodation management techniques. Computerization has aided this process but YM is not wholly dependent on sophisticated technology and can be practised without it (Jones and Hamilton, 1992; Lieberman, 1993).

Accordingly, it might be expected that hoteliers would be familiar with or at least receptive to the concept of YM. However, in the early 1990s this was not the case. Salomon (1990) suggested that YM was still seen as the dark science by 80 per cent of the hotel industry. This point is reinforced by Gamble (1990), who believed that much more than seminars are required to persuade general managers of the benefits of YM. 'At the end of the day, one hundred percent occupancy is safe and any sub-optimal decisions can be explained away. Anything other than one hundred percent is dangerous in career terms.'

As such, this research was carried out in order to determine the levels of knowledge of the concept of YM among hoteliers in Northern Ireland and subsequently in the UK as a whole. It also sought to ascertain if hoteliers operated a formal YM system in full or in part. This required the identification of the key stages/components in a formal YM system (see Figure 16.1) adapted from the work of a number of researchers (Orkin, 1988, 1989a; Kimes, 1989; Rowe, 1989; Jones and Hamilton, 1992).

AN OPERATIONAL FRAMEWORK

Much of the available literature on YM within the hospitality industry has been somewhat repetitive and fragmented. However, it generally agrees that a structured YM system will significantly alter the traditional approach to accommodation management in the following areas:

- data collection;
- determination of optimum guest mix;
- establishment of capacity levels;

- technological input;
- pricing;
- customer/hotel interface;
- human resource implications and training;
- use of incentive schemes;
- management focus.

Taking these into account, Figure 16.1 outlines a ten-stage framework for the effective operation of a YM system in the hotel environment. Primarily, this case study focuses on stages 2 to 6 of Figure 16.1, which are concerned with the accommodation management techniques of rate determination per market segment and rooms inventory management.

SURVEY FINDINGS

At the time of the first survey, in 1993, the hotel industry in Northern Ireland was dominated by small, independently owned hotels. Based on the population of 123 registered hotels, a self-administered questionnaire was distributed to 70 of these hotels. The sample was representative of the spread of hotels throughout the six counties of Northern Ireland and they were located in both urban and rural areas. The sample had an adequate representation of hotels by size and scale of operation incorporating new and well established properties and included both independent and group-owned hotels. In contrast, the second survey in 1996 focused on the UK corporate sector, where it was felt that interest in and application of YM was greatest. A questionnaire was administered to a representative sample of 300 out of 717 hotels drawn from a listing of the top 20 group hotels in the UK (Goymour, 1994). Follow-up interviews were carried out with eight of the respondents who were among a group of 33 managers identified as practising a formal YM system.

Levels of Knowledge of Yield Management

Within Northern Ireland, there was a general lack of awareness in the industry with regard to YM. It was found that the majority (86 per cent) of hoteliers in Northern Ireland were unfamiliar with the concept and its precise function. Only a small number of hoteliers (13.33 per cent) could accurately identify a definition of YM as opposed to definitions of capacity management and that of a hypothetical decision-making strategy. Notably, 20 per cent of managers acknowledge that they were uncertain about the meaning of YM. Set in a European context at the time, this appeared not to be unusual. Gamble (1990) reported that a mere 26 per cent of European hoteliers understood YM. In contrast, in 1996, almost 87 per cent of respondents were able to identify the correct definition of YM. Even allowing for a number of managers who may have selected this definition at random, the data would still suggest that managers in corporate hotels are more familiar with the aims of YM applications than suggested in earlier studies. However, while managers were found to be familiar with what YM claims to achieve, most managers used a rate structure in their hotels which conflicted with the aim of revenue optimization. Only 22 per cent of managers within the total sample were found to be familiar with both the concept of YM *and* the operational aspects of YM as a

---

Stage 1   Personnel
- develop employee understanding
- highlight customer/hotel interface
- appoint forecasting committee
- sort available customer and market data

Stage 2   Analyse demand
- identify competitors and sources of demand
- define hotel's strengths and weaknesses
- predict demand levels and booking patterns
- constantly monitor external factors

Stage 3   Market segmentation
- identify market (existing and potential)
- segment market (demographic, psychographic and geographic)

Stage 4   Determine optimal guest mix
- based on (i) propensity to spend; (ii) volume usage

Stage 5   Analyse trade-offs
- extensive calculations of monetary leakages
- avoid displacing higher spending guests

Stage 6   Establish capacity levels
- set capacity to meet demand of market segments

Stage 7   Introduce YM system
- groups and consortiums need tailor-made systems
- small or independent hotels adopt revised version of above to achieve maximum benefits

Stage 8   Customer reorientation
- training comes into practice by realizing
  - (a) hotels YM objectives
  - (b) meeting customer needs

Stage 9   Operational evaluation
- revise room allocation
- evaluate how demand changes
- identify additional factors which determine demand

Stage 10   Action
- implement any changes required immediately

Figure 16.1 Key stages in a formal YM system

Source: Donaghy and McMahon (1995)

management tool. Therefore, the findings would suggest an increase in the level of understanding of YM as a concept but highlight that managers are somewhat unclear about how to operationalize it.

A Fragmented Approach

An examination of the accommodation management techniques which were being employed in determining rates per market segment and rooms inventory management revealed that none of the hoteliers in the Northern Ireland survey followed the exact procedures outlined in Stages 2 to 6 of the proposed operational framework in Figure 16.1. The UK survey found only 14.6 per cent (32 managers) of hoteliers were deemed to be extensive YM users based on the stages outlined above. The remaining 85.6 per cent were still practising minimal or fragmented techniques. The techniques used by hoteliers will now be examined in detail in comparison with the formal YM framework.

DATA COLLECTION AND DEMAND ANALYSIS

In order for a YM system to operate effectively extensive data are required in quite specific formats. The *Cornell Hotel and Restaurant Quarterly* Conference Report (1990) states that the characteristics of each market segment need to be identified. These include quantifiable demand patterns, booking patterns, booking lead times, propensity to spend, length of stay, check-in and departure patterns. Ideally, this information will allow the hotel manager to quantify future demand from each market on each day of each month. Moreover, to assist accurate forecasting, the manager must take into account any macroeconomic and exogenous factors which may affect demand per market segment, such as weather, holiday patterns, demographic shifts, scheduled forthcoming local and international events. In both surveys it was found that the majority of hotel managers had access to varied forms of data required for demand analysis. With regard to demand patterns, all respondents in the Northern Ireland sample claimed they were able to identify both historical demand and historical booking patterns by market segments and could forecast the total volume of future demand for up to twelve months ahead. However, when asked if they could accurately estimate future demand for each market segment on six specific trading periods (seasonally, monthly, weekly, midweek, weekend and bank holiday), only five managers from the total sample claimed they could do so on all the periods mentioned. These respondents represented the five largest hotels in the sample. Additionally, this group had computerized front office systems which they claimed to use for storage and retrieval of historical guest data. In the UK survey, 63 per cent of the managers claimed that they had extensive data available on the accommodation market in all of the following areas: breakdown of total market segments; historical booking and demand patterns per market segments; duration of stay and spending profiles for all market segments; and the costs incurred in accommodating each segment of the market. Additionally, most of the UK hotels had relatively advanced computerized information systems which had the potential for collecting the data required for a YM system. However, it should be noted that while they held the appropriate information, only 66 managers claimed to allocate a specific number of rooms for sale daily by market segment. Therefore, only limited number of managers are making use of this extensive data for increasing yield. This would support the argument that a good number of managers are YM aware but do not know how to operationalize it.

A significantly large proportion of the Northern Ireland sample (50 per cent of respondents) found it possible to forecast demand for the 'midweek' trading period only. Most hotels within this group were urban located with a strong business market. When asked about future trends, 30 per cent of managers detailed specific methods by which they identified future demand. All of this group examined information which they held on the previous years' occupancy levels. Of these managers, 67 per cent supplemented this with information obtained from fully or partly computerized front office systems, such as extensive guest and company history profiles and frequency of visit data. Only four of those managers who specified methods of identifying future trends used information which reflected changes in the market place. This information was based on Northern Ireland Tourist Board (NITB) projections for the industry on forthcoming events. Additionally, it was interesting to note that the majority of managers within this group continually monitored notices of forthcoming marriages. It is well established that wedding functions in Northern Ireland represent a substantial contribution to hotel revenue both in banqueting and accommodation. The hotels using this market-focused information were the larger urban-based hotels of the Belfast area. These findings tend to highlight a greater awareness among managers in the sample of historical demand than future demand and emphasize the requirement for a strategically focused yield management tool. Historical data merely provide a snapshot of the past and are insufficient for the purposes of forecasting accommodation levels.

In the UK-wide survey, 95 per cent of the managers claimed to forecast accommodation levels on a regular basis. However, of these 208 managers only 27 forecast beyond a twelve-month period. Sixty-five per cent forecast between seven and twelve months, while 136 forecast only six months ahead. Almost 50 per cent of all respondent only forecast four months in advance! This short-term approach to forecasting and planning is contrary to the strategic focus of YM and is surprising given that the hotels in the sample represent a random sample of the top UK hotel groups.

Jones and Hamilton (1992) suggest that hoteliers must identify local competition and, more specifically, be aware of the relative advantages held by each competitor. Further, the management team should clarify the hotel's strengths and weaknesses within the context of each target market to enable the setting of appropriate rates. Managers in the sample were asked if they had information on competing establishments regarding:

- overall rate structures;
- rates achieved per market segment;
- marketing and promotional activities specifically relating to the accommodation sector;
- source of demand for accommodation.

Of respondents in the Northern Ireland survey, 78 per cent claimed they knew the current rate structures of each competing hotel. However, 64 per cent of this group claimed that their reason for gathering these data was primarily to ensure that room rates were structured to be similar to or marginally more competitive than those in competing establishments.

Only 16 per cent of managers in the sample had information on rates available for specific market segments at competing hotels. This information related to the rate structure for three market segments only: conference; tour parties; weekend breaks. While respondents did not indicate their reasons for collecting these specific rates at competing hotels, it may be reasonable to suggest that their motive was to ensure that a similar rate was structured at their own establishments.

Few managers in the sample had information about the accommodation marketing and promotional activities of competing hotels. Of managers, 8 per cent claimed to know of sponsorship associations between competing hotels, leisure and recreational bodies, including golf clubs and activity centres. Of the sample, 21 per cent claimed to have some information on sponsorships by competing hotels of professional business associations such as the Institute of Directors and/or Management. None of the sample was aware of the number of personnel involved in marketing and promotional activities at competing hotels or the budget of competing hotels for marketing and promotional activity.

Managers in the sample were asked if they could classify the source of demand for accommodation at competing hotels by market segment. None of the sample claimed they knew the source of all demand at competing hotels. However, 23 per cent of respondents claimed they could accurately classify the extent to which selected market segments contributed to total occupancy at competing hotels. All the hotels that claimed to have access to this information were urban located. Overall, managers in the Northern Ireland sample appeared to carry out a competitor analysis merely as a benchmark against which the performance of their own hotels could be assessed. Additionally, it would appear that managers in the sample tended to use competitor analysis as a method of affirming decisions on price rather than as a means of identifying opportunities for increasing market share and profit.

A further follow-up survey was undertaken with the 33 managers identified within the UK-wide study as having extensive YM applications. Managers were asked about the information that they had available on competing hotels with regard to:

- overall rate structures;
- rates achieved per market segment;
- marketing and promotional activities specifically relating to the accommodation sector;
- source of demand for accommodation at competing hotels.

The findings show that these hotels attach much importance to having *and using* this information as part of their competitive room sales approach.

All 33 managers had information available on the overall rate structures available at competing hotels. Twenty-seven of these managers (representing almost 82 per cent of the sample) claimed that they knew the rates which competing hotels achieved by market segment. A number of these managers claimed that this information was not highly confidential and was circulated freely among hoteliers in their geographical areas. This finding is in stark contrast to the Northern Ireland sample, where only 16 per cent of managers had information on the rates achieved per market segment within competing hotels. Again, within the context of the Northern Ireland based research, there was no evidence to suggest that managers shared or were aware of the benefits of sharing such information.

While relatively few of the Northern Ireland hotel managers were aware of the marketing and promotional activities undertaken at competing hotels, the British-based managers were much better informed about what their competitors were undertaking in this respect. Of the 33 managers in the survey, 28 claimed that their sales and marketing team were aware of the promotional activities undertaken by competitors with specific regard to the accommodation sector. One factor which may account for this is that the British-based hotels (which were larger in size) had specialist sales and marketing teams who would have the time and expertise available to gather this information.

With regard to the source of demand for accommodation at competing hotels, the British-based managers were much better informed than the managers in Northern Ireland. Twenty-seven managers claimed they had reliable information on the source of demand at competing hotels, though fourteen of these claimed that they had to treat this information 'sensitively'. When probed on this, they claimed that it was not always beneficial to 'poach' this business from competing hotels, and one manager cited an example of where a competitor used this information to target a long established business account who used his hotel. Within a short period of time, several hotel managers excluded the hotelier who used the information to try to poach the business from locally based group meetings.

Shine (1992) states that, ideally, historical data should cover at least the past two years. This timespan enables the identification of demand variables per market segment and assists in the determination of demand sensitivity to exogenous factors. Notably, 70 per cent of hotels in the Northern Ireland sample held registration and accompanying details for more than two years. Some 34 per cent retained them for more than three years. Of managers, 17 per cent claimed to hold information on booked rooms, which were later cancelled. Each respondent in this group recorded the reason for cancellation. Some 78 per cent of hoteliers had information on booked rooms, which end as 'no-shows' (i.e. booked but do not arrive), though only 16 per cent of this group could provide this information by market segment. Only 14 per cent of managers in the sample claimed to document information on enquiries for rooms, which did not follow through with a firm booking. While each manager claimed that the reason for not booking was documented (such as already fully booked or rate too high), the information was not available by market segment and was recorded manually by most of the hotels. While much historical information is stored, relatively little is available by market segment or in a manner which easily lends itself to interpretation by market segment. Therefore, it would be reasonable to conclude that while a good number of hotel managers in Northern Ireland collect relevant data, with some employing basic forecasting techniques, the needs of a YM system would require a somewhat more complex and systematic method of collecting information by specific market segments.

The key differences between the UK and Northern Ireland managers with regard to historical information was found to be the format or extent of refinement of the actual information in itself. While Northern Ireland managers were found to have considerable information available, the information had relatively limited use, as it was not available in an easily usable format, such as by market segment. UK-based managers, however, claimed to gather this information in a manner which would enable them to use the information and only one of the 33 managers claimed that he did not have this information available by market segment.

MARKET SEGMENTATION

Within a formal YM system hotel executives need to be able to define their market into clearly distinguishable segments. Previous research (Dillon, 1991; Bradley and Ingold, 1993) has indicated that hoteliers already practise fragmented techniques of YM and most have divided their customer base into segments such as business, leisure, long and short stay. Initially, this would appear to be the case in hotels in Northern Ireland. All the hotel managers in the sample maintained that they could identify the percentage of business generated from each of the named market segments stipulated in the questionnaire: business, conference trade, short-stay guest (up to two days), long-stay guest (more than two days), wedding/function guest. This claim should, however, be treated with caution. Only 7 per cent of hotel managers in the survey named a segment other than those stipulated in the questionnaire. The remaining 93 per cent identified all of their business within the five categories stipulated. It is probable that the managers 'balanced' their total business proportionately between the named segments. In the 1996 survey, as mentioned previously, 63 per cent of managers in the UK claimed to be able to provide a breakdown of total market segment based on detailed information held in computerized or manual form.

YM does encourage managers to extend and refine the segmentation process to enhance net yield 'through the provision of a more profitable product or service which more accurately meets the needs of more clearly defined groups of guests' (Donaghy *et al.*, 1995). It has been suggested (Warren and Ostergren, 1990; Pannell Kerr Forster, 1992; Donaghy and McMahon, 1995; Donaghy *et al.*, 1998) that this aim can only be achieved by strategically linking YM activities to the marketing function. YM endeavours must be based on a comprehensive awareness of the changing market configurations. Donaghy and McMahon (1995) have developed this idea significantly and have proposed that YM can only be introduced effectively where five yield marketing practices are implemented. These are:

1. Identification of a customer base using a detailed segmentation strategy.
2. Developing an awareness among management of the changing needs and expectations of customers.
3. Estimating the price elasticity of demand per market segment.
4. Responsiveness of management to cope with changing market conditions.
5. Accurate historical demand analyses combined with a reliable forecasting method.

Additionally, the authors proposed a 'yield segmentation process' which enables management to focus more accurately on achieving net yield by segmenting the total market under the following classifications:

- business segments;
- leisure segments;
- geographic area;
- duration of stay per market segment;
- spending profile per market segment;
- expenses/costs of supporting respective market segments.

This approach should give hotels using YM a number of advantages. Primarily, it enables a comparison between market segments in terms of their individual contribution to net yield (thus providing essential information for marketing decisions). The costs, spending profile and net yield per market segment should be highlighted, thus enabling hoteliers to aim for the optimum mix of guests. Finally, it should help to reduce the losses incurred through displacing high spending guests. As this case study indicates, hotel managers could well benefit from the adoption of these more formalized segmentation techniques.

DETERMINATION OF OPTIMUM GUEST MIX

Since the main objective of YM is to maximize profit in the accommodation division, the determination of an optimum guest mix is a crucial stage in a formal YM system. Optimum guest mix refers to the 'systematic selection of the most profitable mix of customers among those requesting accommodation at a given time period' (Donaghy *et al.*, 1994). The availability of comprehensive data, compiled during the demand analysis and market segmentation stages, assists the hotel management team in this selection by allowing them the opportunity to assess:

- the extent of demand from existing markets;
- the potential demand from additional markets;
- the compatibility of hotel resources with market needs.

It is common practice for hotel managers to adjust room rates to changes in the level of demand (Relihan, 1989; Jenner, 1991). It would be expected, therefore, that hoteliers should set rates which reflect the spending propensity of various market segments combined with the availability of accommodation. Clearly, it is sub-optimal to have a segmentation strategy that differentiates customers exclusively on price sensitivity (Dunn and Brooks, 1990). Hotel room prices need to be supported by a segmentation strategy that identifies the varying needs and expectations of different types of customers. In Northern Ireland, the hoteliers appeared to be relatively effective in determining rates for their named market segments for particular trading periods, such as peak/off-peak, midweek/weekend and bank holidays. Of managers who participated in the study, 27 per cent claimed that the rates formulated for peak and off-peak trading periods were determined by the spending propensity of the market segment targeted. Managers were asked if they had information on the spending profiles of individual market segments. Only two hotels in the total sample had a systematic method of collecting these data. Subsequently it is unclear how managers were able to determine the spending profiles of such market segments other than through a personal awareness of market conditions and current economic climate. Clearly the decision on price was not determined from a detailed analysis of historical data combined with an accurate method of forecasting accommodation levels per market segment. While there was strong evidence of room rates being influenced by demand on a seasonal and weekly basis, there was no evidence to suggest that managers would consider changing a particular rate within a particular trading period to maximize revenue on a particular day. In the UK survey, 100 per cent of the managers claimed that they took into account the spending profile of the market segment when setting rates. In particular, they looked at potential guest expenditure in four key areas: restaurant, beverage sales,

Table 16.1 Example of displacement

	Monday	Tuesday	Wednesday
Rooms in hotel	300	300	300
Rooms committed to groups	150	50	200
Expected transient demand	100	100	100
Availability of rooms to new groups without displacement	50	150	0
Groups under consideration	50	50	50
Transient displacement	0	0	50

Source: Donaghy *et al.* (1994)

banqueting and conferences/exhibitions. Of this total, 55 per cent of managers set their rates in conjunction with head office and, interestingly, they also considered the costs incurred by the market segments in room servicing, marketing costs, direct and indirect labour and room maintenance costs. However, it should be noted that only 29.6 per cent of managers claimed to plan the number of rooms for sale each night by market segment. It would seem that the majority of hotels have some way to go before they are practising a formal YM system. Such a system would have the scope and capacity to align room rates more effectively with market forces on an hourly, daily, weekly or monthly basis, thus achieving 'optimum' revenue from an 'optimum' guest mix.

ANALYSIS OF TRADE-OFFS

Hotel managers who operate a YM system must be prepared to accept a YM decision to refuse an advance booking if it is likely to displace high spending guests. Indeed, a substantial block booking for a number of nights six months in advance might be refused even when no other reservations currently exist for those dates. In a YM situation, the hotelier needs to analyse the trade-off between the value of the pro-spective group booking and the loss associated with the probable displacement of transient business. This apparently simple procedure is often more complex and is one of the fundamental building blocks of YM (Berkus, 1988). Using the example of an enquiry for a booking of fifty rooms on three days eight months in advance (see Table 16.1), Donaghy *et al.* (1994) have illustrated the difficulties in deciding whether or not to accept the enquiry.

In the example shown in Table 16.1, accepting the group booking would result in the displacement of valuable business on Wednesday. If the 50 rooms displaced by the group were valued at the average rate of £80 and the prospective group is expected to have an average rate of £60, a trade-off would be calculated as follows:

Revenue gain: 150 group room-nights (50 × 3 nights) at £60.00 = £9,000

Revenue loss: 50 transient room-nights at £80.00 = £4,000

Orkin (1988) suggests that this is not the only type of displacement that occurs. In the context of the above example, Orkin's findings would suggest that a proportion of transients arriving on Monday and Tuesday might perhaps stay through Wednesday with a Thursday morning departure. If Wednesday is unavailable, these people will go elsewhere, adding to the displacement. Furthermore, some of Wednesday's displaced transients may have stayed at the hotel on other days, so management must expect further hidden displacement.

The Northern Ireland survey indicated that a small number of hotel managers appeared to be carrying out some form of basic displacement analysis. Of the hoteliers, 16 per cent recorded that an advance reservation for an individual room would be refused at certain times. The reasons offered in explanation were very clearly revenue-orientated. Factors which determined leasing included written confirmation, advance deposit and, most interestingly, 'booking would be accepted if the room rate was the maximum which was expected to be achieved on that date'.

With regard to block bookings, 20 per cent of hotel managers in Northern Ireland claimed that they would refuse to accept an enquiry if it affected profitability adversely. Comments included: 'if accepting such a booking would inconvenience regular high paying guests' and 'if their budget did not meet what the hotel could achieve from individual guests'. While only a relatively small proportion of the Northern Ireland sample (20 per cent) practise some form of displacement analysis, their reasons are clearly focused on the fundamental aim of revenue enhancement. In a similar fashion, the managers in the UK survey were asked if the room rate would vary over time for a block booking of rooms including dinner. Only 15 per cent of managers stated that it would not differ since they had fixed rates for this type of enquiry. Many of the reasons provided by respondents in accounting for the variation in rates were similar. The two most frequently cited reasons were 'depends on availability' and 'depends on the time of year'. However, those managers classified as having understood YM provided more yield-focused reasons for rejecting the booking, such as 'day of week (high/low demand day), number of low rates already allocated and guest mix. These three reasons are fundamental components of strategic YM decision-making.

Hotels with strategically focused yield operations will identify future business levels and will have allocated specific inventory at specific rate bands.

ESTABLISHMENT OF CAPACITY LEVELS

Orkin (1988) and Jones and Hamilton (1992) have highlighted the strategies that should be employed in order to set capacity levels in the market conditions of high and low demand. When demand is high, they recommend that hoteliers should close availability of low-rate packages, require minimum length of stay and accept block bookings only if groups are willing to pay higher rates. Conversely, when demand is low, managers can offer special low-rate promotions, actively encourage segments that are rate-sensitive and promote limited availability, low-cost packages to the local market. In periods of low demand, Northern Ireland hoteliers recorded that they engaged in one or more of these activities. Notably, just under 80 per cent of the hotels indicated that they used discounting in periods of low occupancy. The single most important reason for discounting at this time was to secure multiple night or block bookings. In relation to periods of high demand, one-third of the sample claimed they minimized discounting but did not rule it out altogether for guests with high spending power in other revenue-generating areas of the hotel, such as restaurant and bar. Hoteliers were found to discount least on the evening of letting. A similar pattern of responses was recorded by most of the hotels in the UK sample not classified as practising extensive YM.

Overbooking is an essential YM technique in optimizing room revenue (Lieberman, 1993). Through overbooking hotels risk being unable to accommodate all those guests who have reservations, and this could result in customer dissatisfaction. Within an effective YM system, overbooking levels are not calculated by mere chance but are set after a thorough and detailed analysis of historical data and projected trends. Predictions of cancellations, no-shows and even early guest departures also form elements of a complex calculation, which facilitates the establishment of capacity levels. However, only approximately 16 per cent of hotels in Northern Ireland had any form of overbooking policy. In the UK sample, 201 managers (91.7 per cent) claimed that they regularly overbook rooms, although, as in Northern Ireland, most hotels in the sample do not appear to have established a formal policy on overbooking. Surprisingly, in 82 per cent of the sample hotels staff still referred to management on a daily basis for instructions on the number of rooms to be overbooked. Twenty-one hotels (17 of which were classified as understanding YM) had computer software which suggested a level of overbooking for each day. As such, while most hotels were seen to overbook rooms, the effective application of YM requires a more formalized approach than those used by the hotels in both samples in order to establish precise overbooking levels.

USE OF TECHNOLOGY

YM is not a computer system or a software package. It is a 'management approach' in which computer-based technology can help the hotel manager to realize the full potential of YM (Lieberman, 1993). YM techniques can be implemented manually but they are dependent upon the extensive accumulation, manipulation and analysis of data. As such, information technology can both simplify the management task and prove more cost-effective in, for example, forecasting demand patterns or calculating the displacement costs of accepting group reservations. One report (International Hotel Association, 1993b) cites that denied reservations were reduced by over 50 per cent through the use of such technology. Goymour and Donaghy (1995) have effectively highlighted the potential advantages of using a computerized YM system:

> Experienced hotel managers have the skills to know whether to let a particular room on a particular night at a cheap rate or to hold out for higher rates. Computerised YM systems do the same calculations but they do it faster and can help less experienced managers to achieve the same thing.

Over recent years there has been much development in the use of technology as an aid to enhancing yield (Nissan, 1987; Sieburgh, 1988; Spano, 1988; Salomon, 1990; International Hotel Association, 1993b; Russell and Johns, 1997; Noone and Andrews, 1999). Both artificial intelligence and expert systems now perform decision-making and problem-solving in a heuristic manner using established rules (set by experienced managers) which are implanted in the software (Berkus, 1988; Russell and Johns, 1997). Indeed, even in the late 1980s both Berkus (1988) and Sieburgh (1988) reported that the development and use of these systems in a YM software package at the Royal Sonesta Hotel resulted in impressive financial, marketing, human resource and product competitive improvements.

In 1993, hoteliers in Northern Ireland had yet to realize the full benefits of computerized YM systems and still relied heavily on management expertise to make pricing and rooms inventory management decisions. None of the managers in the sample claimed to be using a YM software package. In relation to the front office procedures of reservations, guest check-in and check-out, only 20 per cent of hotels operate a fully computerized system. Only seven managers of this group use the output from these computerized front office systems to assist them in forecasting future booking and demand patterns. It would appear that these hoteliers could benefit significantly from information technology. However, managers in the Northern Ireland sample are not the only hoteliers who could gain some advantage from the use of YM computerized technology. Only 56 respondents in the UK survey claimed to have computerized software packages which incorporate a YM programme. None the less, the majority of hotels had extensive computerized procedures within front office, which have the potential for collecting data to enable strategically focused YM decision-making. The more functions within front office that were computerized, the more likely respondents were to *claim* that they operated YM. This strong association between computerization and respondents who *claim* to practise YM might suggest that these managers believe that computerized procedures are an essential component of YM, which, as mentioned above, is not necessarily the case. In 1994, Koss-Feder warned that computerized YM systems will not be the immediate trend, noting that these systems are not regarded as user friendly by many hoteliers. Similarly, this research concluded that managers regard existing computer software for YM to be inadequate and called for industry-specific applications designed to meet user requirements.

STRATEGIES FOR INCREASING PROFITABILITY AND OCCUPANCY

Berkus (1988) stated that YM is a 'process which maximises profit by increasing revenue and occupancy'. If this definition is applied in its widest sense, it can be seen that hotel management teams in Northern Ireland engaged in a number of strategies and tactics which increase occupancy and subsequently profit. These efforts can be categorized under four headings:

- marketing strategies and tactics;
- improvement in facilities and equipment;
- customer reorientation;
- management/financial strategies.

Figure 16.2 details the range of activities that hoteliers reported in their attempt to increase return on investment.

It is interesting to note that the eight managers interviewed after the second survey, and who were classified as practising extensive YM, also identified a similar broad range of strategies and tactics for revenue generation. Yield management, however, was viewed as the most important management/financial strategy. All eight managers noted superior financial performance of their accommodation divisions, which they attributed directly to the application of YM.

A formal approach to YM may be seen as more effective for a number of reasons. From the traditional use of *ad hoc* fragmented techniques identified above, YM has developed into a formalized management tool with planned procedures and policies.

Marketing strategies/tactics	Facilities and equipment
• Trade fairs; tour operator initiatives • Distribution with booking agencies • Advertising • More field marketing • Attracting new market segments • Product modifications • Company account bonus schemes	• Computer reservation system (eg. Gulliver) • Adding a leisure complex • Internal refurbishment • Change menu and room service • Introduce conference facilities • Computerize front office • Modern technology (fax, audio-visual aids, etc.)
Customer reorientation	**Management/financial strategies**
• Customer opinion cards • Examination of guest history details • Return visit reservation cards • Customer care training • Personalization of service where possible	• Cost budgeting • Frequent review of room pricing • Restructuring of room rates • Referral policy (group hotels) • Assessing customer expenditure

Figure 16.2   Disparate strategies used by hotel managers in the case study to increase profitability and occupancy

Source: Donaghy *et al.* (1994)

These aim to achieve clearly defined, long-term, profit optimization objectives. A formal approach can also benefit from the participation of a number of management and staff from various functional areas in the hotel, thus drawing on the maximum professional expertise available. This team effort is more advantageous than the traditional approach, which essentially involved a limited cross-section of the management team. Finally, formal YM applications are customer-led, in that while the focus is predominantly profit optimization, effective YM is contingent upon striking a balance between customer needs and expectations, offering value for money, maintaining a competitive edge and improving overall net return.

IMPLICATIONS OF THE SURVEYS

The investigation of the accommodation management techniques of hoteliers in Northern Ireland in relation to pricing and rooms inventory management has highlighted the fact that some similarities do exist between their current activities and those outlined in Stages 2 to 6 of the formal YM system in Figure 16.1. These practices include attempts at effective data collection, basic demand analysis and market segmentation, determination of optimum guest mix, analysis of trade-offs and the establishment of capacity levels. However, it is clear that their lack of a focused YM approach and their low levels of knowledge of the concept make it unlikely that they will achieve optimum yield. It is encouraging that the majority of managers (87 per cent) in the 1996 survey were able to identify the correct definition of YM but disappointing that only 22 per cent were found to be familiar with both the concept *and* the operational aspects of YM. It would seem that while there has been some increase in the utilization of YM as an effective management tool, there is still a good number of managers even within the corporate sector who need to be made fully aware of the operational aspects of YM and its financial benefits to their hotels.

Consequently, the challenge still remains for educators and management consultants in the UK to find new ways of educating practising managers about YM. It offers significant opportunities to those businesses capable of successfully integrating and applying it as a means of improving the efficiency and effectiveness of their operations. This applies to both corporate and independent hotels. However, it can be seen that many independent hotel operations in the UK currently lack the expertise to adopt formal YM procedures. This is particularly unfortunate, as it is this sector of the industry which faces the greatest difficulties in improving its overall competitiveness through the enhancement of service delivery and product presentation. Northern Ireland, while facing unique opportunities and challenges in the light of recent events, is certainly not alone in having difficulties in making sure that research findings are transferred and applied in relevant companies. Success in what has been described as 'the quest for quality' (NITB, 1994) in current national and international markets will only be gained when the mechanisms elucidated in this chapter are implemented in commercial practice. The development and delivery of methods to help hoteliers to succeed in the integration and exploitation of YM form important elements of ongoing research and industrial collaboration activities.

A Holistic Approach

Besides learning the operational techniques of a formal approach, managers will need to be able to develop a holistic understanding of the implications and demands of supporting such a system. A review of current literature has highlighted the need for changes/developments in the following areas:

- management focus;
- customer–hotel interface;
- staff training and human resource implications;
- use of incentive schemes;
- development of policy and procedural supports.

Management Focus

Within a YM system the price of a hotel room may change several times in one day. The emphasis moves away from the traditional approach of selling room types at a certain price, which is product-driven, to a more complex strategy whereby room price is dictated by customer demand, which is market/demand-driven (Orkin, 1990). The International Hotel Association (1993a) report noted that this new method of selling rooms will involve the following key management activities:

- setting the most effective pricing structure;

- limiting the number of reservations accepted at any given room night or room type;
- reviewing reservation activity to determine whether inventory control is needed;
- negotiating volume discount with wholesalers and groups;
- providing customers with the right product – both room type and room rate;
- enabling reservation agents to be effective sales managers rather than order takers.

The report has indicated that these activities can be most effectively implemented through a 'yield manager'. Considering the fragmented yield approach of the majority of managers in this research, there would appear to be distinct advantages in the development of such a position, which would consolidate the piecemeal departmental objectives of sales, marketing, reservations, front office, financial control and general management into one strategic yield objective. This is supported by the research of Donaghy *et al.* (1997) and McMahon-Beattie *et al.* (1999).

Customer–Hotel Interface

In a traditional booking transaction, the guest will expect to reserve a particular type of room (single, double, twin) at a standard price. Occasionally, this price may be discounted. However, the implementation of a yield-orientated system will fundamentally change the customer–staff reservation dialogue, since the price of a room will be determined by 'just about everything other than room type' (Donaghy *et al.*, 1995). Reservation staff may be required to inform clients that the rate they request is not available on that day or a room is available but at a higher rate, or, even, that the rate they request is available but only if the room is booked and confirmed two weeks in advance. In order to manage this change effectively, hoteliers will require a commitment to the development of a 'yield culture', which Jones and Hamilton (1992) consider to be a fundamental step in developing a YM system.

Staff Training/Human Resource Implications

The implementation of a YM system necessitates that all staff should be familiar with the yield philosophy of the hotel and trained in specific yield techniques. Specialist training will be required for those staff who deal directly with guest reservation and room sales. It was apparent from this research that not only staff but also hotel managers required training in both the operational techniques of YM and the development of its conceptual understanding. Jones and Hamilton (1992) and Donaghy and McMahon-Beattie (1998) have cautioned that an over-dependence upon computer-based YM technology can overshadow the human resource element. While formal YM techniques are enhanced by computer applications, managers need to structure their training programmes so that they include a primary focus on human resource input. Interestingly, five of the eight managers who were interviewed after the second survey reported that YM had increased the productivity of their staff and had resulted in leaner and more cost-effective operations. Four of the managers believed that staff had been empowered by being involved in the planning and decision-making process and by being more accountable for the decision they made. Two managers believed that it had resulted in the reduction of staff turnover. As such, the benefits of YM to staff are slowly being realized.

Use of Incentive Schemes

It may become necessary for hotel managers to reconsider the criteria on which they base their incentive schemes for staff in departments such as sales, marketing and reservations. Traditionally, personnel in these areas have been rewarded for the amount of sales that they make, which is often calculated on achieved occupancy or average room rate. This approach conflicts with the principles of YM, since it implicitly assumes that all room nights are equally beneficial to the hotel. YM involves the use of two approaches, each of which is appropriate for the different levels of demand for hotel rooms. In situations of high demand, management should focus on achieving the maximum revenue from the highest spending guests. Where demand is low, the emphasis is on maximizing room sales 'even if a lower overall rate is the cost with these tactics' (Orkin, 1988). Therefore, a realistic YM scheme must incorporate incentive points which are directly related to sales generated in varying conditions of high, medium and low demand. Since none of the hotels in the Northern Ireland sample was operating a formal YM system, incentives tended to be focused towards increasing volume rather than profitability. Furthermore, only 7 per cent of the hotels in the UK sample were found to be operating a yield-focused incentive programme and a surprising 87 hotels offered a number of incentives at conflict with their revenue aims; for example, sales teams rewarded only on securing new corporate accounts at highly discounted rates or on the number of rooms sold regardless of market segment or rate.

Policy and Procedural Supports

The effective application of YM requires that hotel management establishes a number of policy and procedural supports to be used as guidelines in the decision-making process. Clearly defined policies and procedures aim to support the strategic yield planning process and are essential components of the formal YM system. These supports should be devised for two key areas. The first ensures that relevant data are collected in order that long-term yield decisions can be made effectively. These data include information on the following areas:

- booking cancellations;
- denials (guests who could not be accommodated);
- declines (guests whose enquiry did not result in a booking);
- no-shows (booked guests who did not arrive);
- overbooking levels.

Second, the manager should develop documented support systems for staff. While staff can be trained initially to implement the procedures and adhere to policies, a training, informational and reference support system needs to be available for all existing and new employees.

Huyton *et al.* (1997) have stated; 'If there is one catch phrase for which the hotel and tourism industries will be remembered in the 1990s it will be Yield Management.'

Indeed, there is much evidence to suggest that the application of YM in hotels will continue to increase. Within the context of the Northern Ireland study, hotel managers were clearly seen to be adjusting room rates in relation to demand among broad market segments in an attempt to increase occupancy and profit. While YM seeks to manipulate both the occupancy and rate variables, the formal approach to YM is somewhat more complex and considerably more effective. The formal YM approach has begun to be adopted in a small but growing number of corporate hotels in the UK and it is encouraging that the majority of managers now seem to be familiar at least with the basic concept of YM. In 1992 the International Hotel Association stated that YM will be 'a major decision support tool for the very near future'. If this is to become a reality in the new millennium, practising managers of corporate and independently owned hotels need to develop not only a conceptual understanding of the concept but also the operational and organizational implications of YM. Only then will YM become a strategically focused accommodation management tool.

REFERENCES

Belobaba, P. P. (1987) 'Air travel demand and airline seat inventory management'. PhD Thesis, Massachusetts Institute of Technology.

Berkus, D. (1988) 'The yield management revolution – an ideal use of artificial intelligence'. *The Bottomline*, June/July, 13–15.

Boyce, A. (1991) 'Maximise yields'. *Caterer and Hotelkeeper*, 24 January, 27.

Bradley, A. and Ingold, A. (1993) 'An investigation of yield management in Birmingham hotels'. *International Journal of Contemporary Hospitality Management*, **5** (2), 13–16.

Brotherton, B. and Mooney, S. (1992) 'Yield management – progress and prospects'. *International Journal of Hospitality Management*, **11** (1), 23–32.

Carter, R. (1988) 'Screen dreams'. *The Business Traveller*, April, 34–5.

Cornell Hotel and Restaurant Administration Quarterly Conference Report (1990) 'Yield management magic'. *Cornell Hotel and Restaurant Administration Quarterly*, **31** (2), 14–15.

Dillon, E. (1991) 'In the balance'. *Caterer and Hotelkeeper*, 24 April, 61–2.

Donaghy, K and McMahon, U. (1995) 'Yield management – a marketing perspective'. *International Journal of Vacation Marketing*, **2** (1), 55–62.

Donaghy, K., McMahon, U. and McDowell, D. (1994) 'Yield management: a practised idea or an ideal practice?' Paper presented to the Third Annual Research Conference of the Council for Hospitality Management Education (CHME), Napier University, Edinburgh.

Donaghy, K., McMahon, U. and McDowell, D. (1995) 'Yield management – an overview'. *International Journal of Hospitality Management*, **14** (2), 139–50.

Donaghy, K. and McMahon-Beattie, U. (1998) 'The impact of yield management on the role of the hotel general manager'. *Progress in Tourism and Hospitality Research*, **4**, 217–28.

Donaghy, K., McMahon-Beattie, U. and McDowell, D. (1997) 'Implementing yield management: lessons from the hotel sector'. *International Journal of Contemporary Hospitality Management*, **9** (2), 50–4.

Donaghy, K., McMahon-Beattie, U., Yeoman, I. and Ingold, A. (1998) 'The realism of yield management'. *Progress in Tourism and Hospitality Research*, **4**, 187–95.

Dunn, D. and Brooks, D. E. (1990) 'Profit analysis beyond yield management'. *Cornell Hotel and Restaurant Administration Quarterly*, **31** (3), 80–90.

Fried, L. (1988) 'Hotels join yield management game, linking rates to market demand'. *Corporate Travel*, **1**, 12.

Gamble, P. R. (1990) 'Building a yield management system – the flip side'. *Hospitality Research Journal*, **14** (2), 11–22.

Goymour, D. (1994) 'The top 50 UK hotel groups'. *Caterer and Hotelkeeper*, **3264**, 45–6.

Goymour, D. and Donaghy, K. (1995) 'Reserving judgement'. *Caterer and Hotelkeeper*, 26 January, 64–5.

Hansen, C. N. and Eringa, K. (1997) 'Critical success factors in yield management'. In *Proceedings of the Second International Yield Management Conference*, University of Bath, 9–11 September.

Huyton, J., Evans, P. and Ingold, I. (1997) 'The legal and moral issues surrounding the practice of YM'. *International Journal of Contemporary Hospitality Management*, 9 (2/3), 84–7.

International Hotel Association (1992) 'Yield revenue management'. Report of the IHA Congress, Bangkok, 1–52.

International Hotel Association (1993a) 'The ABCs of yield management'. *Hotels*, 27 (4), 55–6.

International Hotel Association (1993b) 'Technology to the rescue balancing rates, occupancies'. *Hotels*, 27 (8), 37–8.

James, G. W. (1987) 'Fares must yield to the market'. *Airline Business*, January, 16–19.

Jenner, G. (1991) 'Rate relations'. *Caterer and Hotelkeeper*, 9 October, 44–6.

Jones, P. and Hamilton, D. (1992) 'Yield management: putting people in the big picture'. *Cornell Hotel and Restaurant Administration Quarterly*, 33 (1), 88–95.

Jones, P. and Kewin, E. (1997) 'Yield management in UK hotels: principles and practice'. In *Proceedings of the Second International Yield Management Conference*, University of Bath, 9–11 September.

Kimes, S. E. (1989) 'The basics of yield management'. *Cornell Hotel and Restaurant Administration Quarterly*, 30 (3), 14–19.

Kimes, S. E. (1997) 'Yield management: an overview'. In I. Yeoman and A. Ingold (eds), *Yield Management: Strategies for Service Industries*. London: Cassell.

Koss-Feder, L. (1994) 'Yield management software needs to be refined'. *Hotel and Motel Management*, 209 (2), 30.

Larsen, T. D. (1988) 'Yield management and your passengers'. *Asta Agency Management*, June, 46–8.

Lieberman, W. H. (1993) 'Debunking the myths of yield management'. *Cornell Hotel and Restaurant Administration Quarterly*, 34 (1), 34–41.

McMahon-Beattie, U., Donaghy, K. and Yeoman, I. (1999) 'Yield management in hotels'. In S. Verginis and R. C. Wood (eds), *Accommodation Management: Perspectives for the International Hotel Industry*. London: International Thomson Business Press.

Nissan, E. (1987) 'Knowledge-based computer systems for tasks in hospitality management or related areas: accommodation (lodging, alimentation) and leisure'. *International Journal of Hospitality Management*, 6, 191–8.

NITB (1994) *A Development Strategy 1994–2000: Tourism in Northern Ireland*. Belfast: NITB.

Noone, B. and Andrews, N. (1999) 'An investigation into the use of the Internet in revenue management in the Irish hotel industry'. In *Proceedings of the Fourth International Yield and Revenue Management Conference*, Colchester Institute, 5–7 September.

Orkin, E. B. (1988) 'Boosting your bottomline with yield management'. *Cornell Hotel and Restaurant Administration Quarterly*, 28 (4), 52–6.

Orkin, E. B. (1989a) 'Forecasting: crystal ball or CRT?' *Bottomline*, June/July, 21–3, 29.

Orkin, E. B. (1989b) 'Essential yield management'. *Business Travel Management*, December, 60–6.

Orkin, E. B. (1990) 'Strategies for managing transient rates'. *Cornell Hotel and Restaurant Administration Quarterly*, 30, 34–9.

Pannel Kerr Forster Associates (1992) 'Towards success and greater profits'. *International Journal of Contemporary Hospitality Management*, 4 (2), i–iii.

Pfeifer, P. E. (1989) 'The airline discount fare allocation problem'. *Decisional Sciences*, 20, 149–57.

Relihan, W. J. (1989) 'The yield management approach to hotel room pricing'. *Cornell Hotel and Restaurant Administration Quarterly*, 30 (1), 40–5.

Rowe, M. (1989) 'Yield management'. *Lodging Hospitality*, February, 65–6.

Russell, K. A. and Johns, N. (1997) 'Computerised yield management systems: lessons learned from the airline industry'. In I. Yeoman I and A. Ingold (eds), *Yield Management: Strategies for Service Industries*. London: Cassell.

Salomon, A. (1990) 'Yield management – leaders shed light on the "dark Science" '. *Hotel and Motel Management*, **205**, 85, 88.

Shine, M. (1992) 'Yield management: a competitive advantage in the nineties'. *HSMAI Marketing Review*, **9** (4), 13–16.

Sieburgh, J. A. (1988) 'Yield management at work at Royal Sonesta'. *Lodging Hospitality*, October, 235–7.

Spano, S. V. (1988) 'The growing importance of hotel technology'. *Lodging Hospitality*, October, 105–7.

Warren, P. and Ostergren, N. (1990) 'Marketing your hotel: challenges of the 90's'. *Cornell Hotel and Restaurant Administration Quarterly*, **31** (1), 56–9.

17

Application of Yield Management to the Hotel Industry

Jeremy R. Huyton and Sarah Thomas

INTRODUCTION

The principle role of any rooms division manager is not only the maximization of space in particular bedrooms, but also revenue and the use of staff. With labour costs rising and the average spend by customers in the hotel industry declining it is imperative that the gap be closed. However, as Mill (1989) stated, the closing of this gap has created three challenges between cost and spend.

The first is that the hospitality industry is in the 'mature' stage of its life cycle, especially in developed countries. Second, the service industry is a provider of just that 'service', and the service element requires people to carry out such a task. The third challenge is the break with tradition, whereby training and employee development are seen as things to be carried out when times get better. So far it would appear that such times have not yet arrived.

While rooms division managers, on the one hand, wrestle with the cost implications of staff productivity within their departments, they can find solutions to their other challenges, namely rooms and revenue maximization, by looking at them objectively through yield management. Hotel rooms, like airline seats, are a highly perishable commodity. In the case of an aircraft, once the 'plane has taken off the revenue from the unfilled seats is lost forever. The same is true of hotel rooms unsold on any given night. Neither aircraft seats nor hotel bedrooms can be stored for future use. Although yield management is a relatively new term coined by the airline industry, the underlying idea is not. The basic concept is that during periods of high demand for hotel rooms the prices are set at the highest rate so as to maximize revenue; and at times of lower demand the rates are set so as to encourage occupancy.

This yield management strategy is nothing new to the hotel industry and some basic form or another has been used for many years. Many hotels offer special rate packages for periods of low occupancy: weekend rates, mid-summer breaks, Christmas breaks and so on. Many bars and restaurants also offer discounted rates to get their customers to arrive earlier or to stay later, offers such as early diner specials and happy hours, at both the beginning and the end of the evening. Some restaurateurs in the United States have even considered charging a premium for meals served during high demand periods.

Apart from the variety of discount packages being offered by hotels to entice the prospective guest into the hotel during periods of low occupancy, the front office manager has to balance the rooms being sold during high occupancy periods so as to ensure that a 'full house' is achieved.

The following example shows the necessity for an awareness to maximize occupancy. This example highlights lost revenue for one night only, when, in truth, there may be as many as 20 to 30 nights a year when it is possible to miss that 100 per cent 'full house'. For example, if the hotel has 200 rooms with an average room rate of £80, and the rooms division achieved 98 per cent occupancy on 25 nights, then this would equate to a loss of revenue of £8,000.00.

To help to counter such losses through the non-achievement of 100 per cent occupancy historical data have to be used. The main causes for not hitting the 100 per cent target are non-arrival of guests, no-shows, people who cancel their rooms on the day of their actual arrival and cancellations; added to these non-arrivals are those guests who decided to leave earlier than they expected (understays). One also needs to take into account those customers who want to stay on longer than their booked stay (overstays) and those who arrive by chance without a room booking (walk-ins).

A simple method of operating a yield management system is by using the ABC concept, and taking all the historical data into account will enable the rooms division manager to fill with greater accuracy.

Overbooking without Tears

The A of the concept is the simplest way of ascertaining how many rooms there are for sale on a particular night. This looks at the rooms which are let tonight plus the number of arrivals, and does not take into account any past data regarding no-shows, cancellations, etc.

For example, a hotel has 200 rooms, with 40 departures and 55 arrivals:

Number of rooms available	200
Rooms 'on' last night	176
Less departures	40
Rooms now 'on'	136
Plus arrivals	55
Rooms 'on' tonight	191
Rooms spare	9

This simple calculation tells us that there are nine more rooms to sell before the house will be 100 per cent full. However, if one takes into account the variation in customer departures, such as no-shows, cancellations and early departures, it can be seen that this figure of nine is not a true reflection of the actual rooms that one needs to sell to achieve a full-house.

The B aspect of the formula will take into account the data which have been recorded regarding guests who will not arrive or who will not be staying in the hotel any longer. As with all historical information, it takes time to amass, but once the system is in place for collecting and utilizing the data they can be of inestimable value. The percentages which are used in the example below are completely fabricated, but the percentages used in real life will be elicited from facts and figures drawn from the day-to-day operation of the hotel. It is possible to find that, for example, every Tuesday there are more no-shows than any other day, or that the number of cancellations for Sunday is always the highest. Alternatively, the figures may show that no-shows generally are 5 per cent and it can be expected that an extra 1 per cent of your arrivals will be as walk-ins.

Number of rooms available	200
Rooms 'on' last night	176
Less departures	40
Rooms now 'on'	136
(Plus arrivals =	55 but this figure needs amending)
Amendments	
Less	
Cancellations @ 3per cent =	1.65 (a percentage of arrivals)
No-shows @ 10 per cent =	5.5 (a percentage of arrivals)
Early departures @ 1 per cent =	1.36 (a percentage of rooms on)
	8.51
Thus amended arrivals =	55
	−8.5 (Rounded up or down, i.e. 9)
	46

Thus today's rooms 'on' arrivals 136 + 46 arrivals = 182 committed rooms.

Therefore with amendments to the arrivals the number of rooms which are left to let is 18. These figures show that there are not 9 but 18 rooms required tonight to achieve a full house. But to ensure that an accurate forecast is achieved it is necessary to take into account the people who stay on or walk in unexpectedly. This is part C of the formula, and is the combination of all the elements: arrivals, departures, stay-ons, early departures and walk-ins.

Rooms available	200
Rooms 'on' last night	176
Less departures	40
Rooms 'on' tonight	136
Plus arrivals	46
Plus overstays @ 1.5 per cent =	0.6 (a percentage of departures)
Plus walk-ins @ 2 per cent =	1.1 (a percentage of arrivals)
	1.7 (rounded up to 2)
Therefore arrivals = 46 + 2 = 48	
Thus rooms 'on' are 136 + 48 = 184	184
Rooms to sell	16

This means that with all of the arrival and departure data taken into account it is necessary to overbook by seven bedrooms in order that an occupancy of 100 per cent can be reached.

Yield management, whether manual or computerized, endeavours to maximize revenue by adjusting prices to suit market demand. Although this American theory has proved beneficial to both the airline and hotel industry, present day yield management systems have been very slow in gaining acceptance within the British hotel industry.

The focus of this chapter is on the theoretical issues pertaining to a yield management system and then the application of the tools, strategies and tactics involved in implementing and running yield management. Two hotel case studies have been developed to portray 'real' situations, and the problems and benefits of such a system.

SYSTEMS AND STRUCTURES IN PLACE FOR YIELD MANAGEMENT

Yield management will only operate within a hotel that has a mix of market segments with variable rack rates. The property should ideally have over fifty rooms and a computerized reservation/management information system (Orkin, 1988).

The tools and strategies for operating a yield management system are the foundations of any worthwhile yield optimization programme. However, before we analyse the tools and strategies of a yield management system it is necessary to explain the basic yield management formula, as it applies to hotel rooms.

YIELD MANAGEMENT FORMULAE

A rooms yield management formula is established by dividing the revenue realized for a given day by the revenue potential for that day.

$$\text{Yield} = \frac{\text{Room nights sold}}{\text{Room nights available}} \times \frac{\text{Actual average room rate}}{\text{room rate potential}}$$

or

$$\text{Yield} = \frac{\text{Revenue realized}}{\text{Revenue potential}}$$

Revenue realized is variable and revenue potential is fixed. Revenue potential can be calculated by multiplying the number of rooms by the actual rack rate.

TOOLS AND STRATEGIES

Yield management emphasizes high rates on high demand days and high occupancy when demand is low. The focus of yield management is to maximize revenue every day – not for seasons or periods.

The underpinning framework of yield management consists of four steps:

1. Forecasting.
2. Systems and procedures.
3. Strategies and tactics.
4. Feedback.

Forecasting

Forecasting is the key to effective yield management. Forecasting must be done on a daily basis and must encompass more than 30- or 60-day projections. In order to make accurate forecasts a variety of information is required.

The information sources available to the yield management team are:

1. Historical data, both recent and past year, on the number of bookings and knowledge of how transient customers and groups behave with regard to booking events and/or accommodation. This information will give the team details on lead times, wash factors, high and low demand periods, from which the team will formulate the rack rates.
2. Other factors need to be considered when considering forecasting:
   - weather;
   - events in local area;
   - competitors' activities;
   - airlines' schedules and services;
   - limitations of the property;
   - strategies of the property;
   - internal promotions;
   - internal policies on overbooking;
   - consumer behaviour.

Not all the above factors are controllable but they will affect the demand upon a hotel's facilities and the subsequent pricing strategies and decisions.

Yield management is a management decision tool, and even if the forecasts are 'off', decisions are better than if they were made on the basis of no forecast at all.

Systems and Procedures

A computerized system aids the communication of forecast information from the yield management team to relevant departments of a property and in some cases between properties and booking agencies or central reservation systems. A computerized system allows 24-hour input of information and link up to enable efficient circulation of current information. The yield management team and/or analysts can, in some cases, enter the system directly and make phantom bookings to close a rate level in order to stop any reservations clerk or booking agencies selling any more rooms at that particular rate.

The information from the yield management team regarding the various rate levels per number of rooms is input into the computer system. The customer makes a telephone enquiry, the reservations clerk works from the VDU screen, first looking at the days required and then checking the room availability. The reservation clerk, using basic upselling skills (see strategies and tactics), will always offer the highest price room and work down, thus not losing any potential revenue.

The system needs to be flexible to accommodate the 'regular' customer who will expect a continuation of a corporate or 'special' rate. This flexibility is necessary to maintain goodwill, especially for the long-term customer; the organization must retain a human side in yield management. The system cannot take over the role of the manager and many situations may still require to be handled on a case by case basis. A greater understanding of information management in the yield management process is discussed by Johns in Chapter 10 of this volume.

∠ Strategies and Tactics

Decisions are made by the yield management team in relation to pricing policies and market demand. There are two main aims of yield management:

1. On high demand days maximize average room rate to increase revenue.
2. On low demand days maximize occupancy and average room rate.

The strategies identified by Orkin (1988) are as follows.

On high demand days the team will plan for transient reservations (a guest that is not part of a group booking). They will determine the correct mix of market segments so as to sell out at highest rates possible, e.g. the 'walk-in' business man who will pay the highest rate for the privilege of walking in off the street at the last minute and being able to book a room. Once the mix of market segments has been decided the team will assign a number of rooms to each segment of the mix. For example, a hotel has 100 rooms, and allocates the following numbers of rooms to each market segment:

Rate levels

No. 1 (highest)	80 rooms
No. 2	60 rooms
No. 3	40 rooms
No. 4	20 rooms

This means that at all times 80 per cent of the rooms will be held for rack rate guests, and 20 per cent will be held for cheaper clients. Similarly, only 20 per cent of the rooms will be available for the cheapest rates. The operating procedure is simple. The reservations clerk will monitor the pick-up of each room category as she proceeds through the lead time to the day of arrival. If she finds that unexpectedly the high rate categories are filling up faster than anticipated then she would close out the lower rates.

The strategy restricts low profit categories, and limits or eliminates local groups such as local sports teams or women's institutes. The team may also require minimum stays to prevent the early departure factor that often happens when an individual books in advance for six nights but may only stay for four nights, and thus it is often too late for the hotel to resell those remaining nights, even in a high demand period.

The team will also plan for group bookings that fall on high demand days. First of all, the hotel will only sell to groups that are willing to pay higher rates and provide high occupancy per room. A tactic often used is to sell only to a group that books meeting space and hospitality suites as well as accommodation, thus encouraging the guests to stay in-house for meals and to use the bar and other facilities. For more price-sensitive groups, the sales team will attempt to allocate their booking in low demand dates; this is particularly relevant for local clients who want to book function space for a dinner dance or meeting and who wish to have overnight accommodation.

Overbooking Policy

To compensate for late-cancelled bookings, early departures and 'no-show' bookings an overbooking policy is integrated into a yield management system. The yield management team will set a level, i.e. a number of rooms, at which they are prepared to overbook. The level at which the overbooking is set will depend upon the market mix forecast for that period and the associated drop-out rate and the demand for those dates. For example, during a sports world cup, the hotels will be in high demand due to the number of spectators, group supporters, teams, families of teams, officials, media and other promoters. If the world cup tournament lasts four weeks, and the market mix consists of teams and families, the hotel may find it is empty by the end of the second week because many of the teams have lost their matches and are flying home. The yield management team will need to forecast the length of stay of each team and the probability of them staying for the whole tournament despite the possibility of being knocked out. Consequently, the yield management team would use the overbooking policy to ensure the highest occupancy and maximum revenue for the remaining two weeks of the tournament.

On low demand days the team will aim to maximize occupancy and average room rate. They will give the booking agencies and reservations the opportunity of offering alternative rates to price sensitive groups or certain situations, such as weekend leisure breaks or pensioners' group outings, whereby the lower rates will be opened with the possibility of combining an accommodation rate with an evening meal, thus offering bed, breakfast and evening meal for a set rate, enhancing all aspects of the hotel's revenue earning departments. It will also ensure a better utilization of the staff of the hotel. The yield management team will monitor the response to these promotional deals and continually scan the environment for new market conditions and adjust the rates if necessary. The yield management team will also remove high demand restrictions such as a minimum two-night stay and attempt to solicit business from the local community, both group and transient.

A technique that is frequently used by reservations during low demand dates is to upsell. The reservations clerks may offer a standard room first and then offer a more deluxe room at a slightly higher price or offer 'extras' for a minimum cost; for example, £60.00 standard room only, per person, per night, or, for a slight increase in price, £70.00 deluxe room and breakfast per person, per night. The customer is offered an upgraded room at a lower rate than usual. It is good practice to inform the customer that it is a 'one-off' deal, a gesture of goodwill, so the customer does not expect it every time they book.

Feedback

Feedback enables the team to judge the accuracy of their forecasts and form the subsequent month's and year's historical data. More importantly, it gives the team an indication of the responsiveness of the organization's reservation system to their strategies and also the effectiveness of their strategies in response to market demand. Monitoring denials and conversions helps to keep track of the amount of business gained or lost due to yield management effort. Feedback allows everyone involved in yield management to keep updated on strategies and information, as well as acting as a mechanism for praise and assessing individual or departmental performance. These are the structures and basic systems of yield management, but to implement them in a hotel requires a yield management team.

THE YIELD MANAGEMENT TEAM

Before an effective yield management system can be put into place and used it is necessary to have an operations team. They will be the driving force behind its successful implementation and will be the group of people who regularly meet to forecast the forthcoming business of the hotel.

As was previously mentioned, the team will typically consist of the rooms division manager, the sales manager and the reservations manager. This does not mean that anyone else is excluded, but for a speedier and more effective decision-making process it is wise not to make the yield management team too big. In some hotels the general manager likes to be involved or the front office manager may take the place of the reservations department. However, the original three would tend to make the best team. The rooms division manager has the overall control of the department, with targets for maximizing both occupancy and revenue. The sales department must be invited for it is they who go out on a daily basis to sell the hotel's bedrooms. While they are fully aware of the need to maximize revenue, their primary thrust is to get bodies into the hotel. However, working with the rest of the forecast team ensures that the sales and marketing team are fully informed of the peaks and troughs of the hotel's business. The last but still very important member of the team is the reservations department. The reservations manager is the person who is completely *au fait* with all the hotel's bookings, the future booking patterns and the past histories of the hotel's arrivals and occupancies.

The role of the yield management team is fourfold:

1. To predict demand.
2. To assign rooms to transient reservations.
3. To open or close rates as seen fit.
4. To conduct feedback sessions.

The principal role of the team is to predict the demand for rooms into the foreseeable future. It is insufficient simply to take last year's figures and adjust by an agreed percentage figure. According to Orkin: 'Planning for maximum yield takes a different approach. It asks questions like "What would be our mix of market segment if we were to maximize yield?" ' (Orkin, 1988). What was a successful formula for filling bedrooms a few years ago may be completely wrong for today's market mix. Thus it is up to the team to remind each other constantly of the fact that neither the customer nor their expectations remain static.

By trying to predict demand the team assesses what has happened in the past, the time of year, the weather, any exceptional circumstances which surrounded bookings for then and so on. They then look into the future for any similar occurrences which could affect, either positively or negatively, the booking of hotel rooms. While no one can accurately predict what the future may hold, it is still better to conduct such predictions and to make management decisions with limited information than with no information at all. Relihan explains that a worthwhile yield management system depends on accurate demand forecast.

> These [demand forecasts] can be created in several different ways. Some hotels' systems employ sophisticated statistical analyses of reservations history, as the airlines do. Other systems provide a format for hotel managers to 'teach' a computer a set of rules that describe the typical demand pattern of the specific hotel. (Relihan, 1989)

Once a fair estimate has been made of the room requirements for both the near and distant future, the team then has to allocate the right amount of room inventory, i.e. number of rooms, to the various market segments. This is done by discussing, reasoning and deciding what groups will arrive, their room requirements, what will be the volume of corporate rate business, how many walk-ins will arrive, etc. All of these imponderables are examined and, with them, the historical data which management has amassed. The yield team decide which classes or levels of rates to open or close.

The fourth aspect of the yield management team's work is to conduct feedback sessions. These sessions are necessary to help to judge whether or not the forecasts have been accurate and effective. Feedback acts as a measure of responsiveness in terms of systems, strategies and the management of revenue and occupancy. It also acts as a measure of staff performance.

Orkin (1988) gives a simple example of the importance of the need for feedback.

> There are a variety of methods and models for forecasting transient demand. All would gain enhanced accuracy if complete data were available on transient requests that were lost or turned down and why they were not accommodated. Most reservations systems give agents the opportunity to enter lost business, but most do not have a systematic way to ensure that all lost business and related dates are recorded. In forecasting models partial data can mislead or camouflage important trends.

It is necessary for the yield team to strive constantly to have the most up-to-date information and to react quickly to the subtle changes in the accommodation business. It is no longer sufficient to believe that a good overbooking policy is enough to ensure a full house. Unless all the available data are used the rooms division manager can end up with a 100 per cent rooms occupancy but with a yield of considerably less.

TRAINING DEVELOPMENT AND ORGANIZATION CULTURE

A yield management system creates a formalized and efficient procedure for manipulating rates to optimize both market demand and revenue. This presents the individual property manager and the organization with change; that is, a change in both staff attitude and working procedures. An integral part of this management of change process will require managers, reservation clerks and booking agents to be trained. The training and educational process would consist of areas such as new computerized systems, yield management policies and customer enlightenment programmes. For example, reservation clerks will need to be trained to say no to low rates and learn to 'hold out' for the higher rates of late corporate business and the techniques of upselling. Upselling is a strategy whereby reservation clerks are prompted to sell rooms starting from the highest rate and decreasing to lower rates only if they receive price resistance by customers.

The organization may also undergo a culture change in its approach to using yield management. The system actively encourages managers to be proactive in their decision-making, planning and communicating strategies to both staff and booking agencies. Mullins (1992) explains how this change in process, thought and behaviour will need to be developed and nurtured from within a supportive structure and climate. Such an environment stems from senior managers' beliefs and values, which are shown by their commitment to yield management.

THE CUSTOMER

Yield management is a system which is entirely objective in its approach. That is, it places the needs of the customer secondary to those of the hotel. Yield management systems want to maximize both the occupancy and the revenue of the hotel and to do this the yield team open and close room categories at their will and not in accordance with what the customer wants.

For many years the prospective hotel guest has become used to bargaining for room rates or at least expecting that a room at the rate which he or she normally pays will be available. The hotel has been seen by its customers as being simply a provider of room and bed space, and the idea that it is a highly organized establishment whose sole purpose for the owners is to make money appears not to be a part of the hotel guest's thoughts. For as many years as these thoughts have been with the customer, the hotel industry has permitted them by acceding to the needs, wants and whims of their guests. They have given the feeling that they are ashamed of their product and even their profession by rarely questioning the customer or sticking to their guns with regard to room rates. The idea seems to have been that 'We should be grateful for who we can get to come and stay.'

Yield management has turned this aspect of hotel operation on its head. What the system now tells the customer is that we have certain rooms set aside at certain price categories and once they are full you will have to pay more. The initial fear of hoteliers is that prospective guests may choose not to stay with one hotel because of its perceived inflexibility and intransigency over room rates. After all, hotels are not like aeroplanes, they cannot move and therefore have no time schedule to keep, and consequently will sell their rooms at any price so as to ensure that they achieve 100 per cent occupancy. Sheryl Kimes (1989) raised this same point:

> Customers seem to be resigned to the fact that airlines charge different prices depending on how far ahead a ticket is bought and what restrictions were met, but will hotel customers accept this pricing method? The airline industry comprises a small number of major competitors and customers seldom have much choice. Hotels on the other hand, have numerous competitors. If customers don't like having to pay different prices for the same room, they may decide to patronize the competition. Likewise customers may believe it's unfair to pay a higher price for a room than someone who reserved it a few weeks earlier. Hoteliers may face a customer-education problem.

The education problem to which Kimes alluded appears to have been very necessary in the earlier days of yield management implementation. Initially customers rejected the idea that certain room categories were closed out to them. (But that was to be expected because of the sudden curtailment of their previous freedom of choice.) The idea that people could just arrive at a hotel and expect a room of their choice, at a price which they wanted to pay, significantly diminished as the concept of controlling room categories, customer market mix and revenue took hold.

Time will tell whether the hotel industry's newly found cavalier attitude will be maintained, or whether it will revert back to the 'old ways'. Figure 17.1 depicts in a holistic manner the complexity and direction of the information channels involved in a yield management system.

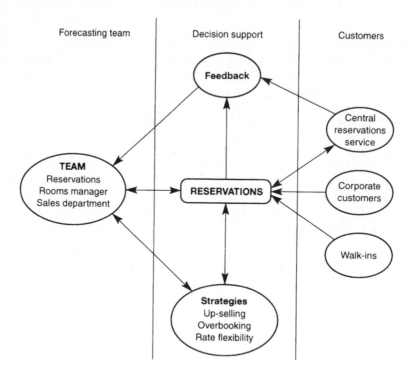

Figure 17.1   Information channels in a yield management system

CASE STUDY: HILTON NATIONAL HOTELS

Within the West Midlands region of Hilton National there are four hotels, Eaton Green, Milton Keynes, Coventry and Warwick. The four hotels range from 150 to 181 bedrooms, with Warwick being the largest of the four. All are strongly corporate businesses.

Prior to a yield management system, Hilton used the CHAMPS management information system, which it acknowledges as a good system for occupancy reports and statistics. For example, it can give the number of rooms a specific company has booked with the hotel, per day or week, for current year or previous years. This, from the reporting point of view, is efficient, but for the demands of today's hotel operations it has become somewhat outdated. The CHAMPS system has a limited use for forecasting (a fundamental element of a yield management system) and thus the rooms division at the Hilton had to make many decisions on gut feeling.

As previously discussed, yield management and the integral forecasting carried out by the rooms division involves many techniques, data and the confidence to 'hang on' for a higher rack rate. This may see the volume of business staying the same or possibly decreasing, but the yield may have doubled because the manager has had enough confidence and knowledge to 'hang on' for the best price for the product offered. Jane, the Hilton's rooms manager, explains:

> We use various charts to aid forecasting, such as 31 day pickups, which consists of; 'A' schedules, which charts what comes in from each market segment per day and at what average room rate. Unsold rooms chart that shows whether the rooms division's forecasting is accurate or not. A regret report to see how much the hotel is regretting. That is the amount of business that the hotel is either turning away or lost through unconverted sales.

The management at Warwick Hilton believes that there are three tools needed in order operate a yield management system effectively.

1. A computerized decision support system (in this case Fidelio).
2. Communications. That is, an internal communication system, as well as the ability of staff to communicate to the customers.
3. Active forecasting. A conscious effort to explore the future booking patterns for the hotel's bedrooms.

The Beginnings of Yield Management at Hilton

Prior to Fidelio, the management at the Warwick Hilton was using yield management in a very naive form, looking at yield in a statistical format, comparing current to historical data and deciding whether the yield had increased by using the following formula:

$$\frac{\text{Rooms revenue achieved}}{\text{Total possible rooms revenue}} \times 100$$

From using this basic form of yield analysis, the management at the Hilton Warwick began to notice a £5.00 yield per room over a year (their first year of using this form of yield management). The management continued to calculate demand for room space, regardless of whether it was for bedrooms or conference rooms, as far out as six months, and in turn was able to instruct reservations to 'hold out' for the full rack rate. Jane, the rooms manager, explained:

> it is very difficult to sit and wait, you wonder what you have done, but it does work. The reservationists sit there and say to perspective clients, we're terrible sorry, we are fully booked, but in actual fact we have got 15–20 rooms to sell. (But because of the rate offered by the client we won't take it.) 'Hanging out' for the full rack rate is worth it, because we are bumping up our yield all the time.

The managers have the knowledge and confidence to 'hold out' because they know that they will get someone else who will pay the full or second highest rack rate.

To operate a yield management system effectively the manager, at unit level, must have a very good knowledge of the hotel's competitive environment and its market mix; for example, how much trade the hotel receives and the average spend from each market segment. The market mix for the Hilton at Warwick is as follows:

- 50 per cent conferences;
- 12 per cent rack;
- 25 per cent leisure;
- 13 per cent corporate.

Such market sector information is vital to all departments of a hotel because of its close ties with profit maximization from the type of customers using the hotel's facilities.

For example, if there are no conferences for three months but lots of corporate trade, the food and beverage department needs to change the menus and packages and sell them 'hard' to the private independent diners. Thus yield management is as applicable to food and beverage as it is to the rooms division.

Yield Management at Hilton Warwick

The forecasting team at the Warwick Hilton consists of the rooms manager, general manager, food and beverage manager and financial controller. Surprisingly, the sales manager is not involved at the hotel but the forecasting team do communicate to the sales department what information they require, such as a market segment analysis and a monthly plan of their rooms and rate targets. Other people who supply information to the yield management team are the front office manager and the reservations manager. The forecasting team meet once a month, towards the end of each operating period, to discuss forecasts made by the rooms manager (who forecasts every week) for the coming months.

The Warwick Hilton has to achieve within 5 per cent of its target sales forecasts. The yield management ethos and process helps to identify demand trends. It immediately picks up what markets are dropping and what are picking up, and flags up whether your selling strategies are working and your lead-in times are correct. Thus yield management is seen by Hilton as making forecasting a much easier thing to do, and making the front office team more aware of the 'business' on the books.

With the introduction of Fidelio, the rooms and reservation staff underwent a seven-day in-depth training with Hilton's trainers. The staff were trained on how to sell, how to deal with the guests, guest history, company history and loyalty.

Working alongside Fidelio is a tool called Northern Demand Pricing. This pricing strategy is concerned with the Hilton global distribution system, HRW (Hilton Reservations Worldwide), which is owned by Hilton International and Hilton Corporation. As a consequence Hilton Warwick now has direct global links to 370,000 outlets selling Hilton hotels. Northern Demand Pricing is used as part of this global reservations system and uses the upselling technique.

Fidelio also allows the rooms manager to close or block out set numbers of rooms at specific rates. For example, the three nights of Monday, Tuesday and Wednesday would be 'closed out' if you have got only 20 rooms to sell and you know on the day the hotel will pick up the required number of people at rack rate.

When forecasting demand, Fidelio helps by identifying potential quiet weekends from its past records. Hilton Warwick's rooms manager gave the following example:

> Friday and Saturday is desperate because we have just had two bank holidays and everybody that wanted to come to Warwick for the weekend have been and gone, so there is not much I can do this weekend. But having said that, if I had been proactive

enough in January and I had Fidelio then, I would have seen this potential quiet spot in June and would have had enough time to book in a coach tour.

Culture Change with Yield Management

The implementation of a yield management system is not just about computerization and forecasting; most companies will need to undergo some form of culture change. Hilton has experienced this change mostly within the sales department. It is the norm for most sales managers to compute success by adopting a 'book by volume' policy rather than by striving to maximize revenue, which is in conflict with the yield management ethos of maximizing revenue to volume. This culture change has to come about by a rethink and a new approach in achieving sales.

Hilton also underwent a change in the way bookings were taken, through having to teach the reservationist to say 'no'. One temporary solution to this problem was the ability of the rooms manager to enter the system and take off blocks of rooms through phantom bookings, thus leaving reservationists with no option but to say, 'I am sorry, we are fully booked.' This denial of accommodation was done even though the hotel has rooms available, but it introduced the 'hold out' policy of yield management to the reservation staff. The reservationists have had to learn not to be afraid of quoting rack rate, as it is easy to reduce the rack rate when faced with price resistance by a customer.

A disadvantage of yield management that Hilton found was that it takes more time and more professional staff to get it right. You need to have well trained reservation staff plus sales staff who will chase potential bookings, develop new business and maintain accurate records of the conversion rate from provisional to confirmed bookings for all business.

To encourage and as an overt display of management's commitment to yield management the staff at the Hilton use incentives to achieve high performance in terms of attaining full rack rate and upselling facilities. For every 5 per cent over estimated occupancy the reservationists get a monetary reward.

Customers and Yield Management

Jane, the rooms manager at Hilton Warwick, explains the difficulty of educating hotel users:

> Say for instance you purchase a bedroom according to either the season or the day, the same as you would buy a train ticket. If you want to go peak time, you pay peak prices and accept the amount of money you have to pay. If you want to go at low time you pay a low price. So therefore, why do companies expect hotels to offer low rates throughout the year? Using yield management we give them an adjusted rate, dependent on the season or time of year, the same as any other service industry. But it is proving very difficult in trying to get the customer around to our way of thinking. Also if companies want more rooms they have to pay the going rate for those rooms, and not expect to get a discount for group bookings. Within the service industry we always have the idea that the 'customer is always right' but now we have got to turn that around. Customers are now paying for the privilege to book a room at the last minute and knowing that hotel will have rooms available, most of the time.

SUMMARY

The long- and short-term benefits of the yield management System at Hilton Warwick may be summarized as follows.

Food and beverage may suffer as a result of the increased proportion of corporate trade, because it is more than likely that a business person will go out of the hotel to eat at night and, therefore, the restaurant revenue will suffer. The opposite is true when a conference is in the hotel and the provision of food and beverage is secured by providing an all-inclusive food, beverage, accommodation and conference package.

Fidelio quickens the pace at which bookings can be taken and also allows for manipulation of the rack rate to achieve maximum yield. It allows the rooms division to be more proactive in forecasting at least eight months out to provide a much clearer picture of potential high and low demand days. This information can then be effectively used by the sales team.

The ability of Fidelio to store guest information and records also provides an improved customer service by allowing the receptionists to use a correct guest history successfully. This the rooms manager sees as being especially important when using brand standards when greeting and checking in a guest to the hotel. The more information a receptionist has about a guest the greater service he or she may offer.

Yield management appears to be providing a treasure chest of high performance yield returns, increased commercial flexibility and a new zest for competitiveness in a dynamic service industry. However, it is only truly efficient when the system is in place and the yield management team use the data. Added to this, the more they practise, the more they forecast, the better and more effective they will become and the higher will be the rooms yield.

REFERENCES

Kimes, S. E. (1989) 'The basics of yield management'. *Cornell Hotel and Restaurant Administration Quarterly*, **30** (3), 14–19.

Mill, R. C. (1989) *Productivity in the Hospitality Industry*. New York: Van Nostrand Reinholdt.

Mullins, L. J. (1992) *Hospitality Management: A Human Resource Approach*. London: Pitman.

Orkin, E. B. (1988) 'Boosting your bottom line with yield management'. *Cornell Hotel and Restaurant Administration Quarterly*, **28** (4), 52–6.

Reliham, W. J (1989) 'Yield management approach to hotel pricing'. *Cornell Hotel and Restaurant Administration Quarterly*, **30** (1), 41–3.

18

Yield Management and the Restaurant Industry

Fiona Whelan-Ryan

INTRODUCTION

In an extremely competitive market, restaurant operators must focus on two important factors: effective capacity utilization and revenue maximization. From these two variables, yield management has become the management technique that offers food service operators revenue and capacity management strategies to ensure long-term survival.

Traditionally, as noted by Kotas and Jayawardena (1994), Van Westering *et al.* (1994) and Strate and Rappole (1997), hotel food and beverage operations have been provided as a secondary product/service that promotes the sale of the primary product: accommodation. Customer perceptions of hotel restaurants have also been quite poor in that such restaurants are perceived to be quite expensive (owing to high cost structures), offering inferior food, relatively 'staid' menus, indifferent service and overall poor value for money compared with competing individual restaurants. These authors recommend that the role that food and beverage operations play in promoting room sales should be acknowledged. They also propose that the hotel food and beverage operation should be seen as an independent revenue-generating centre in its own right. Van Westering *et al.* (1994) and Kimes *et al.* (1998) suggest that hotel food and beverage outlets might benefit from yield management application. Therefore, this chapter focuses on this recommendation and explores the integration of these two departments as part of an integrated yield management system.

The purpose of this chapter is threefold: first, to determine what hotel restaurants do at present to maximize yield within their particular food and beverage department; second, to help food service operators to improve their overall organizational and operational performance levels; third, to develop a yield management model which incorporates yield-orientated practices as part of the broader strategic food service management process.

271

FOOD SERVICE MANAGEMENT

It is essential to evaluate the current role of the food and beverage manager, within the specific operation, as part of the organization as a whole and as part of the yield management team. The responsibilities of the food and beverage manager encompass many of the traditional generic managerial roles, specifically including the following characteristics (as identified by Waller, 1996, p. 25), which are adapted to incorporate the yield management process:

- The provision of facilities for a defined market (defined market segments: residents versus external customers, corporate versus leisure).
- The provision of systems of delivery (sourcing of equipment and raw materials; food production and restaurant; and provision of service to customers).
- Formulation, establishment and maintenance of systems of control to: monitor costs, prices, sales and profitability; provide management information; ensure performance reconciliation.
- Training, motivation and control of staff (encouraging teamwork and sales ability).
- Coordination of resources and activities (with general manager, food and beverage team and YM team).
- Total customer satisfaction (in order that YM be successful, the customer must be satisfied).

Hotel general managers and restaurant managers need to examine and consciously to adopt the above roles when restructuring the role of the restaurant within the organization as a revenue-generating centre in its own right, simultaneously contributing to rooms revenue.

REVENUE AND YIELD MANAGEMENT

Cross (1997, p. 33) defines revenue management as: 'The application of disciplined tactics that predict consumer behaviour at the micromarket level and that optimise product availability and price to maximise revenue growth.' Therefore revenue/yield management is essentially concerned with the application of information systems to predict demand levels and to determine appropriate pricing strategies. Cross (1997) emphasizes the basic principles of revenue management, which include market-orientated pricing, clearer market segmentation, reserving sufficient capacity of the product for the most valuable customers, decision support systems, 'exploiting each product's value cycle' and continual re-evaluation of the revenue management system.

The Yield Statistic

It is important for food and beverage managers to focus on yield profitability rather than costs and gross and net profits, which may be calculated separately by food and beverages. The yield formula is a performance measurement tool, which may be used to measure performance for each hour of each day. It may be used for comparative purposes and is essentially a decision support tool, which may be used to review prices, adjust market mix or increase promotional efforts to certain markets. An adaptation of Orkin's (1988) formula by Van Westering *et al.* (1994) is as follows:

$$\text{Yield} = \frac{\text{Actual covers revenue}}{\text{Covers revenue potential}} \times 100\%$$

$$\text{RevPASH Formula} = \frac{\text{ASPH} \times \text{No. of customers seated at } y \text{ hour}}{\text{Max. SPH} \times \text{Total potential no. of customers seated at } y \text{ hour}}$$

Developing a Revenue/Yield Management System

The process advocated by Cross (1997) and Farrell and Whelan-Ryan (1998) includes creating teams, an evaluation of the markets' needs, evaluating the organization and process, quantifying the benefits, using IT, implementing an effective forecasting system, applying optimization techniques, executing the new system and evaluation. These concepts are included in the broader discussion on the integrated YM model. Kimes *et al.* (1998) point out that many restaurants use a variety of revenue management techniques, but the application of such techniques has mainly been *tactical* by nature. Research findings from Dublin hoteliers highlight this issue.

Characteristics in a Restaurant Operation that YM can Influence Positively

The application of yield management is most effective when applied in operations that have the following characteristics, according to Van Westering *et al.* (1994) and Kimes *et al.* (1998).

Relatively Fixed Capacity

Restaurant capacity may be measured in terms of seating, the capability of the kitchen, the type of menu(s) available and the capability of service staff. As Kimes *et al.* (1998) point out, there are options available to *extend* capacity by adding seats to tables, changing restaurant layout, using outdoor facilities and, of course, turning tables a number of times during that meal period. Kitchen capacity may be effectively increased by changing menu items or production systems or by increasing staffing levels. Service capacity can be further increased by adding additional staff even on a 'casual' or part-time basis or by structuring the service delivery process in a more efficient manner.

Predictable Demand

Overall demand is composed of the following two customer types: guests who make a reservation and walk-in guests. But hotel food service operators must also consider demand from resident versus non-resident guests – both forms of demand can be managed, but different strategies are required. Maintaining an information system to compile information on tracking customer arrival and duration of stay patterns, the percentage of reservations and walk-ins, guests' desired dining times and likely meal duration is prescribed by Sill (1991) and Kimes *et al.* (1998) in order to manage this demand and select the most profitable market mix. Demand from each market segment can be predicted based on analysis of this historical data.

Time-Variable Demand

Customer demand varies by time of year, week and day. Restaurant operators must be able to forecast time-related demand so that they can make effective pricing and table allocation decisions to manage demand, particularly during times of high demand. Estimation of the length of time a party stays once seated (similar to the concept of stay-over) is useful according to Kimes *et al.* (1998) because restaurant operators who can accurately predict meal duration will make better reservation decisions and give better estimates of waiting times for walk-in customers.

Perishable Inventory

A restaurant's inventory should be measured in terms of time, i.e. the time during which a seat at a table is available. Kimes *et al.* (1998) recommend that restaurant operators should measure revenue per available seat hour (RevPASH). This method captures the time factor involved in restaurant seating.

Appropriate Cost and Pricing Structure

Restaurants have relatively high fixed costs and low variable costs, which allows for some pricing flexibility and gives operators the option of reducing prices during low demand times. In hotel restaurants, variable costs are higher than the cost of servicing accommodation product.

DEMAND AND SUPPLY MANAGEMENT

Overview of Strategies for Effectively Managing Demand

Whilst credit must be given to Kimes *et al.* (1998) for their development of yield-orientated strategies for the restaurant sector, it would appear that some 'duration management' strategies suggest that in the vast majority of cases, demand exceeds supply (which is generally not experienced by Irish food and beverage managers). Furthermore, the meal experience in its totality is not considered, and sales techniques for increasing revenues and average spend of customers during their meal are not discussed at all. Defining the duration of a meal by asking customers how long they will need the table would not be appropriate in most restaurants, particularly hotel restaurants.

Table 18.1 Managing demand

Increase	Decrease	Redistribute
Product modifications	Increase prices	Encourage bar meals
Search out new markets	Raise quality	Room service
Alter distribution channels	Reduce seating capacity	Garden barbecues
	Insist on pre-booking	Develop 'slow days' with
Conferences and tours		special promotions
Discount price		Meals tailored to clients
Promotion		needs
Advertising		Differential pricing
Selling		Happy hour
PR		Two-for-one deals

Source: Waller (1996, p. 112)

The most applicable yield-orientated strategies are 'reducing uncertainty of arrival strategies', with internal measures (such as forecasting) and external measures (ensuring guaranteed and confirmed reservations) being used by food and beverage managers for periods of high and low demand (Kimes *et al.*, 1998). Overbooking policies in hotel restaurants or for the majority of independent restaurants in Ireland are rare.

Capacity Management

Effectively managing capacity is central to yield management. Due to the nature of services and hospitality, the number of covers or volume will vary by year, by season, month, week, day and hour. The level of capacity in a particular restaurant is measured not by number of seats in the restaurant, but by the number of customers who can be seated (table turnover) during a particular meal period. The potential volume will vary according to the type of operation, menu(s) available, type of service and so forth. How capacity is managed will depend on organizational and operational policy, which should be clearly determined and communicated to staff and customers as a matter of form.

Tables 18.1 and 18.2 provide an overview of strategies and tactics for effectively managing supply and demand for food and beverage operators. As Waller (1996) points out, decreasing demand and supply are generally unrealistic strategies, as operators will not decrease demand unless fewer customers can generate higher revenue and decreasing supply will only occur where exclusive dishes or special functions are pre-planned. Conversely, supply will only be increased in the medium- to long-term framework, where a hotel operation is planning to break into another market; for example, extending its conference and banqueting facilities.

Overview of Strategies for Effectively Managing Supply

Increasing guest participation, as recommended by Sill (1991), is quite a useful strategy at breakfast times in most hotels, but generally would not be practised during other meal periods in hotels of higher standards. Adjusting service and kitchen, plant or equipment capacity may offer some practical strategies and tactics but may prove to be quite costly in terms of levels of investment and the predominant theme of excess

Table 18.2 Managing supply

Increase	Decrease	Redistribute
Employ more staff	Product modification	Open up new service areas
Buy more equipment	Limit availability	Manage advance bookings
Increase use of technology	Control supply of raw	Manage the queues
Modify the system	materials, part-time staff,	Simplify service procedures
Replicate the system (franchise)	flexible staff	Employ staff with flexible skills
Buy up your competitors (and install your system)		

Source: Waller (1996, p. 112)

demand, which only occurs at certain exceptional times in most hotel restaurants. In tactical terms, 'adjusting employee capacity' is a strategy that is actively used by food and beverage managers within hotel restaurants.

Queuing strategies are also outlined by Sill (1991), and implementation of these strategies would not coincide with customer care policies for *resident guests* in most hotels.

Smoothing demand patterns to accommodate capacity advocated by Sill (1991) include development of a reservations system, forecasting system and guest-tracking system. These strategies stimulate and manage demand in an effective yield-orientated way and are the most applicable to hotel restaurants in Ireland.

Insufficient Capacity/Excess Demand

Sill (1991) and Kimes *et al.* (1998) have provided food and beverage operators with a variety of strategies and tactics to deal with excess demand, from using flexible capacity strategies to accommodate demand, to duration management and queuing systems. In the case of restaurant operations, Davis and Heinke (1994) listed a series of service considerations to minimize queuing dissatisfaction. Customer perceptions of fairness, their level of comfort while waiting, the length of time the customer is waiting, communicating with customers to update them on their estimated wait period and compensating customers if necessary should be considered to provide them with the best level of service possible.

Excess Supply/Insufficient Demand

The scenario of experiencing excess supply has not been adequately considered in the case of hotel restaurants. It may be suggested that the services marketing mix be re-evaluated in terms of the restaurant operation.

- Product: menu modification including introduction of new products.
- Pricing strategies and tactics: for different times of the day and days of the week.
- Place: location of the hotel and restaurant/banqueting rooms.
- Promotional plans: developing special promotions for the restaurant for certain times of the day, week or year.
- Process and service delivery: type and standard of service.

- Physical evidence: refurbishment, seating arrangements, developing a new pre-post meal lounge.
- People: staff, their level of skills in service delivery, selling techniques and customer care. Most importantly, evaluation of customers' wants and needs.

Integration of organizational and operational plans is fundamental to the effective synergy of the two products (i.e. accommodation and food and beverages).

TOWARDS THE DEVELOPMENT OF AN INTEGRATED YIELD MANAGEMENT SYSTEM

Increasing Yield Management Awareness

This will be achieved by organizing seminars and training programmes for management and staff that form part of the yield management team. Regular weekly meetings must take place with this team to review, to forecast and to determine effective strategies and tactics that will maximize yield in all areas of the hotel. These meetings are invaluable as a means of encouraging teamwork and coordination between all departments in the hotel (Figure 18.1).

Historical Data

The food and beverage manager must review past records to determine patterns of demand. Gathering, analysing and maintaining specific information will enable the food and beverage manager to manage capacity utilization and make better decisions in relation to menus, event planning and pricing.

The information required (on a daily basis for each meal period) may be summarized as follows: recording bookings, by type of customer, reservations (residents and non-residents), cancellations, no-shows, walk-ins; recording revenue achieved for each meal period.

Market Segmentation

Market segments that are initially targeted are dependent on the resources available (standard of hotel), such as financial, technological, material and human resources. Segments may include private (individual parties), corporate, independent tourist and group/tour.

Recording and Using Information Effectively

The effectiveness of the system will be largely dependent on the procedures and technology the food and beverage manager has implemented. Historical data must be gathered, structured and analysed, as they will be useful for making future predictions. The current reservations system that gathers data on a daily basis must include functions that allow the reservation taker to record information categories such as

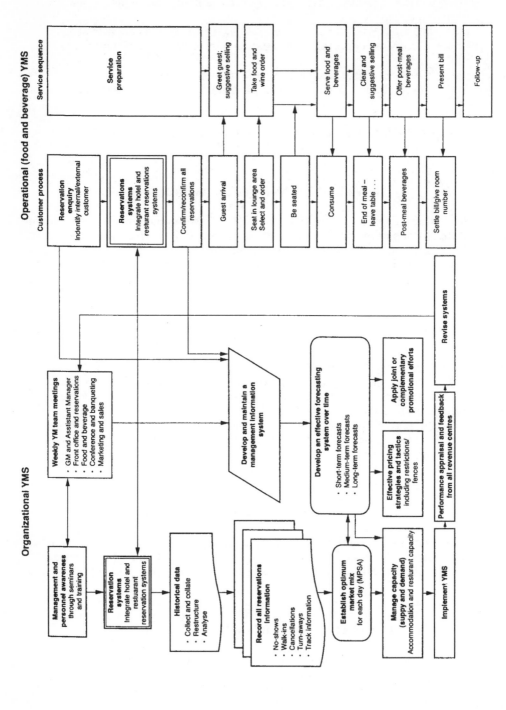

Figure 18.1 Organizational YMS

customer history, credit card numbers, estimated time of arrival, number in party, occasion, special requirements, denials, declines, cancellations and no-shows.

This information will enhance the decision-making process in relation to customer requirements, operational requirements, style of food service and making proactive decisions about promotional efforts concerning the optimum marketing mix to attract on a daily basis for a given meal period.

External Information

External factors must be considered when forecasting, pricing and planning future accommodation packages and special restaurant promotions. Sill (1991) and Kimes *et al.* (1998) do not consider external factors, such as location of the hotel/restaurant, degree of competition, events that have occurred or will occur and current and forecasted occupancy in the hotel.

Forecasting

Forecasts are carried out for a number of reasons, including to predict the number and mix of customers and to predict revenue, i.e. the sales mix from the menu and for analytical and comparative purposes. Other operational reasons include purchasing, stock control, staffing levels and to ensure that supply is consistent with demand (Davis and Stone, 1991; Van Westering *et al.*, 1994; Waller, 1996).

Rolling forecasts that commence a minimum of six to twelve months in advance are most effective. These forecasts should be updated once a week after the yield management meeting and two weeks prior to the date in question, at least twice a week. It is recommended that the final forecast be carried out a minimum of one week prior to the specific date and updated on a daily basis. This allows for all bookings to be confirmed, customers to be contacted so that they can be invited to dine in the hotel restaurant and to have more detailed information on-hand in relation to walk-ins, timing of promotions, etc.

Price Management

Pricing policies will also influence demand. Restaurants will offer different products and services to specific market segments. Menus will vary in price for certain dishes or at certain times of the day and certain days of the week. Special promotions may take place to stimulate overall demand or demand for certain menu items. Meal packaging may take place in lower priced food outlets or for specific high-volume banquets or functions. External considerations, such as location of the hotel and extent of competition from other local restaurants, will also influence price.

Discounting may include the following strategies and tactics: offering early bird specials, speciality meals, wine tastings or special shows or music during slow periods; encouraging group and corporate business and offering bonus points to customers who dine during off-peak periods or to loyal customers.

Price Restrictions

Prices set must be clearly defined, taking into consideration the perceived fairness of prices by the customer (Kimes, 1994). Price fences are required in instances where supply exceeds demand, where management plans to offer discounted packages to encourage capacity utilization and to ensure that higher paying customers cannot easily avail themselves of lower priced packages.

Physical price fences include table location, party size, menu type and the absence or presence of certain amenities. The purpose of the intangible fences is to shift demand from busy to slow periods and to schedule the highest margin business at busiest times.

Marketing Implications

The marketing mix of the restaurant operation should obviously be closely integrated with the organization's overall marketing mix. How the restaurant is marketed as part of the overall hospitality product will to some extent determine its success. The level of independent advertising, promotions and PR the restaurant carries out is also quite important. The types and numbers of packages offered (i.e. accommodation and meals) must be decided upon well in advance by the YM team.

Establishing an Appropriate Mix of Business for Each Day and Meal Period

Based on analysis and evaluation of historical data, an appropriate mix of business from various key market segments should be established for each day and each meal period. This provides clear guidelines for management and staff (particularly, those taking reservations) and assists management in evaluating attainment of goals.

Performance Appraisal

All operational objectives set by the food and beverage manager and banqueting manager (if separate posts exist) must be in line with organizational objectives. Standard operating procedures and budgets – such as revenue, costs, profit and so forth – must correspond with overall financial objectives of the hotel. Performance appraisal is also useful on a micro level because such performance indicators may be used with additional market-orientated information to evaluate operational decisions made by the YM team.

OPERATIONAL IMPLICATIONS OF A YIELD MANAGEMENT SYSTEM

Cousins *et al.* (1995) have modelled three sub-systems of typical food and beverage operations, namely the customer process, the service sequence and the food production process. The former two sub-systems are integrated as part of an organizational yield management system.

The Customer Process

The 'customer process' begins at the enquiry stage, and continues through to reservation and confirmation stage. This process will take longer if it involves an enquiry about a function or banquet. Guests arrive, are then seated, offered a beverage and take time at this stage to examine menus. Their order is taken and guests are seated at their table where the meal is consumed. At the end of the meal guests may adjourn to a lounge (this frees up tables during high periods of demand) to enjoy post dinner drinks and then settle their bill (Figure 18.1).

The Service Sequence

Once the type and level of service has been determined, the service sequence can be properly defined. Managing the service sequence is of prime importance as part of the yield management process (Figure 18.1).

Service Preparation

This involves training one or two key members of staff as 'receptionists' or 'hosts' to deal competently and efficiently with enquiries. Emphasis must be placed on selling techniques from this initial phase. There must be a structured and systematic way of taking reservations, recording details such as denials, declines, cancellations, no-shows and chance customers (walk-ins), and overbooking levels must be constantly monitored.

This part of the process also involves briefing staff on the number of covers expected at a specific mealtime, the number of larger parties that are expected and specified requirements they might have. Staff should be fully briefed on customers and their specific requirements, have full knowledge of the products they are selling, be aware of special promotions that are available to the customer and be aware of effective 'up-selling' and 'suggestive selling' techniques – in order that revenue be maximized.

One member of staff should greet the customers, record that they have arrived and seat them in a lounge area if possible, offering them a pre-lunch/dinner beverage as it allows a table to be prepared for them if there is a high level of turnover at that particular time. The customers should then be escorted to their table and a staff member is signalled to attend to them.

Taking Orders

There are a variety of methods in taking orders. The chosen method will depend on the hotel and its financial control system, the type of restaurant and the proposed billing system. At this stage of the sequence, staff are available to answer any queries the customer might have and must be keenly aware that they have potential to maximize revenue as part of their role in personal selling. Staff must also be aware of the fact that their service forms an integral part of the overall product, i.e. the 'meal experience', and that will clearly influence the satisfaction of the customer.

Service of Food and Beverages

The type of service chosen in most hotels is dependent on the standard of the hotel. The 'type' of restaurant, the mealtime, overall layout of the restaurant, skills of staff and availability of equipment will influence the chosen method(s) of service. The restaurant manager will largely determine the volume of business that might be accommodated in a restaurant at a certain mealtime as a result of the chosen method of service. Methods of service will determine the speed of service, 'turnover' of tables and overall through-put for a specific meal period. Clearly, the type and extent of dishes on menu(s) will also influence the speed of service. A clear communications system and teamwork from all staff involved in food preparation and service are imperative as part of the successful service of food and beverages.

Clearing

In most hotels, with the possible exception of budget hotels, staff clear tables manually. This should be efficiently carried out and will depend on the type of operation, level of demand and number of staff employed (i.e. staff employed specifically to clear and reset tables, staff who serve or staff who perform both tasks). A clear communications system must exist whereby management is aware that tables are ready for customers.

Billing

The chosen billing method will depend on each hotel and restaurant and will vary in terms as to whether the customer is resident or non-resident. The billing system should be linked to an efficient order taking, internal control system. Cousins *et al.*, (1995) suggest that the revenue control system should be conducive to recording and subse-quently analysing data to assist in evaluating performance. Examples include seat turnover for each mealtime, average spend per head on food and beverages, sales mix data, payment method breakdowns, sales per member of staff, sales per available seat hour (RevPASH), sales per square metre and reconciliation of orders taken and payments, at the end of a period.

Follow-up

Direct mail and other promotions can be sent to corporate groups and to loyal guests who stay in the hotel and frequent the restaurant. Special packages and promotions could be offered to these customers, particularly in anticipation of low demand (for accommodation and food and beverages) periods, to increase occupancy and revenues and to smooth demand patterns and levels (Figure 18.1).

Table 18.3 Overview of hotels in Dublin city centre

Classification standard of hotel	Number of hotels
Five star	7
Four star	7
Three star	37
Two star	11
One star	1
Total number of hotels	63

Table 18.4 Response rate from hotels in Dublin city centre, and those that implement a yield management system

Classification standard of hotel	Response rate (%)	Implementation of a YMS (%)
Five star	71	100
Four star	57	75
Three star	49	58
Two star	45	0
One star	100	0

THE DUBLIN HOTEL FOOD SERVICE SECTOR

Background

The Dublin city centre *hotel food and beverage sector* is chosen as the focus of this study. This research explored how yield management in food service operations may be integrated with an organizational yield management system (YMS) in a hotel. General managers were asked whether they had implemented a YMS (and to what extent) in their hotels, whether it was rooms-specific or whether it included other operations, namely food and beverage outlets. To ascertain whether hotel restaurants were profitable or not, hoteliers were asked whether their restaurants were revenue-generating centres in their own right or whether they were just viable (break-even only). The number of hotels that 'sourced out' their food and beverage outlets was also determined.

Research Design and Methodology of the Study

A survey consisting of a semi-structured questionnaire was mailed to 63 hotels in the Dublin city centre registered with the Irish Tourist Board (see Table 18.3). Fifty-one per cent of hoteliers surveyed returned their questionnaires, which was deemed representative and acceptable for the purpose of the study (see Table 18.4).

In-depth interviews were also conducted with a representative sample of respondents that replied to the mail survey. Respondents who had successful restaurants (in terms of revenue generated) were interviewed and a sample (10 per cent of each) of hoteliers who 'broke even' with their food and beverage outlets were also interviewed. The objective of this survey was to elicit more qualitative information from the respondents in relation to maximizing yield from hotel food and beverage operations. Issues that were examined included:

- the level of integration of the organization's YMS;
- strategies and tactics the management team employed in periods of high and low demand;
- the extent to which forecasts were carried out, and levels of information recorded and of historical data maintained;
- pricing policies and marketing strategies and tactics employed.

Findings of the Study

It must be noted that the vast majority of respondents were from the medium to larger hotel categories, i.e. 51–100 bedrooms and 101+ bedrooms. The majority of these respondents were in the three to five star classification strata.

Food and Beverage Facilities

Practically all the hotels surveyed (excluding one and two star hotels) operated more than one food and beverage outlet. Such outlets become more informal in the lower standard classification categories. Almost 50 per cent of respondents from three star hotels stated that their food and beverage outlets were not revenue generating centres. The vast majority of respondents in the three to five star categories indicated that they perceived the food and beverage outlets as services that had to be provided for guests. Fifty per cent of respondents from the two star category stated that they did not offer formal food and beverage facilities – only breakfasts – as there were numerous restaurants in their vicinity and they were unable to compete with them.

Integration of Food and Beverage Operations with YMS

The vast majority of respondents stated that their YMS applied to rooms only and was not integrated with other operations within the hotel (namely, food and beverage). Hotel managers were asked whether they believed that YM of accommodation and food and beverages *could be* integrated. A variety of views emerged. Positive views implied that they had integrated these products to some extent, such as offering special packages, e.g. weekend packages and special event packages; in periods of high occupancy priority was given to higher spend food and beverage customers; and in-house promotion by front office staff of food and beverage outlets was effective. Negative responses also emerged, such as accommodation and food and beverage products/services were 'too separate' to integrate as part of an overall system.

Yield-Orientated Strategies and Tactics Employed in Food and Beverage Operations

It was also important to determine the extent of YM application in hotel food and beverage operations. In periods of high demand the following strategies and tactics were employed:

- maintaining reservations records (manually);
- suggesting alternative date/time for booking;
- encouraging 'spillover' to use alternative food and beverage facilities within the hotel.

In periods of low demand:

- increasing marketing and sales efforts, e.g. sending out mail-shots to local businesses and follow-up calls for bookings;
- special promotions, e.g. special event menus, wine tastings, gourmet evenings;
- promoting banqueting facilities.

Recording reservations information and historical data:

- the vast majority of respondents recorded bookings in a reservations diary;
- historical data were maintained only by the larger properties, particularly those that have a reservations system, while food and beverage managers in medium-sized hotels maintained historical data as hard copy (manually).

Forecasting:

- in most cases, projections for the restaurant were developed from reservations data and were formally updated on a weekly basis for each month and each quarter.

Emerging Trends

Most of the hotels surveyed (91 per cent) operated their food and beverage outlets internally. One notable trend that is emerging is the number of newly established higher standard hotels (specifically four and five star properties) which have success-fully outsourced their main restaurants to high profile chefs who already had their own well established restaurants. This strategy has proven to be very successful for both 'operations'.

Another notable trend is the number of city centre two and three star hotels that do not operate a restaurant in their property, offering accommodation and breakfast in a semi-formal to informal setting. Many of these hotels offer bar food for lunch. The primary reason supplied for not operating a restaurant in the hotel was that it was not a viable option because of the location of the hotel and the number of independently operated restaurants in the vicinity. It was also noted that providing semi-formal to formal meals was not part of the overall product/service offering in some of these properties.

CONCLUSION

The hotel restaurant sector has, to date, been neglected in terms of research carried out in the areas of capacity management, revenue maximization and yield management (Van Westering *et al.*, 1994).

Many YM researchers have addressed the problem of excess demand, particularly those from the USA, where many restaurants experience this phenomenon. However, in the Dublin hotel restaurant sector, food and beverage managers have more often than not had to contend with excess supply.

From recent primary and secondary research (Strate and Rappole, 1997) the following issues are emerging. Hotels are realigning their restaurant products to address their guests' needs and to attract more walk-in business at different times of the day. Hotels are also developing the concept of offering more than one restaurant product to cater for a variety of needs (e.g. formal and semi-formal restaurants). Yield management of the food and beverage operation is tactical by nature and is not integrated with the organization's yield management system. Hotel managers primarily consider integrating their food and beverage system (POS and EPOS) with the reservations system for billing purposes, rather than for data collection and analysis purposes.

Hotel companies are also considering strategic alliances with specialist food and beverage operators to reposition their restaurants, allowing them to become active revenue contributors. Van Westering *et al.* (1994) also notes this trend of franchising out of food and beverage space in hotels. They suggest that rather than this being the only feasible option, YM should be considered. Both strategies could be successfully adopted by many hotels, particularly those in the larger properties' category.

It is clear, therefore, that the development and integration of a food and beverage yield management system and a hotel's yield management system are the way forward for all yield-orientated hotels. Van Westering *et al.* (1994) point out that hospitality industry-specific software companies should develop a yield-orientated food and beverage module as part of the PMS (property management system).

RECOMMENDATIONS

Hoteliers must redevelop their food and beverage outlets and operate them as viable operations in their respective organizations. They must provide products and services that their target markets actually want and must promote this development to existing and potential customers. Providing quality products and services that offer value for money will change customers' attitudes and perceptions of hotel restaurants. Hotel restaurateurs must strive to provide comparable or enhanced products/services to customers to achieve a competitive edge over what their competitors provide.

The restaurant should be treated as an independent operation in its own right. However, cooperation between all members of the yield management team is vital and certain joint promotional packages should be developed to increase yield generally within the accommodation and food and beverage departments.

Hoteliers that have implemented yield management systems in their organizations are strongly encouraged to integrate their food and beverage operation(s) sub-system into the broader organizational yield management system.

Both Kimes (1994) and Van Westering *et al.* (1994) discuss the perceived fairness of yield management by hotel guests. Pricing practices must be seen to be fair and, as discussed above, price fences or restrictions must be clearly set. For yield management to be totally acceptable and successfully practised in the hospitality industry, as it is in the airline industry, education of management, staff and customers is the key.

The hotel restaurant must be viewed as a revenue-generating centre in its own right. The restaurant must complement the hotels' overall product offering. As research has indicated, new hotels in Dublin are developing strategic alliances. The advantages of developing a strategic partnership between the hotel and hotel restaurant include an improved image of the property as a whole, much improved customer perceptions of the hotel restaurant, increased opportunity to attract walk-in business, increased revenues in accommodation and food and beverage outlets and an overall competitive advantage for the hotel.

Hoteliers who are in the process of restructuring their hotel restaurants might consider these approaches, ideas and concepts as part of the development of an integrated yield management system. Obviously, both 'operations' must continue to work closely together – it is management and customer perceptions that must be changed in order that hotel restaurants are seen as viable operations in their own right that actively contribute to increasing overall yield within the organization.

REFERENCES

Bradley, A. and Ingold, A. (1993) 'An investigation of yield management in Birmingham hotels'. *International Journal of Contemporary Hospitality Management*, **5**(2), 13–16.

Breuhaus, B. (1998) 'Handling no-shows: operators react to reservation plan'. *Restaurant Business*, **16**(1), 13.

CERT (1998) *Employment Survey of the Tourism Industry in Ireland*. Dublin: BDO Simpson Xavier Consulting.

Cousins, J., Foskett, C. and Shortt, D. (1995) *Food and Beverage Management*. Harlow: Longman.

Cross, R. G. (1997), 'Launching the revenue rocket: how revenue management can work for your business'. *Cornell Hotel and Restaurant Administration Quarterly*, **38**(2), 77–87.

Davis, M. M. and Heinke, J. (1994) 'Understanding the roles of the customer and the operation for better queue management'. *International Journal of Operations and Production Management*, **14**(5), 21–34.

Davis, B. and Stone, S. (1991) *Food and Beverage Management*. Oxford: Butterworth-Heinemann.

Dillon, E. (1991), 'Yield management – in the balance'. *Caterer and Hotelkeeper*, **24** (April), 61–3.

Farrell, K. and Whelan-Ryan, F. (1998) 'Yield management – a model for implementation'. *Progress in Tourism and Hospitality Research*, **4**(3), 267–77.

Hartley, J. and Rand, P. (1997) 'Conference sector capacity management'. In I. Yeoman and A. Ingold (eds), *Yield Management: Strategies for Service Industries*. London: Cassell.

Jauncey, S., Mitchell, I. and Slamet, P. (1995) 'The meaning and management of yield in hotels'. *International Journal of Contemporary Hospitality Management*, **7**(4), 23–6.

Kimes, S. E. (1989) 'Yield management'. *Journal of Operations Management*, **8**(4), 348–63.

Kimes, S. E. (1994) 'The perceived fairness of yield management'. *Cornell Hotel and Restaurant Administration Quarterly*, **35**(1), 22–9.

Kimes, S. E., Chase R. B., Choi, S., Lee, P. and Ngonzi, E. (1998) 'Restaurant revenue management: applying yield management to the restaurant industry'. *Cornell Hotel and Restaurant Administration Quarterly*, **39**(3), 32–9.

Kotas, R. and Jayawardena, C. (1994) *Profitable Food and Beverage Management*. London: Hodder and Stoughton Educational.

Orkin, E. B. (1988) 'Boosting your bottom line with yield management'. *Cornell Hotel and Restaurant Administration Quarterly*, **27**(1), 52–6.

Orkin, E. B. (1990) 'Strategies for managing transient rates'. *Cornell Hotel and Restaurant Administration Quarterly*, **30**(4), 35–9.

Quain, B., Sansbury, M. and Abernathy, T. (1998) 'Making money at your hotel'. *Cornell Hotel and Restaurant Administration Quarterly*, **39**(6), 71–9.

Sill, B. T. (1991) 'Capacity management: making your service delivery more productive'. *Cornell Hotel and Restaurant Administration Quarterly*, **31**(4), 77–87.

Simpson Xavier Horwath and Restaurants Association of Ireland (1994) *Irish Restaurant Industry Review*. Dublin: Simpson Xavier Horwath.

Strate, R. W. and Rappole, C. L. (1997) 'Strategic alliances between hotels and restaurants'. *Cornell Hotel and Restaurant Administration Quarterly*, **38**(3), 50–61.

Van Westering J., Cooper, C. P. and Lockwood, A. (1994) 'Yield management – the case for food and beverage management'. *Progress in Tourism, Recreation and Hospitality Management*, **6**, 139–47.

Waller, K. (1996) *Improving Food and Beverage Performance*. Oxford: Butterworth-Heinemann.

19

Capacity Management in the Cruise Industry

Julian Hoseason

INTRODUCTION

Yield management (YM) is generally regarded as a technique for managing or balancing demand and supply (Daudel and Vialle, 1994; Cross, 1998; Edgar, 1998; Farrell and Whelan-Ryan, 1998) and includes inventory or capacity management (Kimes, 1997). As a management technique, YM optimizes revenue by using mathematical algorithms (Belobaba and Wilson, 1997) to improve profitability, smooth fluctuations in demand and produce stability through capacity management. YM has been adopted by many service industries, notably in airlines (Larsen, 1988; Ingold and Huyton, 1997), hospitality (Orkin, 1988; Donaghy et al., 1995b) and the cruise industry (Dickinson and Vladimir, 1997; Cross, 1998), as part of their strategic management in a highly competitive industry. While some sectors of the travel and tourism industry have well documented case studies in implementation of YM systems, research indicates that by no means all organizations operating within these sectors have adopted the technique to its full potential.

In order to use YM effectively, the cruise industry has had to improve segmentation by providing purpose-built ships designed to meet demographic and lifestyle changes. By generating greater volumes in new, younger devotees to cruise, YM can be now implemented. Entry into the market place by the launch of *Disney Magic* in 1998 and continued expansion by the leisure-based Carnival Cruises have enabled singles and family-based segments to enter the market (Peisley, 1995). After decades of steady growth in global sales, cruises suffered a mid-1990s crisis when sales temporarily declined (Peisley, 1998a). However, fears of a declining or stagnant market were short-lived. The growth in cruises since 1996 has proven them to be the fastest sector in the UK holiday market and improved performances in other key markets have been particularly noted in Germany and the USA (Anon., 1997a). Continued growth (Anon., 1998) has encouraged fleet expansion and the re-entry of UK tour operators into the market place. Orders for new ships reported by the Passenger Shipping Association (PSA) in 1999 shows plans for 48 new cruise ships with an additional 77,458 berths coming into service by 2003. A capacity increase of 37.8 per cent has been projected upon an expected annual increase in demand of 20 per cent per annum for the next three years, as more holiday-makers switch from land-based inclusive holidays. Historically, major increases in supply have depressed yield (Dickinson and Vladimir, 1997; Holloway, 1998) and have been out of synchronization with demand patterns from key markets, particularly the USA. Thus, despite consolidation of ownership, the cruise industry has a major issue of capacity management looming in the near future as the market matures.

BACKGROUND TO CRUISE

A number of observers dispute the origins of cruise (Burkart and Medlik, 1974; Dickinson and Vladimir, 1997). However, its infancy can be traced back to the mid-1840s when the Peninsula and Oriental Steam Navigation Company (P&O) ran ships to the Iberian peninsula and the Orient. By the 1880s mercantile shipping began to carry greater numbers of leisure travellers, as opposed to those on colonial business or European emigration. By 1900 passenger liners were running regularly between Europe and North America, but they were designed for speed rather than comfort, with a top-heavy profile which made transatlantic crossings uncomfortable for the majority of steerage travellers (Burkart and Medlik, 1974; Dickinson and Vladimir, 1997). Palmer (1971) notes that cruising had become an established alternative vacation by the 1930s when the Shaw Saville Line provided round-the-world voyages.

In 1957 for the first time more people travelled transatlantic by air than sea, marking the death toll for the passenger liners (Yale, 1995). By the 1960s only a very limited schedule of summer-time transatlantic passenger crossings remained (Burkart and Medlik, 1974), but cruise operations suggested themselves as an alternative redeployment for liners. The availability of flights to the Mediterranean and Caribbean meant that cruise ships could operate exclusively in warm waters, without the need to return to colder northern ports to embark and discharge passengers. Liners built for speed proved to be uneconomic to run and difficult to operate in the shallower waters of the Caribbean (Yale, 1995) and, therefore, there was a stimulus for the commissioning of purpose-built cruise ships (Burkart and Medlik, 1974; Yale, 1995). The design emphasis was upon facilities and sun-decks, with hulls built for stability rather than speed. Fly–cruise holidays operated by companies such as Cunard in the 1970s to the Mediterranean and Caribbean attracted over 300,000 passengers (Burkart and Medlik, 1974) to each region drawn from the North American and European markets.

Falling air fares in the 1980s (Yale, 1995; Dickinson and Vladimir, 1997) rescued an ailing industry in which poor perceptions of product caused UK-based tour operators to withdraw from the market. An image of an expensive product, which appealed only to the elderly, forced operators to reposition cruising. Imagery of the cruise product has been a major marketing issue. Dickinson and Vladimir (1997) point out that the TV series *The Love Boat* revolutionized the image of cruise. Initially screened in the United States during the 1980s, the show replaced an image of deck quoits and faded gentility with one of excitement and escapism.

While the 1980s saw the establishment of the North American market dominating cruise, the Mediterranean also remained a core for European based fly–cruise business. Dickinson and Vladimir (1997) observed that this was the period when many of today's main cruise providers began to revolutionize the industry; for example, Carnival Cruise

Line and Costa Cruises both began to show their distinctive branding and corporate characteristics.

THE ECONOMICS OF CRUISE

One predicament facing the industry is non-standardization of cabins or inventory (Bull, 1995, 1996; Dickinson and Vladimir, 1997). Historically, a number of cruise lines opted for smaller and higher density cabins with varying levels of comfort to differentiate the product. In the 1990s Disney Cruise Line increased cabin size because the family market required more space. Deck level and position (inside or outside) alter pricing of the product and this impacts upon selling strategies and revenue management. Airtours recently spent £10 million in a refit converting its first four star ship (RCI's *Song of America*) into the *Sunbird* (Anon., 1999a). Nine penthouse suites were added as part of the general refurbishment, indicating not only a marketing opportunity, but also a trend to reduce capacity and maintain revenue through added value.

Although short-run supply is inelastic (Bull 1995, 1996), cruise owners share similar economic characteristics with other sectors of the travel and tourism industry, i.e. high fixed operational costs and capital investment. The need to maximize and maintain vessel revenue necessitates itineraries in warm waters or seasonal global relocation between different cruising locations (Dickinson and Vladimir, 1997). The age of the ship and crew to passenger ratios may also influence pricing strategies and the differentiation of product (Mentzer, 1989), particularly between budget and quality cruises. Within these constraints, cruise operators have always faced the same dilemma: whether to commission new purpose-built ships, or to make major modifications to older ships (Burkart and Medlik, 1974; Yale, 1995). Both of these imply high capital commitment and operational costs and any gain is only in the short term. However, refurbishment was the route by which many UK tour operators re-entered the cruise market in the 1990s; for example, Thomsons with *Saphire* (Laws, 1997; Anon., 1997b). In order to manage operational costs, cruise lines have sought lower labour cost by crewing ships with foreign nationals (Yale, 1995; Dickinson and Vladimir, 1997), through design and technology making operational efficiencies or through changes in on-board service (Bull, 1995, 1996).

Although management of operational costs has been important in the transformation of the cruise industry, this is not the only factor. Consolidation in ownership (Hobson, 1993; Bull, 1995; Dickinson and Vladimir, 1997) or trading alliances (Peisley, 1995) have also brought benefits through economies of scale in the production and marketing of multinational enterprises. The consolidation of the cruise market has brought huge benefits in purchasing power for global products and services, like insurance and finance, but it has also produced complex trading alliances through share ownership; for example, Carnival's 30 per cent stake in Airtours (Anon., 1997b). Further consolidation (Peisley, 1995) will see not only polarization between owner/operators, but also product repositioning within the market. The exception appears to be Carnival Cruises, whose fleet has been 'boutiqued' into mass and specialist branded markets.

The impact of UK tour operators upon cruising produced a direct fall of 9 per cent in the average price of a cruise in 1995 when Airtours entered the market and a further 5 per cent in 1996 with the arrival of Thomsons (Anon., 1997b). The average price fell to £1,200 during this period. It was widely viewed as an opportunity to expand volume in key market segments and improve the numbers of first-timers, which have always been low (Dickinson and Vladimir, 1997).

MARKETING CRUISE

Various authors (Yale, 1995; Dickinson and Vladimir, 1997) suggest that cruise packages differ from other types of all-inclusive holiday by providing two core elements, accommodation and resort entertainment, rolled into one. As floating hotels, cruise ships are highly competitive compared to land-based packages, where other incremental costs tend to be ignored by travellers when choosing product type and destination (Dickinson and Vladimir, 1997).

The cruise market can be segmented into:

- line voyages (e.g. Southampton to New York);
- river (e.g. the Danube, Rhine or Nile);
- ocean.

Ocean cruising dominates the cruise industry through image (Dickinson and Vladimir, 1997) and operations. For most operators, a comprehensive programme or itinerary in warm waters (Burkart and Medlik, 1974; Dickinson and Vladimir, 1997) with flight connections has long been established as a recipe for success. The establishment of fly–cruises (Burkart and Medlik, 1974; Dickinson and Vladimir, 1997) has not only enabled maximized economic utility (Bull, 1995, 1996), but also assisted marketing. More dynamic itineraries extend the operating and marketing period and reduce the impact of seasonal variation upon revenue (Dickinson and Vladimir, 1997).

According to Burkart and Medlik (1974) fly–cruises have become established since the 1970s in the following regions:

- Mediterranean;
- Caribbean;
- Scandinavia/Baltic;
- Alaska;
- Far East;
- West Coast/Trans-Panama Canal;
- round the world;
- other areas (Black Sea, Indian Ocean, Atlantic Islands).

The proximity relationship between cruise locations and main markets has become well established (Burkart and Medlik, 1974; Peisley, 1995; Dickinson and Vladimir, 1997) and acts as a key factor in mass market cruise. Proximity dependency upon key markets can be explained through the relationship between time–cost and travel demand or the distance decay function (Bull, 1995). The distance decay function measures length of stay in relation to volume, i.e. the greatest demand for travel peaks within a preferred distance from origin. There have been changes in lifestyle (Dickinson and Vladimir, 1997) and the average age of travellers continues to fall, e.g. from 59.1 years in 1992 to 54.6 in 1997 (Anon., 1998). Tolerance of travel by older age groups may remain a major constraint to cruise development, particularly in long-haul destinations. Research by Crouch (1994) identified a relationship between demand elasticity in income, price, exchange rates, transportation costs and promotional activities in the short and long haul markets. He suggests that long haul holidays display higher income elasticities than short haul products, and that there is an exchange rate elasticity of demand which declines as length of haul increases. Long haul markets will remain relatively attractive despite regional variations in economic performance in other markets.

These observations assist in understanding travel patterns behind global and inter-regional movements (Pearce, 1995), but the socio-demographic characteristics of key markets are arguably more important in the short run. In 1995 a Cruise Lines International Association survey (see Dickinson and Vladimir, 1997) identified the chief archetypal characteristics of cruise segments split as:

- restless baby boomers (33 per cent);
- enthusiastic baby boomers (20 per cent);
- consummate shoppers (16 per cent);
- luxury seekers (14 per cent);
- explorers (11 per cent);
- ship buffs (6 per cent).

It has long been accepted that tourist products are offered to highly segmented consumer markets through either behavioural (Cohen, 1979; Plog, 1977) or archetypal characteristics (e.g. Holloway and Robinson, 1995). The key to recent growth in cruising has been matching product development with demographic and lifestyle changes. Marketing has become more focused on developing key segments (Dickinson and Vladimir, 1997) to attract greater volumes. New, purpose-built ships with a wider variety of on-board facilities and activities, together with more dynamic itineraries, have contributed to dramatic growth in demand. However, there is some concern that future expansion by cruise lines like P&O assume continued growth in new markets for quality cruises. The quality cruise market is substantially supported by the increasingly sophisticated 'grey market' (Fry, 1997), who see quality and personalized services as being important (Ananth *et al.*, 1992). In the production–service continuum, service quality will put pressure upon costs, thereby forcing operators to remain competitive through innovation and implementation of YM. While the 'grey market' will continue to grow owing to demographic shifts in population, changes in pensionable age and increases in personal pension and health care provision will alter consumer behaviour within a key market.

Expanding markets straddled with issues of consolidation and polarization (Peisley, 1998a) result in a greater need to improve product positioning and branding. Dickinson and Vladimir (1997) categorized cruise into a continuum of:

- budget;
- contemporary;
- premium;
- speciality;
- luxury.

Holloway (1998) recognized that some cruise operators, notably Carnival Cruises, have positioned themselves across the cruise continuum by using effective branding to differentiate their products and show a clear understanding of niche or micro market behaviour (Cross, 1998). Carnival particularly markets its cruises to mass market segments through theming fun or to micro markets (Fiesta) for Hispanic and Latin

Americans. Excess capacity in the early 1990s (Holloway, 1998) led to greater marketing of cruise in Europe at a time when lower airfares acted as an incentive to travel further and away from the Mediterranean owing to the geo-political instability in the region caused by the Gulf crisis. Bull (1996) recognizes that cruising has a unique economic and operational advantage as a foot-loose industry by being able to switch operational areas to match consumer shifts in demand patterns, thereby being able to present a refreshed product to market into different segments.

YIELD MANAGEMENT

YM has become an essential tool in revenue management of airline, hotel and car rental operations. The cruise industry shares a number of common characteristics with other travel and tourism sectors, since capacity is relatively constrained and demand is both seasonal and highly segmented (Dickinson and Vladimir, 1997; Cross, 1998). However, a number of unique properties make cruises more complex and also quite dissimilar from the YM point of view. For example, the relationship between cabin size, position and deck level affects unit price but is also the value added element in marketing. These properties are not duplicated in other sectors but the relationship is critical in managing yield in cruises.

Research into YM in other sectors of the travel and tourism industry is now quite extensive. They cover primarily the airlines (Larsen, 1988; Smith *et al.*, 1992; Daudel and Vialle, 1994; Belobaba and Wilson, 1997; Ingold and Huyton, 1997) and the hospitality industry (Orkin, 1988; Donaghy *et al.*, 1995a). Studies range from technology impact and implementation studies to marketing, human resource management, revenue and inventory management. There have been a few studies in areas of tour operations (Laws, 1997; Hoseason and Johns, 1998) but hardly any concerned with cruises (Dickinson and Vladimir, 1997).

Kimes (1989, 1997) identifies five necessary conditions for effective YM. These are:

1. Fixed capacity.
2. High fixed costs.
3. Low variable cost.
4. Time-varied demand.
5. Similarity of inventory.

Kimes (1989, 1997) and Cross (1998) supplement these five 'necessary ingredients' for the successfully implementation of YM:

1. Market segmentation.
2. Historical demand and booking patterns.
3. Pricing knowledge.
4. Overbooking policy.
5. Information systems.

A number of YM implementation studies use the analytical framework provided by these two lists. However, Schwartz's (1998) critical review of YM suggests that the perishability of the product and the customer's willingness to pay are in fact the key elements in YM. He claims that the necessary conditions and ingredients identified by Kimes and Cross are overstated or, at best, contributing factors, and that this emphasis reflects misconceptions and misunderstandings of price demand elasticity and consumer behaviour. Schwartz ignores the evidence of Lieberman (1993), Farrell and Whelan-Ryan (1998), Edgar (1998) and others, which suggests that different sectors of the travel and tourism industry share similarities, but apply YM techniques differently (Smith *et al.*, 1992). Indeed, Lieberman (1993) notes that YM can be effectively implemented through the use of YM algorithms and improved customer service quality without sophisticated computer or management systems.

In established markets, consolidation of ownership, together with a chronic over-supply of capacity, tends to make marketing strategies shift towards a price-led approach (Peisley, 1995; Mounser, 1996; Laws, 1997; Skidmore, 1999). When discounting tactics are widely used to maintain sales volume and market share (Hoseason and Johns, 1998), a reduction in yield impacts upon sustainability (Laws, 1997) of the market. Segmentation processes, a greater understanding of micro-market behaviour (Poon, 1993; Cross, 1998) and perishability are important considerations in pricing strategies and subsequent product development (Middleton, 1991, 1996; Edgar, 1997; Poon, 1993). In these market conditions, experienced consumers not only delay purchase (Hoseason and Johns, 1998), but also expect discounting which produces an element of falsehood in demand. Thus capacity management must be given greater importance (Cross, 1998) for revenue and yield to improve than Schwartz (1998) credits.

The cruise market suffers from chronic over-supply in key markets, and discounting has been used extensively (Anon., 1996; Peisley, 1995, 1998a, b; Dickinson and Vladimir, 1997). In 1999, Royal Caribbean International reported a 16.3 per cent increase in net income ($90.2 million) produced by withdrawing ships from service (Anon., 1999b). The company subsequently cross-sold products by utilizing spare capacity in other ships within the fleet, indicating the extent to which capacity can undermine yield at fleet level. Ambitious growth plans by individual fleets may ultimately destabilize the market place and lower yields.

DECISION SUPPORT SYSTEMS IN YM

Computer reservation systems (CRSs) bring a variety of benefits to operations management, ranging from inventory control through to personnel management (Donaghy and McMahon, 1995; Hanlon, 1996; Kimes, 1997; Inkpen 1998). CRS systems from different sectors of the travel and tourism industry have been further linked into global distribution systems (GDSs) (Inkpen, 1998). Continuous improvement of hardware and software technologies has led to a steady fall in system operating costs. These advancements, coupled with effective operational research, have enabled organizations like Sabre Decision Technologies to improve decision support and refine YM (Cook, 1998).

Accurate prediction of revenue through YM modelling is the key to successful revenue management. Research by Jansen *et al.* (1998) indicates the degree to which employee empowerment can lead to a reduction in yield. Decision support systems (DSSs) have been designed to support YM teams in the decision-making process. Use of mathematical algorithms enables complex semi-structured problems to be solved, producing greater consistency in managers' decisions (Russell and Johns, 1997; Proudlove *et al.*, 1998). DSS technology allows greater focus to be placed upon strategic management by easing pressure upon core areas of management (Poon, 1993). This enables managers to develop products focused at micro rather than mass markets, where value added elements within the product are more price sensitive and little differentiation is possible in a competitive market place (Cross, 1997).

Research indicates that use of additional technology, particularly DSSs, appears low for a market worth £785 million in the UK alone, with a number of companies just beginning to recognize the beneficial strategic and operational advantages of modelling yields. Russell and Johns (1997) highlight the advantages of DSS enhancement to YM systems in terms of accuracy and consistency in decision-making. An industry facing greater competition, through consolidation, increases to fleet and overall market capacity, will require DSS technology to give users a greater competitive edge (Belobaba and Wilson, 1997; Proudlove *et al.*, 1998), particularly during periods of poor sales performance owing to geopolitical instability or changes in demand patterns.

Further expansion within the cruise market is likely to polarize ownership as competition for key market segments increases. Greater pressure will be placed upon managing capacity and using technology to support strategic management. Otherwise, simply broadening the base of the market may destabilize the industry. DSS technology enhances management knowledge and moves away from suppositions, giving cruise managers of the future more accurate modelling and better forecasting (Cross, 1997).

YM IN THE CRUISE INDUSTRY

The cruise industry focus is upon management of revenue and cabin availability rather than total cruise revenue, which has historically instilled a pricing strategy of permanent discounting (Dickinson and Vladimir, 1997). Bull (1996) suggests that although price is the strategic variable, little differentiates rates charged by operators within the sectors of the cruise continuum. Pricing behaviour of this nature is typical of oligopolies and continued consolidation will increase competition where excess capacity exists, particularly in the contemporary and premium market segments. Numerous authors, particularly Dickinson and Vladimir (1997), recognize the need for adjustments to pricing mechanisms to manage inventory and improve yield. Cruise, like the long haul holiday market, enjoys long lead times (Hoseason, 1998), which enables yield managers to operate within an extended time frame that other sectors of the travel and tourism industry are denied. Data supplied by the Passenger Shipping Association in 1999 indicate that despite substantial increases in capacity and predatory pricing tactics by UK-based tour operators, there has been remarkable stability and no shortening in lead times since the early 1990s. Stability of this nature enables YM systems to respond and forecast accurate changes to inventory by means of the price mechanism.

There are differences in the experiences of implementing YM by various cruise operators in Europe and the USA, which reflect differences in organizational culture, market positioning and strategic management. Both Cross (1998) and Dickinson and Vladimir (1997) point out the benefits YM has brought to US cruise operators, whose implementation of YM has enhanced their ability to dominate key market segments. For example, Royal Caribbean Cruise Lines' experience of implementing YM demonstrates that there has been a greater level in financial benefits gained through revenue management than through a disproportionate level in effort by management constantly trying to cut operational costs (Cross, 1998). However, UK-based tour operators' use of formalized YM systems for their cruise programmes is much lower in level of implementation. Instead, some use low-cost manual YM systems based on market intelligence and forecasting which relies on discounting to clear unsold cabins. The reason: UK tour operators have only recently entered this market and it may be that market penetration and capacity management are of greater importance for stabilizing their market position in this initial phase.

Many cruise operators have tailor-made computer systems mainly used for operational management and reservations based upon their organizational requirements. Most major cruise lines have reservation systems linked to major CRS/GDS systems, with SABRE and Galileo dominating. Although most cruise lines still use more traditional approaches to product distribution through retailing or direct sell (Dickinson and Vladimir, 1997), changes in technology have enabled cruise lines to alter their distribution techniques and costs. The advanced technology of CRS/GDS assists in managing capacity and cabin availability where YM systems monitor changes in demand and booking lead times. The Passenger Shipping Association reports that only 21 per cent of sales are made within three months of departure, while there has been significant growth (69.2 per cent) in booking lead times of over nine months since the early 1990s. Good historic demand and booking patterns have long been recognized (Kimes, 1989, 1997) as a prerequisite not only for accurate modelling, but also for operationalizing YM systems. In cruise, relatively stable and long booking lead times not only enable greater refinement to YM forecasting, but remain a pattern envied by many other sectors of the travel and tourism industry.

Growth in usage of the Internet has encouraged direct access to reservations and for cruise information via dedicated web pages. However, it is the use of the Internet that differentiates European and American cruise companies' strategies. Europe-based companies have a less sophisticated approach, with web pages that offer little interactivity and concentrate only on providing information. In contrast, USA-based companies have established on-line reservations, with an array of additional services set up to a high standard in design and interactivity. For example, inclusion of real-time share information enables multiple levels in usage from one database, ranging from a single purpose, i.e. a sale, to a wider spectrum of services to meet expanding client needs.

Capacity management has been identified by Kimes (1989, 1998) and Cross (1997, 1998) as an essential element if YM is to be effective. Dickinson and Vladimir (1997) highlight the combined effects of higher cruise costs together with too much capacity being added to premium lines by either traditional cruise lines (Holland America) or newer lines like Celebrity. To compound the problem further, consolidation within the cruise industry (Hobson, 1993), together with product or brand repositioning, has resulted in a top heavy capacity profile which has destabilized the market by trying to defy price elasticities of demand.

Recent trends suggest that optimal ship size and capacity requires the building of mega-ships in order to achieve economies of scale. Data compiled by the Passenger Shipping Association (Anon., 1998) indicate the optimum cruise-ship capacity to be 2,500–3,000 berths. New ships have doubled in size since the 1970s (Holloway, 1998), owing to a combination of improvements in marine technology and economic or operational cost constraints. Evidence suggests that while consolidation of fleet ownership improves economic performance and competitiveness, it is the ratio of ship size to passengers and overall fleet capacity that now needs to be managed if there is to be effective improvement in yield, thus avoiding over-supply. Bull (1996) points out that a

Table 19.1 Cruise ships' capacity ratio

Cruise line	Ship	Tonnage	Maximum capacity	Ratio
Airtours	*Sunbird*	38,000	1,595	23.8
Cunard	*QE II*	66,450	1,800	36.9
Carnival	*Imagination*	70,300	2,594	27.1
Carnival	*Inspiration*	70,000	2,594	27.0
Carnival	*Carnival Triumph*	101,350	3,400	29.8
Celebrity Cruises	*Galaxy*	72,000	2,262	31.8
Disney Cruise Line	*Disney Magic*	85,000	2,400	35.4
Holland-America Line	*Veendam*	55,000	1,400	39.3
P&O	*Oriana*	69,000	1,810	38.1
Princess Cruises	*Sun Princess*	77,000	1,950	39.5
RCI	*Eagle Class*	142,000	3,838	37.0

Source: Passenger Shipping Association (1999). Cited in Anon. (1999c)

single ship may represent between 1.5 and 2 per cent of market capacity. However, it is not ship or fleet size which is the key to future revenue management in the cruise industry. An additional 77,458 berths (an increase of 37.8 per cent) by 2003 (Anon., 1999c) in a consolidated market will cause destabilization and the likelihood of lower revenues. Difficult trading in Europe and the United States during 1999 resulted in selective discounting in budget and luxury cruises being widely used (*Travel Weekly*, 26 July 1999). In the UK, sluggish economic growth, the Balkan conflict and reduced consumer activity in the wake of the 1998 share windfall payments cut growth in cruise to 10 per cent, while capacity increased between 10 and 15 per cent. The short-term impact on the cruise market has forced Thomsons to scrap the charter of *Island Breeze* and *Saphire* for the year 2000. These actions clearly indicate the severity in competition for market share in the budget cruise market.

Capacity management is far more complex in cruise operations than any other tourism-based product. Cabin space, location and comfort all affect unit price (Dickinson and Vladimir, 1997), but it appears that not all cruise lines give equal weighting to space. Table 19.1 shows the capacity ratio of passengers per tonne. It clearly falls as level of luxury decreases towards the mass market. While there are short-run economic advantages in refurbishing older 'dames' of cruise (Burkart and Medlik, 1974), the quality of the cruise experience cannot match that on modern ships. While UK tour operators attempt to compete on price rather than quality, polarization in the market place will produce a 'tiered image' as a by-product. The quality gap between budget and quality cruising will widen, forcing cruise line operators to differentiate the product more along the lines of price and quality, thus reducing average yields even further. To remain efficient, crewing levels need to be less than 1:2.64 passengers (Anon., 1996) and to match the levels in new ships like RCI's *Eagle Class*, i.e 1:3.3 passengers (Peisley, 1998b). With the introduction of budget cruises by Thomson and Airtours, operational costs and hence service levels are under further pressure (James, 1999).

Cross (1997, 1998) puts greater emphasis upon micro-market behaviour and capacity than Kimes (1989, 1998). Planned market growth highlights complex market trends influencing the pricing and marketing of cruises. Companies are targeting younger (40 years old) and more affluent market segments, where price is less sensitive, or families. Disney has exploited changes in micro-market behaviour where themed entertainment and value is at a premium and the ship becomes an extension of their resorts and theme parks. Cruise lines are now more prepared to reposition their products to attract more flexible quality seekers. These companies are more likely to be in a better position to apply YM techniques than those UK tour operators that have become transfixed with market share and price.

Greater demand for more dynamic itineraries, particularly for the more discerning who want port-intensive itineraries, increases the need for more complex YM systems to deal with total cruise revenue where the tracking of on-board revenue needs to be distinguishable from other revenue centres. A more detailed holistic approach to revenue management enables exploitation of micro-market behaviour, whereas previous techniques may have overlooked subtle shifts in consumer behaviour. As a foot-loose industry (Bull, 1996), cruise is unique in being able to switch operating region. Therefore, cruise has the flexibility to respond to shifts in purchasing behaviour and improve its ability to manage yield in a way which is not experienced by other sectors of the travel and tourism industry.

New product development will be a major challenge facing cruise marketers. The Passenger Shipping Association's annual report (Anon., 1998) reveals that although over 60 per cent of cruise clients are repeat business; a steady decline in first-timers since 1995 will cause higher promotional costs and alter the ability to implement YM (Dickinson and Vladimir, 1997). Increasingly, it will be difficult to maintain a balance between valuable experienced clients and a younger more discriminating segment. To encourage repeat business, greater use of early booking offers, loyalty schemes, newsletters, exclusive cocktail parties and priority on lower cost upgrades will be used tactically to maintain competitiveness. However, adverse late booking patterns, as experienced in the late 1990s, may have a greater short-term impact upon ability to improve yield. Increased use of special offers to clear unsold capacity despite the 20 per cent increase in market volume clearly indicates that capacity is not being managed. Indeed, major ocean cruise lines are concerned that budget cruises compete on price alone and do not pay sufficient attention to service quality (James, 1999). Expansion of budget cruise lines will impact upon long-term profitability as tour operators, particularly Airtours, move into the four star market. To maintain stability in revenue, cruise programmes tend to use a combination of price-, market- or revenue-led strategies. Historically, the cruise industry has been price led during periods of excess capacity (Dickinson and Vladimir, 1997). Based upon the experiences of UK tour operating (Mounser, 1996; Skidmore, 1999), the destabilizing effect (Hoseason and Johns, 1998) will impact not only upon the ability to implement YM techniques, but also upon industry-wide yield. In addition, rapid expansion through acquisition by Carnival Cruises has changed the owner/operator profile of the cruise industry to the point where there is a potential imbalance in the cruise continuum. Consolidation in the market place has left large clusters of brand names creating potential excess capacity in the three and four star categories for Carnival Cruises to manage, thereby increasing exposure to predatory moves by UK tour operators or other expanding cruise lines.

Current industry experience suggests that it takes between 13 and 18 months to implement a YM system and this matches lessons from the hospitality sector (Donaghy *et al.*, 1995b). Quality of historic data is a key factor, together with experiential learning of YM systems and subsequent fine-tuning (Gamble, 1990). YM teams need a time-frame to understand and recognize normal and abnormal booking patterns with or without the use of DSSs. Through implementation of YM systems, research within the cruise industry indicates that turnover has increased on average by between 6 and 10 per cent. Net profits have been reported to show an improvement of 6–15 per cent depending upon market position and operational area. There is no doubt that cruise line operators that have implemented YM systems have benefited from the effort. However, this does not explain why the very same operators embarked upon fleet expansion programmes when demand patterns faltered in 1999. In an increasingly competitive environment where pricing strategies become more sensitive to experienced consumers (Cross, 1997, 1998), the case for implementing YM appears to be even stronger.

CONCLUSION

Yield management optimizes revenue. In the cruise industry, the nature and configuration of capacity presents a more intricate and unique product to manage. The behaviour of the micro-market segments is the crux of successful YM implementation. New emerging technologies, especially decision support systems, will play an ever growing role in fleet management and itinerary planning as micro-markets expand and mature. While an ageing population will see an expansion in the so-called 'grey market', cruise lines must not over-compensate in supply at the peril of market stability. Planned changes to pensionable age with higher pension provision will alter purchasing patterns. For growth to continue, yield managers need to consider not only current economic and financial trends but also revenue performance, especially in relation to expansion in capacity in both budget and premium/luxury ships.

Historically, expansion in supply has seen yields fall and, coupled to predatory moves by tour operators, the management of total cruise revenue will become increasingly more important as more value added elements are built into the cruise product. Undoubtedly, many cruise lines will need to change their strategies or implement computer-based YM systems to remain competitive. For budget line operators, the real danger lies in the development of a two-tiered product where the gap between budget and quality cruises widens to the extent that price alone will not be attractive. Thomsons' decision to reduce capacity and partially withdraw from the market may bring temporary relief to other operators. However, plans by fleets to increase capacity remain the core issue within the cruise industry and, until capacity is managed, yield cannot improve.

REFERENCES

Ananth, M., DeMicco, F. J., Moreo, P. J. and Howey, R. M. (1992) 'Marketplace lodging needs of mature travelers'. *Cornell Hotel and Restaurant Administration Quarterly*, **33**(4), 12–24.
Anon. (1996) 'Cruising: pick-up lines'. *The Economist*, 14 May, 88.
Anon. (1997a) 'Cruise market bouyant in both Europe and the USA'. *Travel Industry Monitor Travel and Tourism Intelligence*, **85** (April), 3–5.
Anon. (1997b) 'Impact of tour operators on the UK cruise market'. *Travel Industry Monitor Travel and Tourism Intelligence*, **88** (July), 17–19.
Anon. (1998) *Passenger Shipping Association Annual Cruise Market Digest*. London: Information Research Network.
Anon. (1999a) 'Airtours makes upmarket move with penthouse offerings'. *Travel Weekly*, **13** January, 45.
Anon. (1999b) 'Royal Caribbean sees income rise by 16.3%'. *Travel Weekly*, **3** May.

Anon. (1999c) *Annual Cruise Market Digest 1998*. London: Global Business Research Consultancy, IRN Services Ltd.

Belobaba, P. P. and Wilson, J. L. (1997) 'Impacts of yield management in competitive airline markets'. *Journal of Air Transport Management*, **3**(1), 3–10.

Bull, A. (1995) *The Economics of Travel and Tourism*, 2nd edn. Harlow: Longman.

Bull, A. (1996) 'The economics of cruising: an application to the short ocean cruise market'. *Journal of Tourism Studies*, **7**(2), 28–35.

Burkart, A. J. and Medlik, S. (1974) *Tourism: Past, Present and Future*. London: Pitman.

Cohen, E. (1979) 'A phenomenology of tourist experiences'. *Sociology*, **13**, 179–201.

Cook, T. M. (1998) 'Sabre soars'. *OR/MS Today*, **25**(3), 26–31.

Cross, R. G. (1997) 'Launching the rocket: how revenue management can work for your business'. *Cornell Hotel and Restaurant Administration Quarterly*, April, 32–43.

Cross, R. G. (1998) *Revenue Management*. London: Orion Business Books.

Crouch, G. I. (1994) 'Demand elasticities for short-haul versus long-haul tourism'. *Journal of Travel Research*, **32**(2), 2–7.

Daudel, S. and Vialle, G. (1994) *Yield Management: Applications to Air Transport and Other Service Industries*. Paris: Institut du Transport Aerien.

Dickinson, R. and Vladimir, A. (1997) *Selling the Sea: an Inside Look at the Cruise Industry*. New York: John Wiley and Sons.

Donaghy, K. and McMahon, U. (1995) 'Managing yield: a marketing perspective'. *Journal of Vacation Marketing*, **2**(1), 55–62.

Donaghy, K., McMahon, U. and McDowell, D. (1995) 'Managing yield: an overview'. *International Journal of Hospitality Management*, **14**(2), 139–50.

Donaghy, K., McMahon-Beattie, U. and McDowell, D. (1995) 'Implementing yield management: lessons from the hotel sector'. *International Journal of Contemporary Hospitality Management*, **9**(2), 50–4.

Edgar, D. A. (1997) 'Economic aspects'. In I. Yeoman and A. Ingold (eds), *Yield Management: Strategies for the Service Industry*. London: Cassell.

Edgar, D. A. (1998) 'Yielding: giants v's minnows, is there a difference?' *Progress in Tourism and Hospitality Research*, **4**(3), 255–65.

Farrell, K. and Whelan-Ryan, F. (1998) 'Yield Management – a model for implementation'. *Progress in Tourism and Hospitality Research*, **4**(3), 267–77.

Fry, A. (1997) 'Shades of grey'. *Marketing*, 24 April, 23–4.

Gamble, P. R. (1990) 'Building a yield management system – the flip side'. *Hospitality Research Journal*, **14**(2), 11–22.

Hanlon, P. (1996) *Global Airlines: Competition in a Transnational Industry*. Oxford: Butterworth-Heinemann.

Hobson, J. S. P. (1993) 'Increasing consolidation within the cruise line industry'. *Journal of Travel and Tourism Marketing*, **2**(4), 91–6.

Holloway, J. C. and Robinson, P. (1995) *Marketing for Tourism*, 3rd edn. Harlow: Longman.

Holloway, J. C. (1998) *The Business of Tourism*, 5th edn. Harlow: Addison-Wesley Longman.

Horner, P. (1991) *The Travel Industry in Britain*. Cheltenham: Stanley Thornes.

Hoseason, J. M. (1998) 'Yield management and service quality in long haul tour operating'. In *Conference Proceedings of the Third International Yield Management Conference, Volume 1*, University of Ulster.

Hoseason, J. M. and Johns, N. (1998) 'The numbers game: the role of yield management in the tour operations industry'. *Progress in Tourism and Hospitality Research*, **4**(3), 197–206.

Ingold, A. and Huyton, J. R. (1997) 'Yield management in the airline industry'. In I. Yeoman and A. Ingold (eds), *Yield Management: Strategies for the Service Industry*. London: Cassell.

Inkpen, G. (1998) *Information Technology for Travel and Tourism*, 2nd edn. Harlow: Addison Wesley Longman.

James, L. (1999) 'P&O Cruises MD hits out at budget moves'. *Travel Weekly*, 31 May.

Jansen, M., Swint, F. and Zwaal, W. (1998) 'Perceived empowerment as determinant of yield performance'. In *Conference Proceedings of Third International Yield Management Conference*, University of Ulster.

Kimes, S. (1989) 'The basics of yield management'. *Cornell Hotel and Restaurant Administration Quarterly*, **3**(3), 14–19.

Kimes, S. (1997) 'Yield management: an overview'. In I. Yeoman and A. Ingold (eds), *Yield Management: Strategies for the Service Industry*. London: Cassell.

Larsen, T. D. (1988) 'Yield management and your passengers'. *ASTA Agency Magazine*, June, 46–8.

Laws, E. (1997) 'Perspectives on pricing decisions in the inclusive holiday industry'. In I. Yeoman and A. Ingold (eds), *Yield Management: Strategies for the Service Industry*. London: Cassell.

Lieberman, W. H. (1993) 'Debunking the myths of YM'. *Cornell Hotel and Restaurant Administration Quarterly*, **34**(1), 34–41.

Mentzer, M. (1989) 'Factors affecting cruise ship fares'. *Transportation Journal*, **29**(1), 38–43.

Middleton, V. T. C. (1991) 'Whither the package tour?' *Tourism Management*, **12**(3), 185–92.

Middleton, V. T. C. (1996) *Marketing in Travel and Tourism*, 2nd edn. London: Heinemann.

Moscardo, G. *et al.* (1996) 'Tourist perspectives on cruising: multidimensional scaling analyses of cruising and other holiday types'. *Journal of Tourism Studies*, **7**(2), 54–63.

Mounser, I. (1996) 'Key issues surrounding price-based marketing of breaks and holidays in the UK travel sector'. *Journal of Vacation Marketing*, **2**(4), 367–72.

Orkin, E. B. (1988) 'Yield management makes forecasting fact not fiction'. *Hotel and Motel Management*, 15 August, 112–18.

Palmer, M. D. (1971) *Ships and Shipping*. London: B. T. Batsford.

Pearce, D. G. (1995) *Tourism Today: a Geographical Analysis*. Harlow: Longman.

Peisley, T. (1995) 'Transport: the cruise ship industry to the 21st century'. *EIU Travel and Tourism Analyst*, no. 2, 4–25.

Peisley, T. (1998a) 'The cruise market in mainland Europe'. *EIU Travel and Tourism Analyst*, no. 1, 4–25.

Peisley, T. (1998b) 'The good berth guide: size matters'. *Sunday Times*, 22 February, 67.

Plog, S. C. (1977) 'Why destination areas rise and fall in popularity'. In E. M. Kelly (ed.), *Domestic and International Tourism*. Wellesley, MA: Institute of Certified Travel Agents.

Poon, A. (1993) *Tourism, Technology and Competitive Strategies*. Wallingford: CAB International Press.

Proudlove, N. C., Vaderá, S. and Kobbacy, K. A. H. (1998) 'Intelligent management systems in operations: a review'. *Journal of the Operational Research Society*, **49**(7), 683–99.

Russell, K. A. and Johns, N. (1997) 'Computerized yield management systems: lessons learned from the airline industry'. In I. Yeoman and A. Ingold (eds), *Yield Management: Strategies for the Service Industry*. London: Cassell.

Schwartz, Z. (1998) 'The confusing side of yield management: myths, errors and misconceptions'. *Journal of Hospitality and Tourism Research*, no. 4, 413–30.

Skidmore, J. (1999) 'Powell admits to misjudging travel industry'. *Travel Weekly*, no. 1467, 2.

Smith, B. C., Leikuhler, J. F. and Darrow, R. M. (1992) 'Yield management at American Airlines'. *Interfaces*, **22**(1), 8–31.

Yale, P. (1995) *The Business of Tour Operations*. Harlow: Longman.

20

Capacity Management in the Football Industry

Gerald L. Barlow

INTRODUCTION

The football industry is undergoing radical changes in many of its operations caused by government policies and external changes drawing traditional fans away. There are internal changes too, caused mainly by the constantly increasing levels of transfer fees and wages of the top players. Since 1990 there have been a number of leading English football league teams who have sold their old town- or city-based grounds for new out-of-town grounds, offering better facilities; Sunderland, Derby and Bolton are some of the examples. Combined with this is an increase in the number of clubs who have gone into receivership, Swindon Town being the first in the twenty-first century, but surely not the last. This has meant that these businesses, because clubs investing millions in their future can no longer be considered anything else, have got to approach the whole area of their business as a financial operation. The current First Division of the Football League has clubs like Birmingham City, Blackburn Rovers, Huddersfield Town and Wolverhampton Wanderers that have invested millions of pounds in their premises and teams, not to mention those in the Premiership. If their investors are to see a return on their investment, then they must use all the management tools available, not just those needed to permit them to reach the Premier status they all crave. Through a case study of Birmingham City Football Club, this chapter looks at how yield management could be used to help to manage part of their operation by assisting them in gaining better financial stability.

DEFINITIONS AND OBJECTIVES

Yield management, revenue maximization or revenue management, as it is also known, is the technique used by a number of organizations in the service industries and relates to the need/desire of an organization to maximize its effective use of resources in terms

303

of capacity. Its purpose is to permit the organization to maximize its profits by effective use of supply and demand factors. According to Kimes (1989a), it is 'the process of allocating ... capacity to ... maximize revenue or yield'. Orkin (1988) simply applies a formula:

$$\text{Yield} = \frac{\text{Revenue realized}}{\text{Revenue potential}}$$

Kimes (1989b) suggests that the concept behind yield management is the desire to achieve the best possible (maximum) margin per seat mile or passenger mile, while Lieberman (1993) states that yield management is the practice of maximizing profits from the sale of hotel rooms. Lee-Ross and Johns (1997) point out that major hotel companies, under certain circumstances, consider the investment value of the property higher than the quality of service. Furthermore, the requirement of the shareholders is a healthy dividend in the short term. This all emphasizes the need to achieve a maximum profit, which clearly matches the objectives outlined for yield management.

Kimes (1989b) then identified five core elements needed to be present for yield management to be effective:

1.   Booking patterns.
2.   Knowledge of the demand patterns.
3.   An overbooking policy.
4.   Knowledge of the effect of price changes.
5.   A good information system.

Arthur Andersen Consulting (1997) confirmed the five core competencies identified by Kimes and also recognized four preconditions for the use of a yield management system:

1.   Perishable inventory or seasonal demand.
2.   High fixed costs or sunk costs.
3.   Fixed capacity, either overall or in the short term.
4.   Advanced purchase of the product or service.

Clearly the capacity of a football ground is fixed: it is controlled and fixed by the licence granted in conjunction with the police, fire authorities and local council. In the case of Birmingham City Football Club this is currently 30,500, which includes all forms of seating. This capacity cannot be changed without major rebuilding.

But in the case of a football ground this is not the only available capacity, unlike an airline or hotel. Research has identified the following areas of capacity which management has the opportunity to preside over:

1.   Seating capacity
     ● hospitality;
     ● season tickets;

- match day tickets (all with a range of prices based upon area of seating).
2. Advertising capacity
   - advertising in the ground;
   - advertising in programmes;
   - advertising on the club's kit.

Each of these areas has fixed capacity in the short to medium term and thus is perishable. For example, any unsold seat on a match day is lost revenue, just like a bed in a hotel or seat in a plane or restaurant. Any slot in a programme or around the ground is the same. Similarly, any unsponsored shirt is a lost opportunity, as when it is eventually sponsored, the level of sponsorship will reflect the lost opportunities, or the time available.

An example of maximizing the available capacity in this area can be found in rugby league, where a Yorkshire club has sponsored the tracksuit trouser seat bottom of its physiotherapist to a local radio station for the season.

The question next to be addressed is: how are these areas of capacity managed, and do they fall into the requirement identified by Kimes and associates as requisites for the successful use of yield management?

CAPACITY MANAGEMENT AT BIRMINGHAM CITY FOOTBALL CLUB

Seating Capacity

This area is segmented into two major areas:

1. *Season ticket sales.* These tickets, available for most areas of the ground are sold prior to the start of the season, for the entire season. These include all hospitality, vice presidents' seating and general seats.
2. *Match day sales.* Seats to all other areas of the ground are sold on a match-by-match basis, on the day and in advance. They reflect a similarity to airline seats, theatre tickets, hotel bedrooms and restaurant tables. However, these are fully paid in advance when bought in advance.

Advertising

Ground advertising is the space around the ground, on the pitch perimeter and on the stand front fascias. These areas are sold in advance for the season or the remaining part of the season. *Programme advertising* is sold in advance on the following basis:

1. For the season.
2. For a month.
3. For a single game.

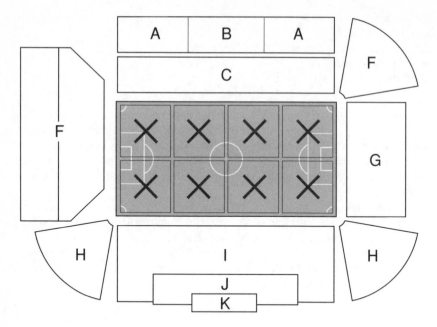

Figure 20.1 Ground seating capacity and segmentation

Pricing Structure

The seating pricing is broken down into two types: season tickets and match day pricing. Season ticket pricing is structured into two types: adult and child. For match day pricing, all ticket pricing is structured according to game types:

> *AA games:* local derby games, e.g. Wolverhampton Wanderers, West Bromwich Albion, and top class teams, e.g. Blackburn Rovers, Nottingham Forest.
> *A games:* top class games, e.g. Charlton Athletic, Fulham, Ipswich Town, Manchester City.
> *B games:* other teams, lower achieving, less popular teams, e.g. Crewe Alexandra, Port Vale.

All ticket pricing is also structured on the basis of ground location and facilities available, as seen in Figure 20.1 and Table 20.1.

Ticket Sales Procedures

Current season ticket holders are given priority for the following season until 30 June. Hospitality seating/boxes are offered to existing customers first and held until 30 June, and then offered on a 'first come first served' basis. Match day tickets are sold on a 'first come first served' basis, with the ticket office opening ten days before kick off. For extra games, cup matches, etc., pricing is based on the same principle of category AA, A and B games, with coupons printed in the programmes for collection to be used in the

Table 20.1 Key to the seating segmentation areas

	Season ticket price		Price per game					
	Adult	Child	AA		A		B	
			Adult	Child	Adult	Child	Adult	Child
Main Stand								
A. Main Stand Wings	288	117.50	17	8.50	16	8	14.50	7.50
B. Main Stand Centre	305	155	18	9.50	17	9	16	8
C. Family Stand	199	119	14	7.50	13	7	12	6.50
Railway Stand								
D. Railway Lower	275	145	18	9	17	8.50	16	8
E. Olympic Gallery	330	165	19	9.50	18	9	17	8.50
Tilton Road								
F. Tilton Corner	240	135	15	8	14	7.50	13	7
G. Tilton Road	255	137	17	8.50	16	8	14.50	7.50
Kop Stand								
H. Kop Corners	310	155	18	9.50	17	9	16	8.50
J. The Kop	325	155	18	9.50	17	9	16	8
K. Club Class	360		22.50		21.50		20	
L. Presidents' Seating	Not available at the time of the research							

future; if the team is successful and reaches the later stages of the FA Cup, when demand is expected to increase, and exceed availability.

Booking Patterns

Birmingham City FC has a pattern of booking for season tickets dating back to the end of the Second World War, with a hard core of fans, and a pattern of sales tied to the team's success, providing a good set of data for forecasting.

For match day tickets a booking pattern is again available based on three issues:

1. Past history of the date, e.g. first Saturday of the season, or first Saturday of a month.
2. Past history of the opposition, e.g. local derby or specific team.
3. Short-term sale history affected by team success, local economics, etc.

Overbooking Policy

Overbooking is not an option. Clearly this is not possible for season tickets, and would not be legal for match day tickets. The only option would be to sell tickets for specific games when season ticket holders confirmed they would not be present. But this does not occur.

Table 20.2 The opportunities to maximize revenue per outlet type

Outlet type	Total available capacity (no. of customers)	No. of opportunities to use per day	No. of opportunities to use per year	Percentage of available use (e.g. maintenance)	Total average available capacity	Effective use of capital
Major inter-national airline	450	2.6	2.6 × 450 × 365 = 427,050 seats	98.9 (four days out per year)	422,370	98.9
Budget airline	159	4	159 × 4 × 365 = 232,140	98.9 (four days out per year)	229,596	98.9
Football ground	30,500	n.a.	30,500 × 30 = 915,000	Used 30 days per year	915,000	8.22
Hotel	500	1	500 × 365 = 182,500	99	180,675	99
Restaurant	80	3.5	85 × 3.5 × 365 = 14,879	100	14,879	100

Note: The areas used for this comparison are: a Boeing wide-bodied aircraft; a Boeing 737–300 aircraft; Birmingham City FC; a 500-bedroom hotel; an average city centre restaurant, based on Café Rouge, Birmingham

Perishability of the Inventory

The seating and advertising capacity of the football industry is highly perishable. For example, if a fan wishes to watch the home game against Wolverhampton Wanderers, but fails to get a ticket, then he or she will have to wait until the following season. But the wait may be far longer should one of the two teams be promoted or relegated. It has been many years since the Birmingham City fans watched a home league game against Aston Villa their nearest geographic rivals. The product is in many ways highly perishable, because every time a seat is not sold for a game it cannot be resold. Similarly, in an airline, revenue capacity is applied on every flight, and thus lost on every flight where the seats are unsold. But the plane might be used four times in one day if on short haul journeys. Similarly, in the hotel sector, the room sale may be lost and cannot be resold if the hotel does not sell its rooms every day. However, the room can be sold twice in one day if there is demand for day lets. The difference is that unlike the hotel industry, which has the opportunity to sell its product on a daily basis, or the airline industry, which might be able to sell its seats up to four times a day, the sales opportunities of the football club are few. Birmingham City has the following opportunities per season (year) to sell its capacity: 23 home league games, and a minimum of three home games in the Worthington Cup. If successful there could be six games, three pre-season friendlies and from nought to four home games in the FA Cup dependent upon the team's success in the cup and the draw. This means that opportunities for using the ground's capacity are extremely restricted, between 29 and 36 games. Table 20.2 indicates the differences within various sectors.

Fixed Costs	£	%	Turnover		%
Match and ground expenses:	1,191,213	17.3	Match receipts and league contribution	4,984,953	59.8
Administration costs	627,916	9.1	TV and radio	245,701	2.9
Staff costs	5,069,448	73.6	Commercial activities	3,106,205	37.3
	6,888,577			8,336,859	
average number of home games	30		average seat price adult	£16.75	5:1
average fixed cost per match	£229,619		average seat price child	£8.39	
average cost per seat	£7.53		average price	£15.36	

Therefore, selling at an average price of £15.36, the club must sell 14,950 seats to break even on fixed costs, or achieve a 49.02% occupancy.

Figure 20.2 Birmingham City FC: summary of finances

THE COSTS OF OPERATING A FOOTBALL CLUB

The finances of Birmingham City plc are available in the annual report for the year ending August 1998. Figure 20.2 outlines the costs and how these relate to the fixed or sunk costs of running this club, and clearly reflect the problems of operating a business, open on so few occasions per year with this level of fixed costs.

The effects of these fixed costs can be seen in Figure 20.3. The striped areas represent the area needed to be sold at average prices to cover the fixed costs per game, using the income from all sources.

The unique aspects of this sector are based around the loyalty of the core customers, lack of seasonality and the fickle nature of the remaining customers/fans.

The 1998–9 season was an overall failure for Birmingham City Football Club. They failed to meet the main goal of the company, and the fans, Premier League status, coupled with failure in all cup competitions. Despite this, the beginning of the 1999–2000 season saw the sale of 16,000 season tickets (54.25 per cent of available capacity), 196 vice president seats (65.33 per cent) and 60 of the hospitality boxes (93.75 per cent). This indicates the loyalty of the fans, in all segments. However, less encouraging were the sales for the remainder of the seats, the match day seating, with 14,500 (44.25 per cent) available for the start of the 1999–2000 season. These tickets are affected greatly by loss of loyalty (if the team is losing games, then the attendance will drop). There are times within the season when other events will attract the same people (Christmas, for example, and other specific events) and poor weather can also affect the sales when the team's level of success is poor. However, this level of customer loyalty (55 per cent) is one that hotels and airlines would clamour for.

Overall the case outlines the situation found in any large professional football club. This case explores the circumstances within this industry. The opening of this chapter outlined the requirements of yield management as identified by Kimes (1989b) and Andersen Consulting (1997). Table 20.3 shows how Birmingham City Football Club matches these requirements.

Clearly Birmingham City Football Club does meet the requirements of yield management, but has not applied the principles of the technique, by frequently modifying

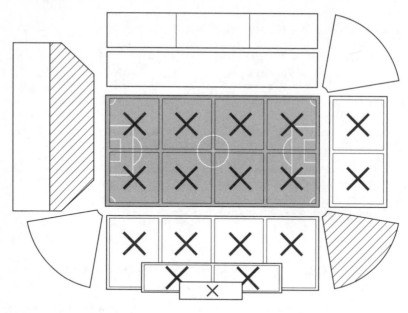

Figure 20.3 Birmingham City Football Club and YM requirements

Table 20.3 Yield management and Birmingham City FC

Requirement	Birmingham City FC
Booking patterns	Know pattern from past history and current season sales.
Knowledge of demand patterns	Past history of sales; history of other clubs available.
An overbooking policy	None.
Knowledge of the effect of price changes	Past history but based on fixed annual price increases; little recent history.
A good information system	For seat demand, little information. Advertising information available but of limited use.
Perishable inventory or seasonal demand	High.
High fixed/sunk costs	High: £7.53 per seat, or 49.02% of capacity.
Fixed capacity	Seating capacity 30,500. Advertising fixed in short and medium term.
Advanced purchase of product or service	55% pre-sold up to nine months in advance; 45% available ten days prior to the match.

the price structures to achieve the highest possible revenue from its available capacity. The club recognizes the different demand patterns as seen in the game classification of AA, A and B types, with different prices. However, it hasn't adjusted the pricing as a result of the actual daily demand. For the past two or three years it has started to look at ways in which this might be done, but may risk alienating 55 per cent of customers, the season ticket holders, who pay up to a year in advance. If the match day prices drop too much, then the season ticket holder might decide that his or her benefits are being eroded. To this end the club decided that it will offer children's tickets for some of the B-type games at the price of £1 if purchased on the day of use for specific seating areas. The aim is threefold.

1. This will bring in new customers, who, it is hoped will become lifelong Birmingham City fans.
2. They will be accompanied by either parents or other adults, and may be accompanied by other children or adults, who may come to other bigger games.
3. They will result in sales otherwise not made (a contribution to the fixed costs).

However, very little use of yield techniques can be found elsewhere, in either seat sales or advertising.

POSSIBLE OPPORTUNITIES FOR THE USE OF YIELD MANAGEMENT TECHNIQUES

Seating Capacity

For one-off or special games, such as cup matches, under the current procedures tickets are sold on the same basis as for league matches, under the club's classification of AA, A or B class and price structure. Therefore, should Birmingham City FC reach the quarter final of the FA Cup and be drawn at home to Manchester United, the ticket price would be the same as for a league game against West Bromwich Albion FC, an AA game. But it is likely that demand would be much higher unless the West Bromwich game was at the end of the season and a deciding game as to whether the club won the divisional championship. The demand for a home tie in the quarter final against Manchester United is likely to be very high, particularly with a maximum availability of 14,500 seats. So the opportunity to gain additional income is clear. The pricing decision under the current policy is based on the aim not to 'rip-off' the fans, who are relied on for the rest of the year. This may appear unusual, but then consider the difference in customers from the average hotel or airline customer and the average football fan. The average hotel or airline customer may use the capacity 10 or 20 times a year or 4–6 per cent of the available time, whereas the football fan would attend 80–100 per cent of home matches, and 55 per cent pay for the whole year in advance. This level of loyalty might be the justification for the lack of use of pricing tactics.

Advertising Capacity

Again, the majority of the ground advertising is sold on an annual basis, with space in the programmes sold on an annual or monthly basis. But what opportunities are available?

Currently the ground advertising is controlled by the available space, with higher priced areas being in the central areas and behind the goals, continuing on around the perimeter of the field.

The programme is planned a month in advance and the advertising is then positioned within the programme, but the capacity can be increased and decreased easily upon demand. Therefore it would be possible to increase the capacity for a high demand game – for example, the possibility discussed of a cup quarter final, where there is a restricted time to plan, advertise and produce. But there should be no problem in producing a larger special cup programme carrying extra capacity.

Can other industries learn from this example? Many would like the opportunity of the high degree of customer loyalty, advance sales and payment and past history, but not the low use of facilities. In many ways football clubs treat their customers with consideration, even if the facilities at times do not reflect this: toilets, catering or queuing, for example.

CAN YIELD MANAGEMENT TECHNIQUES BE USED?

The football industry has a very mixed range of customers, from the dedicated fans to hospitality customers and then the occasional one-off game fan. Could football clubs use the techniques of yield management?

The industry does to some extent use yield techniques in its pricing strategy for both seating and advertising, but Birmingham City appears unprepared to consider applying this technique on a match-by-match or day-to-day basis. The managers believe that they are in a restricted elastic demand situation; stretch it too much and it will break. The break they fear most is with their season ticket holders. For example, May 1998 saw Birmingham City in the first division play-offs for a place in the Premiership. This meant one home and one away game with another of the play-off teams, followed by a possible final at Wembley. The one-off home game could have been seen as an opportunity to use yield-type techniques. However, Birmingham City FC decided to sell the tickets as category A pricing, not even at the top price. The directors decided upon this as a 'treat' or loyalty bonus to its fans. (This from a club whose accounts show a loss of £3 million.)

What would have been the effect of charging a premium? There is no comparison to look at but there were at least four possible results:

1. Birmingham win and go on to Wembley, and again win, and gain promotion.
2. Birmingham win but go on to lose at Wembley.
3. Birmingham win but lose on aggregate, and fail to reach the finals.
4. Birmingham lose, and lose on aggregate.

In the event of a win which resulted in a trip to Wembley, the likely result would be that the fans would initially be unhappy with higher tickets prices, but this dissatisfaction would soon be forgotten if they went on to win at Wembley. If they lost at Wembley the dissatisfaction at the home price might still cause concern. If, however, they had been knocked out at the first stage then the increase in price is more likely to result in unhappy fans. But sufficiently unhappy to stop supporting or not to buy the next season's season ticket? That is the real unresolved question. Similarly, they had the opportunity to sell more advertising as a one-off special event for both the pitch advertising and special programmes, etc., which they again did not do.

The somewhat careful approach to ticket and advertising price management is surprising for a business currently being accused of 'ripping off' its supporters with the price of team kit, a market in which Birmingham City is fully involved.

There is scope for the industry to develop an appropriate type of yield system, which will help to develop a more appropriate approach to its capacity management. Perhaps the use of computer printed programmes will enable a more game-by-game approach to advertising, while still offering incentives to people to subscribe for a whole season. Possibly the use of bigger, better programmes for special games, the AA games, or the later stages of a cup run, will enable a higher rate for advertising and thus generate a higher income.

Whatever their individual circumstances and even with consideration of fans, at the end clubs like Birmingham City need to develop a better approach to their capacity management if they are to have a future. They cannot continue to find investors who are happy with a £3 million loss a year. In an industry where the majority of clubs are not making a profit – under 12 clubs in the first, second or third divisions made a profit in 1998–9, and the most profitable one in the second or third divisions was the second to last in the entire league, Carlisle – how can they not consider some form of yield management or revenue maximization?

CONCLUSION

Given the clear similarity between the requirements for successful yield management and the situation in the football industry, there are few reasons why it could not become a successful tool for the industry, permitting management an opportunity to maximize its ground and advertising revenue. However, the research at Birmingham City Football Club has identified an additional requirement necessary for the successful operation of yield management. That is that the organization must have as one of its aims the achievement of a profit, or more specifically profitability as one of its main objectives. This may seem obvious but there are examples where maximizing profit is not a main aim, Birmingham City Football Club being one obvious example. However, there may be many others, the main one being lifestyle businesses, where the owners consider their lifestyles the main reason for their existence. The hotel industry is one good example where lifestyle business exists, and where the operation of yield management will have a restricted use or benefit.

REFERENCES

Arthur Andersen (1997) *Yield Management in Small and Medium Sized Enterprises in the Tourism Industry*. Brussels: Director-General XXIII, European Commission.

Kimes, S. E. (1989a) 'The basics of yield management'. *Cornell Hotel and Restaurant Administration Quarterly*, **30**(3), 14–19.

Kimes, S. E. (1989b) 'Yield management: a tool for capacity-constrained service firms'. *Journal of Operations Management*, **11**(4), 348–63.

Lee-Ross, D. and Johns, N. (1997) 'Yield management in hospitality SMEs'. *International Journal of Contemporary Hospitality Management*, **9**(2/3), 66–9.

Lieberman, W. H. (1993) 'Debunking the myths of yield management'. *Cornell Hotel and Restaurant Administration Quarterly*, **34**(1), 34–41.

Orkin, E. (1988) 'Boosting your bottom line with yield management'. *Cornell Hotel and Restaurant Administration Quarterly*, **29**(1), 52–6.

21

Conference Sector Capacity Management

Jerry Hartley and Peter Rand

INTRODUCTION

Yield management is not concerned solely with maximizing yield from bedroom stock. Seekings and Farrar (1999) identify conference facilities as also being a major profit generator. Many conferences are residential and consideration of such events will have to be an integral part of a unit's approach to yield management. Yield management systems and the principles underlying such systems must be extended to incorporate consideration of the management of conference capacity for the following reasons:

1. Residential conferences are an additional factor to be considered in a yield management system. Group bookings may, for example, distort available rates offered to other customers if they are treated in the same way as individual reservations (Goymour, 1995).
2. In many hotels, residential conferences have the potential to fill significant amounts of bedroom stock and therefore carry the ability to affect overall yield (positively or negatively).
3. As with the leisure and 'groups' markets, many residential conferences result in multiple night stays – a further challenge within a yield management system.
4. Effective yield management systems cannot focus on accommodation yield only – additional revenue generated by guests during their stay and the costs of providing the services consumed by guests must also be considered. Such factors will vary with different market sectors. Furthermore, different types of conference will carry different revenue and profit generating potential.
5. Maximizing yield from conference capacity, within the context of the unit's overall yield management strategy, is as important as maximizing yield from the sale of bedroom stock.

Kimes stresses this approach in relation to the hotel sector:

> Rooms are certainly not the only thing sold in a hotel. Restaurants, convention space, and other services may contribute substantially to a hotel's profitability. By

concentrating only on the rooms function of a hotel, the yield-management system could be ignoring revenue opportunities in other portions of the hotel. Fortunately, this added function could be built into a yield-management system. (Kimes, 1989)

Two distinct but related elements of a yield management system are room inventory management and a differential pricing structure. The former is concerned with allocating different types of room to the pattern of demand, and the latter with the selection of the 'best' price to charge in a particular situation. This dichotomy is equally relevant when examining the potential applications of yield management to conference demand. These two aspects of yield management are addressed in this chapter in relation to the management of conference capacity. We discuss the effective yield management of conference capacity and suggest how yield might be increased.

However, we contend that effective conference capacity yield management techniques extend beyond room inventory and pricing decisions. The objective of any yield management system is taken to be that of maximizing yield from a given level of stock or capacity over a fixed time period. For a venue having conference, function and/or exhibition space, yield management systems, designed to increase the overall profitability of the venue, must include consideration of many factors beyond room inventory and room pricing. While the yield-related information needed to handle a bedroom booking can be assessed relatively quickly, conference, function and exhibition space can be sold and used in many different ways and for many different purposes – combinations which will produce significantly varying profit potential. Ultimately, yield will be determined by how you sell the total facilities available.

THE 'CONFERENCE CAULDRON'

The conference coordinator will have to consider a wide range of variables when making yield-orientated decisions. How effectively the variables are managed will determine the ultimate yield generated by the venue's conference facilities. The Peter Rand Group has identified a range of twenty factors that must be considered in relation to the conference and allied markets. We label these variables collectively as the 'conference cauldron', the ingredients of which have to be 'stirred and blended together' (managed effectively) if the quality of the resulting 'dish' (the maximum final profit/yield) is to be achieved. The mental image of the 'cauldron' has proved effective during training sessions in helping to reinforce the fundamental point that managing conference capacity is a complex and difficult job, with many variables all having to be combined effectively if yield targets are to be achieved:

Added value	Packaging
Business mix	Profitability
Client's budget	Purpose of event
Competitive edge	Refused business
Dates	Residential requirements
Duration	Risk factors
Future opportunities	Size
Lead time	Space management
Market strength	Timing
Numbers	Vacuums

As we consider how these factors are combined to produce both customer-orientated and yield-orientated approaches, two fundamental questions lie at the heart of the analysis:

- Should the venue take the business?
- If 'yes', at what price?

The first of these questions encompasses two separate aspects of yield management: first, in relation to deciding the proportion of the venue's bedroom stock that can be allocated to the conference market on a particular date (business mix); second, in relation to deciding whether or not to accept particular types of conference booking on specific dates. These decisions relate to the room inventory aspect of yield management. The latter question encompasses the area of a 'differential' or 'proactive' pricing strategy. The ingredients of the 'conference cauldron' are integral components of a yield-orientated approach to the management of conference capacity. The range of factors that has to be considered is complex, but on closer examination a broad structure emerges which forms the basis of a framework against which to examine these issues.

- *Planning conference capacity strategy:* a number of the 'ingredients' must be analysed so that the venue can plan a broad strategy for the management of its conference capacity as an integral part of the overall yield management strategy for the unit.
- *Allocating capacity to particular enquiries:* many of the variables become critical when the conference coordinator has to make decisions as to whether conference/function or exhibition capacity should be released in response to particular enquiries and, if so, at what price.
- *Securing the booking:* having taken the decision to release capacity, securing the business becomes the critical factor (i.e. converting the enquiry into a definite booking).

The ingredients of the 'conference cauldron' can be rearranged to reflect this structure:

1. Planning conference capacity strategy
   - business mix;
   - market strength;
   - competitive edge;
   - profitability;
   - lead time;
   - refused business.
2. Allocating capacity to particular enquiries
   - purpose of the event;
   - numbers;
   - risk factors;
   - profitability;
   - dates;
   - duration;
   - size;
   - residential requirements;

- space management;
- timing;
- vacuums;
- future opportunities.
3. Securing the booking
    - packaging: proactive pricing;
    - client's budget;
    - added value;
    - packaging: customizing enquiry response.

While the structure shown above provides a useful conceptual framework, it should be recognized that this is a guide and not a rigid demarcation of activities. A number of the 'ingredients' must, in practice, be considered at more than one stage of the process. For example, 'profitability' of conference business must be discussed when planning overall conference capacity strategy for the venue, but will also be an important factor when making decisions as to whether to release facilities to a particular type of enquiry. It will also be noted in the structure that 'packaging' has been subdivided to cover a proactive approach to pricing and the customization of responses to conference enquiries.

PLANNING CONFERENCE CAPACITY STRATEGY

Business Mix

Decisions in relation to an appropriate business mix for a specific venue concern the release or non-release of bedroom stock to particular market segments; decisions about whether business should or should not be taken. The venue must consider the total proportion of bedroom stock that can be allocated to the conference market on a particular night. Decisions in relation to business mix clearly have to be adapted to the individual property. In some hotels individual transient accommodation business will drive the occupancy. Such units may look at yield management in terms of the cost to the individual transient market of taking residential conferences. With hotels where residential conferences represent a greater share of the market, the argument is reversed. What will be the cost to the residential conference market of allocating too much accommodation to transient business? What would be the adverse effect on yield? As is stressed in this chapter, venues must also consider the optimum business mix to fill conference, meeting room and function space (sales conferences, training courses, product launches, exhibitions, etc.). Such decisions are made by comparing the relative profitability of the different categories of business that are potentially available on a given occasion. The validity of the decisions made in this respect must depend on the depth and accuracy of information generated by the hotel's management information system.

Market Strength and Competitive Edge

Conference coordinators need an understanding of the strength of the conference market at national level, at local level and in relation to demand for their own venue. An outward looking viewpoint is required to develop an understanding of trends taking place in the national economy and in the conference market place. Active membership of appropriate associations and the development of mutually rewarding relationships with competitors both have a role to play in this respect. Equally, the venue must realistically assess its degree of competitive edge within the market. If the particular venue's strengths are its bedrooms, its meeting rooms or its leisure facilities compared to the competition, then this will influence the ability of the venue to win residential, non-residential or leisure-orientated business.

In relation to the individual property, past sales records, as well as a knowledge of the forthcoming influencing factors which will affect business patterns, are an integral part of yield management systems. As well as data on past sales, data on the level of enquiries for a particular date that have had to be turned away are also required. It is vital that a record of such enquiries is kept, with respect to both individual bookings and conference enquiries made. Not only does such information facilitate the making of decisions in terms of how much bedroom stock to release to conference delegates, it also helps in the setting of tariff rates on particular dates for the various market segments. Once information on the level of demand for particular room categories/ price tariffs is known, the business mix that will maximize accommodation revenue can be calculated.

It is also important to recognize that the market strength for a particular venue will be much greater in some markets than in others. This can have a major impact on both bedroom and meeting room yield. For example, a hotel may have a strong individual corporate accommodation market, due to the proximity of the hotel to thriving local businesses, the quality of the bedrooms or easy access by road, rail and air. Conversely, its meeting rooms may be large and extensive but suffer from external noise, low ceilings or irregular shapes. Hence the demand for bedrooms to be used for residential conferences will be much lower than for individual corporate accommodation, and accordingly the achieved bedroom rate will be much higher from individual corporate accommodation. The reverse can be the case where the facilities and services of a hotel are extremely attractive to residential conferences and much less attractive to individuals. It is not unknown for a breakdown of the residential conference rate to reveal that the accommodation allocation is higher than the published tariff rate for bedrooms, in which case it will be much higher than the achieved corporate accommodation rates.

Profitability

Decisions regarding allocation of bedroom stock to the conference sector cannot be made purely on the basis of accommodation revenue generated. In the case of residential conference delegates the figure is, in any case, somewhat arbitrary, as it is often merely a proportion of an overall residential delegate rate. The relative value of conference business to the rooms division could be increased or decreased according to how the venue allocates the overall delegate rate between profit centres.

The hotel should be equally concerned about how much guests spend on food and beverages and other services during their stay. The expenditure multiplier is identified by Brotherton and Mooney (1992):

> Similarly, it must be recognised that different types of guests possess different expenditure propensities in relation to the other elements of the product mix. If overall profit yield is to be maximised then the length of stay and accommodation

rate are only two components of the total equation. Other categories of expenditure on food and beverage must be taken into account when trying to assess the total yield from a given sale of accommodation.

Hotels need to know how much additional expenditure is generated by conference delegates compared with individual guests. However, there are complexities associated with such calculations. Different types of conference will generate significantly different expenditure multipliers. While the level of expenditure by individual guests will also obviously vary, calculations of average expenditure against room category should be possible.

As yield management systems become increasingly sophisticated it is likely that the focus will switch from a concentration on revenue yield to profit yield, producing a need for clear information about the costs of supply to different categories of business. Donaghy *et al.* (1995) draw upon the work of Dunn and Brooks (1990) in their discussion of the merits of a market-segment profit analysis (MSPA), which, it is contended, allows the venue to base decisions on profit maximization rather than revenue maximization through accurate integration of the full costs of supporting specific markets. The key factors to be identified are therefore seen as being:

- the cost incurred in the provision of the hospitality product;
- the propensity to spend within each sector of the business mix;
- the most desirable mix of guests in terms of incremental costs and profit potential.

> Focusing attention on these three areas will effectively provide a more detailed framework from which hotel managers can more accurately determine the precise contribution of net profit per trigger market. In essence, such an approach is more 'yield' focused than revenue maximisation by virtue of consideration with cost variables. By coupling the costs incurred in providing the hotel service with an awareness of guest spending capacities throughout the hotel, YM moves from a revenue to a profit generating tool. (Donaghy *et al.*, 1995).

The venue's management information system should increasingly provide reliable and accurate information about the direct costs associated with servicing different types of client and different business mixes and hence the contribution generated by different business mixes. Those selling 'space' must be conscious of the different profit rates generated by different categories of guest; for example, rack rate/corporate rate customers, leisure market, package guests, wedding receptions, conference guests (residential/non-residential).

Lead Time

Information on booking lead times underpins the development of a yield management strategy. This is equally so when developing a structured, yield-orientated approach to the management of conference capacity, and reliable information is required in this respect. Care must be taken that lead times are identified by category of business, so that information on conference booking lead times is not, for example, distorted by the inclusion of longer lead times for functions such as wedding receptions or when a year's contract is signed for a series of training courses. Trends in lead times should also be identified. Such information will be an integral part of pricing decisions. For example, if conference booking lead times are becoming shorter; without sufficient knowledge of this fact the conference coordinator might start 'pressing the panic button' too early and commence unnecessary discounting.

Refused Business

Details of enquiries that have had to be turned away owing to capacity being fully booked are also required. Records of refused business are essential when developing a yield-orientated approach to the management of conference capacity. Distinction should also be made between 'unwanted business' (we have the space available but do not wish to offer it for whatever reason), 'cancelled provisional bookings' (we have lost the business) and 'disinterested enquiries' (a general enquiry for a specific date did not materialize into actual business). If the level of refused business is monitored by event and date then high and low levels of demand for specific periods of the year can be tracked from year to year. This will then influence the management of the diary for that period in future years. A comprehensive forecast of patterns of demand and expected lead times is central to the yield-orientated approach.

In summary, an efficient management information system puts the manager in an increasingly strong position to make accurate decisions about allocating bedroom and meeting space inventory to different client groups – on the basis of profit earned as well as revenue generated. Where information systems are not as highly developed, such decisions will still have to be made through judicious reasoning, but on the basis of less precise data.

ALLOCATING CAPACITY TO PARTICULAR ENQUIRIES

Once an overall broad decision has been made as to an appropriate business mix for the venue over a defined time period, decisions have then to be made as to whether conference capacity should be allocated to particular enquiries. Once again, such decisions are made by trying to balance a range of factors. Overall yield generated by the unit's conference stock will be increased when yield-related decisions are made when agreeing to allocate conference capacity to a particular enquiry, and when conference coordinators manage the marketing/selling process so as to generate potentially high yield enquiries and also to ensure that they are successfully converted into firm bookings. Conferences vary significantly in their yield potential and a wide range of factors have to be considered when selling conference, function and exhibition space.

Purpose of the Event, Numbers Attending and Risk Factors

Conferences are held for many reasons and hence there are many different types of potential booking. Some examples are:

- bookings made by corporate organizations for their own staff, dealers or customers;

- bookings made by organizations such as consultants, who may be then 'selling on' places on courses;
- bookings made by national and international associations.

Bookings made by corporate organizations for their own employees include sales meetings, training courses and incentive functions. Conferences and events that are held for the company's customers, potential customers or dealers include exhibitions, product launches and incentive weekends.

In the case of the second category of booking identified above, a consultant company may run various types of training course and book conference facilities and accommodation and then sell places on the course it is proposing to run to other organizations or individuals. Other consultants will have regular clients where the course being run is exclusive to that client's staff.

Associations include all those organizations of a professional, scientific, educational, trade or special interest nature which are made up of individual members or member companies.

The terms 'conference', 'meeting' and 'event' therefore cover such a wide spectrum of possible type of booking that the level of yield generated from selling conference capacity can be extremely variable, depending upon the nature of the event. The 'risk factor' associated with bookings – for example, of cancellation – can also vary widely (Hartley and Witt, 1990).

Hartley and Witt (1992, p. 62) identified four basic items of information that will help the conference coordinator to forecast the potential yield of a possible booking. With some modification, these are as outlined below:

- the organizer of the event, such as a company, association or consultant;
- the purpose of the event – what exactly is the organizer trying to achieve?;
- for whom the event is organized and the likely numbers attending;
- the proposed date(s) of the event, duration and residential requirements.

Corporate events are significant contributors to conference capacity yield, although profit potential will clearly depend upon the nature of the particular event. Where the company is running a conference aimed at its own staff, they are probably told to attend, so estimated numbers are usually reasonably reliable. The corporate conference organizer is likely to be the easiest type of client to work with, as he or she will probably have had at least some previous experience in organizing conferences.

Events organized by associations may also contribute significantly to yield. However, there are many different types of association and one probably has to be more questioning with respect to such factors as numbers likely to attend. Taylor (1979) summarizes the situation well: 'Their delegates are free agents and if they choose not to arrive at all when the association's affairs are being discussed, that is their business.' That said, the committee organizing such an event is normally concerned that the event should be well supported and ultimately voted a success. However, guarantees of attendance are certainly harder for them to provide. The track record of the association is a key factor. Where has the event previously been held? How many members actually attended? How far ahead are delegates required to register? Are non-refundable deposits collected from members by the association?

Bookings generated by consultants who may be 'selling on' places on courses are, again, different in nature. The potential yield generated by such bookings largely depends upon the success of the consultant. Such bookings can represent a welcome source of revenue or be useful 'gap fillers' where the meetings are small in terms of delegate numbers. However, bookings made by less successful consultants can leave the hotel holding empty space if places cannot be successfully sold on the programme, with the implications that brings for yield figures. Furthermore, when available funds are dependent entirely on the response, the chances of a venue securing cancellation fees are much reduced. Again, the importance of establishing the consultant's track record is stressed and establishing a relationship with a reliable consultant will prove beneficial to both parties. Where the booking appears to be higher risk, it may only be worth taking when nothing more secure is available.

Understanding who is to attend the event and the purpose underlying proceedings helps the coordinator to predict both the reliability of the numbers attending and the potential yield-generating capacity of the booking. Where a company's own employees are the delegates, provisional numbers are likely to turn out to be reasonably accurate estimates. Where attendees are invited this may not be the case. However, there will be occasions when customers or dealers, while not actually obliged to attend an event, are clearly likely to wish to do so. Such a situation could arise, for example, where the event is a major product launch. Clues may also be obtained from the organizer's approach to the event. Is the budget so significant as to make this an event that dealers or customers would simply be unlikely to want to miss?

The nature of the event will therefore often reveal its potential yield-generating capacity. A company that has spent millions developing a product will presumably want the launch to be an 'event' in itself, and an appropriate budget is duly allocated. Likewise, if a company is flying in its international dealers from all over the world for a conference, the budget is likely to be considerably higher than for a routine meeting of its own sales representatives. In the former case there is a greater probability of the company choosing special menus for dinner (over and above the standard allocation in the residential delegate rate), selecting more expensive wines, offering the delegates free bar facilities, etc. Releasing conference capacity to bookings with higher expenditure multipliers is a key aspect of yield management of conference capacity.

Dates, Duration, Size and Residential Requirements

The duration of the event, the date(s) on which it is to be held and residential requirements are all important factors to consider when assessing the potential yield of a booking. The attractiveness of a booking may be relative to the dates that the organizer requires, some dates being much easier to sell than others. This should lead to consideration of the tariff to be applied on particular dates and the development of a proactive pricing structure – a typical characteristic of a yield-orientated system. Full discussion of this is developed later in the chapter.

The assumption should not be made that 'big is beautiful' in the conference market. One meeting for eighty delegates is not necessarily better than four meetings of twenty delegates. The one meeting for eighty, with everyone arriving and departing at the same time, can create vacuums at either end of the booking. The larger conference may carry more discounting muscle than the four smaller ones and four conference organizers compared to one means three more future sales leads in the hotel. Other arguments to be considered when weighing up the relative merits of larger events are the implications of one major event cancelling compared with one out of (say) four smaller events, and the increased operational costs of running four smaller events simultaneously rather than one large event.

Residential requirements are an important determinant of likely yield from a conference booking, although there may be many occasions when non-residential conferences are most welcome. If bedroom stock has already been fully booked, possibly at higher rates than would have been generated by conferences, non-residential conferences become of great value to the operation. Conversely, selling all the conference facilities to non-residential bookings and then being left with unsold bedrooms (and having to turn away residential conferences) is a disaster.

Whether the duration of the conference is 'right' depends on the existing pattern of bookings already in the diary and the probability of selling the available space that remains. The potentially available business, in all its disparate forms, has to be combined in such a way that overall final yield is maximized. Fortunately, good management practice can be used to facilitate this process.

Space Management, Timing and Vacuums

Space management is defined here as 'the integration of bookings within the conference diary so that conference space, associated bedroom stock, food and beverage areas and leisure facilities are fully utilized and vacuums are avoided'. The conference diary (whether manual or computerized) is akin to a complicated jigsaw puzzle. The individual conference bookings represent the pieces of the jigsaw. The overall size of the jigsaw is determined by the number of days in a year when facilities are available for letting and the number of bedrooms, meeting rooms and other facilities and/or services provided. Every potential conference booking has a certain 'shape' determined by such factors as arrival and departure times, numbers of delegates, set-up requirements, syndicate rooms needed, residential accommodation requirements and food and beverage needs such as private dining facilities. It is the conference coordinator's task to assess the configuration of each potential piece of the puzzle and complete the jigsaw as fully as possible by fitting together complementary pieces.

Vacuums between events are one of the coordinator's worst fears and may be created in a number of ways. A simple example is shown below.

Assume a conference hotel has the following facilities:

Accommodation	*Conference facilities*
150 bedrooms	One suite holding 40 delegates maximum
	One suite holding 60 delegates maximum

Assume that in a particular week 50 bedrooms are allocated to the individual stay market, with the remaining 100 to be allocated to conference delegates.

Let us suppose the conference coordinator accepts two residential conference bookings, one for 60 delegates and one for 40, both of which start on the Tuesday morning of the week in question and both of which finish at 5.00 p.m. on the Wednesday. Thus both bookings have the same 'shape' or configuration:

Accommodation targets for the Tuesday night are fully achieved, but how does the conference coordinator now sell the 100-room allocation on the Monday and Wednesday nights?

To sell Monday he or she is now reliant on securing a booking for a one-day conference followed by dinner, overnight accommodation and departure the following morning, as no conference capacity exists on the Tuesday. To sell Wednesday night the hotel needs a conference arriving for dinner on the Wednesday night, with the

Figure 21.1 A conference configuration example

	Tuesday		**Wednesday**
Meeting 1	*Meeting 2*	*Meeting 1*	*Meeting 2*
Coffee on arrival × 40	Coffee on arrival × 60	Breakfast × 40	Breakfast × 60
Conference starts	Conference starts	Conference continues	Conference continues
Coffee × 40	Coffee × 60	Coffee × 40	Coffee × 60
Lunch × 40	Lunch × 60	Lunch × 40	Lunch × 60
Tea × 40	Tea × 60	Tea × 40	Tea × 60
Dinner × 40	Dinner × 60	Conference finishes	Conference finishes
Accommodation: 40 bedrooms	Accommodation: 60 bedrooms		

conference itself starting on the Thursday. Thus, bookings requiring the use of conference space for two days but only generating one night's residential accommodation can be problematical if conference space is limited, and may well lead to such accommodation vacuums.

It must be stressed that the timing of arrival and departure is of crucial importance. An arrival, for example, on a Monday evening to start a two-day conference on Tuesday and Wednesday, followed by departure after breakfast on Thursday morning, occupies a meeting room for as much time as an arrival on Tuesday morning and a departure on Wednesday afternoon, but the impact on yield of a three-night stay as opposed to a one-night stay is, of course, critical. Furthermore, in each of these cases, meeting rooms would still be available to be sold to another organization on both the Monday and the Thursday.

Fitting the diary jigsaw puzzle together is a function of experience, training, appropriate interpretation of historical statistical information and knowing the likely pattern of demand for the unit. An appropriate strategy does need to be planned well in advance. If one attempts to obtain back-to-back bookings from the beginning, it is rather easier than leaving it until the month before and then trying to fit the new pieces of the jigsaw around existing bookings. The coordinator must know what the ideal 'model' is for that venue, a model which takes into account the food and beverage areas as well as the actual conference space. The diary charting system must indicate arrival and departure times, room layouts and whether it is possible to move a booking to another room if this becomes desirable. The capabilities of the unit must be known in relation to such matters as room 'turnaround time'. One of the authors has experience of a hotel being able to clear a conference room for 500 delegates and relay it as a banquet for 500 in fifteen minutes.

Most conference hotels have more than one coordinator and those with experience must pass on their understanding of space management to their less experienced colleagues. Otherwise lessons are learned the hard way and at significant cost to the venue.

However, space management will inevitably on occasions involve taking chances. Yield management systems should provide data on patterns of demand. Changing trends to the seasonal pattern of either enquiries or actual business taking place also need to be monitored. Information to this effect should be available if appropriate statistics are maintained by both enquiry and conference date. However, there will be exceptions to anticipated patterns. A booking may be accepted as the diary begins to look worryingly empty as a date approaches and the very next telephone call may produce a more lucrative booking which has to be turned away. Conversely, there will be times when business is refused because forecasts suggest that a higher yield booking is likely to come through and it never does. Things will go wrong sometimes. The knowledgeable and skilful coordinator, applying yield management concepts, increases the chances of keeping such occasions to a minimum.

Managing Provisional Bookings

A word of warning is appropriate at this point. The diary page may look deceptively full if the bookings charted are provisional rather than confirmed. The efficient management of provisional bookings is an important aspect of space management. Many conference organizers will wish to hold facilities on a provisional basis before coming to a final decision. An organizer is likely to view facilities that he or she has not previously used and will require these to be held provisionally pending the inspection visit. It is difficult for the coordinator to avoid holding provisional bookings, but the process must be managed as effectively as possible. Whenever a provisional booking is made, a date should be agreed with the organizer as to when a firm decision will be made. Once that date is reached, if nothing has been heard, contact must be made with the organizer to clarify the situation, and either release of the facilities or a further extension of the provisional booking is agreed. This necessitates the development of an appropriate 'follow-up' system so that the coordinator's attention is drawn to the 'follow-up' date having been reached. Once the booking is confirmed and/or contracted it should be charted as such. It is vital to recognize that when a client confirms a booking on the telephone, it is a verbal confirmation. Only once the client and the hotel have both signed a contract prepared by the hotel is the booking confirmed and contracted. Bookings should be clearly charted as verbally confirmed or contracted.

The coordinator should not automatically concur to hold facilities provisionally or for a particular period of time without an agreement with the prospective client that if another enquiry is received the venue may contact the client to ask for a firm decision or the release of the facilities held. Judgemental decisions will, on occasions, have to be made as to whether it is appropriate or not to agree to hold a provisional booking. Such decisions may be based on the anticipated likelihood of conversion to confirmed and contracted status. Clues to this may be very subtle and can be discerned from the conversation with the potential client. Conversely, there may be occasions when the enquirer does not wish to make a provisional booking, but the conference coordinator may elect to chart that a potentially profitable enquiry has been made for a particular set of dates. If a subsequent enquiry is received for those dates it may be worth a telephone call to the original enquirer just to check whether he or she might wish to take the enquiry further before agreeing to hold the facilities provisionally for the subsequent but less profitable enquiry.

Third Party Enquiries

Conference placement services or agencies, which find venues for organizers, will also often want to hold facilities provisionally. Here, it is important to develop a relationship with the placement service. A good agent will offer a potential client expert advice as to which venue would suit his or her needs and will do the initial work of ascertaining potential availability of dates at particular venues. The agent may also be involved to a greater or lesser extent in the organizing of the detail of the event. Some agents may have a policy of offering (say) three alternative possible venues to a client and will thus make provisional bookings at three venues. Two out of three venues will then face eventual release of those facilities, possibly after holding them for some time as the organizer visits all three venues to view the facilities. Conversely, some agents may have a policy of making an initial recommendation of what they think will be the right venue for a client's needs and of taking the client to see that venue before considering alternatives. The second approach is much more likely to result in a conversion from a provisional to a confirmed and contracted booking. However, the number of options held will often be determined by the client's wishes. The coordinator must develop a relationship with different agencies and take heed of the track record of the agent in converting provisional bookings into actual events.

However, it should be noted that the relationship with an agent and attempts to measure the 'track record' are not simple matters. It is perfectly reasonable for agents to wish to hold provisional bookings. First, they need to be sure that the facilities that they are suggesting to a client will still be available if the client responds positively to the suggestion. Second, an agent will reasonably wish for some degree of protection should the client, having received the written recommendation of a hotel, then choose to contact the hotel direct. If there is a provisional booking under the name of the client and the agency, then the origin of the booking is clear and the agent's commission would normally be honoured. If there is not, the situation may be far from clear as to whether the enquiry was made by the agent in the first place. Such confusion would not be in the interests of either the agent or the venue coordinator, who should be seeking to develop a positive and mutually beneficial relationship with the agent. The track record is obviously important but quite difficult to measure objectively. For example, if an agency is proactive on behalf of a venue, then the relative level of confirmations may be lower, but the absolute number of confirmations may be higher. This could be because the agent is recommending the hotel to his or her clients, when perhaps the hotel does not necessarily fit the client's exact brief. Second, it must always be acknowledged that part of the conversion rate from any client or agent will be dependent upon how specific the client is concerning his or her requirements when making the initial enquiry.

The Meetings Industry Association (MIA) produces a Venue/Conference Placement Agency Code of Practice as part of its 'Meetings Magna Carta'. Compliance with the spirit of the Meetings Magna Carta is a condition of MIA membership. The Code of Practice includes recommended procedures in relation to provisional bookings, which should be of benefit to agents, venues and ultimately clients.

Future Opportunities

On occasions it might, of course, be necessary to balance the value of a current booking against the value of possible future business that may be expected from a client. The venue may have been actively 'courting' a prospective client for some considerable time, but it might be that the first booking that the client shows an interest in placing at the venue is incompatible with the venue's yield management strategy. The configuration of the booking may be wrong in terms of effective space management: wrong dates, wrong timing, etc. Here the coordinator might wish to offset short-term loss against the benefits of long-term gain. Likewise, small meetings from new clients may also be accepted when, ideally, the coordinator might have preferred a larger booking. Introducing a new client to the hotel provides the opportunity of selling the hotel for larger events that the client may be considering holding in the future. However, actual long-term gain from such decisions should be measured. Otherwise it is too easy to use future opportunity as an excuse for taking any new business.

Ultimately, a decision may also be reached that the venue will be unable to release capacity to a particular client type. In an ideal world it may be possible to persuade the organizer to book on alternative dates when the pattern of business is such that the booking becomes relatively more attractive. However, it might be necessary to refuse the business if the contract would displace potentially more lucrative business (Knutson *et al.*, 1995).

SECURING THE BUSINESS

Once a decision has been made that a prospective booking is compatible with the venue's yield management strategy, considerable effort might have to be employed to win the business and convert the enquiry into a firm booking. A transitional point is reached when 'price' is discussed, in that the price the client is prepared to pay partly determines whether the venue will wish to allocate space to that client and the price quoted will partly determine whether the venue is successful in securing the booking. Price and the way the pricing issue is managed by the venue are components of the 'package' that the venue constructs at this stage of the enquiry. The overall relevance and quality of the package will be determining factors in winning or losing the business.

Packaging: Proactive Pricing

Yield management is concerned with market-sensitive pricing of fixed capacity relative to specific market segments. Most authors identify, as a key component of a yield management system, the importance of manipulating rates in a structured fashion, to take into account forecasted patterns of demand (Jauncey *et al.*, 1995).

Determining tariff rates in relation to conference capacity is a relatively complex process, as a 'package' of facilities is usually being purchased covering conference space, equipment, food and beverage requirements and, frequently, residential accommodation. Many events will also have special requirements, such as the involvement of the hotel in the creation of a special theme for the event, or help in organizing appropriate entertainment.

The majority of conference venues gear their conference pricing structure around a delegate rate which takes one of two forms:

- a residential delegate rate, which may include morning coffee, lunch, afternoon tea, dinner, accommodation, breakfast and hire of the conference room;
- a non-residential delegate rate, which may include morning coffee, lunch, afternoon tea and hire of the conference room.

Many venues now also include delegate stationery and basic audio-visual equipment within package rates.

We strongly discourage the sometimes used terminology of 24-hour, 8-hour or day delegate rates. Residential and non-residential rates are far more appropriate. For example, under the term 'residential rate' a venue can specify that this includes the use of the main meeting room between 8 a.m. and 5 p.m. on any one day. This avoids the problem which can arise from use of the term '24-hour rate', when a client might expect a meeting room from midday to midday within one residential rate. In reality the hotel would be unlikely to sell the conference space to anyone else on the morning of the first day or the afternoon of the second day and would thus require additional revenue for the use of the space for what is effectively a two-day period. The terminology also avoids the confusion inherent in the term 'day' delegate rate, there being 24 hours in a day!

The yield generated by a conference booking is, however, not solely a function of the delegate rate paid by the client. One of the main themes developed in this chapter is that there is no such thing as a 'standard' conference booking. Each booking must be examined on its own individual merits. The essence of the coordinator's task is to ensure that high-yield bookings are taken on peak dates with lower yield-generating bookings accepted, if necessary, on less popular dates or where space is still available at short notice.

The overall yield generated by the booking will depend on a variety of factors, such as the number of delegates, the delegate rate paid, the value of additional expenditure incurred over and above the delegate rate and the extent to which the booking fits in with the existing pattern of bookings (actual or forecast). While some of these issues are examined in the next section, the key aspect under consideration here is the actual price or delegate rate to be charged.

This will be governed to some extent by the published tariff, in that the coordinator can hardly charge a higher delegate rate than that published in brochures or other literature. One possible approach is to publish a differential conference rate structure where higher rates are charged in peak periods and lower rates offered in off-peak periods. It could be argued that such a differential approach to pricing establishes a clear, published and logically developed conference tariff structure. Higher yields can be generated in times of peak demand and a more competitive rate is published in times of lower demand. However, a published lower tariff in off-peak periods can be problematical as the rate has then to be offered to all customers, including those for whom budget is not a determining factor. It is important that managers are aware of what effect a price change will have on demand. Assumptions could be made, for example, that publication of a lower tariff in January or February would generate an increased level of enquiries. However, it is relevant to ask how often those making conference enquiries know the advertised conference rates before they telephone. Regulars will be aware of them but it is possible that the overall percentage of enquirers with such knowledge is low. Therefore a low price in a period of low demand may seldom in itself generate more enquiries and any gains could be more than offset by those customers who would have paid the full price. Certainly, cheaper rates on less popular dates should not automatically be offered.

A radical but still potentially flexible approach is the 'up to' tariff, where the maximum rate is quoted as the published rate but it is apparent that a reduced tariff may be available, dependent on the overall attractiveness of the booking to the venue (its lead time, numbers, duration, additional spend, dates required, etc.). The essential feature of this approach is that those persons handling the enquiries should have authority, having established appropriate information from the customer, to negotiate on the services, facilities and prices offered in order to maximize yield.

Establishing a proactive pricing structure is therefore a complex operation, but one which moves the operation away from a discount-orientated approach to one of synchronizing the quotation with the needs of the client, and the needs of the venue, to maximize yield. The informed and empowered coordinator is able to make a decision not to release capacity to a particular market segment in times of high demand (the cost-conscious customer) through appropriate design of a pricing structure, but can manipulate rates in a structured fashion when required.

Client's Budget and Added Value

The 'up to' proactive pricing structure enables the venue to quote in line with the parameters of the yield management strategy, while taking due account of the needs of the client for that specific event. The 'up to' system has another advantage in that it does not commit the venue to quoting a final rate for an event until details of the event are known. As has been stressed throughout this chapter, the ultimate value of a conference depends on many contributing factors. The delegate rate paid is merely one of these factors and may be adjusted by the coordinator to take account of other factors, such as the value of likely additional spending which gives 'added value' to the core booking. While meeting a client's budget may be an important determining factor in securing a booking, it is not something that may necessarily be addressed at an early stage of an enquiry and the 'up to' tariff retains flexibility and avoids the dangers of the 'from to' tariff, where the client may automatically begin to think in terms of the lower figure as the starting point for negotiations. When negotiating on price it is important to avoid this kind of downward spiral which can be caused by quoting a price too quickly before client needs have been discussed and before the configuration and ultimate value of the booking have been ascertained. Ideally, the new client should see the venue before a firm price is quoted so that the coordinator can promote the benefits of the facilities and services directly to the potential customer and begin to develop a working relationship. If the initial contact or meeting is handled appropriately, it is more likely that the prospective client will think in terms of 'value for money' rather than merely cold 'price'.

Conference coordinators should also take the opportunity, where appropriate, to promote the discount on full tariff rate that the residential conference rate offers. Conversely, when quoting a non-residential delegate rate, care must be taken that the room hire element within the delegate rate broadly matches the advertised room hire charges for the appropriate meeting room if quoted separately. Most venues will quote a non-residential delegate rate as subject to a minimum attendance. Otherwise, if delegate numbers fall too low the room hire element in a non-residential delegate rate results in a very low room hire charge being levied. Conversely, thought should be given to the implications of charging a non-residential rate when numbers of attendees are high. The client can work out an approximation of the room hire element within the rate and where delegate numbers are high the resultant room hire charge can be very significant, possibly resulting in a higher charge than that published as the 'room hire only' charge for hiring the suite without any commitment to lunch and the other elements of the non-residential delegate package. A logically constructed and consistent tariff structure is required. Careful consideration must also be given to the matter of VAT. The client's budget will invariably exclude VAT. If a venue quotes to match a client's budget figure but on the basis that all prices are inclusive of VAT, a significant amount of revenue is being sacrificed unnecessarily, all of which is profit.

Packaging: Customizing Enquiry Response

Planning a yield-orientated conference capacity management strategy and identifying the appropriate types of booking to take on particular occasions are fruitless activities if the 'right' types of enquiries are not converted into contracted bookings. Empirical work has suggested that venues miss opportunities to convert conference enquiries into firm bookings (Hartley and Witt, 1992, p. 74).

Problems can arise when the organizer contacts the venue to make an initial enquiry about holding a conference or event at the venue. This is a critical moment; a 'moment of truth' (Carlzon, 1987) in the sales/marketing process where marketing and selling should fuse together to lead to a profitable yield-generating sale through the anticipation and meeting of customer needs. The yield management system falls apart if this customer contact moment is not managed effectively. Yield-generating business is lost.

When the potential customer contacts the venue with an initial enquiry, maximum effort must be made to achieve three objectives:

1. To find out whether the venue can meet the customer's requirements.
2. To find out whether the venue wishes to secure the booking. For example, is the booking compatible with the venue's yield management strategy? Is the booking attractive in terms of likely yield generated? Is it a high- or low-risk booking? How does the booking fit in with the existing bookings in the diary on a particular set of dates? Might it become a more attractive booking if the organizer would agree to switch to alternative dates?
3. To maximize the venue's chances of converting the enquiry into a contracted booking.

Hartley and Witt (1992) carried out an empirical study of the response of 83 conference hotels in the UK to a general telephone enquiry requesting information to be sent on their conference and function facilities. Results from the survey indicate that hotels may be missing opportunities to convert enquiries into sales. The following points from the survey were particularly significant:

1. Of enquiry calls, 35 per cent were not directed beyond the person who answered the telephone (the switchboard operator or receptionist), with the result that these hotels did not put the enquirer into contact with a specialist conference coordinator.
2. Of the hotels, 77 per cent did not attempt to ascertain any details about the event during the enquiry call and consequently were unable to send a written response that was in any way personalized with regard to the potential client's specific needs.
3. Only 2 per cent of the hotels surveyed took the opportunity during the enquiry call to invite the potential client to visit the hotel and view the facilities.

In a subsequent study, Hartley and Witt (1994) suggested specific areas that conference coordinators might explore as a route to achieving a higher success rate in converting conference enquiries into definite bookings.

The need for a personalized response to enquiries is seen as a key factor. All conferences and events are unique to some extent. It is vital that venues personalize their responses to enquiries. A key factor leading to the successful conversion of an enquiry into a definite booking is to show how the venue can meet the client's particular needs. A customized or personalized response should be given, as otherwise the only option is to send a standardized pack of information with a standard letter. Makens (1990) points out the inadequacies of such packs:

> Each prospect or client represents a unique buyer with customised needs. Unfortunately, these needs are seldom heard by the sales representative. Instead of

listening for clues that describe specialised needs, the sales representative finds it easier to send a standard packet and hope the prospect will pick out something useful. Meeting planners and conference organisers often complain that it is virtually impossible to differentiate among a stack of hotel 'fulfilment kits'.

A further problem that can arise with conference packs is that the message the client is really interested in (i.e. can this venue successfully manage 'my' conference or event) is further hidden by the plethora of additional material that venues include in their packs.

One does recognize that the conference or event organizer has a variety of roles to play in life and may be a potential customer for a weekend break or Christmas party but, in our opinion, 'selling-on' is not an appropriate strategy while the original sale is yet to be secured. Anecdotal evidence suggests that, on occasions, organizers may toss away up to half the contents of the pack before finding items that really interest them. When only a small proportion of those making enquiries are the final decision-maker, it is important that the written sales proposal reflects the reasons why this particular venue should be selected. It may be the only communication a venue has with the ultimate decision-maker.

A customized response (in terms of how the coordinator responds during the enquiry call and subsequently in writing) will display a number of characteristics which will increase the chances of converting the enquiry into a sale:

1. It will highlight benefits of the venue location and stress facilities and services appropriate to the client's event, rather than purely listing features and details of the facilities being held.
2. The response will clearly show that the venue is taking a real interest in the event and is focusing on the potential client's particular needs. A simple example would be to ask an organizer planning a conference for 100 persons whether or not a back projection set will be used. If so, the size of room needed to accommodate such a booking will be larger than a conference not using back projection. By asking the question, the coordinator is showing that he or she is professional enough to clarify such issues at an early stage. The client may have rung five other venues who have not bothered to do so, and now the client may have to take the initiative to ring them back to double check. It is up to the venue to show initiative, not the potential client. It has actually been known for an organizer to travel 150 miles to look at a venue, only to find at that stage that the suite is too small to take the specified delegate numbers and a back projection set.
3. Currently available dates should be shown.
4. The response should always include an invitation to visit the venue and see the facilities at first hand.

The Peter Rand Group suggests a number of key issues which should be covered with potential customers. These emphasize the importance of finding out the background to the event, which illustrates interest in the client and also helps to identify how best the venue can help to support the event. The client can be asked various questions which signal client benefit:

- 'What is the purpose of your meeting/conference/event?'
- 'How often do the meetings take place?'
- 'Who are the delegates that will be attending?'

The client can clearly see the reason behind the questions and will appreciate that the venue is taking a real interest in his or her event. However, the answers also provide signals to the venue as to the likely potential profit or yield that will be generated by the booking. Given that it is sensible not to discuss the client's budget too soon during an enquiry, these alternative clues are important indicators for the conference coordinator.

In a similar fashion, location will play a large part in the client's decision and questions can again be asked:

- 'Where will your delegates be travelling from?'
- 'How will they be travelling?

These enable the venue to point out how its location meets the client's need for ease of access or how potential travel problems may be overcome. Simultaneously, the coordinator receives further information about potential yield. For example, if delegates are travelling from overseas, the potential for the 'add-ons' that one receives to a greater or lesser extent from a conference, such as account rather than cash bars, menu supplements, bedroom upgrades and various special items, is likely to be higher than for a purely local meeting.

The conference coordinator will also find it valuable to know which venues clients have previously used, what factors they feel are particularly important in selecting their venue, what extra services they may require which the venue might help in providing or organizing and if and when they last visited the venue. It is also important to know who will actually make the final decision on choice of venue. This may not be the person making the enquiry call, so perhaps the decision-maker should also be invited to visit the venue.

Of course, sending customized or personalized responses to potential clients is more time-consuming than sending standardized packs and letters. Coordinators may respond that they simply would not have time to reply to each enquiry in a personalized way. Hartley and Witt (1994, p. 280) cover this issue:

> Two points may be made here. First, not every sales enquiry necessitates such a detailed response. Some organisers will not already have an outline programme for the event or specific dates in mind. In such cases the degree of customisation will be less. The fundamental point, however, is that it is in the hotel's interest to find out during the original enquiry call what the situation actually is and so be able to produce a response with an appropriate degree of customisation. The more the client has formulated his/her ideas about a particular event, the more customised the enquiry response letter should be. Secondly, IT makes such letters possible at minimum cost and with only minor additional time expenditure. It is still, in effect, a standard letter, but with customised additions at various points. However, the standardisation must be sophisticated. The letter must read as a customised whole, and not as a series of standard paragraphs with a few personalised additions. Otherwise the wrong message is again conveyed, and the chances of convincing the customer that the hotel is focusing on his/her particular event and set of needs are diminished.

Information technology (IT) is the key factor here and its incorporation in the conference office does not need to be limited to word processing packages. For example, customer databases allow conference coordinators quickly to identify whether enquirers are new or existing customers, and references to past events and particular individual requirements may be usefully addressed in response letters. Additional information should also be available to assist the yield management process. What was the value of the previous business? What was the take-up of numbers? What was the feedback? To what extent was it 'good business'? Hence IT comes to the forefront of the yield management system once more. It is the tool that is used to increase the chance of securing an identified high-yield booking and can be applied to gain competitive advantage. IT systems must be used as a means to customization rather than merely standardization.

The term 'potential client' not 'client' has been used consistently in the paragraphs above. An organizer is not a client until the booking is confirmed and contracted. The essential message, then, is that yield from conference facilities will not be maximized unless the selling process is managed effectively. IT packages help in this process but they are the servant, not the master. Ultimately, successful yield management techniques depend upon the capability and motivation of the people managing the systems.

To manage effectively – for example, by producing customized rather than standardized responses and adopting a sophisticated proactive pricing strategy – does certainly call for a higher calibre of staff and an effective staff development programme. Gill Smillie (1991) of Conference Venues CountryWide succinctly stressed the importance of the role of the conference coordinator: 'For any specialist meetings venue this job is the most crucial of all. It could mean a difference of literally hundreds of thousands of pounds in turnover for a company.' Investment in high-calibre staff is a prerequisite of successful selling. Coordinators are salespersons, not order takers. They are at the 'cutting edge' interface between venue and client and sophisticated yield management pricing systems will count for little if enquiry calls are not managed correctly.

Recruitment of the right calibre of person for the conference office and an effective programme of staff training and development are as vital a part of a yield management system as any of the other components. Ultimately, it is the actions of people that will lead to success or failure.

MEASURING SUCCESS

Yield management systems culminate in the production of yield statistics which measure the performance of the operation. The basic yield statistic (Orkin, 1988) is relatively easy to apply when considering yield in relation to accommodation revenue alone. It becomes more complex when introducing cost and profit factors and has to be further refined when attempting to measure yield from conference capacity because of the wide range of variables involved. Yield statistics in relation to conference/function and exhibition capacity must measure:

- the degree of success in selling the bedroom capacity allocated to the conference market over a fixed time period;
- the degree of success in selling conference space.

Conference Sector Bedroom Yield

Yield generated can be measured using the normal yield management statistic. For example, if over the period of one month 1,000 room nights are allocated to the conference sector at a target rate of £70 per night and in reality 700 rooms are sold at an average rate of £65 per night the yield statistic is:

$$\frac{\text{Rooms sold}}{\text{Rooms available for sale}} \times \frac{\text{Average rate of rooms sold}}{\text{Average rate potential}} = \frac{700}{1,000} \times \frac{65}{70} = \frac{45,500}{70,000}$$
$$= 65\%$$

In the above example the room rate would normally be the accommodation allocation within the residential delegate rate.

Yield from Conference Space

This is the yield generated from conference space excluding bedroom yield. Yield from conference space, as with yield from bedroom capacity, is a function of two variables (occupancy and rate), more usefully called 'revenue generated'. These factors can be measured separately but under a yield management approach a single integrated statistic must be produced. Occupancy can be measured in two ways:

- meeting session occupancy;
- delegate occupancy.

Meeting Session Occupancy

Attainment is measured in terms of the percentage of the total available sessions that were actually sold over a fixed time period.

For example, a venue has ten meeting rooms which could each be sold over three sessions in any one day (morning, afternoon and evening), making 210 available sessions in any one week. If 147 sessions were actually sold the meeting session occupancy is 70 per cent.

The venue would need to define what constitutes 'evening session occupancy'. For example, if a conference room was sold for a residential conference it might be reasonable to define this as covering the evening session even though the delegates were not using the room. Normally, the hotel would not be able to sell the room to another client for that evening session.

Delegate Occupancy

Delegate occupancy takes into account the capacities of the various conference rooms. A high meeting session occupancy could be achieved but at the expense of selling conference rooms below the capacity of the suites (i.e. putting 30 delegates in a suite which will hold 50).

For example, the venue with ten meeting rooms might have five rooms which hold 30 delegates and five rooms which hold 50 delegates, making a total delegate capacity over a week of:

$$(5 \times 30 + 5 \times 50) \times 3 \text{ (sessions per day)} \times 7 \text{ days} = 8,400 \text{ delegate capacity.}$$

If 4,200 delegate places are sold over this period the delegate occupancy is 50 per cent.

Revenue Earned

The second factor to be monitored when measuring yield from conference capacity is the 'rate' earned. This might be calculated by using the average delegate rate obtained but, as has been argued throughout this chapter, this would be a simplistic figure given the importance attached to additional spending over and above the basic delegate rate. However, yield management statistics, based on revenue yield, compare revenue realized against revenue potential. In order to calculate this a venue must produce an estimate of the revenue that would be produced by the 'ideal' configuration of bookings in the conference diary. This would be a function of occupancy rates and revenue generated and could conveniently be shown as revenue yield per square metre of conference and function space. It should be noted that the 'ideal' occupancy rate might well be less than the theoretical maximum due to consideration for resultant demands on food, beverage and other areas. Thus, if the target revenue yield per square metre is £20 and the actual achieved over a time period is £15, the yield statistic is 75 per cent.

Conference Capacity Yield Statistic

Combining the revenue yield per square metre with the conference sector accommodation yield produces an overall conference capacity yield statistic as illustrated below. Assume that a venue is attempting to measure conference capacity yield over a period of one week. The potential and realized figures might appear as shown below:

	Target (potential) (week)	*Actual realized (week)*
Accommodation		
Number of bedrooms (allocated to conference sector)	400 rooms	325 rooms
Accommodation rate	£70	£65
Conference space (capacity of 850* sq. m.) *inc. private dining facilities		
Revenue per square metre	£93	£75

Conference sector bedroom yield

$$\frac{\text{Rooms sold}}{\text{Rooms available for sale}} \times \frac{\text{Average rate of rooms sold}}{\text{Average rate potential}} = \frac{325}{400} \times \frac{65}{70} = \frac{21,125}{28,000} = 75\%$$

Conference space: revenue earned

$$\frac{\text{Revenue per square metre realized} \times 850}{\text{Potential revenue per square metre} \times 850} = \frac{£75 \times 850}{£93 \times 850} = \frac{63,750}{79,050} = 81\%$$

Conference sector capacity yield

$$\frac{\text{Accommodation revenue realized} + \text{Conference space revenue realized}}{\text{Accommodation revenue potential} + \text{Conference space revenue potential}} \times 100$$

$$= \frac{21,125 + 63,750}{28,000 + 79,050} \times 100 = \frac{84,875}{107,050} \times 100 = 79\%$$

Yield statistics not only measure performance but are an important aid to future planning. There is clearly scope for further research in terms of the development of conference capacity yield statistics and models which incorporate detailed consideration of cost factors and profitability.

SUMMARY

Conference facilities are a major profit generator and yield management systems must therefore incorporate consideration of this aspect of the venue's overall capacity. Conference, function and exhibition space can be sold and used in many different ways and for many different purposes – combinations which will result in significantly varying profit potential. Therefore, the conference coordinator will have to consider a wide range of variables when making yield-orientated decisions. Room inventory aspects of yield management will apply when determining the business mix and the proportion of total bedroom stock that can be allocated to the conference market.

Additionally, careful consideration will have to be given when allocating capacity to individual enquiries in order to ensure that yield is maximized. Professional space management, a proactive pricing structure and the use of effective marketing and selling techniques are integral components of a yield-orientated approach to the management of conference capacity.

It must be recognized that yield management of conference capacity is a complex process necessitating the recruitment of high-calibre staff, a structured approach to staff development and an organizational culture which gives authority to staff handling enquiries so that yield-orientated decisions can be made.

Suggestions have been developed in the chapter for the measurement of yield generated from conference capacity, an area which might prove fruitful for further research.

REFERENCES

Brotherton, B. and Mooney, S. (1992) 'Yield management – progress and prospects'. *International Journal of Hospitality Management*, **11**(1), 28.

Carlzon, J. (1987) *Moments of Truth*, Cambridge, MA: Ballinger.

Donaghy, K., McMahon, U. and McDowell, D. (1995) 'Yield management: an overview'. *International Journal of Hospitality Management*, **14**(2), 142.

Dunn, D. and Brooks, D. E. (1990) 'Profit analysis beyond yield management'. *Cornell Hotel and Restaurant Administration Quarterly*, **31**(3), 80–90.

Goymour, D. (1995) 'Yield management. room to manoeuvre'. *Caterer and Hotelkeeper*, 2 February, 60–1.

Hartley, J. S. and Witt, S. F. (1990) 'Cancelling conferences and functions: how should hotels respond?' In *Proceedings of European Marketing Academy 19th Annual Conference*, Innsbruck, May.

Hartley, J. S. and Witt, S. F. (1992) 'Hotel sales management: turning conference and function enquiries into sales'. *Journal of Hospitality and Leisure Marketing*, **1**(2), 62.

Hartley, J. S. and Witt, S. F. (1994) 'Increasing the conversion rate of conference and function enquiries into sales'. *International Journal of Hospitality Management*, **13**(3), 275–85.

Jauncey, S., Mitchell, I. and Slamet, P. (1995) 'The meaning and management of yield in hotels'. *International Journal of Contemporary Hospitality Management*, **7**(4), 23–6.

Kimes, S. E. (1989) 'The basics of yield management'. *Cornell Hotel and Restaurant Administration Quarterly*, **30**(3), 14–19.

Knutson, B., Malk, M. and Schmidgall, R. S. (1995) 'When it's smart to turn away business'. *Cornell Hotel and Restaurant Administration Quarterly*, **36**(4), 56–61.

Makens, J. C. (1990) 'Follow-through: the way to added sales'. *Cornell Hotel and Restaurant Administration Quarterly*, **31**(2), 66.

Orkin, E. B. (1988) 'Boosting your bottom line with yield management'. *Cornell Hotel and Restaurant Administration Quarterly*, **29**(1), 52–6.

Seekings, D. and Farrer, J. (1999) *How to Organise Conferences and Meetings*, 7th edn. London: Kogan Page.

Smillie, G. (1991) 'Upgrade meetings staff'. *Caterer and Hotelkeeper*, 5 December, 31.

Taylor, D. (1979) *How To Sell Banquets: The Key to Conference and Function Promotion*. London: Northwood Books.

Endnote

Sir Rocco Forte

MANAGING THE YIELD MANAGER

Yield management is not new. Indeed, it may be entering its third millennium as a management technique. We are told that Joseph and Mary had to be accommodated in a stable two thousand years ago because there was no room at the inn. But perhaps the innkeeper had identified them as customers who could not afford a premium rate on a night of peak demand and had decided to hold out for better business. After all, he might have known that there were three kings in town who had yet to find accommodation.

Whatever the truth about the Bethlehem hotel market on the first Christmas Day, most good hoteliers have been practising yield management for many years, although they may not have known it. Setting rooms aside for value-added packages at busy times, creating special deals at quiet times and giving preference to regular customers who pay the best rate have long been considered good management. The two things which have changed in recent years are the conversion of best practice into a recognized business technique and the emergence of IT solutions which increase the accuracy with which we can apply that technique.

In this respect, the hotel industry has been slow. The airlines set the pace in developing yield management twenty years ago and saw dramatic increases in profitability as a result. The bigger hoteliers are catching up, led by companies from North America, but the European companies have established a good record in recent years.

One of the myths about yield management is that it is relevant only to big, mid-market, chains. Certainly it can bring obvious benefits there, but its application goes much wider. When I was chairman of the old Forte company, we developed software for the budget hotels, even though they were operating a single price policy. The reservations systems set aside rooms on the busy Saturdays, which were released only to those also booking Sunday, the quietest day. Rooms were also set aside for families because, although they paid the same rate, they spent more in the adjacent Little Chef restaurant.

I am now focused on the luxury sector with my new company, RF Hotels. Yield management is key to us here too. The Balmoral in Edinburgh is the best hotel in a strong market. We have just completed a £7 million refurbishment and need to see the benefits through higher rates at peak times. But there is plenty of new supply at four star level which creates vigorous competition at quieter times and so we need to have price-driven offers then. The Astoria in St Petersburg was our most profitable hotel until the Russian economy hit problems. It has had to make rapid adjustments to its strategy for 48 weeks of the year, but still retain its price integrity for the famous White Nights period when there is still a significant excess of demand over supply.

As a relatively small company, RF Hotels does not have large armies of corporate staff to run central sales and marketing activities. This is not a cost issue, it reflects our philosophy that resources should be deployed as near to the customers as possible. That philosophy is particularly relevant for yield management in the luxury sector, where decisions are often more complex and can be taken only by the person on the spot.

This does not mean that my fellow directors and I ignore yield management. I believe that our role is to set the framework and processes, to recruit and motivate the right people and to monitor performance so that we learn from failures and reward success. With this in mind, I have set out below ten rules which I would recommend to managers wanting to ensure their business gains from yield management.

- My first rule is to delegate the day-to-day decisions. Managing yield is about thousands of individual judgements, such as whether to take a decision over the telephone or when to close out on the global distribution systems. These decisions cannot normally wait while the person on the front line checks with his or her boss, other than for the very big bookings. Today's customers are increasingly learning to shop around. They will go elsewhere if they do not receive an answer when they call.
- To delegate with confidence it is necessary to have clear guidelines, authority levels and accountabilities. Yield decisions can often have a bigger effect on revenue than decisions on published prices. So the senior people in a hotel company should make it their business to see and approve the rules within which yield management is being performed. The manager should be reviewing decisions and looking at close-outs each day. In larger hotels there should be a senior manager whose job is to look at yield and see the wider picture. At the Balmoral we have promoted one of our brightest and most experienced sales executives into this role.
- It is an over-simplification, I know, but the essence of yield management is to understand what has happened in the past and to apply those lessons to the future. Yet so often we fail to record the present and end up having to make decisions based on guesswork. Lack of data on reservations denied is the most common failing. Of course there are difficulties in obtaining a complete picture, not least because the GDS has gaps in information here. But without knowing how many customers were put off by yield management decisions we will not know how brave to be next time, or indeed how ambitious to be when setting prices. So my third rule for managers is to ensure that the systems needed to record necessary data are in place.

- Computers have the potential to be the greatest asset to the yield manager or the biggest threat. The danger is that the computer will be seen as the technique itself rather than simply a tool to aid the manager. Once they buy the latest piece of IT managers can make the grave mistake of believing that they no longer have to supervise yield management so closely. But the IT is only as good as the data that are put into it and so more sophisticated IT places an even greater premium on the need for historic data. It also means that there must be very clear guidelines on when the computer's decisions can and cannot be over-ridden. Properly used, some of the yield management packages can bring dramatic results but my fourth rule is to use IT to the full without letting it become a substitute for good management.

- My next three points relate to operational aspects, which are all too often neglected in discussions about yield management. One objective of yield management is to maximize price at times of high demand. However, people who pay high prices rightly have high expectations. We can all charge a high price at certain times. But if that is not linked to value, customers will not come back at a time when you need them more than they need you. So my fifth rule is that when your yield management allows you to charge a premium price, make sure your operations are geared up to provide a premium service.

- Similarly, my sixth rule is to be particularly careful with regular customers. It is all too easy to yield out someone who visits ten times a year because a one-off customer is willing to pay a pound more on a particular day. Clearly this is short-sighted but it is all too easy to do if you are working with an automated programme. Yet another reason to recognize that the computer can help, but not replace, the manager on the front line. Of course, a yield management programme linked to a multi-unit loyalty programme will reduce your risks here, but this is becoming an expensive option for smaller businesses and is far from foolproof even for larger ones.

- Of course, yield management is not just about maximizing rate. Volume is an equal partner in the equation and, even in the luxury sector, there are times when it is better to sell rooms cheaply than to leave them empty. The skill here is not to undermine your core pricing. The traditionally accepted way has been to 'hide' the room price within a package deal. I suspect that many of today's customers are becoming too sophisticated for this and we need to recognize it. Why not offer the off-peak bargains to those who pay premium rates at peak times? It means more work in communicating the offers, but it sells the rooms and builds loyalty at the same time.

- Most yield management discussions focus on rooms, which reflects too many hoteliers' weakness of regarding food and beverage as a necessary nuisance rather than a profit opportunity. Conference and banqueting in particular is just as likely to benefit from yield management as the rooms business. Yet how many managers regularly monitor function rooms let as a percentage of potential, let alone cash yield per square metre? A good rule for number eight is that if you believe in yield management, apply it to the whole business.

- This brings me conveniently to my point number nine. It is always a temptation to maximize yield in one part of the hotel at the expense of others. The classic is rooms versus conference and banqueting. Is it better to accept £10 less on the room price if it brings in £30 of banqueting revenue? Of course it is, but this means that you need to design your management structure so that the person making final decisions has the overview of the whole hotel, or in a multi-unit

operation is even able to sacrifice yield in one property if there is a bigger
benefit elsewhere.

- My final recommendation is perhaps the most important. Yield management is,
like the rest of business, about taking risks in order to out-perform the
competition. You can maximize your chance of success through skill and hard
work, but sometimes a risk will not pay off. The manager must therefore judge
those managing yield on their successes, not their failures. If someone outwits
the competition nine times but loses out on the tenth, he or she should be
praised for the nine, not pilloried for the tenth. Otherwise he or she will become
risk-averse and your performance will go back to average. When someone does
not succeed it is important to discover why and to learn the lessons. But yield
management is a lonely business without a supportive manager and, provided
your team has stuck to the agreed rules and been as professional as possible, you
must accept that everyone will come unstuck occasionally. If they don't, it
probably means they are losing out the rest of the time by not being bold
enough.

I hope these suggestions are helpful. I have certainly found it useful to go through the
issues in this way and will manage our own yield better as a result of Ian Yeoman asking
me to write this piece.

Ian asked me to say a little about our experience of yield management at RF Hotels
during 1999. The Balmoral in Edinburgh ended the year with the highest rooms yield in
the city and a 25 per cent premium over the number two hotel. We led in 11 months and
came a little unstuck in one. We still have much to do as far as yield management of
conference and banqueting business is concerned, but we are on the case. The St
David's Hotel and Spa was not only in its opening year but was also the first five star
hotel in Wales. So history was hard to come by! We made some mistakes, normally by
going for a little too much rate before we had built up volume, but where there was
significant volume the team yielded very well indeed. The Rugby World Cup was an
outstanding example. The Astoria in St Petersburg saw volumes in the market decline
and responded more quickly than the competition. Perhaps that is the advantage of a
small company. Whatever the reason, they moved from number three on yield in the
city to number two and maintained a very respectable level of profitability in difficult
circumstances.

Looking to 2000, we have hotels in Brussels, Rome and Florence to add to the
collection. Yield will become even more important to us, as it will to all hoteliers. One
final tip? Watch out for the Internet. It allows smaller companies like us to play in the
big league at a manageable cost. With some imagination and a lot of hard work even a
team as small as ours can develop its own Internet-based tools to push yield. But that is
the making of competitive edge and I am sure you would not expect me to share that
with my competitors in a piece like this!

Sir Rocco Forte
Chairman, RF Hotels

Index